Twelve fragments of bronze were found near Urbino in the late fifteenth century, engraved with Roman laws – on one side a law concerning extortion, on the other an agrarian law. The text, when complete, would have been much longer and more complex than most other Latin documents known to us. Dating as they do from the time of the Gracchi and of Marius in the later years of the Roman Republic, the laws are of considerable interest to Roman historians and are important evidence for the understanding of the revolutionary period which led to the overthrow of the Republic.

In this volume, Dr Lintott offers a complete re-edition of these complicated and fragmentary texts, including a revision of the relationship between the fragments and full discussion of the manuscript sources of those now lost. The texts are accompanied by facing English translations and the commentary which follows discusses in detail the issues involved in establishing and restoring the texts. A series of introductory chapters, written as far as possible in non-technical language, give a summary of the context of the laws from both a legal and an historical viewpoint.

This is an edition of major importance whose publication will be welcomed by ancient historians and legal historians alike.

Judicial reform and land reform in the Roman Republic

A new edition, with translation and commentary, of the laws from Urbino

Judicial reform and land reform in the Roman Republic

A new edition, with translation and commentary, of the laws from Urbino

ANDREW LINTOTT

Fellow and Tutor in Ancient History
Worcester College, Oxford

CAMBRIDGE
UNIVERSITY PRESS

CAMBRIDGE UNIVERSITY PRESS
Cambridge, New York, Melbourne, Madrid, Cape Town, Singapore,
São Paulo, Delhi, Dubai, Tokyo

Cambridge University Press
The Edinburgh Building, Cambridge CB2 8RU, UK

Published in the United States of America by Cambridge University Press, New York

www.cambridge.org
Information on this title: www.cambridge.org/9780521130882

First published 1992
This digitally printed version 2010

A catalogue record for this publication is available from the British Library

Library of Congress Cataloguing in Publication data

Lintott, A.W. (Andrew William)
Judicial reform and land reform in the Roman Republic. – New ed., with
translation and commentary of the laws from Urbino / Andrew Lintott.
p. cm.
Latin texts with English translations and commentary.
Includes bibliographical references and index.
ISBN 0 521 40373 1
1. Extortion (Roman law) – History – Sources. 2. Land reform – Law and
legislation – Rome – History – Sources. 3. Law reform – Rome – History –
Sources. I. Title.
KJA3461.L56 1992
340.3'0945'632 – dc20 91-36641 CIP

ISBN 978-0-521-40373-3 Hardback
ISBN 978-0-521-13088-2 Paperback

Additional resources for this publication at www.cambridge.org/9780521130882

CONTENTS

Part two: The texts

ILLUSTRATIONS

Figures

Plates

FOR MY CHILDREN

PREFACE

I was first shown the main group of bronze fragments,[1] with which this book deals, by my classics master James Howarth, at a time when they were still on public exhibition in the Museo Nazionale at Naples. My interest in the extortion court I owe to my tutor in Ancient History at Oxford, Dacre Balsdon. However, my curiosity about the epigraphic problems was only awakened by H.B. Mattingly's attempt, after some pioneering investigation by G. Tibiletti, to overthrow Mommsen's arrangement of the fragments and his identification of the extortion law. The rebuttal of Mattingly's views by A.N. Sherwin-White and the thesis of K. Johannsen on the agrarian law made me realise the need for a proper re-edition of the bronze as a basis for future scholarship. This led me back to Naples in 1977 (where the fragments were now in a store), the first of a number of visits. I also inspected the Vienna fragments and pursued manuscripts and early editions in the Vatican and other libraries. Impressed, as I inevitably was, by Mommsen's achievement, I did not immediately realise how much needed to be done with the texts and how far revision of the texts would lead to new questions about their substance and implications. I received immense help and encouragement from Michael Crawford and other members of the group concerned with the revision of the texts of Roman laws. However, it became apparent that the only way that justice could be done to the work of over a decade was a book devoted to the laws on the Urbino fragments, and I am grateful to the readers of the Cambridge University Press for preliminary advice on the form of the work and to the Syndics of the Press for accepting it for publication.

My other debts of gratitude are numerous and warmly felt. Financial assistance for travel abroad and for photographic work has been provided by the Wolfson Foundation, the British Academy, the Craven Committee in Oxford and the Moncrieff Fund in Worcester College. For the production of the texts and translations and other help I owe much to a series of tolerant and

[1] The fragments have been commonly referred to by classical epigraphists as the *tabula Bembina* after their one-time owner, Cardinal Bembo. Unfortunately this term, as Dr Cecil Clough kindly pointed out to me, is also used by Renaissance scholars for another possession of Bembo's – a Roman bronze table-top with Egyptianising motifs. Hence I have preferred the term 'Urbino fragments' after their provenance.

indefatigable secretaries in the Classics Office at Oxford. The final plans of the ensemble of the fragments were realised through the draughtsmanship of Marion Cox and the photographic skill of Paolo Scremin. I am grateful to the directors and staff of the Museo Nazionale at Naples and to Dr Alfred Bernhard-Walcher and his staff in the Kunsthistorisches Museum at Vienna for photographs and help in my visit there, also to the staff of a number of libraries, especially the Biblioteca Apostolica Vaticana and the Bibliothèque Nationale in Paris, and to the British School at Rome for support and encouragement, while I was in Italy. I have learnt a great deal from my contemporaries, not least from those, like Harold Mattingly, with whose views I came to disagree profoundly. However, I am also more conscious than before of what classical scholars today owe to their predecessors, in particular to Renaissance humanists. They cannot be thanked: we can only do our best to develop what they began.

ABBREVIATIONS

Abbreviations of periodicals in general follow the system of *L'Année Philologique*, with one important exception: *ZSS* for *Zeitschrift der Savigny-Stiftung für Rechtsgeschichte, romanistische Abteilung.*

ANRW — *Aufstieg und Niedergang der römischen Welt*, Festschrift J. Vogt, ed H. Temporini and W. Haase. Berlin and New York, 1972–

Bruns — G. Bruns and O. Gradenwitz, *Fontes Iuris Romani Antiqui*, 7th edn. Tübingen, 1909

CAH — *Cambridge Ancient History*

CIL — *Corpus Inscriptionum Latinarum*

Degrassi — A. Degrassi, *CIL Auctarium. Inscriptiones Latinae Liberae Rei Publicae. Imagines.* Berlin, 1966

EJ — V. Ehrenberg and A.H.M. Jones, *Documents Illustrating the Reigns of Augustus and Tiberius.* 2nd edn. Oxford, 1975

FGH — F. Jacoby, *Die Fragmente der griechischen Historiker.* 3 parts, 11 vols. Berlin and Leiden, 1923–58

FIRA — S. Riccobono, *Fontes Iuris Romani Anteiustiniani.* 3 vols. 2nd edn. Florence, 1940–3

IG — *Inscriptiones Graecae*

IGRR — R. Cagnat *et al.*, *Inscriptiones Graecae ad Res Romanas Pertinentes.* Paris, 1906–27

ILLRP — A. Degrassi, *Inscriptiones Latinae Liberae Rei Publicae.* 2 vols. 2nd edn. Florence, 1966

ILS — H. Dessau, *Inscriptiones Latinae Selectae.* 4 vols. Berlin 1892–1916 (repr. 1954)

Mitteis, Wilcken *GCP* — L. Mitteis and U. Wilcken, *Gründzüge und Chrestomathie der Papyruskunde.* 4 vols. Stuttgart, 1912 (repr. Hildesheim, 1963)

Mommsen, *Ges. Schr.* — Th. Mommsen, *Gesammelte Schriften.* 8 vols. Berlin 1904–13

Mommsen, *Staatsr.* — Th. Mommsen, *Römisches Staatsrecht.* Vols. I and II, 3rd edn; vol. III, 1st edn; Leipzig, 1887–8

Mommsen, *Strafr.* — Th. Mommsen, *Römisches Strafrecht.* Leipzig, 1899

MRR — T.R.S. Broughton, *The Magistrates of the Roman Republic.* 2nd edn

OGIS W. Dittenberger, *Orientis Graeci Inscriptiones Selectae*. 4 vols. Leipzig, 1903 (repr. Hildesheim, 1960)

ORF H. Malcovati, *Oratorum Romanorum Fragmenta*. 2 vols. 4th edn. Turin, 1976–9

P.Teb. B.P. Grenfell *et al.*, *The Tebtunis Papyri*. London, 1902–76

RE A. Pauly, G. Wissowa and W. Kroll, *Real-Encyclopaedie der klassischen Altertumswissenschaft*

RRC M.H. Crawford, *Roman Republican Coinage*

SEG *Supplementum Epigraphicum Graecum*

Sherk, *RGDE* R.K. Sherk, *Roman Documents from the Greek East*. Baltimore, 1964

Syll.^{3} W. Dittenberger, *Sylloge Inscriptionum Graecarum*^{3}. 4 vols. 3rd edn. Leipzig, 1915 (repr. Hildesheim, 1960)

The following legal texts may be referred to without further reference.

Frag.Atest. *Fragmentum Atestinum, CIL* I^2, 600; *FIRA* I, 20

Frag.Tar. *Fragmentum Tarentinum*, R. Bartoccini, *Epigraphica* 9 (1947), pp. 3–31

Lex Ant.Term. *Lex Antonia de Termessibus, CIL* I^2, 589; *FIRA* I, 11

Lex Corn. XX quaest. *Lex Cornelia de viginti quaestoribus, CIL* I^2, 587; *FIRA* I, 10

Lex de Delo *Lex Gabinia Calpurnia de insula Delo, CIL* I^2, 2500; C. Nicolet, ed. *Insula Sacra*. Rome, 1980

Lex Flav.mun. The combined text of *Lex mun. Mal.* and *Lex Irnit.* (see below)

Lex Gen.Urs. *Lex Coloniae Genetivae Ursonensis, CIL* I^2, 594; *FIRA*, I, 21

Lex imp.Vesp. *Lex de imperio Vespasiani, CIL* VI.1, 930; *FIRA* I, 15

Lex Irnit. *Lex Irnitana*, J. Gonzalez, *JRS* 76 (1986), 147–243

Lex Iul.agr. *Lex Iulia agraria* (or *Mamilia Roscia Peducaea Alliena Fabia*), *FIRA* I, 12

Lex lat.Bant. *Lex latina tabulae Bantinae, CIL* I^2, 582, cf. I^2 (1986), pp. 907–8; *FIRA* I, 6; Bruns, 9

Lex mun.Mal. *Lex municipii Malacitani, CIL* II, 1964; *FIRA* I, 24.

Lex mun.Tar. *Lex municipii Tarentini, CIL* I^2, 590; *FIRA* I, 18.

Lex osca Bant. *Lex osca tabulae Bantinae, FIRA* I, 16; Bruns, 8; new fragment, D. Adamesteanu and M. Torelli, *Arch. Class.* 21 (1969), 1–17

Lex prov.praet. *Lex de provinciis praetoriis (de piratis), FIRA* I, 9; new fragments, M. Hassall, M. Crawford, J. Reynolds, *JRS* 64 (1974), 195–220

Lex Rubr.Gall. *Lex Rubria de Gallia Cisalpina, CIL* I^2, 592; *FIRA* I, 19

S.C. Calvisianum *FIRA* I, 68, V (pp. 409–14); *SEG* IX, 8

S.C. de Asclep. *Senatus Consultum de Asclepiade, CIL* I^2, 588; *FIRA* I, 35

S.C. de Bacch. *Senatus Consultum de Bacchanalibus, CIL* I^2, 581; *FIRA* I, 30

Tab.Heracl. *Tabula Heracleensis, CIL* I^2, 593; *FIRA* I, 13

BIBLIOGRAPHY

Lex Repetundarum

Inscribed on one face of twelve bronze fragments, eleven of which were apparently discovered towards the end of the fifteenth century, probably near Urbino, the twelfth discovered in the nineteenth century, on one account at Fossombrone (Forum Sempronii) nearby. Two pieces are known only from a number of humanist copies. The fragments, which form four complexes, will be designated here by letters, following Mommsen's notation: Aa + Ab; Ba + Bb + Bc; C + E; Da + Db + Dc + Dd + F. For a discussion of the discovery, transmission and early publications of the fragments see chapter 5 below (pp. 66–70).

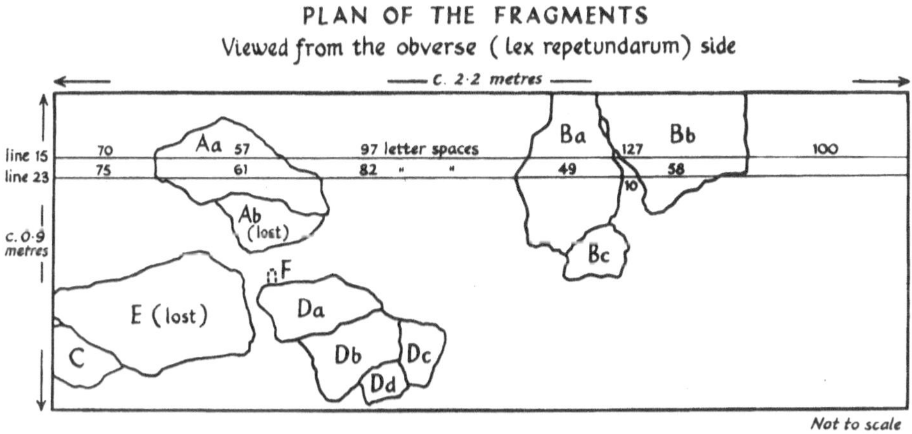

Fig. 1 Plan of the fragments

A Only the top half (Aa) preserved. Naples, Museo Nazionale, inv. 2636. Max. height – 26.3 cm; max. width – 35.5 cm. Degrassi, *Imagines*, 384c. Early copies of Aa + Ab in Mazzochi, *Epigr. Ant. Urb.*, fo. 180r; Sigonio, *De Iudic.*, II.27; Pinelli, Vat. lat. 6531, fo. 179r; Orsini, *Notae*, *Syll.*, no. XI; P. Dupuy, Paris, BN, Dupuy 461, 69.

B Naples, inv. 2636. Max. height – 50 cm; max. width – 66 cm. Degrassi, *Imagines*, 384a–b. Early copies of Ba + Bb in Sigonio, *De Iudic.*, II.27; Pinelli, Vat. lat. 6531, fos. 183v–184r + 179v; Orsini, Vat. lat. 6037, 52v and *Notae*, *Syll.*, no. VIII; Vettori, Munich lat.

743, fos. 107v–108r. Copies of Bc in Orsini, Vat. Lat. 6040, fo. 34v; Borghini, Florence, Bibl. Magl. II.x.70, p. 2; Vettori, Mun. lat. 743, fo. 112v.

C Vienna, Kunsthistorisches Museum, inv. III.172 (= Noll, *Griech. u. lat. Inschr. d. Wiener Antikensammlung* (1962), no. 421). Max. height – 17.8 cm; max. width – 18 cm. Degrassi, *Imagines*, 384e. Bronze replica (? *c.* AD 1600) – Naples, inv. 4611 (Fiorelli, *Cat. Mus. Naz. Nap. -Iscr. lat.*, II.2054). Early copies in Orsini, Vat. lat. 6040, fo. 35r and *Notae*, *Syll.*, no. x.

Dabc Naples, inv. 2636. Max. height – 32.5 cm; max. width – 48.1 cm. Degrassi, *Imagines*, 384d. Early copies of Da + Dbc in Orsini, Vat. lat. 6040, fo. 34v + 6037, fo. 53v and *Notae, Syll.*, no. XII; Borghini, Bibl. Magl. II.x.70, pp. 1–2; Vettori, Mun. lat. 743, fo. 112r. Copies of Da in Pinelli, Vat. lat. 6531, fo. 180v; Brisson, *De formulis et sollemnibus populi Romani verbis* (Paris, 1583) II, p. 172 (from Claude Dupuy); copy of Dbc in Pighius, *Annales Urbis Romae*, III, pp. 137–8.

Dd Vienna, inv. III.173 (= Noll, *Inschr. Wien. Ant.*, no. 422). Max. height – 11.3 cm; max. width – 12.8 cm. Degrassi, *Imagines*, 384–5. Copies in Orsini, Vat. lat. 6040, fo. 35r and *Notae*, *Syll.*, no. IX.

E Lost. Copies in Peiresc (from the *ecmagma* of Henri de Mesmes), Paris, BN, lat. 8958, fo. 167v; Orsini, Vat. lat. 6040, fos. 36v–37r and *Notae*, *Syll.*, no. XIV; Vettori, Mun. lat. 743, fo. 111v; Borghini, Bibl. Magl. II.x.70, p. 1; Scaliger, Vat. lat. 6531, fo. 175r (154); P. Dupuy, Paris, Dupuy 461, fos. 89–89bis; Brisson, *De Formulis*, II.173–4; Boissard, Stockholm, S.68, fo. 143v; *Romanae Urbis Topographiae et Antiquitatum*, III, 105.

F Naples, inv. 112521. Max. height – 5.2 cm; max. width – 3.7 cm. Concave, when viewed from the *repetundae* face. No previous photograph. Best copy in Garrucci, *Sylloge*, no. 2311 (= Bormann, *CIL* XI, 364a). Cf. *CIL* I², p. 444, *CIL* XI Add., p. 1234 for accounts of the fragment then believed to be lost. The copies in J. Gruter's *Inscriptiones Antiquae Totius Orbis* derive from Orsini and Brisson. The illustrations in F. Ritschl, *Priscae latinitatis monumenta epigraphica*, though helpful in portraying the distribution of the text over the fragments, cannot be treated, like photographs, as evidence for the text independent of the scholars who actually copied it.

Editions and discussions of the reconstitution of the text cited in chronological order

Orsini, F., 1583. *Leges et Senatus Consulta quae in veteribus cum in lapide tum ex aere monumentis reperiuntur*, in *Notae ad Leges*, a supplement to: A. Agustin, *De Legibus et Senatus Consultis*. Rome, 1583

Klenze, C.A., 1825. *Fragmenta legis Serviliae repetundarum*. Berlin, 1825

Rudorff, A.A.F., 1861. *Ad legem Aciliam de pecuniis repetundis*, Abh. d. kgl. Akad. Wiss. phil.-hist. Kl. Berlin, 1861, 411ff

Ritschl, F., 1862. *Priscae latinitatis monumenta epigraphica*. Berlin, 1862, nos. XXI–XXV

Mommsen, Th., *CIL* I¹ (1863), no. 198 = *Ges. Schr.*, I, 1ff

Girard, P.F., 1889. *Textes de Droit Romain*. 2 vols., 1st edn. Paris, 1889, I, no. 6

Hesky, W., 1903. 'Anmerkungen zur *lex Acilia repetundarum'*, *Wiener Studien* 25 (1903), 272–87

Brassloff, S., 1904. 'Beiträge zur Erläuterung der *lex Acilia repetundarum*', *Wiener Studien* 26 (1904), 106–17

Bormann, E., 1905. 'Zur römischen Urkunden der Zeit der Republik', *Festschrift für O. Hirschfeld.* Berlin, 1905, 432–9

Lommatzsch, E., *CIL* I² (1908), no. 583

Hardy, E.G., 1911. *Six Roman Laws.* Oxford, 1991

Bruns, C.G. and O. Gradenwitz, 1919. *Fontes Iuris Romani Antiqui.* 7th edn. Tübingen, 1919, no. 10

Tibiletti, G., 1953. 'Le leggi *de Iudiciis Repetundarum* fino alla guerra sociale', *Athenaeum* 31 (1953), 5–100, esp. 21–31

Riccobono, S., 1968. *Fontes Iuris Romanae Anteiustiniani.* 2nd edn. 1968, no. 7

Mattingly, H.B., 1969. 'The Two Republican Laws of the *Tabula Bembina*', *JRS* 59 (1969), 129–43

Eder, W., 1969. *Das vorsullanische Repetundenverfahren.* Munich, 1969, esp. 120–231

Girard, P.F. and F. Senn, 1977. *Textes de Droit Romain,* II *Les Lois des Romains.* 7th edn. Paris, 1977, no. 7

Venturini, C., 1979, *Studi sul crimen repetundarum nell'età repubblicana*, Milan, 1979

Krummrev, J., 1986. *CIL* I.2.iv², Addita Tertia. 1986, pp. 908–10

Other discussions

Alexander, M.C., 'Repetition of Prosecutions and the Scope of Prosecutions in the Standing Criminal Courts of the Republic', *CSCA* I (1982), 141–66

'*Praemia* in the *Quaestiones* of the late Republic', *CPhil* 80 (1985), 20–32

Badian, E., '*Lex Acilia Repetundarum*', *AJPhil* 75 (1954), 374–84

'E.H.L.N.R.', *MH* 45 (1988), 203–18

Balsdon, J.P.V.D., 'The History of the Extortion Court at Rome 123–70 BC', *PBSR* 14 (1938), 98–114

Behrends, O., *Die römische Geschworenverfassung*, Gött. Rechtswiss. Stud. 80. Göttingen, 1970

Buckland, W., 'Civil Proceedings against Ex-Magistrates in the Republic', *JRS* 27 (1937), 37–47

Ewins (Hall), U., '*Ne quis iudicio circumveniatur*', *JRS* 50 (1960), 94–107

Ferrary, J.-L., 'Recherches sur la législation de Saturninus et de Glaucia II', *MEFR* 91 (1979), 85–134

Review of Venturini (1979), *Labeo* 29 (1983), 70–7

Fraccaro, P., *Opuscula* II. Pavia, 1957

Gabba, E., 'Rome and Italy in the Second Century B.C.', *CAH* VIII. 2nd edn. Cambridge, 1989, 197–243

Garnsey, P., 'The *Lex Iulia* and Appeal under the Empire', *JRS* 56 (1966), 167–89

Griffin, M., 'The *leges iudiciariae* of the Pre-Sullan era', *CQ* ns 23 (1973), 108–26

Gruen, E.S., *Roman Politics and the Criminal Courts, 149–78 B.C.* Cambridge, Mass. 1968

Hassall, M., M. Crawford, and J. Reynolds, 'Rome and the Eastern Provinces at the End of the Second Century B.C.', *JRS* 64 (1974), 195–220

Henderson, M. I., 'The Process *De Repetundis*', *JRS* 41 (1951), 71–88

Herrman, P., 'Die Stadt Temnos und ihre auswartigen Beziehungen in hellenistischer Zeit', *MDAI (Istanbul)* 29 (1979), 239–71

Jones, A.H.M., *Studies in Roman Government and Law*. Oxford, 1960

'*De Tribunis Plebis Reficiendis; De Legibus Iunia et Acilia Repetundarum*', *PCPS* ns 6 (1960), 35–42

Kelly, J.M., *Roman Litigation*. Oxford, 1966

Kunkel, W., *Untersuchungen zur Entwicklung des romischen Kriminalverfahrens in vorsullanischer Zeit*, Abh. Bay. Ak. Wiss. phil-hist. Kl. n. f. 56. Munich, 1962

Quaestio, RE 24 (1963), 720–68

Levick, B.M., 'The *Senatus consultum* from Larinum', *JRS* 73 (1983), 97–115

Liebs, D. 'Die Herkunft der Regel, *Bis de eadem re ne sit actio*', *ZSS* 84 (1967), 104–32

Lintott, A.W., 'The Offices of C. Flavius Fimbria', *Historia* 20 (1971), 696–701

'Imperial Expansion and Moral Decline in the Roman Republic', *Historia* 21 (1972a), 626–38

'*Provocatio*. From the Struggle of the Orders to the Principate', *ANRW* 1.2 (1972b), 226–67

'Notes on the Roman Law inscribed at Delphi and Cnidos', *ZPE* 20 (1976a), 65–82

'The Procedure under the *Leges Calpurnia* and *Iunia de repetundis* and the *actio per sponsionem*', *ZPE* 22 (1976b), 207–14

'The *quaestiones de sicariis et veneficis* and the Latin *lex Bantina*', *Hermes* 106 (1978), 125–38

'M. Caelius Rufus and Pausanias', *CQ* ns 30 (1980), 385–6

'The *Leges de Repetundis* and Associate Measures under the Republic', *ZSS* 98 (1981), 162–212

'Le procès devant les *recuperatores* d'après les données épigraphiques jusqu' au règne d'Auguste', *RHD* 68 (1990), 1–11

Mantovani, D., 'Il pretore giudice criminale in età repubblicana', *Athenaeum* 77 (1990), 19–49

Il problema d'origine dell' accusa popolare (Dipartimento di scienze giuridiche, Università di Trento 6). Padua, 1989

Mattingly, H.B., 'The Extortion Law of the *Tabula Bembina*', *JRS* 60 (1970), 158–68

'*Lex Acilia Glabrionis*', *Hermes* 107 (1979), 478–88

'A New Look at the *Lex Repetundarum Bembina*', *Philologus* 131 (1987), 71–81

Meyer, Ed., *Caesars Monarchie und das Prinzipat des Pompeius*. 3rd edn. Stuttgart, 1922

Meyer, H.D., 'Die Strafklagekonsumption beim Repetundendelikt und die Rechtsregel – *bis de eadem re ne sit actio*', *ZSS* 95 (1978), 138–57

'Der Civis Romanus als Kläger im Repetundenprozess', in *Studien zur antike Sozialgeschichte. Festschrift F. Vittinghof* (Köln. hist. abh. 28), ed. W. Eck *et al.* Cologne, 1980, pp. 145–56

Mommsen, Th., *Römisches Staatsrecht*. 3rd edn. Leipzig, 1887–8

Römisches Strafrecht. Leipzig, 1899

Nicolet, C., *L'Ordre équestre*. Paris, 1966, I, esp. pp. 467–515

'Les lois judiciaires et les tribunaux de concussion', *ANRW* 1.2 (1972), 197–214

Pontenay de Fontette, E., *Leges Repetundarum*. Paris, 1954

Pugliese-Carratelli, G., '*Tabulae Herculanenses*', *PP* 3 (1948), 165–84

Richardson, J.S., 'The Purpose of the *lex Calpurnia de repetundis*', *JRS* 77 (1987), 1–12

Rosenberg, A., 'Die Entstehung des sogenannten *Foedus Cassianum* und des Lateinischen Rechts', *Hermes* 55 (1920), 337–63, at 346–9

Schmidlin, B., *Das Rekuperatorenverfahren.* Freiburg, 1963
Serrao, F., 'Appunti sui *patroni* nei processi *repetundarum*', *Studi in onore di Pietro di Francisci.* Milan, 1956, II, 473–511 = *Classi, partite e leggi nella repubblica romana.* Pisa, 1974, 233–75
Sherwin-White, A.N., '*Poena Legis Repetundarum*', *PBSR* 17 (1949), 5–25
'The Extortion Procedure Again', *JRS* 42 (1952), 43–55
'The Date of the *lex repetundarum* and its Consequences', *JRS* 62 (1972), 83–99
The Roman Citizenship. 2nd edn. Oxford, 1973
'The Political Ideas of C. Gracchus', *JRS* 72 (1982), 18–31
Stockton, D.L., *The Gracchi.* Oxford, 1979
Strachan-Davidson, J.L., *Problems of the Roman Criminal Law.* 2 vols. Oxford, 1912
Venturini, C., 'La repressione degli abusi dei magistrati romani ai danni delle popolazioni soggette fino alla *lex Calpurnia* del 149 a.c.', *BIDR* 72 (1969), 19–87
Zumpt, A.W., *Das Criminalrecht der römischen Republik.* 2 vols. Berlin, 1868, II
Zumpt, C.T., *De legibus iudiciisque repetundarum.* Berlin, 1845, I

Lex Agraria

Inscribed on the other face of the twelve fragments on which the *lex repetundarum* was inscribed. These fragments, which form four complexes, will be designated here by letters, following Mommsen's notation: Aa + Ab; Ba + Bb + Bc; C + E; Da + Db + Dc + Dd + F. For a discussion of the discovery, transmission and the early publications of the fragments see chapter 5 below (pp. 66–70).

A Only the top half (Aa) preserved. Naples, Museo Nazionale, inv. 2636. Max. height – 26.3 cm; max. width – 35.5 cm. Degrassi, *Imagines*, 385c. Early copies of Aa + Ab in Mazzochi, *Epigr. Ant. Urb.*, fo. 180v; Sigonio, *De Antiquo Iure Italiae*, II.2; Pinelli, Vat. lat. 6531, fo. 181r; Orsini, Vat. lat. 6037, fo. 54v and *Notae, Syll.*, no. IV; P. Dupuy, Paris, BN, Dupuy 461, 68.

B Naples, inv. 2636. Max. height – 50 cm; max. width – 66 cm. Degrassi, *Imagines*, 385a–b. Early copies of Ba + Bb in Sigonio, *De Antiquo Iure Italiae*, II.2; Pinelli, Vat. lat. 6531, fos. 181v–183r + 179v; Orsini, Vat. lat. 6037, fo. 52r + 6040, 34r and *Notae, Syll.*, no. I. Copies of Bc in Orsini, Vat. lat. 6040, fo. 34v and *Notae, Syll.*, no. XI; Vettori, Mun. lat. 743, fo. 130r.

C Vienna, Kunsthistorisches Museum, inv. III.173 = Noll, *Gr. u. lat. Inschr. d. Wiener Antikensammlung* (1962), no. 422. Max. height – 17.8 cm; max. width – 18 cm. Degrassi, *Imagines*, 385e. Bronze replica (? *c.* AD 1600) – Naples, inv. 4611 (Fiorelli, *Cat. Mus. Naz. Nap. iscr. lat.*, II.2054). Early copies in Orsini, Vat. lat. 6040, fo. 35r and *Notae, Syll.*, no. III.

Dabc Naples, inv. 2636. Max. height – 32.5 cm; max. width – 48.1 cm. Degrassi, *Imagines*, 385d. Early copies of Da + Dbc in Orsini, Vat. lat. 6040, fos. 34r + 6037, 53r and *Notae, Syll.*, no. V; Vettori, Mun. lat. 743, fo. 130r. Copies of Da in Pinelli, Vat. lat. 6531, fo. 180r; Brisson, *De formulis et sollemnibus populi Romani verbis* (Paris, 1583), II, 172–3 (from Claude Dupuy); copy of Dbc in Pighius, *Annales Urbis Romae*, III, 137.

Dd Vienna, inv. III.173 = Noll, *Inschr. Wien. Ant.*, no. 422. Max. height – 11.3 cm; max. width – 12.8 cm. Degrassi, *Imagines*, 385–6. Copies in Orsini, Vat. lat. 6040, fo. 35r and *Notae, Syll.*, no. II.

E Lost. Copies in Peiresc (from the *ecmagma* of Henri de Mesmes), Paris, BN, 8958, fos. 168r, 178r; Orsini, Vat. lat. 6040, fos. 36r–v and *Notae, Syll.*, no. VII; Vettori, Mun. lat. 743, fo. 129v; Scaliger, Vat. lat. 6531, fo. 176r (149); P. Dupuy, Paris, Dupuy 461, 88; Brisson, *De formulis*, II, 174–6; Boissard, Stockholm, S.68, fo. 144r and *Rom. Urb. Top. et Ant.*, III.104.

F Naples, inv. 112521. Max. height – 5.2 cm; max. width – 3.7 cm. Convex, when viewed from the agrarian face. No previous photograph. Best copy in Garrucci, *Sylloge*, no. 2311 (= Bormann, *CIL* XI, 364a). Cf. *CIL* I², p. 444, *CIL* XI, p. 1234 for accounts of the fragment then believed to be lost.

Editions and discussions of the reconstitution of the text cited in chronological order

Orsini, F. 1583. *Leges et senatus consulta quae in veteribus cum in lapide tum ex aere monumentis reperiuntur*, in *Notae ad leges*, a supplement to: A. Agustin, *De legibus et senatus consultis*. Rome, 1583

Rudorff, A.A.F., 1839. 'Das Ackergesetz des Spurius Thorius', *Zeitschr. f. geschichtl. Rechtswissenschaft* 10 (1839), 8–194

Huschke, P.E., 1841. Review of Rudorff, *Ackergesetz* – *Krit. Jahrb. f. deutsch. Rechtswiss.* 5 (1841), 579–620

Ritschl, F., 1862. *Priscae latinitatis monumenta epigraphica*. Berlin, 1862, nos. XXII, XXVI–XXVIII

Mommsen, Th., *CIL* I¹ (1863), no. 200 = *Ges. Schr.*, I, 55–145

Girard, P.F., 1889. *Textes de Droit Romain*. 2 vols., 1st edn. Paris, 1889, I, no. 7

Lommatzsch, E., *CIL* I² (1908), no. 585

Hardy, E.G., 1911. *Six Roman Laws*. Oxford, 1911

Bruns, C.G. and Gradenwitz, O., 1919. *Fontes Iuris Romani Antiqui*. 7th edn. Tübingen, 1919, no. 11

Saumagne, C., 1927. 'Sur la loi agraire de 111', *Rev. Phil.* 53 (1927), 50–80

Zancan, L., 1935. *Ager Publicus*. Padua, 1935

Burdese, A., 1952. *Studi sull' ager publicus*. Turin, 1952

Hinrichs, F.-T., 1966. 'Die *lex agraria* des Jahres 111 v. Chr.', *ZSS* 83 (1966), 252–307

Riccobono, S., 1968. *Fontes Iuris Romani Anteiustiniani*. 2nd edn. Florence, 1968, no. 8

Mattingly, H.B., 1969. 'The Two Republican Laws of the *Tabula Bembina*', *JRS* 59 (1969), 129–43

Johannsen, K., 1971, 'Die lex agraria des Jahres 111 v. Chr.' Dissertation. Munich, 1971

Girard, P.F. and F. Senn, 1977. *Textes de Droit Romain*. II *Les Lois des Romains*. 7th edn. Paris, 1977, no. 8

Other discussions

Accame, S., *Il dominio romano in Grecia dalla guerra acaica ad Augusto*. Rome, 1946

Adamesteanu, D. and C. Vatin, 'L'Arrière-Pays de Métaponte', *CRAI* (1976), 110–23

Asheri, D., *Distribuzioni di terre nella antica Grecia* (Memorie dell'Accademia di Torino, 4th ser. no. 10. Turin, 1966)

Badian, E., 'The *lex Thoria*. A Reconsideration', in *Studi in onore di Biondo Biondi*. 4 vols. Milan, 1963, I, 187–96 = *Studies in Greek and Roman History* Oxford, 1964, 235–42

'Tiberius Gracchus and the Roman Revolution', *ANRW* I.1 (1972), 668–731

Barker, G., 'The Archaeology of the Italian Shepherd', *PCPS* 35 (1989), 1–19

Bauman, R., 'The Gracchan Land-Commission: Four Questions', *Historia* 28 (1979), 385–408

Lawyers in Roman Republican Politics. Munich, 1983

Blümel, W., *Die Inschriften von Mylasa*. 2 vols. Bonn, 1987–8

Bozza, F., *La 'possessio' dell' ager publicus*. Naples, 1938

Bradford, J., *Ancient Landscapes*. London, 1957

Broughton, T.R.S., *The Romanization of Africa Proconsularis*. Baltimore, 1929

Brown, F.E., *Cosa. The Making of a Roman Town*. Ann Arbor, 1980

Brunt, P.A., *Italian Manpower*. London, 1971

Buckland, W.W., *A Textbook of Roman Law*. 3rd edn; rev. P. Stein. Cambridge, 1975

Burdese, A., 'Le vicende delle forme di appartenza e sfruttamento della terra nelle loro implicazioni politiche tra IV e III secolo a.C.', *BIDR* 88 (1985), 39–72

Caillemer, A. and R. Chevallier, 'Les centuriations de l'Africa Vetus', *Annales* 9 (1954), 433–60

Capogrosso Colognesi, L., *La struttura della proprietà e la formazione dei 'iura praediorum' nella età repubblicana*. 2 vols. (Ist. dir. rom. Univ. Roma, 42. Milan, 1969)

'Max Weber e Eduard Meyer sulla storia romana arcaica', *BIDR* 88 (1985a), 83–107

'Comunità agraria in Roma antica', *Quad. Stor.* 11 (1985b), 77–97

Carandini, A., *Settefinestre. Una villa schiavistica nell' Etruria romana*. 3 vols. Modena, 1985

Carcopino, J., *Autour des Gracques*. Paris, 1928 (2nd edn 1967)

Cardinali, G., *Studi Graccani*. Rome, 1912

Chevallier, R., 'Essai de chronologie des centuriations romaines de Tunisie', *MEFR* 70 (1958), 61–128

Chouquer, G. *et al.*, *Structures agraires en Italie meridionale – cadastres et paysages ruraux* (Coll. Ec. fr. de Rome, 100, 1987)

Corbier, M., '*Fiscus* and *Patrimonium*: The Saepinum Inscription and Transhumance in the Abruzzi', *JRS* 73 (1983), 126–31

Cotton, M.A. and G.P. Metraux, *The San Rocco villa at Francolise*. London, 1985

Crampa, J., *Labraunda* III.1. *The Greek Inscriptions*. Lund, 1969

de Martino, F., '*Ager privatus vectigalisque*', in *Studi in onore di P. di Francisci*. 4 vols. Milan, 1956, I, 557–79

'*Gromatici* e questione graccane', in *Nuovi studi di economia e diritto romano* (*Scritti di diritto romano*, III); Rome, 1988, 163–87

de Neeve, W., *Colonus*. Amsterdam, 1984

Dilke, O.A.W., *The Roman Land-Surveyors*. Newton Abbot, 1971

Douglas, A.E., 'The Legislation of Spurius Thorius', *AJP* 77 (1956), 376–95

'The Legislation of Sp. Thorius. Corrigenda', *AJP* 78 (1957), 89

Engelmann, H. and D. Knibbe, 'Das Zollgesetz der provincia Asia', *Epig. Anat.* 14 (1989)

Fentress, E., '*Via Aurelia, via Aemilia*', *PBSR* 52 (1984), 72–6

Fraccaro, P., 'La colonia romana Dertona e la sua centuriazione', *Opuscula* III.1 (1957), 123–50

Frederiksen, M., *Campania*. London, 1984

'The contribution of archaeology to the agrarian problem in the Gracchan period', *DArch* 4–5 (1970–1), 330–67

'I cambiamenti delle strutture agrarie nella tarda repubblica: la Campania', in Giardina and Schiavone (1981), I, 265–87

Frier, B.W., *The Rise of the Roman Jurists: Studies in Cicero's Pro Caecina*. Princeton, 1985

Gabba, E. and M. Pasquinucci, *Strutture agrarie e allevamento transumante nell' Italia romana (III–I sec. a.c.)*. Pisa, 1979

Garnsey, P.D.A., 'Where did Italian peasants live?', *PCPS* 25 (1979), 1–25

Gelzer, M., review of Carcopino (1928), *Gnomon* 5 (1928), 648–60

Giardina, A. and A. Schiavone, eds., *Società Romana e Produzione Schiavistica*. 3 vols. Rome–Bari, 1981

Gohler, J., *Rom und Italien*. Breslau, 1939

Granet, J., 'La loi agraire épigraphique de 111', 'La loi agraire et l'élevage', *Pallas* 36 (1990), 125–54

Gsell, S., *Histoire ancienne de l'Afrique du Nord*. 7 vols. Paris, 1914–30

Hardy, E.G., 'Were the *Lex Thoria* of 118 B.C. and the *Lex Agraria* of 111 B.C. reactionary laws?', *Journ. Phil.* 31 (1910), 268–86

Hatzfeld, J., *Les Trafiquants Italiens dans l'Orient Hellénique*. Paris, 1919

Helly, B., *Gonnoi*. 2 vols. Amsterdam, 1973

'Les Italiens en Thessalie au IIe et au Ie siècle av. J.-C.', in *Les Bourgeoisies Municipales Italiennes aux IIe et au Ie siècles av. J.-C.*, Centre Jean Bérard. Naples, 1983, 355–80

Heurgon, J., 'Inscriptions Étrusques de Tunisie', *CRAI* (1969), 526–55

Hinrichs, F.-T., 'Die römische Strassenbau zur Zeit der Gracchen', *Historia* 16 (1967), 162–76

Die Geschichte der gromatischen Institutionen. Untersuchungen zu Landverteilung, Landvermessung, Bodenverwaltung und Bodenrecht im römischen Reich. Wiesbaden, 1974

Hopkins, K., *Conquerors and Slaves*. Cambridge, 1978

Jones, C.J. and Ch. Habicht, 'A Hellenistic Inscription from Arsinoe in Cilicia', *Phoenix* 43 (1989), 317–46

Kaser, M., 'Die Typen des römischen Bodenrechts', *ZSS* 62 (1941), 1–81

Das römische Privatrecht. Munich, 1955

Das römische Zivilprozessrecht. Munich, 1966

Kelly, J.M., *Studies in the Civil Judicature of the Roman Republic*. Oxford, 1976

Keppie, L., *Colonisation and Veteran Settlement in Italy 47–14 B.C.* London, 1983

Kniep, F., *Societas Publicanorum*. Jena, 1896

Labruna, L., *Vim fieri veto. Alle radici di una ideologia*. Camerino, 1971

Laffi, U., 'L'iscrizione di Sepino (*CIL* IX, 2438) relativa ai contrasti fra le autorità municipali e i *conductores* delle gregi imperiali con l'intervento dei prefetti del pretorio', *Stud. class. e orient.* 14 (1965), 177–200

Levi, M.A., 'Intorno alla legge agraria del 111 a.c.', *RFIC* 57 (1929), 231–40

Lewis, D.M., 'Public Property in the City', in *The Greek City from Homer to Alexander*, ed. O. Murray and S. Price. Oxford, 1990, 245–63

Lintott, A.W., review of Johannsen (1971), *CR* ns 25 (1975), 98–101
Manacorda, D., 'The *Ager Cosanus* and the Production of the Amphorae of Sestius. New Evidence and a Reassessment', *JRS* 68 (1978), 122–31
Maschke, R., *Zur theorie und Geschichte der römischen Agrargesetze.* Tubingen, 1906
Meister, K., 'Die Aufhebung der gracchischen Agrarreform', *Historia* 23 (1974), 86–95
Mertens, J., *Alba Fucens.* Brussels/Rome, 1969, I
Misurare la terra. Centuriazione e coloni nel mondo romano – Catalogo della mostra, 11 dic. 1983–12 febb. 1984. Modena, 1983. (Further volumes of *Misurare la terra* have appeared – three, relating to Modena, Mantova and the Veneto, in 1984, and one, relating to Rome and its suburban territory, in 1985.)
Molthagen, J., 'Die Durchführung der gracchischen Agrarreform', *Historia* 22 (1973), 423–58
Panella, C., 'La distribuzione e i mercati', in Giardina, and Schiavone (1981), II, 55–80
Pani, M., 'Potere di *iudicatio* e lavori della commissione agraria Graccana dal 129 al 121 A.C.', *Ann. Fac. Lett. Fil. Bari,* 19–20 (1976–7), 131–46
'Su un nuovo cippo graccano dauno', *RIL* 111 (1977), 389–400
Ch.-Picard, G., 'L'administration territoriale de Carthage', in *Mélanges d'archéologie et d'histoire offerts à A. Piganiol.* Paris, 1966, III, 1257–65
Piganiol, A., *Les documents cadastraux de la colonie romaine d'Orange* (*Gallia*, Supp. XVI, Paris, 1962)
Potter, T.W., *The Changing Landscape of South Etruria.* London, 1979
Rawson, E.D., 'The Ciceronian Aristocracy and its Properties', in *Studies in Roman Property*, ed. M.I. Finley. Cambridge, 1976, 85–102
Intellectual Life in the Roman Republic. London, 1985
Richardson, J.S., 'The Ownership of Italian Land. Tiberius Gracchus and the Italians', *JRS* 70 (1980), 1–11
Romanelli, P., *Storia delle province romane dell'Africa.* Rome, 1959
Rostovtzeff, M.I., *A Social and Economic History of the Hellenistic World.* 3 vols. 2nd edn. Oxford, 1957
Salmon, E.T., *Roman Colonisation in the Republic.* London, 1969
Salviat F. and C. Vatin, 'Le cadastre de Larissa', *BCH* 98 (1974), 247–62
Seager, R., 'Cicero *Brutus* 136', *CR* ns 17 (1967), 12–13
Solazzi, S., *Il concorso dei creditori in diritto romano.* Naples, 1937, I
Steinwenter, A. 'Precarium', in *RE*, XXII.1814ff
Tchernia, A., 'Italian Wine in Gaul at the End of the Republic', in *Trade in the Ancient Economy*, ed. P. Garnsey, K. Hopkins and C.R. Whittaker. London, 1983, 87–104
Teutsch, L., *Das Städtewesen in Nordafrika in der Zeit von C. Gracchus bis zum Tode des Kaisers Augustus.* Berlin, 1962
Tibiletti, G., 'Il possesso dell' *ager publicus* e le norme *de modo agrorum* sino ai Gracchi', *Athenaeum* 26 (1948), 173–236 and 27 (1949), 1–41
'Ricerche di storia agraria romana', *Athenaeum* 28 (1950), 183–260
Toynbee, A.J., *Hannibal's Legacy.* 2 vols. London, 1965
Uggeri, G., '*Kleroi* arcaici e bonifica classica nella *chora* di Metaponto', *PP* 24 (1969), 51–71
Vallet J. *et al.*, *Fouilles de Megara Hyblaea.* Rome, 1976
Watson, A., *Rome of the XII Tables.* Princeton, 1975
Weber, M., *Die römische Agrargeschichte.* Stuttgart, 1891
Willcock, J.S.M., 'The *lex Thoria* and Cicero, *Brutus* 136', *CR* ns 32 (1982), 474–5

Wilson, A.J.N., *Emigration from Italy in the Republican Age*. Manchester, 1966
Wiseman, T.P., '*Viae Anniae*', *PBSR* 32 (1964), 21–35
'*Viae Anniae* Again'; *PBSR* 37 (1969), 82–91
Yavetz, Z. *Julius Caesar and his Public Image*. London, 1983
Zumpt, A.W., *Commentationes Epigraphicae*. Berlin, 1850, I

General bibliography

Behrends, O., 'Tiberius Gracchus und die Juristen seiner Zeit', in *Das Profil des Juristen in der europaischer Tradition*, ed. K. Luig and D. Liebs, (Ebelsbach, 1980), 25–121
Bleicken, J., *Lex Publica. Gesetz und Recht in der romischen Republik*. Berlin, 1975
Bloch, G. and J. Carcopino, *Histoire romaine*. Paris, 1926–29, I–II.i
Broughton, T.R.S., *The Magistrates of the Roman Republic*. 2 vols. 2nd edn, including supplement. New York, 1960
vol. III, 2nd supplement. Atlanta, 1986
Brunt, P.A., *The Fall of the Roman Republic*. Oxford, 1988
Coarelli, F., *Il foro romano. Periodo repubblicano e augusteo*. Rome, 1985
Crawford, M., *Roman Republican Coinage*. 2 vols. Cambridge, 1974
Coinage and Money under the Roman Republic. London, 1985
'The Laws of the Romans: Knowledge and Diffusion', in *Estudios sobre la Tabula Siarensis*, ed. J. Gonzalez and J. Arce. Madrid, 1988, 127–40
de Martino, F., *Storia della costituzione romana*. Naples, 1958, I–III
De Meo, C., *Lingue tecniche del Latino*. 2nd edn. Bologna, 1986
Farrell, J., 'The Distinction between *Comitia* and *Concilium*', *Athenaeum* 64 (1986), 407–38
Frederiksen, M.W., 'The Roman Municipal Laws: Errors and Drafts', *JRS* 55 (1965), 183–9
Gabba, E., *Appiani Bellorum Civilium Liber I*. 2nd edn. Florence, 1967
Greenidge, A.H.J., A.M. Clay and E.W. Gray, *Sources for Roman History B.C. 133–70*. 2nd edn. Oxford, 1960, rev. 1986
Hansen, M.H., *The Athenian Assembly*. Oxford, 1987
Harris, W.V., *Ancient Literacy*. Cambridge, Mass. and London, 1989
Jones, A.H.M., *Athenian Democracy*. Oxford, 1957
Lintott, A.W., *Violence in Republican Rome*. Oxford, 1968
'The So-Called *Tabula Bembina* and the Humanists', *Athenaeum* 61 (1983), 201–14
'Democracy in the Middle Republic', *ZSS* 104 (1987), 34–52
MacDowell, D.M., *The Law in Classical Athens*. London, 1978
McCuaig, W., *Carlo Sigonio. The Changing World of the Late Renaissance*. Princeton, 1989
Malcovati, H., *Oratorum Romanorum Fragmenta*. 4th edn. Turin, 1976
Marouzeau, J., 'Sur deux aspects de la langue du droit', in *Mélanges Henri Lévy-Bruhl*. Paris, 1959, 435–44
Millar, F., 'The Constitution of the Roman Republic', *JRS* 74 (1984), 1–19
Niccolini, G., *I fasti dei tribuni della plebe*. Milan, 1934
Nicolet, C., 'L'inspiration de Tiberius Gracchus', *REA* 67 (1965), 142–58
Ogilvie, R.M., *A Commentary on Livy I–V*. Oxford, 1965
Reynolds, J., *Aphrodisias and Rome*. *JRS* monographs I. London, 1982
Schulz, F., *History of Roman Legal Science*. Oxford, 1946

Serrao, F., *La 'iurisdictio' del pretore peregrino.* Milan, 1954
Stockton, D.L., *The Gracchi.* Oxford, 1978
Taylor, L.R., *Roman Voting Assemblies.* Ann Arbor, 1966
Wallace-Hadrill, A., ed., *Patronage in Ancient Society.* London, 1989
Williamson, C., 'Monuments of Bronze: Roman Legal Documents on Bronze Tablets', *CSCA* 6 (1987), 160–83

PART ONE

BACKGROUND

1

Introduction

The Urbino fragments and Roman history

The subject of this book is twelve fragments of bronze inscribed with Roman legal texts, one relating to robbery and extortion by magistrates and those in authority, the other to land-distribution in Italy and the provinces. These once formed part of a large 'table' (perhaps in fact two plates, not one) set up in the late second century BC in the forum of an Italian town, probably in the region of Urbino (Urvinum Metaurense). It was in Urbino *c.* AD 1500 that they first entered the world of scholars and antiquarians as a feature of the library of Federico da Montefeltro, duke of Urbino, the redoubtable *condottiere* who was patron of the painters Piero della Francesca and Uccello among others. The fragments were subsequently given to Cardinal Pietro Bembo: hence they are referred to by some classical scholars as the *tabula Bembina*. Their varied fortunes as objects of curiosity and antiquarian interest from then onwards provide a fascinating insight into the world of classical scholarship.[1] But that is not the justification of the present publication, nor is the fact that the fragments constitute a puzzle, presenting a great number of technical problems to those who try to make sense of them. It is that they are of fundamental importance for anyone who seeks to understand that revolutionary period in Roman history, which led to the overthrow of the Republic by internal forces at a time when it dominated the external world known to the Romans.

To begin with, these texts have the merit of bringing us into direct contact with the era of the Gracchi and C. Marius. The sources for Roman history in the period 146–70 BC are at first sight comforting in their bulk, when compared with the evidence available for much of ancient Greek history for example, but this bulk results not from the survival of good contemporary or near contemporary histories, but from a vast heap of very disparate material, much of it fragmentary and almost all of it highly tendentious. Works such as Appian's *Civil Wars* and Plutarch's *Lives* suffer from their distance from the actions they describe (upwards of 200 years) and the fact that they were never intended to be general political histories of the period. The epitomators of Roman history, who wrote under the emperors, chiefly but not exclusively basing their work on the, now lost, later books of Livy, attempted to package brief and simple

[1] See below 'History of the Texts' and Lintott, 1983.

accounts, often with a message about Republican corruption, which derived from earlier biased narratives. *Obiter dicta* of Cicero and fragments of other late Republican writers are precious for the historian, but it is often hard to measure the distortion imported by the political motivation of the authors, since we have simply an *exemplum* in a speech or, worse, an excerpt from a speech or narrative that otherwise does not survive, and not a coherent account. In the face of this it might have been expected that any first-hand documentary evidence would have been seized on with relief as a surer basis for understanding what was actually happening at the time, especially if it consisted of laws relating to corrupt practices by the elite in governing the empire and to land-distribution at home and abroad. If Attic inscriptions could be used to supplement and even correct Thucydides' account of the Athenian hegemony of the fifth century, surely Roman inscriptions could do the same for the political life of the late Republic?

A number of reasons may be suggested for the comparative neglect of these laws. One is that the inscriptions that survive are fragmentary and difficult to handle (but that is of course true of many Attic inscriptions). Another, somewhat disconcerting for a reflective historian, is that they lack points of contact with literary sources, even when they can be found a plausible historical context. It is fair to say of the judiciary law (*de repetundis*), which is on one face of the Urbino fragments, that, unless it had been discovered, there would have been no reason to suspect its existence in the form we have it or the existence of its particular provisions. As for the agrarian law on the other face, the existence of its general provisions about Italy is mentioned in the most summary of notices, which hardly does them justice, while its provisions about provincial land could not have been anticipated by a historian versed in the surviving literary evidence. Equally unmentioned in the literary tradition is another important epigraphic document, recently re-edited in the light of new discoveries, the law about the praetorian provinces of 101–100 BC, found first at Delphi and now at Cnidos.[2]

The historian, then, who seeks to study Roman history between the destruction of Carthage and the Social War without proper attention to epigraphy (or indeed to archaeological evidence) is balancing precariously on one unsound leg. If the present edition leads to inscriptions being more frequently and thoughtfully used, it will have performed a service. However, the laws are also evidence of a less political kind. They reveal the development of Roman law – in one case procedure in criminal matters, in the other the law of real estate and taxation – and especially the development of techniques of legislation. As statutes, the *lex de repetundis* and the *lex agraria* are more complex than anything that survives from the Greek classical period and indeed from the Hellenistic world, except for the tax-regulations of the Greek rulers of Egypt, the Ptolemies. They are also far more complex than anything that

[2] Hassall, Crawford and Reynolds, 1974.

survives of earlier Roman law (clearly here the accident of preservation may be misleading but not, it will be argued, significantly). Thus we have in these texts a milestone in the history of legal draughtsmanship. Finally, they contain the largest quantity of second century BC Latin prose outside Cato's *De Agri Cultura*. This edition is not intended to provide a commentary on matters purely linguistic, but the fact that two considerable tracts of sophisticated Latin could be first drafted and then engraved is a historical fact of importance for the mentality and linguistic capabilities of both the political elite and some of the *populus Romanus* at large.

More detailed references to the political background will be found in the discussions of the two laws that follow, but a few words about their general context may not be out of place in this introduction. They fall in the period which followed the remarkable seventy-odd years, during which the Romans, in the words of the contemporary Greek historian Polybius,[3] became masters of almost all the known inhabited world. These conquests produced wealth and the temptations of power, not only for the Roman people as a whole but for individuals. Among the elite these were the magistrates and military officers, but there were also the Romans and Italians who used the umbrella of Roman power to shelter their business activities – real estate, moneylending and trade throughout the Mediterranean. Much of the wealth yielded by war or peaceful exploitation came back to Italy, where it fuelled political ambition (which was advanced by ostentatious expenditure and a bountiful lifestyle) or grew as capital investment, above all in property. In consequence, as Roman writers from Sallust onwards (if not earlier) pointed out,[4] the greed for resources stimulated by this purchasing power created simultaneously luxury for the rich and impoverishment for the humble. This would not have been true of all the humble, since those who served the requirements of the wealthy – from architects and craftsmen in stone, metal, glass or pottery, to building-labourers and porters, men who tended to be found in Rome or other urban centres, such as Capua – must have had a livelihood and varying degrees of prosperity. However, those who worked the land found themselves competing for its possession with men of greater resources, who did not even necessarily want them as labourers, except at harvest time, since much of the regular work was done by slaves. How far the process of dispossession of the poorer peasants by the wealthy had gone in the late second century BC is a matter of debate, to which I will return, but it was already under way on land in the public domain, where the holdings of the rich were exceeding the legal maxima.

Major aims in the legislation of Tiberius and Caius Gracchus were a fairer allocation of public land in Italy, tighter control over the exploitation of Rome's allies by senators abroad and greater accountability for the senatorial elite as a whole. The *lex repetundarum* illustrates the second and third aims, while the *lex agraria*, though not itself a Gracchan law, reflects the efforts of the

[3] Pol. 1.1.5; 3.9; 3.1.4; 4.2. [4] Sall. *Cat.* 10–11; *Jug.* 41; Lintott, 1972a for the tradition.

Gracchi to achieve the first aim.[5] The radical nature of their legislation is apparent in these laws; so is the subtlety with which the legislators operated, even though they could have had few precedents to guide them. In many ways these bronze fragments are the best monuments to the two politicians that have survived.

The constitutional status of the laws

Both these laws were *plebiscita*, resolutions made by an assembly of the Roman plebs (the small number of patricians were excluded from such an assembly), voting in thirty-five divisions (*tribus*) under the presidency of a tribune of the plebs. Such resolutions had the force of law without qualification since the *lex Hortensia* of 287 BC. Laws or plebiscites passed in assemblies had been an important ingredient of Roman political life since the early Republic, if we can trust the evidence of the Roman annals. In the middle Republic they were used to enact reforms in the constitution, criminal and private law and religious practices, also grants of citizenship, land-distribution, economic and social measures and the creation of special magistracies. Furthermore, assemblies voted on formal declarations of war and treaties. The *populus Romanus*, therefore, or that part of it which actually attended assemblies, had a significant part to play in the workings of the Roman constitution.[6]

However, one should not interpret this democratic element as an equivalent to classical Athenian democracy or even the more restricted democratic constitutions of the Hellenistic period. Materially, assemblies did not concern themselves with the details of foreign and military policy, as they did at Athens: these were settled by the senate or by the commanders on the spot. Formally, Roman assemblies did not debate as the Athenian *ekklesia* did. They were not seated gatherings, whose ordinary members might be called to speak from the rostrum, but public meetings which stood to hear the convenor or other eminent men whom he permitted to speak. This applied whether the meetings were *comitia*, formal assemblies which could vote on a measure (the plural *comitia* is used for a singular meeting, the singular *comitium* refers to a specially constructed place of assembly), or *contiones*, informal gatherings at which the convenor gave his proposal an airing.[7]

The measures inscribed on the bronze tablets would thus have been presented as drafts by the relevant tribune to informal public meetings before they were read and voted on in *comitia*. They may have been modified before the final vote as a result of suggestions made to the legislator by speakers at meetings or privately. However, the essence of a Roman assembly is conveyed by the words of a legislator introducing a bill (*rogatio*) for voting: 'Velitis iubeatis, Quirites?', 'Citizens, are you going to approve and order?' The Roman people said 'yea' or

[5] See below pp. 166–9, 282–6 for the arguments over the identity of the two texts.

[6] Millar, 1984; Lintott, 1987. [7] On the meaning of these terms see Farrell, 1986.

'nay' to what was put before them. It was not a matter, as it frequently, if not always, was in the Athenian assembly, of 'The Council has decided to hold a meeting about X, what is to be done about it. Who wants to speak?'[8]

The laws of the Gracchi have a special radical glamour, in that they were passed in spite of being against the interests of many senators and in defiance of majority opinion in the senate. There has been much argument about the constitutionality of legislation contrary to the will of the senate.[9] Certainly, it was not forbidden by law. As for *mos*, constitutional custom, this was a flexible concept which could be interpreted in more than one way. It might be used to describe innovations to an over-rigid ancestral tradition or, conversely, to appeal to an idealised past against current reforms, believed to be too revolutionary, especially those introduced by statute, such as those of the Gracchi.[10] Between the *lex Hortensia* of 287 BC, which gave full force to *plebiscita*, and 146 BC most known laws were passed with senatorial approval, if not at the senate's instigation. However, there were notable exceptions – the agrarian law of C. Flaminius of 232, the *lex Claudia* of 218, which restricted the size of ships senators were permitted to own, the *lex Terentia* of 189 about the children of freedmen and the *lex Valeria* of 188, which gave three towns (including Cicero's birthplace Arpinum) full Roman citizenship.[11] In the decade before Ti.Gracchus' agrarian law there had been two laws about secret ballot, the *lex Gabinia* of 139 and the *lex Cassia* of 137, about whose political context we are unfortunately badly informed. These were, however, radical initiatives, on whose merits the senators were divided and which are highly unlikely to have resulted from preceding decrees of the senate.[12] In fact the number of laws passed directly by an assembly in the Gracchan period created a tradition themselves, which was regarded as part of the existing political fabric by Cicero, though, as a politician committed to the prevalence of senatorial authority, he disapproved of it.[13]

The publication of the laws

Although no chapters relating to the publication of these two laws survive in the texts as we possess them, it is probable that, like Athenian laws and other Roman laws of this period, they included such provisions. Indeed it may be conjectured that the mention of the *praetor peregrinus* and perhaps local magistrates in the last two surviving lines of the *lex repetundarum* indicates that

8 Cic. *Dom.* 44, 47 and 80; *Pis.* 72; Livy 22.10.2; 38.54.3; cf. 31.6.1; *lex de Delo* (*CIL* I², 2500), line 5; *lex de Flamonio divi Iuli* (J. Keil, *Forschungen in Ephesos*, IV.3.281–2, no.24 = EJ, 377, line 1; cf. Jones, 1957, 110ff; Hansen, 1987, 54ff.

9 Recently summed up by Badian, 1972, at 694–701.

10 Bleicken, 1975, 368ff. Cf. Livy 26.2.7ff; 27.8.4ff.

11 Pol. 2.21.8; Cic. *Inv.* 2.59; Livy 21.63.2; Cic. *Verr.* 5.45; Plut. *Flaminin.* 18.2; Livy 38.36.7.

12 Cic. *Amic.* 41; *Leg.* 3.35–7; *Brut.* 97 and 106; *Sest.* 103; Asc. 78C; *Schol.Bob.* 135St; PsAsc. 216St.

13 *Acad.* 2.13; *Har.Resp.* 43–4; *Sest.* 96; 103.

the law there was dealing with publication. Clauses relating to publication can be detected in the *fragmentum Tarentinum*, which contains part of a law about criminal justice, probably another *lex de repetundis* a little later than that on the Urbino fragments, and in the Roman criminal law on the *tabula Bantina*. The law of 101–100 BC about the praetorian provinces provided for copies to be sent for publication to communities in Asia.[14] Publication in writing was an essential part of the process of legislation. By the *lex Licinia Iunia* of 62 BC legislators were required to deposit copies of their bills in the *aerarium*, before they were passed, and earlier it was customary to post a text, probably on a wooden board rather than bronze.[15] In the late Republic, once the bill had become law, a copy was kept in the *aerarium* engraved on bronze and one or more texts would have been put on display publicly in Rome.[16] The *fragmentum Tarentinum* indicates that other communities might be sent or encouraged to take for themselves copies to be displayed in their own forum or *agora* and it, like the Urbino fragments, is itself the result of this process. The aim of such publication was in part to inform – though it would have taken a skilled man to read a legal text so posted, it was not so difficult to read as is often supposed, if it was indeed put up 'in a position from which it could be correctly read from ground level' (cf. *lex rep.* 65–6; *frag.Tar.* 14). Its other function was to establish and assert the law's existence.[17] The validity of a law was demonstrated by the existence of its text in public and its abolition entailed the dismantling or destruction of any such published text.[18]

Although a law engraved on bronze in a fixed location was important as an ultimate source and guarantee of authenticity, it was not the most convenient one for those who were frequently concerned with its provisions. We hear of copies made – presumably on papyrus or wooden tablets. W.V. Harris has taken Cicero's complaint that the texts of laws were not guarded by an archivist at Rome, so that copies depended on slaves and public attendants, as evidence that there were no authoritative texts in the treasury or elsewhere. However, this was not Cicero's point, nor is it a safe inference from Cicero. He was not saying that there were no legal texts that could be used as sources, but that they were not properly looked after, so that acquisition of a reliable copy depended on the honesty and diligence of the man sent to find the text: he might copy for

[14] *Frag.Tar.*, lines 13–14; *lex lat.Bant.*, lines 30–1; *lex prov.praet.* Delphi C.22–6 (in Hassall *et al.* 1974). Cf. Falerio, frag. 1A (*CIL* I², 2677), line 6, also the instructions for the engraving of Roman treaties (e.g. *SEG* 35 (1985), no. 823, lines 41–3; *OGIS*, 762, 14–15; *IG* IV².1.63, 6–9; *IGRR*, 1028b, 23–4; *ILLRP*, 516, 13–14), other evidence in Williamson, 1987, 171, n44; and see the comments of Frederiksen, 1965.

[15] *Lex Licinia Iunia* – Cic. *Att.* 2.9.1; *Sest.* 135; *Vat.* 33; *Schol.Bob.* 140St. Cf. *Leg.Agr.* 2.13; *Att.* 3.23.1ff; Crawford, 1988, 132.

[16] Cic. *Phil.* 1.26; *Mil.* 87; Suet. *Jul.* 28. Cf. Williamson, 1987, 170–2; Crawford, 1988, 139–40.

[17] On the readability of the inscription, see Crawford, 1988, 133; cf. Jos. *AJ* 19.291 (an edict of Claudius) for the phrase about reading from ground level; on the symbolic display of the inscription, see Williamson, 1987.

[18] Plut. *Cic.* 34.1; *Cato mi.* 40.1; Dio 39.21.

you the wrong text or indeed, if he found the search tiresome and had enough skill, invent one. Nevertheless, the whole point of the attendant's mission was that in theory an authoritative text was available.[19] Harris is on surer ground when he argues that we cannot draw any secure conclusions about general literacy from the publication of these laws on bronze.[20] There was certainly a professional literacy among those concerned with the law and, no doubt, a lower grade literacy among those who needed to know legal texts for their own purposes (the kind of literacy that can be ascribed to the engravers on the basis of their work is discussed below, pp. 64–5). There are implications, however, in the references to recitation aloud and the degree of rhetoric in the texts (see below, pp. 61–2): these do suggest in the urban population a widespread aural appreciation of elaborate and complex prose – a form of sophistication as interesting as literacy.[21]

[19] Cic. *Leg*. 3.46; Harris, 1989, 164ff, 206ff.

[20] Harris, 1989, 163ff. Cf. his general arguments in chs. 1–2.

[21] For the recitation of laws, once passed, see *frag. Tar*. 13–14 and 25 (cf. *CIL* I², 2677, IA, 12); for a treaty, see *IGRR*, 1028, a14–15. Importance of recitation is to be seen in *lex rep*. 15–16; *S.C. de Bacch*. (*FIRA* I, 30), 23–4.

2

The *lex repetundarum*

The nature of Roman criminal law

Although at first sight the judiciary law on the fragments contains features that are reassuringly familiar – a president of a court, a jury whose verdict is decisive, the provision of advocates, the collection of evidence and the estimation of damages – other features, such as large juries and rewards for accusers, are unusual in present-day procedure. Moreover, much of the familiarity is in fact superficial and conceals a form of criminal justice which is foreign to our experience, rooted, as it was, in the Romans' own history. To begin with, although the Romans had a concept of public law which included the prosecution and punishment of bad behaviour, offences which we would now regard as part of the public domain, such as theft, were left to private prosecution and the procedure of private law. It was primarily political crimes which were treated as offences against the community and subjected to prosecution by a procedure quite distinct from that used in cases of theft, debt or the failure to honour a legal obligation, for which the forms of private law were appropriate.

Even before their first and fundamental law-code, the Twelve Tables enacted in the mid-fifth century BC, the Romans probably had magistrates, the *duumviri perduellionis*, who prosecuted public offenders, and, in order to secure a verdict they believed to be justified, submitted the issue to assemblies of the citizens of Rome. The Twelve Tables ratified this, providing further that in capital trials the verdict should be referred to the *comitiatus maximus*, that is, the military assembly (the *comitia centuriata*), which also had the function of electing the senior magistrates.[1] The capital cases were those generally considered to fall under the heading of *perduellio* (i.e. being an enemy of the community, treason), but there were also less grave offences, some of them arising from specific statutes, others from magistrates failing to perform their duties as they might be expected to do. Investigation of and argument over such charges took place under the supervision of the prosecuting magistrate in informal public meetings, before a formal assembly was proclaimed in which a vote was to be taken on the verdict. Any Roman citizen present was entitled to vote on such occasions but his vote was merely part of a complex system of block voting by

[1] *XII Tab.* IX.1–2 = Cic. *Leg.* 3.11 and 44.

the *tribus* or *centuriae*, so that a majority of these 'tribes' or 'centuries' was required to secure a conviction.[2]

Trials before an assembly continued to be a feature of the middle Republic (though we have very few examples of a capital trial leading to a conviction). Prosecutions were no longer entrusted to the *duumviri perduellionis* but to tribunes of the plebs or, in non-capital cases, to aediles (there is also some evidence for prosecutions by *quaestores*). The paradox of this was that the tribune of the plebs could not himself convene the assembly which delivered the verdict in the *comitia centuriata*. This curious practice may perhaps be explained by a desire to shift the embarrassment of prosecuting leading members of Roman society from their peers in the senate to the official representatives of the plebs as a whole, who, whatever their social origins, were committed to guarding plebeian interests in their year of office.[3]

Procedure before an assembly was primarily used against ex-magistrates. Common people who committed treason or threatened the community in a particularly heinous fashion – such as the Bacchanalian 'conspirators' in 186 BC – tended to be tried by magistrates with an advisory tribunal (*consilium*). Capital sentences arising from such trials were occasionally referred to assemblies. However, they were also put directly into effect.[4] The early struggles of the Roman plebs had won protection for its members from arbitrary execution by a Roman magistrate, at first *de facto*, later *de iure*. Originally springing from the mutual physical support of the plebs, *provocatio*, the right to appeal against capital sentences, was enshrined in Roman law by a *lex Valeria* of 300 BC. Later laws introduced sanctions against those who ignored *provocatio* and instituted a ban on the flogging of Roman citizens. However, in practice even in the late Republic magistrates entrusted with a tribunal of investigation (*quaestio*) by the senate executed those whom they regarded as enemies of the community without reference to a popular assembly, presumably on the ground that they had made no appeal and the plebs had no interest in protecting the alleged criminals. Such was the fate of the members of the Bacchanalian conspiracy of 186 BC, the female poisoners in 181 and 152 and the followers of the Gracchi, first in 132 and then in 121.[5] Some temporary tribunals, however, were established by a law passed in an assembly, for example that which investigated the corruption of Hostilius Tubulus in 141. A

[2] Pol. 6.14.6–7; Cic. *Dom.* 45; *lex osca Bant.* (Bruns, no. 8 = *FIRA* I, 16), lines 13–15.

[3] Pol. 6.14.6. For the interpretation of the use of tribunes to prosecute, see Lintott, 1987, 44–8; on quaestorian prosecutions, see Lintott, 1971.

[4] Pol. 6.16.2 (referring to the tribunals sponsored by the senate in cases with political implications). On these special tribunals, see Kunkel, 1962, 75ff; Strachan-Davidson, 1912, I, 225ff; Lintott, 1972b, at 238–46. I do not discuss here the thorny question of procedure in non-political criminal cases, where the traditional view that these cases too were tried before an assembly has been attacked by Kunkel (1962, 97ff). My own views are in Lintott, 1972b. Cf. Mantovani, 1990 for recent support for Kunkel's view in general.

[5] Lintott, 1972b, 253–61; 1968, 161–8.

natural development of this was to establish a permanent tribunal to deal with a particular type of offence against the public interest. A further stimulus in this direction was provided by a law of C. Gracchus, which forbad any capital condemnation of Roman citizens without prior sanction from an assembly, thus tightening the constraints created by the *provocatio* laws.[6] This was one important element in the genesis of the *quaestio perpetua*, the characteristic criminal court of the late Republic, where offences, procedure and the nature of the jury were defined by the enabling statute and this statute authorised the court to pass and enforce verdicts without being subject to appeal or further reference.

However, the development of the *quaestio de repetundis* itself, a court established to investigate illegal exactions by magistrates and senators, was also a major factor in the growth of this new criminal procedure. The loss of property of any kind through theft or fraud was generally a matter for civil, as opposed to criminal, actions in Roman law. It has been argued that it was illegal to bring a civil action against senior magistrates, after they had left office, over alleged delicts committed while they were in office.[7] Certainly, at the time of our laws *imperium* represented by the *fasces* had come to protect the holder in theory, while he actually was a magistrate, to say nothing of the practical problem of bringing a man with lictors to court against his will.[8] However, there was no general statute or constitutional principle granting ex-magistrates immunity from private actions. This is clear from the procedure in 171 BC (to be discussed more fully below, p. 13) when the senate encouraged the private prosecutions by allies of ex-governors of Spain. Nevertheless, to mount a prosecution of a powerful man would have been a daunting task for a humble Roman citizen, let alone a non-Roman with little knowledge of the Latin language or Roman law, who would have needed the services of a Roman patron to help him in the procedure required.

In fact, early attempts to gain redress against delinquent magistrates have their origin in diplomacy by communities and the enlistment of the support of the senate (which had a general concern for the loyalty of allies and the tranquillity of Rome's empire) or else in an initiative by the senate itself. For example, in 204 a Locrian embassy protested against the conduct of Q. Pleminius, the man appointed prefect of the city by Scipio the previous year, and secured the appointment of a special tribunal, which actually investigated on the spot the offences against the Locrians and the associated mutiny of Roman soldiers (such a tribunal was on our evidence unique). This led to Pleminius and thirty-two others being condemned to death, after some restitution of stolen property had been made to the community.[9] In 172 it was

[6] Cic. *Fin.* 2.54; *Nat.Deor.* 3.74; *Rab.Perd.* 12; Kunkel, 1962, 51ff, 61ff.

[7] Buckland, 1937; Serrao, 1956, 486–7; for a more cautious approach, see Richardson, 1987, 9ff.

[8] *Lex rep.* 8–9; Gell. 13.13.4.

[9] Livy 29.8–9; 16–22. Cf. Lintott, 1972b, 256ff, arguing that Livy's narrative is correct in substance; a different version in Venturini, 1969, 31ff. On the prehistory of *repetundae* in general see Lintott, 1981, 164–76; Venturini, 1969; Eder, 1969.

proposed that a praetor should investigate at Rome the conduct of the proconsul M.Popilius Laenas, who as consul the previous year had attacked a Ligurian people, the Statellates, and sold into slavery ten thousand men who had surrendered to him.[10] In 170 embassies protested about the actions of two praetors, C.Lucretius and L.Hortensius, in Chalcis during the third Macedonian war. There was also a protest embassy from Thisbae in Boeotia. In consequence two tribunes prosecuted Lucretius before an assembly and secured his condemnation to a fine of one million asses. A number of Greeks, who had been improperly enslaved, were freed; we have no evidence of any financial compensation, but Lucretius' receipt of silver coin, as a bribe or ransom money, was discussed in the senate. In the same year P.Licinius Crassus (*cos.* 171) was condemned to pay a fine in a trial, whose details are not preserved for us.[11]

Meanwhile, in 171 the senate received complaints from Spanish communities about three former governors – M.Titinius (*pr.* 178), M.Furius Philus (*pr.* 174) and M.Matienus (*pr.* 173). The Spaniards alleged that they had been robbed and humiliated. Instead of encouraging a prosecution by tribunes in an assembly or establishing a special tribunal, the senate resolved in this case that there should be a special form of civil procedure, to be supervised by the praetor who had just been allocated Spain as his province. After a preliminary hearing by the praetor, five *recuperatores* were allocated by him to each defendant, who were to hear the evidence brought by all those with a claim against that man. The plaintiffs were allowed to choose Roman *patroni* to plead their cases and selected some major personalities, including Cato the Censor and Aemilius Paulus. However, one defendant was acquitted at the third hearing, while the other two went into exile before a verdict could be reached, thus frustrating the exaction of adequate compensation.[12] In spite of its failure to provide justice for the Spaniards, this procedure is interesting because it concentrated on the problem of recovering money and viewed the offences from the point of view of the injured parties.

Recuperatores, a small panel of judges (an odd number, in order to facilitate a majority decision), were comparatively rarely used in civil cases during the Republic, where the standard method was to appoint a single judge (*unus iudex*), who would himself in turn collect a *consilium* of advisers. Antiquarian tradition maintained that *recuperatores* originated in the commissions set up according to treaty to settle mutual compensation for public and private losses, which had been sustained while states had been at war with one another or perhaps permitting brigandage and piracy by their citizens against one another. So this sort of jury would have been especially appropriate to deal with the Spaniards' complaint.[13] More generally, they seem to have been used in a number of cases in the late Republic where the public interest was at stake, on

[10] Livy 42.7–8; 21–22.

[11] Livy *Per.* 43; 43.4.1–6 and 7.5–8.10; Zon. 9.22.6; *FIRA* I, 31 = Sherk, *RGDE* 2, lines 50–2.

[12] Livy 43.2. [13] Festus 342–3L. Cf. Schmidlin, 1963; Lintott, 1990.

occasions when there was no individual injured party, but a magistrate or other citizen was seeking to enforce administrative law.[14] Mommsen regarded cases of this sort as the precedent for the later procedure of the *lex repetundarum* and *quaestiones perpetuae* in general. He has been rightly criticised for ignoring the influence of criminal tribunals, such as those which condemned the Bacchanals and Hostilius Tubulus.[15] However, there does seem to be a procedural similarity between actions before *recuperatores* and those in a non-capital *quaestio* – most obvious in the procedure described on the fifth Cnidos tablet of the law about the praetorian provinces of 101–100 BC – and we should not discount the possibility of mutual influence between them.[16]

There is a brief reference to provincial governors being condemned for taking money in the 150s, but we do not know what procedure was used, whether prosecutions before an assembly or investigations by a special tribunal or civil actions like those undertaken in 171. A report of the trial of consul L. Cornelius Lentulus Lupus 'under the Caecilian law' may mean that a special tribunal was set up for him.[17] With complaints of maladministration and extortion becoming commonplace, there was a need for a regular and well-known legal process, adapted to the needs of Rome's allies and subjects, which would make the improvisation of special procedures unnecessary and be a good advertisement of Rome's care for the welfare of her allies. Even if the legislation was enacted by a tribune in the assembly of the plebs, and the senate itself as a body was to have nothing to do with the legal process created, it would probably have gained credit among Rome's allies from the introduction of a new court because, in the eyes of foreigners, it was the council which ruled the empire. It is generally assumed that the *lex Calpurnia de repetundis* of 149, which, according to Cicero, established the earliest *quaestio perpetua*, was the first legislation designed to meet this need.[18]

The most important allusions to this law are in the epigraphic *lex repetundarum* itself. The *lex Calpurnia* is cited in conjunction with an otherwise unknown *lex Iunia* as the predecessors of that law (lines 74 and 81). They were in force at least up to the time when the epigraphic law was passed and some features of them may have remained valid afterwards. The penalty they imposed seems to have been simple restitution of the sums taken (line 59) and the procedure they employed was not that of the epigraphic text, where denunciation (*nominis delatio*) before a magistrate introduced an elaborate trial before a large jury, but an ancient, though not outmoded, form of civil procedure, the *legis actio sacramento* (line 23). It is this last characteristic which

[14] E.g. *lex agr.* 37–9; *lex lat.Bant.* 9–10. Cf. Schmidlin and Lintott cited above, note 13.

[15] Mommsen, *Staatsr.* I, 168 for the *quaestio* as a 'sharpened' civil process; contrast Kunkel, 1962, 51ff, though he accepts the influence of trials before *recuperatores* at 61.

[16] For a discussion of the procedure on Cnidos v, see Lintott, 1976a, 73ff, where it was suggested that the text did describe *quaestio* procedure, now revised in Lintott 1990.

[17] Livy *Per.* 47; Val.Max. 6.9.10. For the private actions through the *actio per sponsionem*, see Lintott, 1976b.

[18] Cic. *Brut.* 106; *Off.* 2.95; *Verr.* 3.195; 4.56.

raises the fundamental question about these two laws: were they in fact any use to the allies and subjects of Rome at all?[19]

In the *legis actio* the ritual statements by the prosecutor leading to the wager (*sacramentum*) included an invocation of the law of Roman citizens and so would have only been valid for Roman citizens and those who shared their legal rights, the Latins. When foreigners sued Romans at this time, it was under the still comparatively new procedures introduced by the edicts of the praetors, in which a fiction of citizenship could be introduced. The implication of the employment of the *legis actio sacramento* in the *leges Calpurnia* and *Iunia*, then, is that the allies were not intended to sue in their own persons under this law. Could they not, however, have been represented by *patroni*, like the plaintiffs from Spain in 171? In fact, the only prosecutors known to us in the period 149–123 are leading Romans, Scipio Aemilianus, P.Cornelius Lentulus and C.Rutilius Rufus,[20] and it seems plausible that the legislators should have sought to channel prosecutions in such sensitive cases through members of the Roman governing class. Yet there is an objection to this in the technicalities of the *legis actio sacramento*. The plaintiff normally sued here in his own name: in an action about property he said 'I claim that this is mine according to the law of Roman citizens (*ex iure Quiritium meum esse aio*)', in an action about obligation he said 'I claim that you should give to me.' There was an ancient maxim, 'No one can bring a *legis actio* on another's behalf.' However, exceptions were made to this in certain cases where the plaintiff had not the capacity to sue.[21] Some scholars have been sufficiently influenced by the argument from the *legis actio sacramento* as to hold that this procedure was not intended for foreigners but only for Roman citizens and possibly Latins. Non-Latin allies seeking redress would have simply had to operate like the Spaniards in 171: they would have approached the senate and sought some *ad hoc* private process.[22] Such measures cannot, however, have been positively prescribed by the *leges Calpurnia* and *Iunia*,[23] since the actions under these laws are characterised in *lex rep.* 23 as being by *sacramentum*. It would follow on this view that any actions undertaken to gain redress for foreigners before the epigraphic *lex repetundarum* would have been authorised by the senate, without the assistance of any law, as in 171. (The case of D.Iunius Silanus, who committed suicide in 141 after his natural father, the consul T.Manlius Torquatus, had taken over the investigation of complaints against him by a Macedonian embassy to the senate, is perhaps not relevant, since we cannot be sure that he was not liable under the *lex Calpurnia*.[24])

While recognising the force of the argument from the *legis actio sacramento*,

19 See Richardson, 1987.

20 Cic. *div.Caec.* 69; *Font.* 38; *Brut.* 81; *Mur.* 58; Val.Max. 8.1.11.

21 *Dig.* 50.17.123. Cf. Gaius 4.82; Just. *Inst.* 4.10.pr.

22 Apart from Richardson, 1987, see A.W. Zumpt, 1868, II.1.42ff; Eder, 1969, 68ff.

23 As Zumpt thought.

24 Cic. *Fin.* 1.24; Livy *Per.* 54; *Oxy.Per.* 54; Val.Max. 5.8.3. Cf. Eder, 1969, 75ff.

I prefer to believe that the *leges Calpurnia* and *Iunia* were intended to be of value to allies:[25] they could well have included an exception to the rule that one could only bring a *legis actio* in one's own name, similar to those made for prisoners of war and men improperly enslaved.[26] The *socii* would have been permitted under these laws to have an eminent *patronus* to bring a civil action on their behalf, in which the wager (*sacramentum*) first led to a judgement about the guilt of the accused and later perhaps a separate action decided the actual amount of damages.[27] It remains something of a puzzle why the *lex Calpurnia* prescribed the *legis actio*, especially in the light of the less formal procedure employed in 171. One might think that it was intended to be a deterrent against frivolous and vexatious suits or, more cynically, that it was designed to keep prosecutions of all kinds to a minimum. Even if there had been so far only a trickle of allied complaints, the legislator may have foreseen and feared an undesirable increase. Yet in any case members of allied communities did not take lightly a prosecution of a member of the elite that effectively ruled the Mediterranean world. It may have been believed that, because it required the prosecution to be channelled through a Roman *patronus*, the use of the *legis actio* would do less damage to Rome's reputation than another form of private action (or a tribunician prosecution). But this belief, if it existed, was probably mistaken. The later history of the court showed that a Roman prosecutor would not hesitate to bring his country into disrepute, if thereby he could win his case.

Whatever view is taken of the aims of the *leges Calpurnia* and *Iunia*, it appears that the prosecution of a delinquent magistrate as a result of complaints by allies remained something which required a considerable degree of support from members of the Roman elite. It was not easy to bring a case to a successful conclusion and the reward for success was limited – merely the recovery of what had been lost. The legislators had taken care that such magistrates should be handled in a way which caused the minimum breach of the solidarity of the governing class and the minimum pain to their families and friends.

The content of the lex repetundarum

The technical arguments for identifying the *lex repetundarum* on the Urbino fragments with a law passed in C.Gracchus' tribunates are discussed in a separate section, and in what follows it is assumed that we are dealing with a law of 123 or 122 BC, probably the latter,[28] passed some twenty-five years after the

[25] Even if one should not rest too much on Cicero's statements in *Div.Caec.* 17–18 and 2 *Verr.* 2.15 that the whole *quaestio* was established on behalf of the allies, which may reflect perceptions of the court in 70 BC. [26] Gaius 4.82; Just. *Inst.* 4.10.pr.

[27] This would have been a precedent for the separate *litis aestumatio* in the *lex repetundarum* (lines 58ff).

[28] See pp. 166–9, 'Identity of the *Lex Repetundarum*' and on the chronology Fraccaro, 1957, II, 30.

first creation of the *quaestio de repetundis*. This was a time when there was dissatisfaction over acquittals of guilty men under the *leges Calpurnia* and *Iunia* and C.Gracchus, who in his tribunates was asserting the sovereignty of the popular assemblies over the administration of Rome, decided to enlist the support of wealthy men outside the senate (the *equites* or 'knights') as jurors in the trials of delinquent senators.[29]

The law, as it survives, may be analysed into the following sections:

I Definition of who is allowed to sue whom for what offences under the law (lines 1–5)

II Procedure (a) before trial (lines 6–35)
(b) during the main trial (lines 36–56)
(c) during the calculation of damages and execution of condemnation on the defendant's property (lines 57–69)

III Miscellaneous provisions regarding enforcement, transfer of official obligations, the relation of this law to previous laws and collusive prosecutions (lines 70–5)

IV Rewards for prosecutors (lines 76–88)

V (probably) Provisions for publicity (lines 89–90)

The law must have continued after the last surviving line. There may have been further provisions about publicity and there was certainly a *sanctio*, that is, a clause or series of clauses requiring the observance of the law on pain of prosecution (this is mentioned in lines 55–6, see the commentary there). We may also suppose the existence of clauses dealing with collisions with previous legislation, such as are found in *lex agraria* 41–2, and the formula used to avoid conflicts with sacred law, which appears at the end of the *fragmentum Tarentinum* and the *lex Gabinia Calpurnia de Delo*.[30]

The law, like all Roman laws, began with a prescript, now lost, which identified it and stated its title to obedience (see the commentary to *lex agr.* 1). This included the name of the proposer, the nature and place of the assembly, the date and the names of the first *tribus* and the first voter within that *tribus*. The latter seems to have been cited as witness to the formal correctness of the voting procedure.

The first line of the text proper lists the potential injured parties whose losses are to be remedied. What survives is a phrase covering any foreigner in a peaceful relationship to the Roman people, including former enemies who had surrendered. Whether offences against Roman citizens were also covered, is a moot point (see commentary on *lex rep.* 1), but there is no good evidence against this possibility and it seems plausible that the law should have tried to provide a special avenue for redress to Roman citizens injured by men in authority.

29 App. *BCiv.* 1.22.93ff; Diod. 34/5.25–7; 37.9; Varro, ap.Non.Marcell. 728L; Livy *Per.* 60; Vell.Pat. 2.6.3; Pliny *HN* 33.34; Plut. *C.Gr.* 5.2–3; *Compar.* 2.1.

30 *Frag.Tar.* 26; *lex de Delo* 36, cf. C. Nicolet, ed., *Insula Sacra* (Paris, 1980), 9ff.

What offences are covered? Essentially the improper acquisition of property above a certain minimum sum through force, menaces, fraud or the solicitation of favours by Roman magistrates, senators or senators' sons (lines 2–3). Official brutality is not covered, except in so far as it produced financial loss, nor is the receipt of unsolicited bribes or gifts. The fixing of a minimum sum may seem to have been unfair to a man who had not possessed much but was robbed of what he had. However, as will appear, provision was made for the injuries committed by one man against a number of victims to be prosecuted together, and it was undesirable that an elaborate procedure should be deployed in a small matter.

The categories of potential offenders (lines 2–3) deserve comment. Magistrates were of course the representatives of the Roman people, whose power and authority rendered their improper actions difficult to resist. Other senators normally only left Italy either on official business, as members of a magistrate's staff or ambassadors, or when they were permitted to travel unofficially on a religious pretext – this was called *libera legatio*[31] – but they were allowed to travel throughout Italy on their private affairs. Their status might be expected to put citizens and foreigners in contact with them at a disadvantage. Sons of senators, especially those still in the power of their fathers (*patria potestas*), were regarded as their fathers' representatives, and their insertion by the legislator is an attempt to plug an obvious loophole for evasion. Nevertheless, it may be argued that foreigners in particular were also at a disadvantage when dealing with Roman businessmen with the prestige of the imperial power behind them, most commonly the tax-collectors who were independent contractors to the Roman people. The latter were not drawn from those inside the senatorial order and thus were not covered by this law. It appears that this is an instance of the legislator deliberately favouring the wealthy men outside the senate, many of whom were members of the order of *equites* (knights), at the expense of senators – a possibility consistent with the later provisions about jurors and with the complaints about C.Gracchus in literary sources.[32] From the legislator's point of view the whole thrust of his legislation was to restrain the corrupt practices of the highest order of society and it may have seemed undesirable to broaden the target and dissipate the concentration of fire.

The right to prosecute (lines 3–4) was granted first to the victims themselves and their relatives, secondly to men acting for an allied king, an allied community or a fellow-citizen in that community (the use of representatives, *cognitores*, was already accepted in Roman civil law). The important feature here is that in theory a wronged foreigner was given direct access to Roman law in a suit against an ex-magistrate or other high-ranking Roman, whether he was acting for himself or others. How many non-Romans availed themselves of this

[31] Cic. *Leg.Agr.* 1.8; 2.45; *Flacc.* 86; *Att.* 2.18.3; *Leg.* 3.18; Plut. *Mar.* 31.2.

[32] Varro, cit. note 2; App. *BCiv.* 1.22.96–7; Diod. 34/5.25–7; Vell. 2.13; Pliny *HN.* 33.34.

opportunity is hard to guess. We know of two prosecutions *de repetundis* by Latins before 90 BC,[33] but these, though not Roman citizens, had the advantage of knowing the Latin language and coming from communities which regularly had access to Roman law. A man who spoke little or no Latin could ask for a *patronus* (lines 9ff). Nevertheless, this was only permitted after the denunciation (*nominis delatio*) had been made and accepted by the praetor, thus setting in motion the machinery of the *quaestio*, and the man who performed the denunciation remained the plaintiff and accuser, whose personal involvement was essential right through the case. Clearly this was a major departure from procedure before the present law, since then the complaints of Rome's allies could only be brought to bear with the aid of high-ranking Romans, perhaps after a preliminary hearing in the senate.[34] We may still wonder how far a non-Roman could have managed the summons of his opponent without aid from a Roman friend or patron ('patron' in the sense of a personal connection, not formally appointed by the praetor). The change may have been more dramatic in theory than in practice. It was linked, however, with the provision of rewards for successful prosecutors and was surely intended by the legislator to be an important change. It should be noted that requests for *patroni* were not allowed in the short procedure, resembling those in regular civil law, provided for in lines 6–8. It is likely that this was reserved for the simpler cases, when men sued on their own behalf.

Those who wished to sue under the main provisions of the law had, as was generally required by the Twelve Tables,[35] to bring their opponent before the praetor in the forum and denounce him formally (lines 6 and 19). Why should the accused have appeared in the first place, since the authority of a magistrate had not yet been brought to bear on him? This is a problem with all suits in Roman law, where the accuser was inferior in power and status to the accused.[36] The Twelve Tables prescribed that, on occasions when a man resisted summons, witnesses should be called to his recalcitrance and ultimately physical force might be used. When a Roman senator was being summonsed, as under this law, perhaps the most important sanction available to the prosecutor was the creation of scandal by informal accusations. In the last resort it might have been necessary to bring a complaint before the senate. If the accused ran away, which was tantamount to a confession of guilt, or if he stayed at home and refused a summons, this would have entailed the cessation of public activity, which was a living death for a senator or would-be senator and might have led to formal loss of status through degradation by the censor. Once accuser and accused had appeared before the praetor, if the suit was accepted by that magistrate as competent, the accused normally was required to provide sureties (*vadimonia*) for future appearances.[37] However, this law went further

[33] Cic. *Balb.* 53. [34] Cf. Serrao, 1956. [35] *XII Tab.* I.I. [36] Kelly, 1966, ch. I.
[37] Cf. *lex agr.*, lines 34ff.

by permitting trial of absentees (line 29), thus countering any attempt by the accused to jump bail. The frustrations suffered by the Spanish plaintiffs in 171 were not to be permitted.

After the suit had been accepted by the praetor, the plaintiff (lines 9–12) could ask him for a *patronus*. The term in this context refers to an advocate, but one who would not take over the responsibility for bringing the action from the plaintiff himself. This was no doubt how men, who were *patroni* in its more general sense – i.e. protectors of dependants in Roman society – traditionally assisted their clients in court. The choice was at the praetor's discretion. He might choose someone with an existing connection with the plaintiff. However, the right accorded to the plaintiff to repudiate a *patronus* who was no use to him, suggests that the legislator had in mind the precedent of 171, when it was rumoured that the *patroni* of the Spaniards had obstructed their wish to call on the evidence of powerful and noble men.[38]

The complex procedure for assembling a jury was also set in motion (lines 12–19). The law instructed the relevant praetor (in the first year the praetor supervising civil suits involving foreigners, in subsequent years one specially selected to preside over the court) to select and record a panel of 450 jurors. The positive qualifications for membership of this panel do not survive on the bronze that remains. The literary tradition about C.Gracchus suggests that these jurors were *equites*, either in the strict sense that they held the public horse or because they had an equestrian census qualification. The correct spectrum of meaning of the term *eques* in the late Republic has evoked a great deal of scholarly debate. Even if it is held that the term strictly referred to members of the Roman cavalry, not to men merely possessing a certain property-qualification, a problem remains over who were the cavalry – the eighteen centuries of *equites equo publico* (who by now may have numbered 2,200, but are unlikely to have numbered many more), or the 19,000 odd Roman cavalrymen, that Polybius maintains were available to Rome in the year 225 BC. It is probable that the source of recruitment of the new jurors was wider than the eighteen centuries, since large numbers of them would have been disqualified by connection with senators or absence from Rome on public and other business. Moreover, according to the elder Pliny, the members of the Gracchan juries were originally called *iudices* (judges) rather than *equites*, the latter term being reserved for members of the equestrian centuries.[39]

[38] Livy 43.2.11.

[39] The sources relevant to C.Gracchus cited in notes 29 and 32 above. For numbers of *equites*, see Pol.2.24; Cato, *ORF*, frag., 86 for 2,200 *equites equo publico*. The view of Nicolet, 1966, that the term *equites* only applied to members of the centuries, has been best criticised by T.P. Wiseman (*Historia* 19 (1970), 67ff). On the character of the *ordo* see Brunt, 1988, 144ff, 515–16. For the phrase *iudices Gracchani* see Cic. *Brut.* 128. On the tradition that C.Gracchus passed a general jury-law, which prescribed a mixed panel of senators and *equites* see Brunt, 1988, 194ff.

What our inscription makes clear is that not only senators and former holders of minor magistracies were excluded, but also the close relatives of senators. This would have eliminated the upper strata of the equestrian order, who were either too young to be senators or, though of senatorial family, had decided to stay out of public life – indeed the very people who had traditionally formed the core of the public horse.[40] Ex-senators stripped of their rank were also ineligible. The legislator evidently aimed to create a body as unconnected as possible with any senatorial defendant. It is only later, during Cicero's lifetime, that *equites* became the standard name for non-senatorial jurors, and this may be linked with the fact that by then the leading members of the equestrian order, those close in standing to senators and linked by family to them, would have joined the juries in the *quaestio de repetundis* – probably for the first time through Servilius Caepio's bill of 106 BC (if we do not believe the *lex Acilia* to be separate from C.Gracchus' legislation and so a further law of the period 121–107, see below pp. 166–9).

The concern for impartiality can also be seen in the procedure for selecting a trial jury (lines 19–26). The defendant had first to reveal to the plaintiff (line 20) any members of the panel who were relatives of his as close as cousins, together with stepfathers, stepsons and relatives by marriage, also members of the same club or association (*collegium* or *sodalitas*). Interestingly, nothing is said about patron–client relationships at this point. It may have been assumed that the jury were men of sufficient substance for that relationship not to be significant, or perhaps that such a relationship at that level of society would have entailed membership of the same *sodalitas*. With this information the plaintiff had to select 100 potential jurors, who were in no wise connected with himself (line 22) – the law clearly refers to the plaintiff here, not to any *patronus*, and this is a strong indication that Roman citizens might sue. If he selected men known to him to be connected with the defendant, that was his affair. The defendant was permitted to reject fifty of these, leaving a trial jury of fifty (line 24). If he failed to do so, the plaintiff was to perform this reduction himself (line 25).

In Roman civil law it was a principle that a single judge was acceptable to both parties in the case and also that, where a jury of *recuperatores* was empanelled, the plaintiff and defendant were accorded a limited right of rejection, but the procedure used here goes far beyond such requirements. Although it is designed to ensure that a defendant will not be acquitted because of the personal obligations of jurymen towards him (thus providing an additional indication of what had been wrong with previous senatorial juries in the *quaestio de repetundis*), the law also self-consciously requires impartiality among the jurors towards the plaintiff. A noteworthy feature throughout the chapters on jury-selection is the concern for publicity. The praetor had to have his list of jurors read out at a public meeting and swear that he had chosen fairly.

[40] Cf. Sherwin-White, 1982, 21–2.

The list had subsequently to be written in black on a white board and kept available for copying throughout his magistracy (lines 14–15, 18–19).[41] The defendant had to swear publicly that he had declared any potential jurors connected with him, the plaintiff similarly that he had chosen jurors unconnected with himself and according to the rules of the law (lines 20–3). The names of the trial jury were to be kept on record and available for copying (lines 26–7).

The praetor was required to give the trial jury notice of the day on which they had to be present in Rome early in the morning (line 30). The jury was not to be supplemented and had to remain on the case until it was finished. It is possible that some sort of attendance allowance was paid to them in certain circumstances (lines 27–8). If the defendant died or went into exile, the suit could be brought against a connection of his, an heir or a close relative who would have had the control of his money (line 29).

Before the trial opened, the praetor, if necessary, organised the collection of evidence and witnesses in Italy (lines 31–4). This was conceived as an inquiry to seek substantiation of the plaintiff's claims. There is no mention of gathering evidence abroad, as happened in the procedure known as *inquisitio*, first attested while the later law of Servilius Glaucia was in force (see below, pp. 28–9) and employed by Cicero when he prosecuted Verres,[42] or of the summoning of witnesses from abroad.[43] This may be ascribed to a desire of the legislator to provide speedy procedure and his expectation that any plaintiff from outside Italy would bring his witnesses with him. It also reflects the nature of the prosecution as a private suit rather than the general investigation of the conduct of a magistrate. The law enjoined that magistrates in Italian communities should assist in the collection of evidence (line 31). Up to forty-eight witnesses could be formally summonsed by the plaintiff (patrons and clients of the defendant were excluded from the obligation to testify) and the production of public and private documents could be demanded (line 34). The use of praetorian authority to summons witnesses, though alien to private law-suits entrusted to a *iudex*, is also a feature of trials before *recuperatores* (see below, p. 30), but the provisions known to us there do not attain the complexity of the *lex repetundarum*.

Not much survives of the instructions for the trial itself. The jurors had to swear oaths before the case began, that they would listen to the evidence and not absent themselves, and again, before they voted, that they should not try to discover each other's votes (lines 37, 44). Elaborate routines were prescribed for jurors who wished to be excused from attendance and for the determination by the praetor whether sufficient of the jury had made up their minds to enable a vote to be taken (lines 45–8). Regarding this last point, if more than a third of

41 On the concern for publicity, Sherwin-White, 1982, 21.

42 Cic. *Scaur.* 23ff; *Verr.* 1.6; Asc. 19C; still used in the time of the younger Pliny (*Ep.* 3.9.6; 5.20.2; 6.5.1–2) but operated by the provincials themselves.

43 Cic. *Flacc.* 14; 36ff.

the jury said '*non liquet*', i.e. that they were unable to decide, the praetor was required to prolong the hearing until this was remedied, but jurors who refused to give a verdict on more than two occasions were to be fined 10,000 sesterces (lines 47–8) – 2½ per cent of the census qualification of *equites* and a considerable sum by the standards of that time (it was almost double what was regarded as an excessive annual rent for a house in Rome).[44]

The mechanics of voting were laid down in detail (lines 49–54). After those who had stated that they could not make up their mind had been removed, the remaining jurors were each given a slip of boxwood, four fingers in length, with the letter A for *absolvo* on one side and C for *condemno* on the other (line 51). The juror was required to delete the letter he did not want and deposit the slip in a voting jar, keeping his arm bare, so that there was no question of his inserting more than one vote, but concealing the surviving letter with his fingers (line 52). Once the votes had been all cast one by one, they were withdrawn one by one by a juror selected by lot, who displayed the surviving letter to the court and the surrounding crowd, while reading out its verdict. The voting ballots were then passed on to the presiding praetor (lines 53–4).

The law still recognised the possibility that some jurors at this stage would record a no-vote, but this was taken as strictly neutral. If there were more votes to condemn than either votes to acquit or no-votes, considered separately, then the defendant was condemned, although an overall majority had not voted to condemn him (line 55). It would have been assumed, however, that no-votes would be kept to a minimum through the preceding examination of the jurors on their readiness to vote. The vote was final. Whether a man was condemned or acquitted, he could not be tried again *de repetundis* under this law, unless collusive prosecution was proved or he committed fresh offences after the trial (lines 55–6). As to the retrial of a condemned man, it should be noted that the law of the Roman Republic, like the law of Athens, did not normally allow for appeal as part of the judicial process. *Provocatio* (see above), which might also involve appeal to tribunes, was possible against capital condemnations outside a *quaestio perpetua*, and the help of other magistrates might be invoked in private cases, where it was alleged that there had been a miscarriage of justice by the magistrate who had heard the pleas.[45] However, the present law specifically forbad any obstruction to its execution by other magistrates (lines 70–1).

Immediately a man was condemned, the presiding praetor had instructions either to obtain guarantors (*praedes*) from the defendant or to confiscate publicly his property (lines 57–8). This was to ensure that the defendant could not hide his resources in the ensuing period, when the jury carried out the *litis aestumatio*, that is, calculated the precise amount of damages to be paid to each victim. The payments were to be double the loss sustained by the victim for any offence committed after the passage of the law, simple restitution for previous

[44] The view of the censors of 125 BC, Vell.Pat. 2.10; cf. Val.Max. 8.1.*Damn*.7.

[45] Lintott, 1972b, 238ff; Jones, 1960, 72ff; see also Asc. 47C, 84C.

offences (line 59). This seems to be a partial concession in face of possible objections against retrospective legislation, something to which the Romans were not in fact opposed on principle. The legislator was quite prepared for this new procedure to be used to deal with earlier offences, even by men acquitted under previous *leges de repetundis* (lines 74, 81), but not to go beyond the penalty required by previous laws in such cases.

During the *litis aestumatio* every party to the suit was expected to make his claim for damages separately (lines 59–60). If the sum available to the treasury from the defendant was equal to the total damages involved, then payment would be made almost immediately (line 61). If not enough money was available at the end of the *litis aestumatio*, a distribution was made to the claimants involved of what money there was, presumably in proportion to the damages in theory due to them, on a day appointed in advance (lines 62–6). However, this did not extinguish the defendant's liability, and future quaestors at the treasury were required to continue to pursue the money and pay it to the claimants (lines 66–9). Sums uncollected by the claimants after five years were to remain in the treasury as the property of the Roman people (line 66).

The provisions for trial, estimation and allocation of damages are at this point complete. The immediate sequel in the text is a number of supplementary provisions. First, magistrates were forbidden to delay proceedings in the court, except when these clashed with a formal assembly or a meeting of the senate (lines 70–2). The duties of one year's magistrates were to devolve on their successors (lines 72–3, cf. lines 79–80). Men condemned under the previous *leges de repetundis*, the *lex Calpurnia* and the *lex Iunia*, were not to be tried again for the same offences (lines 73–4). There was also a chapter dealing with occasions when the jury had decided that a collusive accusation (*praevaricatio*) had been made, intended to ensure the acquittal of the defendant (line 75).

Most of the remainder of the surviving text of the law concerns rewards for successful prosecutors and therein lies one of the most interesting features of the law. Rewards for informers are attested earlier in Roman history – most conspicuously at the time of the Bacchanalian conspiracy of 186 BC – but these were associated with tribunals of inquiry in which magistrates investigated without the need for formal prosecution.[46] We also find them mentioned in the agrarian law on the reverse of the tablet and in a literary source regarding agrarian legislation (*lex agr.* 90–1 with commentary). In the *lex de repetundis* rewards are given to those responsible for 'denunciation' (*nominis delatio*) – the same term that is used for laying information – but the man who denounced in this court actually brought the prosecution himself. Rewards were offered to Roman citizens (line 87, cf. also lines 83–4?), probably including freedom from the obligation of military service. More strikingly, non-Romans were offered

[46] Livy 2.5.9; 4.45.2; 8.18.4; 22.33.2; 26.27.9; 27.3.4ff; 28.46.5–6; 32.26.14; 39.19.3–4. Cf. Cic. *Scaur.* 41; *Sulla* 51; *Inv.* 2.110; and on the Catilinarian conspiracy later *Cat.* 4.5,10; Sall. *Cat.* 50.1.

full Roman citizenship and freedom from military service (lines 76–7). Alternatively, they might remain in their previous communities but be granted *provocatio* in their relations with Roman magistrates and freedom from public obligations in that community (lines 77–9). As Cicero pointed out later, this kind of reward must have been particularly repugnant to members of the senatorial order, because, whatever their attitude to the extension of Roman citizenship, it could only take effect at the expense of the ruin of a senator.[47]

The implications and consequences of the lex repetundarum

The *lex repetundarum* on the Urbino fragments was not the first law on this subject nor the first law to set up a permanent criminal tribunal (*quaestio perpetua*). Nevertheless, it was revolutionary in more ways than one. The tribunal's operations were strictly governed by the plebiscite passed by the assembly and there was little discretion for those who operated in the court as to procedure. The most conspicuous feature of the court was the large jury-panel, which was an innovation both in its size and because anyone connected with the senate was rigidly excluded from it. Although the president of the court had important functions in supervising the trial and ensuring the observance of the statute (including perhaps the right to interrogate witnesses, lines 35–6), the initiative rested with the prosecution and the important decisions – over not only the guilt of the defendant (lines 44ff) but the size of the damages (lines 57, 60) and the question of collusive prosecution (line 75) – were left to the jury.

This *quaestio perpetua* was not a people's court drawn by lot from the citizens, as at Athens, but it was a court with a jury from outside the elite, controlled by regulations approved by the people, whose proceedings were to be as public as possible and in which the victims themselves could prosecute. The general comments preserved in the literary sources, including some attributed to C.Gracchus himself, which portray his reforms as the creation of a new source of power and conflict in the Republic, do not seem in this light exaggerated.[48] The actual threat posed to senators as individuals may seem less dramatic and the images ascribed to Gracchus – a sword hanging over the senate and a knife thrust into the senate's side – excessively lurid.[49] Those condemned for robbery and corruption were only to suffer financially: there was no capital penalty nor damage to status and reputation through the automatic infliction of *infamia*, that is, the loss of senatorial dignity or further degradation. Yet there was a penal element in the sums paid by convicted men and, arguably, any system of justice, which made the conviction of men of senatorial rank more probable, would have been felt as a stab in the flesh of that order. Gladiatorial contests were held in the forum in the late Republic.[50] The

[47] Cic. *Balb.* 54.

[48] Cic. *Leg.* 3.20; Varro, cit. note 2; Diod. 34/5.25–7; 37.9; App. *BCiv* 1.22.97.

[49] Cic. *Leg.* 3.20; Diod. 34/5.27; 37.9. [50] Plut. *C.Gr.* 12.5–7.

trials in the *quaestio de repetundis* were to be another public spectacle, whose climax would be political, rather than physical, death.

The law was revolutionary in making its procedures available to allies and rewarding them for success. In principle this was a major break with the earlier custom, according to which foreigners could only obtain justice for offences by Roman officials through seeking patronage among the elite. How effective the law would have been in this respect is open to question. Much would have depended on the ability and good faith of any *patronus* appointed by the presiding praetor. It would still have been a formidable task for a non-Roman to tackle a man of senatorial rank without informal assistance from a Roman with legal expertise in the period before the acceptance of the denunciation, the point at which a *patronus* could be formally appointed.

The law formed part of what was arguably the greatest package of reforms passed in the popular interest during the Roman Republic. The main features of C.Gracchus' politics were: (a) to make the plebeian assembly both the source of reform and the central reference-point in politics; (b) to secure *commoda* (welfare) in the shape of land and cheap corn for the Roman plebs through the profits of empire; (c) to maintain the liberty of the plebs by measures safeguarding *provocatio* (the right of the plebs to call for protection against the coercive power of magistrates); (d) to break the judicial monopoly of the senate and to prevent abuses of power and corruption among the magistrates, most of whom were either senators already or soon would be; (e) to improve the status of Rome's allies in Italy by giving citizenship to the Latins and some privilege involving voting rights to the latter. As a judicial measure, the *lex repetundarum* should be grouped with Gracchus' law about *provocatio* (which forbad capital trials without the assembly's approval), his law against conspiracies by magistrates and senators to secure capital condemnations[51] and probably a general judiciary law creating a jury-panel for public and private lawsuits out of a mixture of senators and *equites*.[52] Clearly it is consistent with other measures which sought to make senators more accountable and bring their abuses into the public gaze. The legislator's continual concern with publicity in the legal process he was creating is striking – in the selection of the jury-panel and the trial-jury (lines 14–15, 18–19, 20–3, 26–7), the jurors' oath (36–8), voting procedure (53), the distribution of money recovered in damages (65–6) and rewards for accusers (79). The non-senatorial jury reflects Gracchus' desire to diminish the senate's traditional position as the chief source of authority in all public matters. If the law was available to Roman citizens (see commentary on line 1), it may be seen as a contribution to the protection of the Roman plebs against exploitation by their superiors. The rewards the law offered to successful non-Roman accusers are in the same spirit as the proposal for

[51] Plut. *C.Gr.* 4; Cic. *Rab.Perd.* 12; *Clu.* 148, 151 and 157; *Brut.* 48; Ewins, 1960; Lintott, 1968, 163ff; Brunt, 1988, 224ff.

[52] See below pp. 168–9 and commentary on *lex agr.* 37; Brunt, 1988, 194ff.

extending Roman citizenship to the Latins and for giving improved status to the Italian allies, though, if that bill had been ratified by the assembly and put into effect, the rewards proposed for non-Romans by the *lex de repetundis* would have looked comparatively insignificant beside it. As to the provision of justice for Rome's allies, it would be naive to pretend that the aim of this law was easily reconcilable with C.Gracchus' devotion to the interests of the Roman plebs. From that point of view ruthless exploitation of the Roman empire would have been in order, and we can detect in Diodorus (almost certainly following Poseidonius and, through him, conservatively minded Romans) precisely this criticism: C.Gracchus created a conspiracy of the 'worst' people at Rome, above all the equestrian tax-collectors, to exploit the allies.[53] In fact the law said nothing about non-senatorial collectors of taxes: it sought to prevent extortion by magistrates and officials, while placing no restraint on those collecting the revenues of the Roman people.

Some inferences about the success of the law can be drawn from the subsequent history of this and other courts. First, the form of the *quaestio de repetundis* was transferred to courts dealing with other crimes, whether newly created, such as the *quaestio de maiestate* established by L.Saturninus, or already existing, such as the *quaestio de ambitu* and other courts reformed by Sulla. The pattern of a permanent tribunal regulated by statute, with a large jury and an adversarial format, in which the initiative lay with the prosecutor, was repeated in courts dealing with treason, public violence, murder, embezzlement and bribery. The recruitment of the jury remained a matter of political controversy.[54] Senators were brought into the *quaestio de repetundis* by Servilius Caepio in 106 BC, but removed from it within a few years. The bill of M.Livius Drusus in 91 BC restoring the court to senatorial juries was annulled. The *lex Plautia* of 89 allowed some senators into the album of jurors, and Sulla handed over the court exclusively to senators in 81. Finally, after the *lex Aurelia* of 70, the jurors were one third senators and two thirds non-senators, although among the two thirds must be counted a number of future senators and close relatives of senators whom C.Gracchus had excluded. These had probably been introduced to the court for the first time by Caepio, as it would have been illogical for him to include in his jury-album senators and Gracchan jurors, but not the *equites* closely connected with the senate that Gracchus had excluded. The question then arises whether these leading *equites* were eliminated from the juries together with the senators by Glaucia. It may be that they were not, and this would have encouraged the use of the term *equites* for non-senatorial jurors from then on.

Allegations were made of bias and corruption among the non-senatorial jurors in the pre-Sullan period. The burden of such allegations was that innocent men were condemned (the most notorious case was that of P.Rutilius

[53] Diod. 34/5.25–7. For a useful general account of C.Gracchus' legislation, see Stockton, 1979, 114–205. [54] See e.g. Brunt, 1988, 194ff; Balsdon, 1938.

Rufus in *c.* 92 BC, who may in fact have been guilty as charged).[55] However, examination of the results of cases shows a conviction rate of about 50 per cent.[56] It is reasonable to believe that any corruption did not always work in one direction. The provisions of the *lex Aurelia*, which established mixed juries, were a final compromise in which the dignity of the senatorial order was as important as honest verdicts. Non-senators, remarkably, remained exempt from charges of receiving bribes as jurors throughout the Republic. This was something which C.Gracchus took no measures to deal with in his judiciary laws, perhaps because he did not wish his new jurors to be vulnerable to senatorial hostility. By the late Republic some of the cutting edge of non-senatorial jurors had been blunted, but in this respect their vested interests were preserved. Senatorial jurors, by contrast, were threatened by Gracchus' law against conspiracy to create capital condemnations and became liable for receiving bribes under the provisions of later *leges de repetundis*.[57]

Modifications were made to the procedure of the *quaestio de repetundis*, not always in the same spirit as the Gracchan legislation. By 100 BC the provision for up to three rehearings without penalty to the jurors had been replaced in Glaucia's law by a compulsory two-part trial (*comperendinatio*). Glaucia had also introduced the pursuit of damages from those to whom the convicted defendant had passed on his ill-gotten gains (*quo ea pecunia pervenerit*).[58] Both these reforms may be regarded as furthering C.Gracchus' aims. Another reform changed the direction of the court. To deal with the situation, when a man was denounced by a number of parties for his conduct in a particular term of office, a procedure called *divinatio* was introduced, whereby a jury selected the prosecutor who should handle all the alleged crimes together. This seems *de facto* to have led to accusations being undertaken by Romans, who were not personally involved in the injuries but were versed in the ways of the forum, while the actual plaintiffs, Roman or non-Roman, acted as their advisers.[59] Associated with this was the introduction of *inquisitiones*, tours of investigation in the provinces conducted by the prosecutor. Here the prosecutor could collect evidence from documents and find witnesses; indeed he could discover

[55] Cic. *de Or.* 1.225; *Clu.* 140; Vell. 2.13; App. *BCiv* 1.22.96; 35.158; and on Rutilius Rufus, see Cic. *Brut.* 115; Poseidonius F27 (Jacoby) = 78 (Edelstein-Kidd); Livy *Per.* 70; Val.Max. 2.10.5; Dio fr. 97.1; Lintott, 1981, 194–5. [56] Lintott, 1981, 209–12.

[57] Cic. *Clu.* 104, 148 and 152; *Att.* 1.17.8; *Rab.Post.* 16. Cf. on Gracchus' law Ewins, 1960; on the development of bribery charges *Ibid.*, 100; Lintott, 1981, 193–6, 202–5; Venturini, 1979, 472ff.

[58] Cic. *Rab.Post.* 9; *Fam.* 8.8.3; *Verr.* 1.34; 2 *Verr.* 1.26; *Scaur.* 29–30; PsAsc. 230–231St.; Balsdon, 1938, 110–11; Lintott, 1981, 189f.

[59] Cf. Cic. 2 *Verr.* 2.32; *Flacc.* 22; 42ff; *Fam.* 8.8.2, on which see Lintott, 1980. Venturini, 1979, 422, has argued that this change was *de iure*, but the principle of admitting accusations by non-Romans is accepted as already existing (under the *lex Iulia de repetundis* of 59) in the *S.C. Calvisianum* (see below, note 62).

petitioners with a claim against the accused so far unknown to him.[60] It may be argued that this led to more efficient and comprehensive prosecutions, but the part that might be played by non-Roman plaintiffs especially was reduced. The centrality of compensating victims who had suffered loss was also diminished, when the remit of the *quaestio* was extended to cover the receipt of freely given bribes (probably by 100 BC) and to various breaches of rules laid down for the behaviour of magistrates in provinces.[61] Complaints still came from the allies, but the prosecution became more of a piece of Roman self-regulation and the injured parties more distanced from the workings of the law. Ultimately, a straightforward process for recovery was reinstated by the *S.C. Calvisianum* of 4 BC, in which the allies could obtain simple restitution for their losses in a comparatively short time with the minimum of judicial complexity (in this decree the method of providing *patroni* for plaintiffs resembles the measure in the *lex repetundarum*).[62]

Under the late Republic the working of the *quaestio de repetundis* became even more elaborate than it was under C.Gracchus' law. It was also inevitably distorted by political considerations and various forms of corruption. Nevertheless, it remained one of the chief arenas in which a member of the elite, who had exercised power over Rome's subjects and allies, was forced to face the fact that his authority and dignity were not impregnable.

The origins of the legal procedure in the *quaestio* established by the lex de repetundis

Earlier in this chapter (pp. 11–14), two forms of Roman legal process were mentioned which have some claim to paternity of the *quaestiones perpetuae* as a whole – first, the special tribunal (*quaestio*) set up to investigate and punish particular offences, such as the Bacchanalian conspiracy or the corruption of Hostilius Tubulus, secondly, the private, or quasi-private, process before a jury of *recuperatores*, which was used to deal with delicts like theft, when the public interest was at stake, or with offences against administrative law. We know little detail about procedure before the special tribunals. What is clear is the importance of the president (or presidents) of the court in conducting the investigation and the fact that the verdict was their responsibility, even though it was reached by the consultation of a quasi-jury, a *consilium* of assessors.[63] It should also be stressed that these special tribunals were held in public (the

[60] Cic. *Verr.* 1.6; 2 *Verr.* 1.30; *Flacc.* 13ff; *Scaur.* 23ff; Asc. 19C.

[61] Lintott, 1981, 191–7, 202–7; Venturini, 1979, 472ff and 515ff.

[62] *SEG* IX, 8 = *FIRA* I, 410ff = EJ, 311, V, esp. lines 100ff.

[63] On these courts see Kunkel, 1962, 59ff. However, his view that the responsibility for the verdict lay with the *consilium* as jury was rightly criticised by Garnsey, 1966, 177ff; cf. Lintott, 1972b, 228 with n9.

investigation in 138 BC of the murders committed in the Silva Sila took place before a large and appreciative crowd).[64]

We are better informed about trials before *recuperatores*. The detailed evidence begins in the period immediately following the *lex de repetundis* and there is no reason to think that the characteristic features of such trials had recently changed. In a number of respects the procedures here resemble in principle those of the *lex repetundarum*, even if the detail and indeed the scale of operations is different. First, the jury of *recuperatores* itself was formed by selection from a previously created panel of jurors, followed by a limited amount of rejection of unwanted jurors, alternately by prosecution and defence. This can be seen in the *lex agraria* of 111 BC and in the law about the praetorian provinces of 101–100 BC.[65] In this last and a number of other texts relating to *recuperatores* we find provision for the summons of a limited number of witnesses on behalf of the prosecution,[66] and on some occasions when the prosecution has been undertaken in the public interest there are rewards for accusers.[67] A further feature of trial before *recuperatores* was that the magistrate who appointed them seems to have taken responsibility for exacting the damages, as did the praetor in the *quaestio de repetundis*.[68]

Yet the Gracchan *quaestio* also shows major differences from private law procedure of all kinds. Although those liable to prosecution and the delicts involved were closely defined by the law at the start, each case was not usually confined to a single issue, which could have been determined in a formula given by the praetor to the judge or judges in a private suit, e.g. 'if it appears that Manius Aquillius has unjustly exacted five statues from the city of Pergamum . . .' Prosecutions were characterised by the linking of a multiplicity of pleas, indeed by a plurality of plaintiffs, since, even if one man originally performed *nominis delatio*, he may have been acting as the representative of a number of people (*lex rep.* 4 and 60), and it appears from the rules about rewards (*lex rep.* 76ff) that a number of prosecutors could be in line for a reward on account of a successful prosecution, since a choice had to be made of the man most responsible. The rule forbidding the retrial of a man acquitted or condemned under the Gracchan law (*lex rep.* 55–6 with commentary) did not, as Mommsen thought, lay down that a man could not be tried twice on a single issue, but that he could only be brought back to court *de repetundis* if he did something actionable after the verdict. The implication is that the trial was expected to embrace any possible damage to any victim (even perhaps in different regions or

64 Cic. *Brut.* 85–9.

65 *Lex agr.* 37; *lex. prov.praet.* (Hassall *et al.*, 1974), Cnidos V.15–24. See also *ed. Aug. de aq. Ven.* (note 67 below). Cf. *lex rep.* 12ff.

66 Cnidos V.30; *lex Iul. agr.*, ch. LV; *lex gen. Urs.*, ch. XCV; *ed. Aug. de aquaeductu Venafrano* (Bruns, 77), 65ff. Cf. *lex rep.* 32ff.

67 Cnidos V.44ff; *lex Iul.agr.*, ch. LV; *ed. Aug.* (Bruns, 77), lines 65ff. Cf. *lex rep.* 76ff.

68 *Lex agr.* 39; Cnidos V.40ff; *lex Iul.agr.*, ch. LV. Cf. *lex rep.* 56ff. See, in general on this topic, Lintott, 1990; Mantovani, 1989, 121ff.

provinces) up to the time of the trial, and this is in fact the impression we get from cases under later *repetundae* laws, whether our evidence is a Ciceronian speech or a report in Tacitus or Pliny: prosecutors deliberately accumulated every charge possible.[69]

The corollary of this was the *litis aestumatio*. The notion of *aestumatio* of appropriate damages was common enough in private law; what was unusual about the *quaestio de repetundis* was the allocation of a separate part of the trial to this (*lex rep.* 58–60), in which individual claimants came to the fore and the jury decided by majority verdicts what damages should be assigned to each. It is evident that, without this second stage, the procedure would have been of limited value to the injured parties and it would have been better for them if they had been allowed to press their claims separately.

A strong case has been made recently for the effect of Greek philosophy, especially political theory, on the Gracchi and their advisers.[70] It has similarly been argued that Greek ideas influenced lawyers friendly to the Gracchi – P.Mucius Scaevola (*cos.* 133) and P.Licinius Crassus Mucianus (*cos.* 131) – though the context in which this has been suggested is the rules about *ager publicus*.[71] Speculation is not, therefore, out of order about the likely impact of Greek judicial practice on the Gracchi. It is difficult to find similarities in detail for the somewhat surprising reason that inscriptions have preserved few judicial texts from the Greek world similar to a law establishing a Roman *quaestio*. Certainly, the elaborate voting procedures in fourth century Athens described to us by the Aristotelian *Athenaion Politieia* (chs. 68–9) have a general similarity to those in the *lex repetundarum* (49ff). The trial jury of fifty in the *quaestio* was unusual by traditional Roman standards (there was of course the civil court of 100 men, the *centumviri*, but we do not know how many of these were empanelled for a particular trial), but it can hardly be related to the mass juries of 500 or more used by the classical Athenian democracy: the *repetundae* jury is more directly comparable to the fifty-one *ephetai* drawn from the Areopagus.[72] Provisions like the oath taken by the jurors and the sealing of evidence can be paralleled at Athens and Cnidos.[73] More striking are the recently published regulations for trials, comprised in the second century BC *sumbolai* (judicial convention) between Clazomenai and Temnos. Here there are not only oaths, but a clause disqualifying from jury-service relatives of the parties, which in content, if not in style, is close to the rules in the *lex repetundarum* (lines 20 and 22).[74] If we knew more about Greek legal procedure in the Hellenistic period, it is likely that further parallels with the *lex repetundarum* would emerge, though it would not follow that it was the Gracchi themselves who had imported all features of procedure which apparently had Greek ancestry. Oaths by the jurors, for example, may have been required in

69 Alexander, 1982. Cf. Meyer, 1978.

70 Nicolet, 1965. Cf.Badian, 1972, 679ff.

71 Behrends, 1980; Bauman, 1983, 249ff.

72 MacDowell, 1978, 116ff.

73 *Ath.Pol.* 67; *Syll.*³, 953, 2ff and 22ff.

74 Herrman, 1979, 253–4, lines 37–41.

quaestiones before C.Gracchus' time. Nevertheless, the probability remains that this court was to some extent the product of crossbreeding between Greek and Roman judicial stock.

Appendix *Additional note:* Mantovani's view of the *lex repetundarum*

In a powerfully argued work (*Il problema d'origine dell' accusa popolare*, Padua, 1989) – which unfortunately came into my hands after the typescript had been sent to the publisher, but for which I am grateful to the author – Dario Mantovani has tried to argue that the *actio popularis*, that is, accusation by anyone who wished, originated before the era of *divinatio* under the *leges Serviliae*, in fact under C.Gracchus' *lex repetundarum*. He believes that this provision, limited (he conjectures) to Roman citizens, existed in addition to those visible in the surviving text, whereby wronged individuals and their relatives and representatives of communities could prosecute (lines 3–4).

His arguments (pp. 71ff) are partly from sources external to the *lex rep.*, partly from the text itself. Central among them is the speech L.Crassus delivered in favour of the *lex Servilia Caepionis* of 106 BC, in which Crassus aroused odium 'in iudicum et accusatorum factionem, contra quorum potentiam populariter tum dicendum fuit' (Cic. *Brut.* 164; cf. *de Or.* 1.225). In my view, he misinterprets the word *factio* as 'the faction (of judges and accusers)', when it is naturally taken in its original abstract sense of unofficial power and influence (cf. R. Seager, '*Factio*: Some Observations', *JRS* 62 (1972), 53–8), in effect a synonym for *potentia*. The passage may still be thought to imply that the court had been dominated by professional accusers. Arguably this is what Crassus was trying to suggest, but, of course, this may have been a blatant misrepresentation. Mantovani also points (pp. 76 and 97) to the accusations undertaken by men of the senatorial and equestrian orders in the decade after the *lex rep.* – L.Crassus himself, T.Albucius, M.Brutus and M.Antonius. However, it is perfectly possible for these to be representatives of an injured community (Albucius may have been particularly acceptable to the peoples of Asia through his familiarity with the Greek world – Lucilius, 88–94M). Nor can it be excluded, in cases other than that of Crassus versus Carbo (Cic. *Verr.* 3.3; *de Or.* 3.74), that Cicero has treated as an accuser a man who was the plaintiff's *patronus* appointed by the court.

Even if Mantovani's argument was so far sound, it would only prove, as he admits (pp. 79ff), that the *actio popularis* was introduced before the *lex Servilia Caepionis*, perhaps by the *lex Acilia*, if this was not identical with the *lex rep.* However, he believes that he can find traces of the *actio popularis* within the *lex rep.* itself. He begins with the chapter about the exhaustion of the action after the verdict, unless the defendant committed some new offence (line 56). This in effect required that all claims against a magistrate after his term of office should be assembled in a unitary action, if they were all to succeed. But how could this be, he asks, if individual injured parties were expected to bring individual suits?

Clearly, he is right that, if claims were fragmented, the result would have been that at most one injured party would have received satisfaction. However, when actions originated in a non-Roman community, they would probably have been handled by a single representative, and indeed there were other considerations that might have induced a plaintiff to put forward other complaints than his own. There was a minimum sum of damages required for the activation of the *quaestio* procedure. Moreover, in order to make an impact on the judges sufficient to secure a condemnation, the more evidence the prosecutor could secure, the better. If there were other potential plaintiffs, he could employ them as witnesses. Obviously, injustices could have occurred through the exclusion of deserving plaintiffs from undertaking an action, but the same might have resulted from an *actio popularis* (especially if there was not as yet a system of *inquisitio* in the provinces). For the legislator this method of prosecution combined giving to Rome's allies direct access to a criminal court with the simplicity and publicity afforded by a single spectacular trial.

This said, Mantovani's other arguments lose most of their force. Certainly, *petitio* belongs to a single man (pp. 86ff), but this does not help Mantovani's case. The argument (p. 89) that *quoius eorum opera unius maxume is condemnatus erit* (in lines 76ff) does not imply that more than one person actually brought the action is true, but the word *eorum* (not present in the parallel phrases from *lex Iulia agraria* ch. LV and *Frontinus de aquis*, 127, which he quotes) suggests that the prosecutor formed part of a group. The argument from *praevaricatio* (p.93) seems baseless. Evidently, if it was desirable to exclude *praevaricatio* in the later period, when an *actio popularis* was intended to embrace all complaints, it was equally desirable to do so, when a man might collusively bring a limited action which only covered his own alleged wrongs.

Mantovani suggests (pp. 112ff) that the *actio popularis* was provided as an alternative to prosecutions by injured parties or their representatives in lines 6ff. His problem is that he is proposing to insert, not a new clause, but a new chapter, and the prolix style of the law requires a great deal of space for this. (He wishes to eliminate the restoration *ali]eno nomin[e* in line 6 on grounds that seem to me more theoretical than textual.) Unless such speculations are given definition by an *exempli gratia* supplement, they are literally without substance and one cannot consider the problems that they entail.

3

The Lex agraria

Public and private land in Italy

Land owned by the people as a whole plays a far larger part in the history of the Roman Republic than in that of any other ancient city. The relative unimportance of public and temple land in the Greek city is well demonstrated in Aristotle's discussion of common ownership of property in the *Politics*. His only examples of the maintenance of public land (as opposed to the regulation of private holdings) are from Crete and south Italy, where this was used to sustain the common houses of the men (*andreia*).[1] Whether the existence of publicly owned land was a major feature of the Roman economy in the Regal and early Republican periods is a much debated but unanswerable question. The first good evidence we have of conditions of land tenure is provided by the Twelve Tables in the mid-fifth century BC. Here we find a well-articulated organisation of private property, accompanied by certain formal means of bequest, which allowed the testator to make legacies and probably to name heirs with a different effect to that resulting from intestate succession.[2] Nothing in the surviving fragments relates to rights on any public or common land.

It has been held since the early nineteenth century that the control of property by fathers of families at the time of the Twelve Tables had evolved from a system of ownership by villages (*pagi*) or clans (*gentes*). The former was the view, for example, of Savigny, Mommsen, Maine and Weber. The clan theory was developed by Bonfante and has remained a firm tenet of most Italian jurists and ancient historians since.[3] It has to be admitted that the evidence for either of these propositions is weak. It is true that under the Twelve Tables members of the *gens* have tertiary rights in cases of intestate succession (and are involved in cases of madness).[4] However, although this shows the importance of extended families in early Roman times and how they might become involved

[1] *Ar.Pol.* 2.1268a; 7.1329b–30a. A useful discussion of the evidence for all kinds of public land in Greece in Lewis, 1990; for an interesting example of public land in a Hellenistic city in Asia Minor see Jones and Habicht, 1989, 319–20, at lines 26ff.

[2] *XII Tab.* V.3–5, 8–10; VI.3; VII; VIII.7. For the problems regarding the nature of wills at this time, see Watson, 1975, 52–70.

[3] See the review of modern discussions in Capogrossi Colognesi, 1969, I, 71ff.

[4] *XII Tab.* V.3–4; 7a.

in the transference of property, it does not prove that the *gentes* originally owned the property. The fact that certain rural *tribus* are named after great patrician *gentes* need mean no more than that the *gens* had considerable holdings in those areas. As for the story in Livy that land was allocated to the Claudii and their clients on their arrival from Sabine territory,[5] it should be remembered that in the story the donor is the *res publica* itself (at face value the story is an argument for the ultimate ownership of land by the whole community), nor is it stated that the Claudii subsequently held this land collectively as a clan. There are, moreover, considerable problems in formulating a theory to explain how the later attested dominance of the *pater familias* (head of the nuclear family) derived from an earlier regime, in which it is supposed that the clan head was dominant and all males in the clan subordinate to him were of similar status, without any right of property vested in them.[6] It is easier to conceive how land owned by a village community, controlled politically through some kind of village council, became subsequently parcelled up as private property under the heads of nuclear households. This is an argument in favour of the view of Mommsen and Weber, but positive evidence for this view is hard to find.[7]

There was later in Roman law relating to property the concept of *precarium*, whereby a man might hold property on sufferance from its owner, so having rights against third parties but not against the owner himself. This, it has been suggested, may have derived from a custom of wealthy men with a surplus of land lending it without rent to clients.[8] However, we do not know how antique this concept is and it must be doubtful whether it was a basic feature of early land-tenure. The existence of common pastures and woods (*pascua*, *ager compascuus*, *silvae*), on the other hand, can be assumed with some confidence. The small size of what by tradition was the original allotment (*heredium*) – 2 *iugera* = $\frac{1}{2}$ hectare[9] – is an argument that farmers were expected to make use of common land as well. But the relative economic importance of the enjoyment of common land cannot be estimated. In particular, no argument can be safely drawn from the existence of a certain kind of *ager compascuus* attested in the Principate, where land was shared by a limited number of neighbours, for the system of grazing in the late Republic, still less that of the earliest times (*lex agr.* 14–15, 23–4 with commentary).

[5] Livy 2.16.5. The land of the Mucii (*Mucia prata*) was similarly said to be a gift by the senate (*patres*), see Livy 2.13.5–6; Festus 131L; Pliny *HN* 2.211.

[6] Capogrosso Colognesi, 1969, I, 147ff.

[7] Mommsen, *Staatsr.*, III.23; Weber, 1891, 49ff, 125ff. Cf. Capogrossi Colognesi, 1985a and 1985b.

[8] *Lex agr.*, line 18 with commentary; examples of *precarium* relating to rights of way, *ILLRP*, 491–2; in general Steinwenter, '*Precarium*', in *RE*. Cf. Festus 288–9L; Weber, 1891, 89ff; Zancan, 1935, 14ff; Brunt, 1988, 410–11. For a sceptical view, see A. Drummond, 'Early Roman *Clientes*', in Wallace-Hadrill, 1989, 89–115, esp. 98–9.

[9] Varro *RR* 1.10; Livy 8.21.11; Frontinus *Lim.* 13–14 Thul = 29–30 Lach.

Cicero claims in *De Re Publica* that King Numa had first turned Romans to peaceful pursuits by distributing conquered land. This statement is unparalleled in our other sources, though it may be connected with the rules ascribed to Numa concerning boundary-stones (*termini*).[10] Whatever its validity as a statement of fact, it is important because it reflects two beliefs, first that the public authority was the original owner of land conceded to individuals, secondly that the source of land was military conquest. It was also held that originally members of the *populus Romanus* were permitted to occupy public land at will and farm it. Varro believed that the so-called *ager arcifinius* – which in the late Republic was land outside the formally measured territory, defined by reference to natural features like hills, rivers and trees – derived its name *ab arcendis hostibus*, by being a buffer against enemy invasion. This view was maintained by the writers on Roman land-surveying, who believed that originally land seized by a victorious Roman army was left for occupation by Roman settlers without rent (*ager occupatorius*), simply to ensure that it did not fall back into enemy hands.[11] A tradition was also known to these writers, according to which a man was only allowed as much public land as he could cultivate himself. This was associated with the *lex Licinia* of 367 BC restricting holdings of public land, which, it was alleged, the author of the law himself disregarded.[12] However, these writers recognised that the tradition had been broken, once occupation for prospective use was tolerated. Traces of the ancient attitude may be seen in the permission to turn public land into private land by occupation and cultivation up to the limit of 30 *iugera* (*lex agr.* 13–14).

If the writers on land correctly describe the principle of occupation of *ager publicus*, the annalistic tradition about the protests of the *plebs* over patrician monopolisation of the land in the early Republic may be basically sound (see below, p. 37). However, doubts have been raised about whether this kind of occupation was completely uncontrolled by any magistrate.[13] Questions have also been raised about the status of any land occupied in this way. Although it has been maintained that in the early Republic the possession of *ager publicus* had the nature of ownership and was neither revocable nor subject to the payment of any rent or tax, it is more generally believed that this possession was simply occupation and enjoyment, revocable by the community though protected against disturbance by other private citizens. As to the payment of rent, the statement in Appian (below), that land left for occupation was so liable, is usually accepted as the theoretical position, whatever the practical problems in collecting rent.[14]

10 Cic. *Rep.* 1.26; cf. Dion.Hal. *AR* 2.74; Plut. *Numa* 16; Festus 505L.

11 Frontinus, *Lim.* 2 Thul = 6 Lach (Cf. Agenn. Urb. 53 Thul = 2 Lach); Hyg. 78 Thul = 284 Lach; Sic.Flacc. 102 Thul = 138 Lach. Cf. Bozza, 1938, 38ff.

12 Colum. 1.3.10f; Sic.Flacc. 100 Thul = 137 Lach.

13 Bozza, 1938, 11ff.

14 Against Zancan, 1935, 8ff, who held that occupation had the nature of ownership see e.g. Bozza, 1938, 43ff, 71ff; Burdese, 1952, 62–5. Neither of the latter believed, however, that the land was originally subject to tax (cf. Bozza, 21ff; Burdese 64–5), *contra* Tibiletti, 1948, at 182–90.

In Appian's summary of the background to the Gracchan reforms in the first book of the *Civil Wars* we are told that the advance of Roman power in Italy was accompanied by the seizure and expropriation of land from the defeated. Some was used for the foundation or refoundation of cities, i.e. *coloniae*, some for allocation to individuals, either by gift or sale, the rest was retained as public land, being either formally rented or left for occupation against payments to the community.[15] Distributions of land are recorded by the annalists in the first century of the Republic against a background of plebeian protest about patrician greed. Although, as we have seen, distributions are not *per se* implausible, if we accept that *ager publicus*, as it was understood later, existed in the early Republic, the accounts have been frequently viewed by scholars with scepticism, since their colouring is drawn from the late Republic.[16] The founding of colonies is the most credible item, especially those that were joint undertakings with members of the Latin League.[17]

The redistribution of land after the seizure of Veii in the early fourth century can be accepted with greater confidence, since its effects would still have been visible at the time of the earliest annalists and it is consistent with the results of archaeological survey.[18] Furthermore, the law of Licinius and Sextius in 367, which restricted the exploitation of *ager publicus*, is well established in a variety of sources, even if there is room for argument over whether the figures given for the maximum size of land holdings (500 *iugera*) and numbers of animals (100 large and 500 small beasts) are anachronistic.[19] At all events the pattern described by Appian seems to be as old as the fourth century. Colonies, whether in effect new cities (originally with Latin status) or smaller fortresses, were founded regularly in Italy from the aftermath of the siege of Veii down to the middle of the second century; men were also settled without becoming members of a colony, especially in Sabine territory and the *ager Gallicus* on the Adriatic coast.[20] Land granted or sold to individual Roman citizens seems to have become fully private land. The territory of a colony was ceded to that community and most of this became the private land of the citizens of that colony.

We do not hear of any political controversy over the founding of colonies. There is a hint of trouble in the account of M'.Curius Dentatus' settlement in Sabine territory in the early third century after the Samnite wars, and the bill of C.Flaminius in 232, which distributed land captured from the Gauls on the Adriatic coast, apparently produced an almost violent reaction from political

15 App. *BCiv.* 1.7.26–7.

16 Livy 2.31.4, 41.3, 44.1, 48.2, 52.2, 54.2, 61.1, 63.2; 3.1.22; 4.43.6, 47.8, 49.11, 51.5; 5.12.3; Dion.Hal. *AR* 6.43.1, 44.2; 9.73. Cf. Ogilvie, *Commentary on Livy I–V*, on 2.41.

17 Salmon, 1969, 40–54; Toynbee, 1965, I, 115–41.

18 Livy 5.30.8. Cf. Potter, 1979, 94–6.

19 Livy 6.35.4ff, 7.16.9; Varro *RR* 1.2.9; Colum. 1.3.10ff; Pliny *HN* 18.17. Cf. Tibiletti, 1949, at 7ff, rejecting all details; Burdese, 1952, 56–7; 1985, at 52ff, accepting the figures for land-holdings but not for grazing.

20 *Lib.Col.* 2.253,349L; Pol. 2.21.8; Salmon, 1969, 55–81; Toynbee, 1965, I, 141–71.

opponents.[21] It should be noticed that the redivision of land (*ges anadasmos*), which had become anathema in the Greek world and was only undertaken in revolutionary situations, was an equally unpopular idea in Roman society.[22] Roman expansion through military conquest in Italy allowed her for the most part to satisfy the land-hunger of her humbler citizens and to prevent their impoverishment without damaging the vested interests of land-holders.

The Hannibalic invasion led to great, if temporary, disruption of Italian agriculture and Hannibal's defeat brought dire consequences to the peoples who had sided with him.[23] A striking measure was taken by the senate in 200 BC, when, since it needed to repay those who had lent the Roman people money during the war and had no money in the treasury, it conceded to these men a large quantity of public land within the fiftieth milestone from Rome for exploitation at a token rent, until such time as monetary repayment could be made. This land – called *trientabulus* or *in trientabulis*, because it related to a third of the sum owed to the creditors – was still at least in part in their possession in 111 BC (*lex agr.* 31–2 with commentary). Other land near Rome was used to place deported Campanians, especially the territory formerly of Veii and that belonging to the colonies of Sutrium and Nepet.[24] The captured Campanian territory, apart from that assigned to the colonies of Puteoli, Liternum and Volturnum, was for a long time left open for occupation, but in 172, after the senate had recommended an investigation by L.Postumius (*cos.* 173), a plebiscite was passed requiring that in future this land should be rented out according to contracts let by the censors. An elaborate survey was consequently carried out by a praetor, P.Lentulus, probably in 165, which led to the recovery of public land by purchase and its division into rented smallholdings[25] (see further commentary on *lex agr.* 1–2 and 32). Major colonisation occured in peninsular Italy in the second century and there is some evidence for allotments to individual Romans and non-Romans as well. There was also considerable settlement in the fertile land of Cisalpine Gaul from 218 BC onwards, both through colonies and individual allotments, and the principle of exploiting conquered territory outside Italy was established, to be taken yet further in the Gracchan period.[26] In Spain by contrast, although Romans were

[21] App. *Samn.* 5; Cic. *Inv.* 2.52; Val.Max. 5.4.5.

[22] Cic. *Off.* 2.78–82, showing the continuity of attitude between Aratus of Sicyon and himself. On Greek attitudes in general, see Asheri, 1966.

[23] Brunt, 1971, 269ff, criticising Toynbee, 1965, II, 10–35.

[24] Livy 26.34; 31.13.6ff.

[25] Livy 42.1.6, 19.1; Cic. *Leg.Agr.* 2.82; Gran.Lic., pp. 9–10 Flem; Frederiksen, 1984, chs. 11–12.

[26] Latin colonies: Copia = Thurii (193); Vibo Valentia = Hipponium (192); reinforcement of Placentia, Cremona (190); Bononia (189); Aquileia (181); Luca (180). Citizen colonies: Volturnum, Liternum, Puteoli, Salernum, Buxentum, Pyrgi, Sipontum, Tempsa and Croton (194); Potentia and Pisaurum (184); Mutina, Parma, Saturnia (183); Graviscae (181); Luna (177); Auximum (157). For settlement on individual allotments see Livy 31.4.1–3; 40.38.2ff; 42.22.5ff. See in general Tibiletti, 1950.

settled at Italica in 206 BC, the urban foundations in the second century were for Spaniards or those of mixed race: Roman settlement there would have been on a private basis.

The restriction of the exploitation of *ager publicus* by occupiers remained an issue. One of the reasons why action was taken over the *ager Campanus* in 173 was that some private citizens had vastly added to their holdings out of public land and were concealing the difference between what was public and what was private. Six years later in a speech on the Rhodians Cato the Censor sought to prove that one should not punish people for alleged wishes by adducing as an analogy the Romans' own wish to disregard agrarian laws: no law was so harsh as to punish people for wanting to hold more than 500 *iugera*, no law punished people for wanting more cattle grazing than was permitted; 'we all want to have more and we do so with impunity'.[27] It has been argued that the limits on grazing mentioned by Appian are likely to be a second-century development of the Licinian law.[28] We also hear of prosecutions of cattle-owners for offences whose exact nature is not made plain[29] – either for exceding the maximum number of beasts or failing to pay pasture dues (*scriptura*) or perhaps fencing in public pasture as private land (cf. *lex agr.* 24–6 with commentary). The builder of the road from Rhegium to Capua *c.*132 BC, either P.Popilius Laenas or T.Annius, boasted that he was the first to make herdsmen give way to ploughmen on the public land, but the depredations of errant herds were still the subject of debate (and humour) in the late second century.[30] Many areas unsuitable for agriculture but suitable for cattle-raising were *ager publicus*, as were the *calles*, the drove-roads which linked winter and summer pastures (*lex agr.* 14–5, 24–6 with commentary).

Even if sections of conquered territory had been given to colonies or permanently alienated to private individuals, the 'public land of the Roman people' remained a major feature of the Roman economy in the second century BC. The example of Campania shows how it could be neglected for a long period. Nevertheless, according to Appian, it was in theory either let out formally to contract or subject to tax on occupation. Although much of the land had been devastated in the Hannibalic War and may have been left undistributed for that reason, this does not mean that it was permanently infertile: it was still potentially an important asset to the Roman people.

Roman land-surveying

The characteristic form of Roman surveying, the division of land into a grid of squares (*centuriae*), is still embedded in the landscape and can be detected by

27 *ORF*, frag. 167.

28 Tibiletti, 1948, at 191ff; 1949, at 12ff and 30ff; 1950, at 261ff; Burdese, 1952, at 57ff.

29 Livy 33.42.10; 34.53.4; 35.10; cf. 10.13.14, 23.13, 47.4; Ovid, *Fasti* 5.285ff.

30 *ILLRP*, 454, lines 12–14; cf. Wiseman, 1964; 1969; Cic. *de Or.* 2.284.

air-photography, even when it is not obvious on the ground or from a study of maps.[31] The *centuriae* and their sub-divisions (cf. *lex agr.* 7 and 66 with commentary) were used to allocate new territory or to redistribute existing territory in public possession. The earliest known traces of it are associated with the colony of Terracina, founded in 329 BC.[32] Before the use of centuriation land was divided by *strigae* into long strips, sub-divided by baulks crossing them (*scamna*), and this system was still employed where it was thought appropriate (e.g. at Cosa and Alba Fucens), after centuriation had been introduced elsewhere.[33] There is no certain equivalent of centuriation in the Greek world (though a system of this kind has been postulated for Larissa in the late third century BC). Elaborate geometry, on the other hand, was common, especially in newly founded cities, and we should not discount the possibility that this influenced the Romans. A town grid is physically attested at archaic Megara Hyblaea in Sicily and there is evidence for a rural division into strips at Metapontum and Heraclea in south Italy.[34]

Centuriation, whether urban or rural, was applied to reasonably flat and open territory. Mountains and thickly wooded land were excluded and the irregular spaces between the formal grid and natural features, over which it could not be extended, were recorded as *subseciva* (*lex agr.* 66 with commentary). Surveying was carried out with a cruciform instrument fixed at right angles to a pole (*groma*). From this, sight-lines were taken, which became the lines of the grid. Points on which the *groma* had been placed and were thus each a junction of four squares of the grid were marked by a *terminus* (boundary-stone). The examples that survive from the Gracchan period are upright cylindrical stones, frequently with a cross representing the junction of the squares on the upper circular face and usually the names of the commissioners who were dividing the land inscribed round the stone.[35] The position of the stone relative to the grid as a whole was also indicated. This was based on one central *groma* point, like the central point (x = 0, y = 0) of a graph. In theory the north-south line through this point was the (chief) *kardo*, the east-west line the (chief) *decumanus*, though there were exceptions to this, notably in Campania.[36] The surveyor was assumed to be facing down the *decumanus* (either eastward or westward) and the squares were then labelled according to whether they were *V(ltra)* or *K(itra) K(ardinem)*, beyond or inside the *kardo*, and whether they were to right or left of the *decumanus, D(extra)* or *S(inistra)*

[31] See Bradford, 1957; *Misurare la terra*, 1983; Chouquer *et al.*, 1987.

[32] Livy 8.21.11; Chouquer *et al.*, 1987, 105ff, arguing for the existence of squares with 71 m sides within *strigae*.

[33] Front. *Lim.* 1 Thul; Chouquer *et al.*, 1987, 108, 135ff; Mertens, 1969, 47ff.; Brown, 1980, 18, figs. 9–10.

[34] Salviat and Vatin, 1974 (cf. *Id.* in *Cadastres et espace rural*, ed. M. Clavel-Leveque (Paris, 1983), 309–11); Vallet, 1976; Uggeri, 1969; Adamesteanu and Vatin, 1976.

[35] Hyg. 71ff, 158ff Thul; *ILLRP*, 467–74 (cf. *CIL* I^2, 639–45 and 719); Pani, 1977.

[36] Hyg. 132ff, cf. 71–2 Thul.

D(ecumanum).[37] With each of these two indications a figure was given indicating how many squares each line was from the main axes.

Each *centuria* contained 400 square *actus* (an *actus* is 120 Roman feet, hence the side of a *centuria* square is 2,140 feet) or 200 *iugera*. One *iugerum* is about ⅔ acre or ¼ hectare, thus in area equivalent to a square of 50 metres by 50 metres. The work of surveying, together with information about the allotment of land, was recorded and entered in the plans of the surveyors (*formae*); these might then be exhibited, engraved on bronze or stone (*lex agr.* 7 with commentary), as Lentulus' assignment of Campania was. The best evidence for such publicly displayed *formae* is those set up in Vespasian's time at the Caesarian colony of Arausio (Orange).[38]

The agrarian problems of the second century

In the well-known passage of his *Civil Wars*, mentioned earlier, Appian states that the Romans exploited the land they conquered in war in order to build up a population of farmers, who would also be their warriors. He lists the various forms of land-management – the foundation or augmentation of towns (*coloniae*), the allocation *gratis* or sale of land to individuals (both Roman and Italian), the renting of land by contract – and adds that land which had fallen out of cultivation through war was left to be used by anyone who wanted, in return for a rent based on produce – 10 per cent on arable produce, 20 per cent on fruits.[39] Such rents would not have been a severe imposition, once land had been restored to cultivation. However, it remains a question how far the amount of rent could be properly calculated by any officials concerned with public land and thus whether the Roman people were getting a fair return on their property. It was this unallocated land, according to Appian, which was monopolised by the wealthy: they removed previous possessors by negotiation or force and farmed vast tracts through chattel-slaves, who were a more convenient labour-force than free men, since they were not liable to military service.[40]

The majority of modern historians have seen this as only one aspect of the change which came over Italy in the second century BC. For they believe that there was a general trend to greater accumulation of land by the wealthy and its exploitation in a more efficient and systematic fashion. They infer this from two general considerations, the undoubted growth of capital in Italy and the ready availability of slaves – both products of empire – but they also adduce two specific pieces of evidence. These are the handbook on agriculture written by Cato the Censor in the second century and the archaeological evidence for the existence of 'villas' – i.e. large farm-houses with storage space for crops and presses for wine and oil, which also have comfortable living-quarters suitable

[37] Hyg. 12, 14, 71 and 131–2 Thul. [38] Gran.Lic. pp. 9–10 Flem; Piganiol, 1962.
[39] App. *BCiv.* 1.7.26–7. Cf. Plut. *Ti. Gr.* 8.1. [40] *BCiv.* 1.7.29–30; cf. Sall. *Jug.* 41.8.

for at least temporary residence by an owner of the highest class.[41] It is argued that the nature of agricultural production was transformed from one of a subsistence economy to large-scale production for a market and in this process the peasant-cultivator became outmoded. He was driven off the land by economic forces as much as, or more than, by the *force majeure* of the large landowners.

This view cannot be accepted without certain reservations. First, it is untrue to say that there was a technological revolution in agriculture, as Rostovtzeff admitted, even though he strongly supported the thesis of an economic revolution.[42] Apart from the invention of a new olive-press (*trapetum*), agricultural methods differed little from those in archaic Greece. What Cato and other agricultural writers did preach was a more calculated organisation of farming with attention to costs, yields and profits. How far this entailed a 'capitalist' attitude in the strict sense – a belief in the augmentation of capital for its own sake – and how far production was geared to meeting specific markets remain difficult questions, though we may be reasonably confident about market-production in certain areas, for example Campania and the *ager Cosanus*.[43]

As regards the creation of large-scale farms at the expense of peasant holdings, the classic examples of 'villas' belong to the first century BC, largely the post-Sullan period, and survey evidence suggests the persistence of smallholdings in a number of areas, although of course we cannot be sure that a small habitation represents an independent proprietor rather than a tenant.[44] From the literary evidence (see above, p. 41) it appears that some of the earliest accumulation of land was by cattle-owners, whose expansion would have left no archaeological traces. In general, Appian seems to present as well developed, if not complete, a process which was still in its formative stages in 133 BC. It was an era of competition and conflict between peasant and rich proprietor, in which the latter's complete dominance of production was not yet established.

The wealth derived from empire did not only affect the Italian economy: it was also invested back in the provinces. We have scattered evidence for Romans and Italians resident or doing business in the East from the mid-third century BC onwards.[45] They are first attested in Sicily in 205 but probably had begun to settle from the end of the first Punic War (Italian mercenaries had been

41 See for example Carandini, 1985; Cotton and Metraux, 1985; and in general on the incidence of villas in Republican Italy, Carandini, 1985, I, 15ff and the contributions in Giardina, Schiavone, 1981, I.

42 Rostovtzeff, 1957, II, 1186ff.

43 Republican writers on agriculture, Varro, *RR* 1.1.10, 16.5, 18, 19; Rawson, 1985, 135ff. For market-production, see e.g. Tchernia, 1983; Manacorda, 1978; Frederiksen, 1981; Panella, 1981.

44 Frederiksen, 1970–1; Garnsey, 1979. On tenants, de Neeve, 1984.

45 Hatzfeld, 1919; Helly, 1983. See e.g. *ILLRP*, 245; *IG*, IX.2.858; XI.2.115; XI.4.642; L. Moretti, *Iscr. Stor. Ell.* II, 95; Helly, *Gonnoi*, II. no.42.

employed and given land in Sicily by the tyrants of the classical period).[46] By the time of the first Sicilian slave-revolt – contemporary with Ti.Gracchus' tribunate – the Italian landowners were a significant part of Sicilian society.[47] As we have seen, men had settled in Spain after the Roman defeat of the Carthaginians there in 206. Attempts to estimate the total amount of emigration abroad during the Republic show wide variations. The figures given for the 'Romans' massacred in 88 BC on the orders of Mithridates VI in what has been termed the 'Asiatic Vespers' – 80,000–150,000 – are likely to be exaggerated.[48] The term 'Romans' surely includes Italians of all ages and both sexes and conceivably any imported slaves in their households. Nevertheless, it is certain that many men from Italy acquired property abroad, whether they intended to live there themselves or manage the estate through a son, freedman or partner. This process was to be advanced by legislation of the Gracchan period.

Mention has already been made of colonisation and individual allotments in Cisalpine Gaul, not yet a part of Italy, in the second century (see above, p. 38). In the period immediately preceding the law of 111 BC we find that land in Africa had been both allocated to colonists and sold (*lex agr.* 49–90); a colony was placed in 118 at Narbo in Transalpine Gaul,[49] and a settlement near Dertona in Cisalpina perhaps belongs to this period;[50] in Greece a distribution of Corinthian land was contemplated, if not already begun (*lex agr.* 96ff) and land may have already been sold elsewhere in Greece (*lex agr.* 91ff with commentary). Free distributions of provincial land diminished the hunger for land in peninsular Italy, and sales of provincial land deflated the pressure that would otherwise have been created by free-floating money on the Italian land-market. Whether impoverished peasants directly benefited is another matter. The allotments in Africa under C.Gracchus' *lex Rubria* were large – if not 200 *iugera* for every man, perhaps 100 (*lex agr.* 60 with commentary) – and would have required a labour-force greater than a *pater familias* and his immediate family. Indeed it is alleged that they were intended for respectable citizens.[51] However, any genuine emigration to Africa (as opposed to purchases by would-be absentee landlords) may have had the secondary effect of making more public land in Italy free for new distributions.

[46] Livy 29.1.10; *ILLRP*, 320. Cf. e.g. Diod. 13.44.2, 80.4, 85.4; 14.15.3, 58.2, 68.3.

[47] Poseid. *FGH* 87, F108 = Diod. 34/5.2, 2ff (though probably overstated), cf. Diod. 36.2, 2a, 3.4, 4.1 for Roman or Italian landlords during the second slave revolt of 104–101 BC.

[48] Val.Max. 9.2.3 *ext*; Memnon, *FGH* 434, F22; Plut. *Sulla* 24. For estimates, see Brunt, 1971, 209ff (conservative); Hopkins, 1978, 68–9. For a general survey, see Wilson, 1966.

[49] Vell.Pat. 2.7; Cic. *Brut.* 160; *Clu.* 140; *de Or.* 2.223.

[50] Vell.Pat. 1.15.5; Fraccaro, 1957, III.1.123–50.

[51] Plut. *C.Gr.* 9.2. Figures for labour required for the cultivation of olives and vines in Cato. *Agric.* 10 and 11.

The policies of the Gracchi

According to our sources, Tiberius Gracchus advocated his agrarian law of 133 BC on moral and demographic grounds: it was to give their just reward to the men who had helped to build the empire and to create a sound reservoir of future military manpower. However, solving any general agricultural problem lay outside the scope of the law: its target was the injustice perpetrated on Roman public land, the excessive holdings of the wealthy there. The existing limit of 500 *iugera* per person was reasserted, but there was an added concession of a further 250 *iugera* for each child of the landholder.[52]

There is a suggestion that he originally intended to buy back surplus land – not so implausible, since this is apparently what was done by P.Lentulus in Campania *c.* 165 BC. However, the final version of the bill had no mention of this: instead, Gracchus argued that for the rich, secure tenure of their legitimate holdings, as prescribed by his law, was fair compensation for the loss of any public land held to excess.[53] The land not assigned to prior possessors was to be distributed to the poor by a commission of three men, 'changing their position each year' – perhaps, then, subject to re-election (it has also been suggested that there was a rotating chief executive).[54] These new allotments could not be alienated by sale and, in Appian's view, it was this provision combined with the supervisory powers of the commission which frustrated the rich, since they were unable to evade the law by taking back the land they had lost. They were also required to register their holdings of public land and, when they neglected to do so, the commissioners invited information to be laid against those who ignored this regulation.[55]

References to a separate judicial law may mean that it was after creating the commission that Gracchus found it necessary to confer on it judicial powers, in order to cope with disputed holdings and boundaries. On the boundary-stones (*termini*) the commissioners appear as *A(gris) I(udicandis) A(dsignandis)*.[56] Such powers would not have been necessary for a commission distributing land in virgin territory. Many other points remain obscure about the agrarian law of Ti.Gracchus. However, some inferences may be drawn from the law of 111 BC on our bronze. It appears that Ti.Gracchus did not give new allotments to individual non-Romans nor give permanent security to holdings of non-Roman prior possessors (*lex agr.* 1–10 with commentary). This is not to say that the legislator envisaged expelling all non-Romans from *ager publicus*. Those with censorial leases would not have been affected. As for the rights conceded

52 App. *BCiv.* 1.9.36–7, cf. 8.33; Plut. *Ti.Gr.* 10.4.

53 Plut. *Ti.Gr.* 9.2; Gran.Lic. 9–10 Flem; Cic. *Leg.Agr.* 2.82; App. *BCiv.* 1.11.46.

54 App. *BCiv.* 1.9.37; 13.55; Carcopino, 1928, 149ff. Cf. Bauman, 1979, at 406, n138.

55 App. *BCiv.* 1.10.38 (cf. 27.111); 18.73.

56 Livy *Per.* 58; Macr. 3.14.6 = *ORF*[4], no. 9, fr. 30; *ILLRP*, 467–74; Pani, 1977 = *AE* 1973, 222; Bauman, 1979, 391ff.

by law or treaty to non-Roman communities or individuals as occupiers or possessors (*lex agr.* 21 and 29 with commentary), Gracchus is unlikely to have revoked them explicitly – Cicero says he overlooked them[57] and some at least were still in force in 111 – but the allies seem to have suffered from the workings of the commission later, and this would have been inevitable if they held land in excess of the legal limits reaffirmed by Gracchus.

The status of both the new allotments and the recognised holdings of prior possessors seems to have been uncertain at the time. New allotments certainly did not become fully private land, alienable by sale, until 111 (*lex agr.* 18–19 with commentary), in spite of what Appian says. As for the holdings of prior possessors, who had been given 'special tenure without payment, secure for ever', these were alienable by sale before 111, perhaps as a result of the first agrarian law after Caius Gracchus' death.[58] Nevertheless, it may still have been thought that the Roman people were the ultimate owners of these lands, until they were specifically declared private in 111 (commentary on *lex agr.* 7 and 10). The Gracchi themselves seem to have wanted to maintain a residual public authority over the land which was being assigned and distributed, without perhaps realising the problems that this might cause in Roman law. And indeed there was a specific reason for doing so: if they had allowed the existing holdings of prior possessors immediately to become private, the possessors would then have become entitled to occupy a further 500 *iugera* of public land under the provisions of the *lex Licinia* (and any other relevant agrarian legislation), as renewed in the *lex Sempronia.*

In spite of the death of its author, the agrarian law was not rescinded or modified, but was vigorously executed in a number of regions, as the *termini* found in Campania, Samnium, Lucania, Apulia and the *ager Gallicus* in Picenum show. The claim of the road-builder in the inscription from Polla that he first made herdsmen give way to ploughmen attests by implication the rival activities of the Gracchan *tresviri.*[59] Their operations were, however, limited in 129, when there were complaints from leading Italians about their treatment at the hands of the commission. It seems likely that they were being stripped of land alleged to be in excess of the legal limit or their holdings were being

[57] Cic. *Rep.* 1.31, 3.41. Hardy, 1910, 273–4, believed that the commissioners could legally have resumed land in the possession of colonies and Latin towns but did not do so in fact; that it had not been Ti.Gracchus' intention to deprive Latins and Italians of all public land and that their possession of their legitimate holdings was confirmed by the second post-Gracchan law.

[58] App. *BCiv.* 1.27.131, cf. 11.46. On the status of the land of new settlers, see also Cardinali, 1912, 182. Hardy, 1910, 271, held, somewhat improbably, that Ti.Gracchus wanted prior possessors to have their permitted holdings as private property but failed to embody this in his law. The fact that the land of new settlers was not yet private property is an argument in support of the view that the increase in the census figures of 125 BC cannot represent new *assidui*, i.e. those reaching a property qualification, as a result of Gracchan allotments, cf. Brunt, 1971, 15–25.

[59] *ILLRP*, 454, lines 12–14.

adjusted in order to create clearer boundaries and easier mapping. In consequence the senate recommended that lawsuits over the land involving the allies should be referred to the consul of 129, Sempronius Tuditanus.[60] This would not have affected lawsuits which only concerned Roman citizens. However, it is arguable that in the end even the political protagonists of the commission's work decided that judicial activity was best left to magistrates other than the land-commissioners themselves. In the law of 111 cases arising from the land-legislation were to be referred to any consul, praetor or, where the land was public, any censor (*lex agr.* 24, 33–6). The land-commissioner, *IIIvir a(gris) i(udicandis) a(dsignandis)* on the Gracchan boundary-stones, was described as *a(gris) d(andis) a(dsignandis)* both in the law of 111 and earlier in the *lex repetundarum* of 123–2. It is probable that under C.Gracchus' law of 123, if not earlier, the commissioners were relieved of all judicial functions, including those relating to Roman citizens: only this seems to explain the disappearance of *i(udicandis)* from their title. In any case there is no warrant for believing that the work of the commission was completely frustrated by the *senatus consultum* of 129. Initially, at least the commission would still have had control of cases involving Roman citizens only, while cases involving allies would have been referred to a consul or praetor of the year, as prescribed in the law of 111.[61]

A further agrarian law about Italy was passed by C.Gracchus. It was not simply a repetition of the law of 133, as one source alleges.[62] Apart from probably modifying the functions of the commission, it also excepted certain land from division (*lex agr.* 1–2 with commentary). This incidentally shows that the work of the commission was still proceeding and that all available land had not yet been surveyed. It is most likely that this was a concession to the Italian allies, exempting from redistribution the *ager publicus* they occupied, especially perhaps their ancestral land, which they were still allowed to enjoy through treaties or other enactments (*lex agr.* 29), although it had become Roman territory through conquest. Some land was taken at the expense of both Romans and non-Romans for C.Gracchus' own colonies, but they were compensated for this and their tenure of land received in exchange was later secured in the law of 111 (*lex agr.* 20–3). It is also at this time that we first hear of

60 App. *BCiv.* 1.19. Cf. Cardinali, 1912, 161ff (though I cannot agree with his view that the majority of Italians had *commercium*).

61 *Lex agr.* 15; *lex rep.* 2, 13 and 16. Cf. *ILS*, 49 on M.Livius Drusus in 91 BC. Cf. Bauman, 1979, 406–8. For the continuation of the work of the commission and of the judicial hearings by consuls after 129, compare Hardy, 1910, 273.

62 Livy *Per.* 60; Plut. *C.Gr.* 5.1; Vell.Pat. 2.6.3; *lex agr.* 1 and *passim*. The view of Molthagen, 1973, that C.Gracchus passed no agrarian law separate from his colony legislation should be discounted. The general exception of certain land from division applying to a succession of categories in lines 1–10 is inappropriate for a colony law. In fact, when land was needed for founding colonies, C.Gracchus took the land, but provided compensation (*lex agr.* 20–3).

a rent being required from holders of land-allotments – a rent which M.Livius Drusus (*tr.pl.* 122) legislated to remove.[63] Colonies were planned by C.Gracchus for Tarentum (Neptunia) and Scyllacium (Minervia) in Italy, perhaps also for Capua.[64] There was also a programme of road-building, which would have assured communications for those farming or grazing far from towns (*lex agr.* 26–7). Associated with this was the allocation of land to *viasiei vicanei*, villagers by the roads (*lex agr.* 11–12), whose job was probably to help maintain the roads and provide hospitality for travellers – not a complete innovation, since the stone from Polla seems in fact to indicate the same activity by the builder of the *via Popillia* or *Annia* here.[65]

The *lex Rubria* about Africa provided for the refounding of Carthage as a Roman colony. According to Appian, 6,000 colonists were enrolled, more than originally was permitted in the bill (*lex agr.* 58–61 with commentary). The enterprise set in motion a massive surveying operation – if this had not already been started in the years following the creation of the province in 146 (commentary on *lex agr.* 67). Land outside the colonial territory was also sold by the quaestors at Rome – perhaps to Latins and Italian allies, as well as to Roman citizens (*lex agr.* 50, 76, 83, cf. commentary on line 55). This must have been either provided for by C.Gracchus himself, whether in the *lex Rubria* or in an obscure *lex Sempronia* mentioned in the law of 111 (*lex agr.* 82), or have been a measure of the period before C.Gracchus. A possible occasion for this is the plague of locusts, which struck Africa in 125 and may have caused the evacuation of much territory in the province (in view of King Mikipsa's gift of corn to C.Gracchus, when he was in Sardinia, it is unlikely to have caused serious devastation in Numidia).[66]

The *lex Rubria* was repealed (*lex agr.* 55, 59ff) and the town of Carthage was not rebuilt (line 81),[67] but the distribution of land to colonists was not abandoned (lines 58ff) and a *terminus* shows a land commission operating there after 120 BC.[68] As for the provisions of the Gracchan legislation about Italy, it appears that Appian gave an inaccurate and probably over-pessimistic picture of their fate. Appian says (*BCiv.* 1.27) that there were three agrarian laws after that of C.Gracchus:

> Shortly afterwards [i.e. after the end of the uprising of the younger Gracchus] a law was passed enabling those who possessed the land in dispute to sell it. For this also had been forbidden by the elder Gracchus. And immediately the wealthy began to buy from the poor or they used force under this pretext. And the outcome was even worse for the poor until Spurius Borius, while tribune, introduced a law, that they should no longer

[63] Plut. *C.Gr.* 9.4. [64] Plut. *C.Gr.* 5.1; 6.3; 8.3; Vell. 1.15.4; Livy *Per.* 60; *Vir.Ill.* 65.

[65] Plut. *C.Gr.* 6.3; 7.1–4; App. *BCiv.* 1.23.98; *ILLRP*, 458, cf. 454, line 15.

[66] App. *BCiv.* 1.24.102–4; *Pun.* 136.644; Plut. *C.Gr.* 10.2; 13.1–3; Vell.Pat. 2.7.8; Eutrop. 4.21; Oros. 5.12; cf. *ibid.* 11.2–5; Plut. *C.Gr.* 2.5. [67] Cf. Plut. *C.Gr.* 13.1–3.

[68] *ILLRP*, 475.

> distribute the land, but that it should belong to the current possessors and rents should be paid for it to the people, this money to go towards distributions. This was a consolation to the poor because of the distributions, but of no value in increasing population. Once the Gracchan law had been rescinded by this device – a law which would have been excellent and beneficial, if it could have been executed – the rents also were abolished soon afterwards by another tribune and the people were dispossessed of everything. As a result of this they suffered a still greater shortage of citizens and soldiers, rents and distributions and laws simultaneously, fifteen years after the legislation of Gracchus, in a state of idleness through being embroiled in lawsuits.

The agrarian law on the bronze fragments can be firmly dated to 111 BC (see 'Date and Identity of the Lex Agraria', pp. 282–6 below). If we try to relate Appian's account to the surviving text of this law, we find that Appian is vague or misleading in three respects. First, the new assignees of land distributed by the Gracchan commission cannot have been allowed to sell their land under the first post-Gracchan law, since purchase from them is not recognised as granting title to land in the chapter of the law of 111 providing for judicial confirmation of these holdings (*lex agr.* 15–16); by contrast, those who had bought their land from prior possessors (*veteres possessores*) could get confirmation of their title in 111 (*lex agr.* 16–17): their land, therefore, had been legally purchasable before 111. Secondly, *veteres possessores* were not legally permitted to hold on to public land without limit under the second law, since the law of 111 only recognises holdings no greater than those permitted under the *leges Semproniae* (*lex agr.* 2). (It should be noted that this undermines the view of Niccolini that it was on the excess holdings of public land only that rent was demanded.[69]) Thirdly, the impression given that all rents were removed under the third law is misleading, whether we identify the law of 111 on the bronze with this third law of Appian or with a subsequent one unmentioned by Appian. The law of 111 abolished any rents on Gracchan allotments or the recognised holdings of prior possessors (*lex agr.* 19–20), but other land, which remained public, continued to yield rent or pasture tax (*scriptura*), for example common pasture land and *ager patritus* (*lex agr.* 25 and 28).

If the commission in Italy ceased to exist in the middle of the decade 120–110 BC after the second post-Gracchan agrarian bill, this is not so surprising. What Appian means by saying that under the law of Spurius Borius 'the land should belong to the current possessors', is not clear. It may simply mean that there was to be an end to regularising land-holdings by surveying and the creation of grids of centuriation. By this time most illegal holdings would have been corrected and there may not have been the same demand for new allotments as earlier. It should be stressed that the limit on the amount of *ager publicus* which prior possessors could legally retain (ultimately as their private property) was never abolished in this period. The legislator of 111 was, in my view, faced not with

[69] Niccolini, 1934, 179ff.

the collapse of Gracchan legislation but with a situation, where much had been accomplished at the expense of a considerable amount of legal confusion about conditions of land-tenure. Detailed examination of the law will suggest a consolidation of the Gracchan achievement, rather than the ratification of its failure. Though I do not agree with Hardy's assessment of the Gracchan legislation as an honourable failure, I cannot but endorse his remarks about the *lex agraria* itself: 'this great and weighty law, which shows that even in the revolutionary period, amid all the corruption and strife of the time, great questions could still be dealt with in a spirit of equity, compromise and statesmanship'.[70]

The contents of the agrarian law of 111 BC

There are two main parts of this law: the first (lines 1–42) deals with land in Italy, the second (lines 43–105) with land outside Italy. Within the second part a section from lines 48 to (probably) 91 concerns Africa, and following this is a section about land in Greece. The text from lines 43 to 48 has been attributed variously by scholars to the Italian and African sections. A case will be made in the commentary that it belongs to neither, but is in fact a small independent section about land in another part of the empire. The Italian section ends with chapters relating to potential conflicts with preceding legislation, which enforce respect for the new provisions (lines 40–2). The last fragment of the law, whose purport is intelligible (line 102) seems to be part of a *sanctio*, imposing penalties on those who breach the law (cf. commentary on *lex rep.* 55–6). No trace survives, however, of any clause relating to publicity, and the text may have continued on the bronze for a number of lines under the last surviving letters.

The Italian section begins with a list of categories of land (lines 1–7), to which no instructions are immediately attached. The basis of the definition in each case is public land in Italy in 133 BC, the year of Ti.Gracchus' agrarian law. Land exempted by C.Gracchus from division (see above, p. 46 and commentary on line 1) is excluded from consideration, and each chapter then describes a particular operation which has changed the nature of this public land since 133. These are (a) the secure acquisition of land by prior possessors within the maximum permitted by Ti.Gracchus (lines 1–2); (b) the new assignation of land to Roman settlers by the land-commission (lines 2–3); (c) some form of exchange (lines 3–4); (d) assignation by the commission of land in a town or village outside Rome (lines 4–5); (e) assignation of buildings and building-sites by the commission to prior possessors and new settlers (lines 6–7). All these categories of land and building are declared to be private and to have the same status as other private land and buildings. The censor is instructed to take them into account as such in his register (lines 7–8), and the owners' continued enjoyment of the land is guaranteed against any action by magistrates, the senate or anyone else (lines 9–10).

There follow chapters concerned with special problems arising out of the

[70] Hardy, 1910, 286. For another positive assessment, cf. Cardinali, 1912, 206ff.

foregoing enactments. The first topic is land assigned to *viasiei vicanei* (villagers by the roads). Their enjoyment of the land assigned to them is also guaranteed, but it is expressly stated that the land should not become private (lines 11–12). Regarding the land which is still public after the provisions of lines 1–10, it is enacted that if a man occupies no more than 30 *iugera* of this for cultivation, this land is to become private (lines 13–14). Further, grazing on common pasture land (*ager compascuus*) of up to ten large beasts and a number of small beasts unspecified in the surviving text is to be free of tax (lines 14–15).

The law then lays down judicial procedures, whereby current possessors of land assigned by the commission or properly retained by prior possessors may get legal recognition of their holdings. These procedures were available to assignees and their heirs, prior possessors and their heirs, and also to those who had purchased from prior possessors (lines 15–18). There is a special procedure for men who have been ejected by force from land in their possession, so that they may obtain restoration to their holdings (line 18). One or two chapters follow (lines 19–20), which declare the land made private by this or earlier legislation to be immune from rent, tax or pasture tax (this provision may have been extended to the *viasiei vicanei*).

This concludes the main provisions about land in Italy. The general thrust is clear: private status and immunity from tax is to be granted to the bulk of formerly public land, which the agrarian commissioners had investigated and assigned in the years after 133, whether the holder was a new assignee or a prior possessor. This is not, however, a casual concession. It is stressed that Gracchan limits on the holdings of prior possessors should not be exceeded, reference is made to the plans and records drawn up by the commission and the law foresees the need to establish the legality and security of land-holdings in the courts.

We then find one or two complex chapters also concerned with the ratification of holdings and their conversion into private land (lines 20–4). Their separation from the main body of enactments of this kind in lines 1–10 may be explained in part by the fact that they relate to specific tracts of territory, some of which had been taken for the creation of *coloniae*, but it is more significant, in my view, that non-Romans are involved as well as Roman citizens. Those who had received public land in exchange for land surrendered to a commissioner for the foundation of a colony, were apparently granted secure enjoyment of this land and for some of them, presumably Roman citizens and probably Latins, it was to be private property. As in lines 15–18, a chapter was added, which specified the judicial procedure to be used to secure legal recognition of their holdings for assignees or their heirs.

The chapter following (line 24–5) has a new introductory formula referring to land which would be still public after the passage of the law, and public land is the main concern of the next eight lines of text. Land kept for public use and land rented out by censorial contract, like the *ager Campanus*, seem to have been excluded from discussion here. The first category for which regulations are given is pasture land: this was to remain open to anyone's herds and flocks and not to be fenced off on pain of a fine. The limit on free grazing was repeated (lines 25–6), but there is no trace of any general upper limit on numbers of animals to be grazed. It was held sufficient to forbid monopolisation by enclosure and to tax large numbers of animals. However, in the next chapter (line 26) it is provided that no tax shall be paid by cattle on the public roads or drove-roads. At this point there are inserted two parallel chapters dealing with exchanges of public for private land and *vice versa* (lines 26–7), the effect of which is simply to declare that land so affected should become fully private or fully public respectively. Arguably these were occasioned by the previous reference to public roads, whose construction would have required the requisition of private land and the grant of former public land in compensation (commentary on line 27).

The law next confirms the status of a puzzling category of land, *ager patritus* (lines 27–8), which seems to be a form of public land let out on long leases. There is a general injunction about keeping public rights of way clear (line 28), and a chapter extending the rights available to Roman citizens on public land to those Latins and *peregrini* (i.e. non-Roman allies) who had the right to enjoy public land in 112 BC (line 29). This does not seem to relate to the conversion of public land to private but rather to matters like pasturage and transport. Similarly, Latins and *peregrini* are granted access to the same legal procedures relating to the land as Romans (line 30). We now reach the two last types of public land in Italy to be discussed (lines 31–2). First, land granted to *coloniae, municipia* or their equivalent for exploitation. This would have been either rented out by these communities for revenue or made available *gratis* to their own citizens for farming. Linked with this is the land in the *trientabula*, the land ceded to wealthy men who had lent Rome money in the second Punic War (see above, p. 38), which was in effect on a long-term lease with a token rent to attest its public nature. The legitimacy and security of occupation of these two types of land are confirmed.

The provisions of substance about land-tenure in Italy are now complete and the text returns to jurisdiction. There are parallel chapters about public and private land, in which jurisdiction is confined to regular magistrates (lines 33–6) – for private land consuls and praetors, for public land consuls, praetors and censors (the latter, no doubt, because they were in charge of letting contracts for public land and the collection of rents there). There appears to be a clause in each chapter which does not exclude appeal against the jurisdiction of these magistrates. The message of the law is that litigation about the land should follow normal procedure. However, in the next chapter concerning tax-cases (lines 36–9), there seems to be some innovation: an accelerated process involving a jury of *recuperatores* could be initiated by the tax-collector approaching either a regular magistrate or a pro-magistrate, and we have a reference to the selection of this jury from members of the first class (*classis prima*) – men of considerable substance, but not members of the equestrian centuries of public horse nor even necessarily holders of the equestrian census, as it seems that the jurymen in the *quaestio de repetundis* were.

The coda of this part of the law is two chapters designed to enforce its execution. The first absolves a man from any oaths required by previous legislation, whose regulations about land-tenure conflict with those of the present law, and from any penalty accruing through failure to take the oath (lines 40–1). The second (lines 41–2) stresses the right and duty of magistrates to make judicial decisions according to this law and to disregard contrary provisions in earlier laws, guaranteeing them immunity from any penalty on account of their neglect of these laws on this ground.

The overall impression left by the Italian section of the law is one of variety. Even if several categories of former public land are made private in the opening lines, a number of types of public land subsist – land occupied by the villagers by the roads, pasture land and drove-roads, land leased to communities, the land in the *trientabula*, land occupied by non-Romans and some land apparently still available for new occupation and cultivation. A law is of course not necessarily a mirror of reality, but it is hard to imagine a law like this being passed, if the public land of Italy had irrevocably passed into the hands of a minority of private citizens and public control of it was a thing of the past.

We also have the impression of an attempt to balance interests. The prior possessors got formal and final confirmation of their holdings as private property free from rent, together with a right to unrestricted pasturage (subject to a pasture tax on the number of animals above a certain minimum). The Gracchan assignees also got confirmation of their holdings as private property free from rent, again with the right to pasturage on the remaining *ager publicus*. Moreover, the possibility was offered to anyone, including apparently someone who had already been assigned land, to convert up to 30 *iugera* of the remaining *ager publicus* into private property by cultivation. Thus, in theory the interests were served of both substantial landowners and those who had been recently landless or indeed still were. The price of this was the abolition of the old agrarian regime, where up to 500 *iugera* of public land could be taken over for long-term private use. A small amount of enclosure for cultivation (30 *iugera*) was allowed those with less than the maximum permitted amount of former *ager publicus*, but pastoralists were specifically prevented from fencing off public land (line 25). Of course there was nothing to prevent rich men expanding their private property, provided that they did so by the purchase of other people's private property. Equally, although at one point the law provided a magistrate with a remedy against violent expulsion (line 18), a peasant, who was trying to cultivate 30 *iugera* of *ager publicus*, would have had practical difficulties in asserting his right against a pastoralist seeking free range for his animals. Nevertheless, the law was not only backward-looking in its clarification and consolidation of rights on the land in the wake of the Gracchan reforms, it was also forward-looking. It provided some means for the landless to make a living off public land without the intervention of the commission, and it put an end to the creeping monopolisation of public land through large-scale occupation by the rich, while safeguarding their existing interests. Though the legislator cannot have excluded the possibility of future distributions or colonisation in the land remaining public, it was a settlement meant to last.

The second part of the law is devoted to the provinces and with this change of focus its character changes. Whereas before we have been dealing with the conversion of public to private land and regulations about the land remaining public, what follows is primarily concerned with the settlement of men and the sale of land. Great uncertainty surrounds the small section of poorly preserved text (lines 43–8) which comes immediately after the enforcement chapters. In the commentary there will be found my arguments for believing that this section does concern land in a province, but is equally not part of the African section. We find here references to the assignation of land to colonists by virtue of a *lex Baebia* and the sale in Rome of land to purchasers who make the appropriate provision of guarantors and securities.

The African section begins (lines 48–58) with land publicly sold, whose future status is to be private and subject to tax (*ager privatus vectigalisque*, line 49). A commission of two men (*duumviri*) is to be set up (line 52) and one of these is first required to compile a register of all holdings properly deriving from the public sale of land, including those arising from subsequent private sales of this land or the seizure of property by creditors (lines 52–8). The impression is given that public sales and subsequent transfers of this property have been going on for some time. A commissioner was also to review holdings created by the repealed *lex Rubria* and to ensure that these did not exceed the allotments prescribed by that law either in number or in quantity of land assigned (lines 58–62). Correctly assigned holdings were to be ratified. Similarly, the tenure of land properly bought through public sale or bought or inherited from the purchaser was to be ratified (lines 63–5). When a man had bought in good faith land publicly sold to someone else, he was to be compensated with an equivalent piece of land (lines 65–6). Where a man had not received his correct colonial allotment, he was to be given it out of undistributed land (lines 66–7). Through error the parallel procedures of public sale and distribution of land to colonists must on occasions have either been inexact in themselves or have overlapped, so frustrating one of the recipients. Even men who had taken land as colonists which was not properly theirs were perhaps to receive compensation (lines 67–8). Equally, those who had been sold land which was in fact part of a colonial allotment, were to be compensated for its loss out of unsold land (lines 68–70).

Land obtained by purchase, though in private ownership, was to remain subject to tax (*vectigal*), and we find at this point the regulations for the collection of this *vectigal*, as well as those for the collection of any money owed to the treasury from the purchase-price (lines 70–4). The commissioner is further instructed to compensate the non-Roman friends of Rome in Africa for any losses of land resulting from the grants to Roman citizens (lines 74–7) and to ensure that Rome's old enemies there, the tribute-paying peoples (*stipendiarii*), possess the quantity of land originally assigned to them (lines 77–8). His final duty in that province is probably to make a record of all land left over from all the purchases and allocations (lines 78–82).

There was still land in Africa, neither privately owned nor colonial land, which was to be leased, mainly for pasturage. This is the next item (lines 82–3) and it is followed by regulations about future tax-contracts in Africa (lines 83–9). These would have embraced all land which was *vectigalis*, whether sold or retained as the property of the Roman people. The last chapters that certainly belong to the African section relate first to freedom of movement on roads and the *limites* (paths) between the centuries and secondly to false declarations of land-holdings (lines 89–91).

Arguments will be found in the commentary that what follows probably belongs to the section about Greece, which is first securely attested in line 96. Initially the law deals with public sales of land and their consequences. Possessors unjustly deprived of land should be compensated; holders of certain land which had been public were not to be liable to tax (lines 91–2). The text becomes more fragmentary and we can only glimpse the operations envisaged by the law. Tenure of land granted by senatorial decree is confirmed (line 93) and there is a reference to the vintage and olive-harvest in 111 BC (line 95). A commissioner is to organise the surveying of land and erection of boundary-stones in Corinthian territory (lines 96–7). Some land is to be sold (line 99) and provision is made for the taking of security from the purchasers (lines 100–1). Overall the same basic patterns appear as in the African section. Land in Greece is being purchased from the treasury. Some land is still liable to tax or pasture tax; other land is exempt. The centuriation in Corinthian territory suggests that a colony may have been planned, and Roman citizens are certainly among the existing beneficiaries of land-distribution (line 94).

Like the Italian section, the African section is mainly concerned with stabilisation after a period of turbulence and confusion. But it is not a matter of a reaction against Roman settlement and land-ownership abroad. Rather, the impression given by the law is that it is embracing such settlement and positively encouraging land-purchases by Romans. What survives of the Greek section similarly implies the continuance of land-purchases by Romans and the creation of a new colonial settlement. Against the perspective that has been sketched earlier there is nothing surprising about this. Traditionally, the Romans had exploited military victory so as to provide their citizens with land. The scene for this was no longer Italy alone but the Mediterranean. The hostility to C.Gracchus' refoundation of Carthage, ill-omened and a bogey to Rome for over a century, should not make us think that the Romans or the Roman upper class on principle disapproved of the establishment of Roman citizens overseas or beyond the Alps. Given that one of the purposes of colonisation was military – to provide fortresses which would secure Roman territory against external threat or internal subversion – it is natural that their colonial ventures were at first confined to Italy, and then to Italy and Cisalpine Gaul. However, by now consolidation of Roman control had taken place on either side of the Po, especially since the construction of the *via Postumia* from Genua to Aquileia by the consul of 148.

The agrarian law of 111 was passed about the same time that the Romans finally declared war on Jugurtha. It showed a Roman commitment to settlement and investment in Africa that was incompatible with a *laissez-faire* policy towards the Numidian king. The Romans could not tolerate a potentially hostile power as a neighbour to land into which so much Roman capital was being ploughed. Equally, the maintenance of colonists in Africa, even when they had no urban centre, suggests a desire to reinforce the Roman presence in Africa as a limit to any Numidian ambitions. Economic advantage for individuals and security for Roman dominion went hand in hand. There may have been senators who were, so to speak, little Italians, reluctant to see Romans living or holding property overseas either on moral grounds (through fear that they would become morally corrupted) or because they feared political consequences from the dispersal of the citizen body, since it destroyed the notion of Rome as a city-state. Yet such views do not seem to have been influential at this time. By 111 BC exploitation of the empire was an item on the political agenda shared both by supporters and opponents of the Gracchi.

Agrarian epilogue

In the period between 111 and the Social War in 90 BC interest in redistribution of Italian land and settlement overseas did not disappear. In his *elogium* on stone M.Livius Drusus, the tribune of 91 BC, is recorded as one of a commission of ten for the distribution of land under his own law and one of a commission of five for the same purpose under the otherwise unknown *lex Saufeia*.[71] Drusus' own agrarian bill, proposed when he was tribune, apparently disturbed some powerful Italians, who feared to lose land that they were currently occupying. There is no reason to think that this was illegal or arose from an oversight by previous commissions. The bill may in fact have threatened the land occupied under law or treaty (*lex agr.* 29), which C.Gracchus had probably excluded from division.[72] Also under Drusus' law, colonies were apparently established in Italy and Sicily, something which had been voted into law long before but had not been put into effect – perhaps the twelve colonies proposed by Drusus' father in 122.[73]

Land had earlier featured in the legislation of the tribune L.Appuleius Saturninus in 103 and 100, in this case land outside peninsular Italy. Probably in his first tribunate, Saturninus legislated to give time-served veterans of Marius 100 *iugera* each in Africa (in the writer's view most probably within the centuriated area in the province).[74] Then in 100 BC he proposed to distribute to

[71] *ILS*, 49. [72] App. *BCiv.* 1.35.136; 36.162–3. Cf. commentary on *lex agr.* 1.
[73] App. *BCiv.* 1.35.136; cf. 23.101. [74] *Vir.Ill.* 73.1.

Romans and Italians land recovered after the invasion of the Cimbri in Cisalpine Gaul. He also planned colonies in Sicily, Macedonia and Achaea.[75] In the last instance he would have been able to take advantage of the surveying operations mentioned in the law of 111. We also hear of the founding of Eporedia in north-west Cisalpina in 100, and it is attractive to connect the founding of Mariana in Corsica with this legislation.[76]

The years after 91 BC, in which the Romans first fought their Italian allies and then each other in Italy, and in the East were in a major conflict with Mithridates VI, produced a great tear in the fabric of agrarian history. When at last victorious, Sulla settled few of his men overseas (we only hear of Aleria in Corsica, though it is of course possible that some existing settlements were reinforced). There were, however, massive settlements in Italy on land expropriated from his opponents, especially in Etruria and Campania.[77] A great deal of property was, moreover, made available through the proscription and execution of alleged Marians and this was sold, usually cheaply, to Sullan supporters. Other land may have been simply seized without the intervention of any Roman magistrate.[78] There are two important aspects of this. First, the type of Italian land-distribution regular in the Gracchan period, which sought to benefit needy individuals without excessive disruption to previous holdings, was superseded by large-scale allocation to veterans. Secondly, private holdings, already disturbed by civil war, were thrown into greater confusion and it was easy for influential men on the victorious side to accumulate land. Sulla's aims in concentrating settlement in Italy were probably revenge on his enemies and security, for himself and the regime that he had placed in power, against any reaction from those Marians who survived. Men did migrate abroad, but the majority of these would have been Marian refugees, especially those who sided with Sertorius in Spain.

A law was passed, the *lex Plotia*, to give land to Pompey's veterans in 70 BC, but it seems not to have been put into effect[79] and, although the full powers of the tribunate, emasculated by Sulla, were also restored in that year, it was some years before another agrarian bill was proposed. This was the *rogatio* of Servilius Rullus, proposed in late 64, whose passage into law was successfully resisted by Cicero in his consulship. Thanks to Cicero's denunciations of the bill, we are better informed about it, even if tendentiously and obliquely, than we are about any other item of agrarian legislation in that century. Some of the items are familiar. A ten-man commission was to be elected – though by an unusual procedure – for a five-year period with the same rights in relation to the

[75] App. *BCiv.* 1.29.130–2; *Vir.Ill.* 73.5; cf. Cic. *Balb.* 48.

[76] Vell.Pat. 1.15; Strabo 4.6.7(205); Pliny *HN* 3.123; 3.80.

[77] Pliny *HN* 3.80; App. *BCiv.* 1.96.447; 100.470; 104.489; Cic. *Cat.* 3.14; *Mur.* 69; Florus 2.9.27. For other literary and epigraphic indications see Greenidge, Clay and Gray, 1960, pp. 216–8.

[78] Cic. *Quinct.* 76; *Rosc.Amer.* 6, 43 and 125–6; *Leg.Agr.* 2.56; Sall. *Hist.* 1.55.18M; Pliny *HN* 36.116.

[79] Dio 38.5.1–2; Plut. *Luc.* 34.4; cf. Cic. *Att.* 1.18.6.

founding of colonies as under the *lex Sempronia* (contrary to what Cicero implies in his discussion, this must have been Caius', not Tiberius Gracchus' law). However, unlike the Gracchan commission, these men were to be granted praetorian *imperium* with the judicial power inherent in it. Their staff was also to be numerous: apart from the usual attendants necessary for surveying, transport animals and the equipment necessary for staying in the field, they were to have 200 surveyors of equestrian rank.[80]

Their job was twofold: first, to sell land in order to raise money; secondly, to use this money to acquire land for settlement. What was to be sold? Land designated for sale since 81 BC, chiefly, no doubt, territory confiscated by Sulla;[81] more generally, public land in Italy or abroad, including the former royal estates of Hellenistic kings, most of which would have been currently leased out by the censors.[82] In spite of Cicero's presentation of this last proposal, it seems likely that this land was to be sold, like the land in Africa in the Gracchan period, on condition that it became *ager privatus vectigalisque* – still liable to tax, though not directly owned by the Roman people. Remaining public land was to be subject to heavier rents or taxes.[83] With this money and the product of the booty brought back by generals, cultivable land was to be bought to be distributed to new settlers and colonies were to be founded, in particular one at Capua in the *ager Campanus*.[84]

Pace Cicero, there was much that was plausible and sensible in the bill, given the room available for manoeuvre by the legislator. However, over it hung the shadow of Sullan expropriations and profiteering, exemplified by C.Quinctius Valgus, Rullus' father-in-law and a magistrate in three Campanian towns[85] – a point which Cicero ruthlessly exploited. Any public assignations since 82 BC were ratified by the bill.[86] Any territory, which according to senatorial decree should have been publicly sold since 81 BC, was in fact to be sold (this would have mainly concerned lands confiscated from Marian supporters, including the territory of Volaterrae and Arretium).[87] By contrast with the Gracchan period, confiscation and purchase were the chief means to make land available for distribution. We hear little of disposable public land in Italy, except for land rented out by the censors in the *ager Campanus* and pasture-areas such as the *silva Scantia*.[88] There is no question of restricting the exploitation of public land any more. Most has apparently passed into private hands, but there seems to have been little attempt to undo the effect of Sulla's victory or to pursue public land illegally occupied by his supporters.

Remarkably, the overthrow of the *status quo* was actually proposed by the tribune L.Flavius in 60 BC. He proposed to take the same starting-point as our law – land public in 133 BC (*P.Mucio L.Calpurnio consulibus*) – and to challenge

[80] Cic. *Leg.Agr.* 2.31–2; cf. 16–18. [81] *Leg.Agr.* 2.35. [82] *Leg.Agr.* 1.3–6; 2.48–51.
[83] *Leg.Agr.* 1.10; 2.56–8. [84] *Leg.Agr.* 1.10; 2.66–7, 73, 75–6, 79, 85 and 96.
[85] *Leg.Agr.* 3.3, 8 and 13–14; *ILLRP*, 523, 598 and 645–6.
[86] *Leg.Agr.* 3.4 and 11. [87] *Leg.Agr.* 2.35; cf. *Att.* 1.19.4; *Fam.* 13.4.2.
[88] *Leg.Agr.* 1.3.

the right of Sullan possessors to their holdings. Both of these features of the law were opposed by Cicero in the interest of his wealthy supporters.[89] Only the purchase of land with the revenues accruing from Pompey's conquests in the East was acceptable to Cicero then, and this was the chief feature of Caesar's first agrarian law of 59 BC (which Cicero also opposed). However, to judge from Cicero's later correspondence about Volaterrae, Caesar's commissioners also had power to dispose of land which was still theoretically public.[90] Caesar's second law, the *lex Campana*, provided for the redistribution of the *ager Campanus*, which had up to now been rented out by the censors.[91] It had become clear that the large holdings of land built up in the Sullan period were politically impregnable and policies on the Gracchan model had little scope left in Italy. In his dictatorship Caesar still exploited his measures of 59 BC, but the bulk of his settlement of veterans occurred abroad.[92] It took the civil war after Caesar's murder and a new round of proscriptions to liberate land for distribution once more – not with the happiest consequences.[93]

Let me conclude with a comparison. In 111 BC, in spite of the conversion of much public land into private, a number of categories of land remained in the public sector in Italy. Moreover, the acquisition of land from the public sector by individuals was required to conform to rules which could be tested in the courts. In the late Republic the amount and variety of public land had been greatly reduced; there were still smallholdings in colonies and the *ager Campanus*, but the only route to the re-establishment of peasant proprietors lay through purchase by the treasury or a new round of confiscations. Moreover, there had been a period during the social and civil wars and their aftermath, when the safeguards envisaged by the legislator of 111 regarding the occupation of certain types of public land must have been completely at a discount. At the same time it had been easy to acquire, either by unauthorised occupation or by legal purchase, large quantities of private land, especially land seized from the Italian enemies of Rome or proscribed Romans. It is perhaps not a coincidence that it is precisely in this period that the luxurious 'villa' becomes well attested archaeologically. It was not the Hannibalic war or an economic crisis in the second century, but the ten years of Italian and civil war, which brought about an irreversible revolution in agriculture.

[89] *Att.* 1.19.4.

[90] App. *BCiv.* 2.10.31; 3.2.5; Dio 38.1.4–6. Cf. Cic. *Fam.* 13.4.1–2 (Cicero stresses the exemption that Volaterrae had received under the law of 59 BC).

[91] Cic. *Att.* 2.16.1–2; Dio 38.5.2.

[92] On Caesar's measures see Cic. *Fam.* 9.17.2; 13.4.1–2; *Phil.* 2.101–2; App. *BCiv.* 2.94; Suet. *Jul.* 38.1; Dio 42.55.1; Yavetz, 1983, 137–43. On Caesarian and triumviral settlements, Brunt, 1971, 319–32; Keppie, 1983.

4

The Laws as Texts

Grammar

The two laws[1] generally express their instructions in third person imperatives, singular or plural. There are, as the text stands, two examples of the use of a future indicative for this purpose, a construction normally regarded as informal (*lex rep.* 25 and 66). A more common variant is that the imperative *facito* is used with dependent subjunctives (these are sometimes, but not necessarily, introduced by the particle *utei*). The construction with *facito* is especially appropriate when a magistrate is ordered to ensure that someone else does something (e.g. *lex rep.* 15 and 30). However, it is also used for variety, when the man addressed could well have been instructed with a simple imperative, since he was going to be the agent in law, even if he did not carry out all the physical actions involved (*lex rep.* 8, 12 and 26; *lex agr.* 77–8).

It is characteristic of Republican legal texts that the separate instructions are strung together in series, either in asyndeton or linked by simple connectives such as *-que* or *neive*.[2] Participles are not used to subordinate any of the commands. Subordinate clauses are only used to define more closely the nature, time and place of the separate instructions. The tendency of the text, therefore, is to have a sequence of verbs in the same mood, imperative or subjunctive. Alternative nouns or verbs are listed either in asyndeton (*dederunt adsignaverunt reliquerunt*) or with *-ve* linking the last two or three items (e.g. *lex rep.* 3: *ablatum captum conciliatum aversumve*; *lex agr.* 7: *dedit adsignavit reliquit inve formas tabulasve retulit referive iusit*).

By far the most common kind of subordinate clause is the relative. Definitions which condition the application of each instruction precede the instruction itself and usually take the form of a series of relative clauses, including sub-relative clauses (e.g. *lex agr.* 4–5; *quei ager publicus populei Romanei . . . fuit, extra eum agrum, quei ager . . . divideretur, quod eius agri . . . in terra Italia, quod eius extra urbem Romam est, quod eius in urbe . . . est, quod eius III vir . . . adsignavit; lex rep.* 75: *praetor, quei . . . quaeret, qua de re ei praetori eisque ioudicibus, quei . . . adfuerint, quei vivent, . . . satis factum erit*). Comparatively few chapters are introduced by conditional clauses. The

[1] For a general study of legal Latin see De Meo, 1986, 67–131.

[2] Cf. De Meo, 1986, 73.

examples are almost entirely at the end of the *lex repetundarum* (lines 72, 76, 78, 79 and 83; cf. perhaps *lex agr.* 41). On other occasions conditional clauses introduce new items within a chapter (*lex rep.* 19; *lex agr.* 25 and 38). Otherwise, the conditional clauses are secondary to the original defining relative clauses (*lex rep.* 11, 39 and 56).

The tense and mood of verbs in those relative clauses which define future instructions are generally either future or future perfect indicative. The perfect is occasionally used for events which have taken place before the passage of the law, but this may be equally rendered with a future perfect (contrast *lex rep.* 74: *fuit fueritve ex lege ...*, with *lex rep.* 10: *quoiave in fide is erit, maioresve in maiorum fide fueri⟨n⟩t*). However, we also find present and perfect subjunctives. Sometimes these may be explained as resulting from their position in virtual *oratio obliqua* (e.g. *lex rep.* 20). Sometimes the context of the subjunctive is a negative definition (e.g. *lex rep.* 69: *quod sine malo pequlatu fiat*, *lex agr.* 2: *quod non modus maior siet*). However, a consistent pattern is hard to find. Note *lex rep.* 10: *dum nei quem eorum det ..., quoiei is ... at⟨t⟩igat, queive eiei sodalis siet*, but at the end of that same chapter (line 11) *neive eum quei ioudex ... erit, neive eum quei patronus datus erit*; also *queive trans mare erit* (line 17, cf. 14) following a series of subjunctives dependent on *dum ne quem eorum legat, quei.*

Relative clauses tend to precede their corresponding demonstrative pronoun, but the noun with which the demonstrative agrees may precede the relative pronoun or be incorporated in the relative clause (e.g. *lex rep.* 12: *pr(aetor) quei inter peregrinos ious deicet, is ...*; *lex rep.* 54: *ex qua sorti pronuntiaverit, eam sortem ....* The more general stylistic equivalent of this is the position of the defining relative clause or clauses before the instruction itself. A variation on this device on a gigantic scale is the list of various types of land at the beginning of *lex agraria* (lines 1–7) without any instruction attached, followed by a chapter containing instructions, commencing *Ager locus aedificium omnis quei supra scriptus est.*[3]

Within the texts we find *oratio obliqua* (e.g. *lex rep.* 4, 15, 18, 40, 42 and 47; *lex agr.* 37 and 64) and a variety of adverbial clauses. There are temporal clauses depending on *ant(ea) quam, post(ea) quam, donec, quotiens* and *ubei* = when (*lex rep.* 44, 48, 49, 63 and 65; *lex agr.* 89; *quom* as a temporal conjunction is only found in *lex rep.* 71); comparative clauses following *ita utei* (*lex agr.* 27), *quasei sei* (*lex rep.* 41), *siremps quasei sei* (*lex rep.* 77). Negative provisos are introduced by *dum nei* (*lex rep.* 10, 15, 30 and 63). Negative result clauses introduced by *quo minus* are common in *lex agraria* (lines 9–11, 20, 25, 36 and 84; cf. 87–8; *lex rep.* 61 and 71). The converse, a positive result clause introduced by *quo magis*, is found occasionally (*lex rep.* 74 and 81; *lex agr.* 12). Also of interest are two uses of the gerundive agreeing with a noun in the genitive used to define the object aimed at – *lex agr.* 27: *quod eius] rei ioudicandae maxsume verum esse comperrit*; *lex rep.* 32: *quod eius rei quaerundai censeant refere* (the

[3] Cf. De Meo, 1986, 67ff and 87ff.

first gerundive construction seems to be dependent on *verum*, the second on *re* in *refere*).

Style

As Marouzeau (1959) and Crawford (1988) have pointed out, there are two styles of Roman legal language. One is the austere language of early Republican laws, which to a certain extent is paralleled in the crisp and succinct phraseology of the classical jurists, seen to best advantage in the edict of the *praetor urbanus*; the other is the ponderous and pleonastic language of legal draughtsmen in the middle and late Republic. Our texts are supreme examples of this second style. The grammatical elements out of which the texts of the laws are composed are comparatively simple, but the sentences and chapters, which they generate, are prolix and frequently tortuous.[4] One contributory factor is the use of extensive definitions, in which all the exceptions are included, and their repetition *in toto* at almost every opportunity. Another is the exact itemising of each action which the laws prescribe, for example in the regulations for selecting a jury-panel (*lex rep.* 12–19) or the voting-procedure (*lex rep.* 49–55). On occasion the law uses the formula, *utei quod recte factum esse volet* (*lex rep.* 30), which allows a magistrate some discretion as to method, or *utei e re publica fideque eius esse videbitur* (*lex agr.* 35 and 78), where the discretion may involve legal or moral judgements. On the whole, however, actions to be taken are spelt out in detail.

On the other hand, there also seems to be an element of rhetoric, which seeks to stress the solemnity of the statutes and the grandiose nature of their subjects. The slow introduction to the *lex agraria* with its elaborate catalogue of types of land-assignment is an affirmation of the importance of land in Italy to the Roman people and the actions taken about it in the last twenty years. Similarly, at the beginning of the *lex repetundarum* the reader is made aware of the various conditions of men who formed the *imperium Romanum* and the range of offences (perhaps more impressive in appearance than in fact), which the law sought to repress. Even if we allow that clarity and precision were more fundamental aims for the draughtsmen than rhetorical effect and that they occasionally preferred brevity (in *lex rep.* 13 and 16 all former magistrates of senatorial rank are not listed, but the text refers simply to senators after the minor magistrates), there is a tendency to redundancy in vocabulary. There are pairs where it is hard to find a distinguishing legal nuance – *dedit adsignavit, deduxit conlocavit, factus creatusve* – and series in which one term at least seems unnecessary – *agrum locum aedificium possesionem.*[5]

By the late Republic there were professional legal draughtsmen (Cic. *Dom.* 48) and it is reasonable to postulate an accepted common style of legal draughtsmanship (one of whose other eventual consequences was a greater attention to orthography).[6] How new was the style we are discussing? The

[4] Cf. Schulz, 1946, 96–8. [5] Cf. De Meo, 1986, 80ff. [6] Cf. De Meo, 1986, 96.

remains of the Twelve Tables and the laws attributed to the kings are sufficient to show the laconic, pregnant style of early Roman statutes, whose statements seem like maxims expressing an eternally valid justice. The few fragments of laws passed between the time of the Twelve Tables and 200 BC suggest that they tended to ape their renowned predecessors. The fact that Cicero borrowed the style of these early laws for his ideal Roman constitution in the *De Legibus* (2.7) shows their attraction to later generations, especially to the temperamentally conservative. A deliberately laconic style was to be found in other texts intended for public consumption, such as *elogia* and military reports (Marouzeau, 1959, 442).

For surviving examples of legal draughtsmanship of the second century BC we must turn to the *senatus consulta*, especially those preserved in Latin. Of these the most interesting is the *S.C. de Bacchanalibus* (*FIRA* I, 30), because it was intended to be a recommendation valid for an indefinite time in the future and, furthermore, because what the senate recommended was the edict which the consuls should publish on a matter of public order. *Senatus consulta* of this period normally read like the minutes of a meeting, which indeed they were – see for example the Greek texts relating to Thisbae (*FIRA* I, 31) and to the Dionysiac artists (*FIRA* I, 34), where the actual decrees were brief and practical. The *S.C. de Tiburtibus* (*FIRA* I, 33) is, though brief, unusually clumsy and ponderous, but this seems to have resulted from a deliberate attempt to create an impressive document, when there was only one point to make, namely that the senate accepted the excuses of the people of Tibur. The *S.C. de Bacchanalibus* is generally crisp and to the point, but it also shows signs of striving for effect – to be expected, when the edict it contained was intended to impress a wide public – for example in lines 13ff: *Neve post hac inter sed conioura[se ne]ve convovise neve conspondise neve conpromesise velet. Sacra in oqultod ne quisquam fecise velet; neve in poplicod neve in preivatod neve extrad urbem sacra quisquam fecise velet*... There is evidence here of a verbosity which prefigures the texts of the *lex repetundarum* and the *lex agraria*. The same thing can be seen in a parody of legal pronouncements from the same period – the *edictiones aediliciae* of Ergasilus in Plautus' *Captivi* (791ff). But these examples still fall some distance short of the style of our two laws. By contrast, contemporary examples of *leges* in another sense, i.e. private contracts, which are to be found in Cato's *De Agricultura* (144–50), do not waste words, although they are immensely detailed and precise.

We must also consider the possible influence of Greek models. Reference was made in the introduction to the ordinances of the Ptolemies. The surviving regulations of Ptolemy Philadelphus and Ptolemy Euergetes II[7] certainly provide a parallel in length and complexity of material. However, the structure of these texts is comparatively simple and, although there are similarities with our laws, when a series of instructions is being given linked by simple

[7] B.P. Grenfell, *The Revenue Laws of Ptolemy Philadelphus*, 1986; *P.Teb.* I, no. 5.

connectives (e.g. *lex rep.* 12ff), there seems to be no equivalent to the inversion of relative clauses and their appropriate demonstratives nor to the deferred impact created by the location of the imperative at the end of its main clause and the relevant subordinate clauses (see e.g. *lex rep.* 4, 19, 63–4, 74–5 and 76–7). If we turn to the classical Greek world, it is tempting to compare the detailed prescriptions about voting in *lex rep.* 49ff with those in the Aristotelian *Athenaion Politeia* (chs. 64–5 and 68–9) regarding the allotment of jurors and voting in Athenian courts. It must, however, be conceded that this resemblance is created by the similar necessity incumbent on the draughtsmen of both Athenian and Roman laws to itemise a complex procedure, so that there could be no possibility of error or confusion at a vital point.

The law is not the only field where this is necessary; another is religion. A fine Greek example is the first century BC revision and republication of the Messenian law about the mysteries at Andania (*Syll.*³, 736). Though there is no equivalent religious law extant from the Roman Republic, the imperial texts regarding the Arval Brethren (*ILS*, 5032ff, esp. 5035, 5039–40) give us some idea of the form in which Roman religious rituals might have been written down, as do the Umbrian *Tabulae Iguvinae*[8] and the recently expanded dossier of honours voted by *senatus consultum* and *lex* to honour the dead Germanicus in AD 19–20, where a major concern is the correct performance of ritual.[9] The composers of religious texts also exploited rhetorical pleonasm in order to achieve solemnity (Macr. *Sat.* 3.9.7; Cato, *Agric.* 141).

A contrast is provided by a second century BC Greek text concerned, like the *lex repetundarum*, with detailed judicial procedure.[10] The second document on this stone relates to an agreement between Clazomenae and Temnos about long-term arrangements to settle disputes between inhabitants of the two cities. The regulations here find an echo in our *repetundae* text. There are two (lines 24ff and 47ff) references to oaths – by the jurors and by the opposing parties – something which was part of a long tradition in the Greek world (*Ath. Pol.* 67; *Syll.*³, 953, lines 2–9). Moreover, we find a catalogue of those disqualified from jury-service: 'a father must not be juror to a son, nor a son to a father, nor cousins on the paternal or maternal side, nor stepsons nor stepfathers'. This is a striking parallel to the regulations of *lex rep.* lines 20 and 22. However, in spite of the material similarities, the two documents are far apart stylistically, the Greek compressed and matter of fact, the Latin prolix and ponderous – perhaps self-consciously so. Note for instance the repetition in *lex rep.* 22 of *queive-siet* clauses and the phrase *quoi is queive ei, quei petet, gener socer vitricus privignusve siet*, where the initial variations are unnecessary, since the clause mentions both fathers-in-law and sons-in-law, stepfathers and stepsons.

The influence of Greek law on Roman was detectable in the Twelve Tables

[8] I. Devoto, *Tabulae Iguvinae*. 2nd edn. Rome, 1940.

[9] EJ 94a (cf. 94b) with *Tabula Siarensis* (J. Gonzalez, *ZPE* 55 (1984), 55–100).

[10] Herrman, 1979, 253–4.

(*Tab.* VII.2, X.2–3), whether we believe the story of the Roman embassy to Delphi or not.[11] That the Romans in the second century learnt something from the Greek world about framing regulations for law-courts and agrarian matters is very plausible, if with the paucity of our present evidence unprovable. However, the style in which they chose to express these regulations was their own. It partly sprang from the desire of the legislators to be thorough and effective. But there was also a concern for an impressive rhetoric, traces of which can be seen earlier in the *S.C. de Bacchanalibus*. Lastly, one should not forget that these laws were read aloud to the assembly which was to vote on them: some of the more rotund phrases may have been chosen because they would sound well.

A note on the engraving

Details of the different styles of engraving of the two laws may be found in the introductions to the two texts (see below, pp. 74, 171–2). Each face of the bronze seems to have been engraved consistently in one style, which is distinct from that of the other face, even if the letter-forms used do not fundamentally differ. The inscription of the *lex de repetundis* is in a confident, elegant hand, which shows considerable difference in the space allocated to different letters. M and Q sprawl in a grandiose fashion, E, T and S are tightly compressed. A similar style can be found on the Guardia Vomana fragment of a judiciary law (*CIL* I², 598). The agrarian face has a more evenly spaced but much less attractive text. The engraving of individual letters is slipshod and often very shallow. It may be wondered if this was entirely the fault of the engraver and may not have resulted from his having to work on a bronze placed in an inconvenient position, on which the edge of the chisel could not get a firm purchase.

If we eliminate the faults deriving from poor engraving, more prevalent on the agrarian face, we find that the errors, which result from the inadequate transmission of the text from the copy of the law provided to the mind and hand of the engraver, are similar in number on the two faces but arguably different in character. On the *repetundae* face some errors may result from attraction to a preceding word or phrase – for example *ipsei parente for ipse parens* in line 3 (where *ipsei parente* must have stood earlier in the line); *fuerit* following *erit* in line 10, although the subject is now plural. The latter might also arise, however, from the mishearing of a text read to the engraver. This may be the explanation for the inscribing of *courato* for *iourato* in *lex rep.* 21. Other possible examples of this are in *lex rep.* 20 – *propiusve eum ea cognitione{m} attingat* – and *lex rep.* 41 – *ut eius* for *utei is*, though a graphic error is perhaps equally likely in the last case. It is possible that this engraver was listening to the text being read, as he engraved, even if he also looked at the master-copy himself from time to time. The existence of an assistant, or supervisor, whose duty it was to read the text,

[11] Dion.Hal. *AR* 10.52.4, 54.7; Livy 3.31.8 with the commentary *ad loc.* of Ogilvie, 1965.

may also be indicated by the suprascript corrections (*lex rep.* 3, 7, 22, 28 and 33; *lex agr.* 17). It would have been very difficult for the engraver himself to have recognised these errors, before he had moved so far on in his work that they would no longer be apparent.

When the engraver of the *repetundae* face writes *hominis* for *nominis (delatio)* in line 41, this is more probably a mishearing than a graphic error. It seems particularly careless, since he had already met the phrase *nominis delatio* earlier in the text, and suggests that he did not recognise *nominis delatio* as a standard legal phrase with a well-known meaning. However, it is not entirely stupid, since *hominis* is a noun in the right case, which could in certain circumstances have depended on *delatio*. Again, where he substitutes *deiuraturum* for *deferatur* in line 74, this is nonsensical and ungrammatical, but could not have been perpetrated by a man with no grasp of Latin legal vocabulary. It seems to be a combination of a mishearing and the retention in the memory of the word *deiuraturum* or a similar form of *deiuro* from a previous occasion, when he was inscribing a legal text. Other examples of errors that suggest that the engraver was not copying mechanically are those involving abbreviations. In line 74 he (or his reader) expanded *mag* into *magistratus* without realising that this was a clause introduced by *quo magis*. Again, in line 80 *praetor* and *quaestor* are probably expansions of the abbreviations *pr* and *q* in the original, which take no account of the proper case of the nouns.

The engraver of the agrarian face, however, does not make this sort of semi-literate error, but commits some mistakes which cast grave doubts on his basic literacy. Examples are *de]crrnito* in line 16, *A.D.X.E.K. Octobris* in line 21, *vieiqae* in line 26, not to mention the bizarre introduction of 'W's in lines 25, 82 and 88 (the first example is a reversed M, the second a reversed N, but the third defies explanation). In spite of this he was on the whole remarkably accurate, and it may be that we should suppose a man, who copied mechanically a text before his eyes, without much sense of what constituted plausible spelling, or a man who engraved what was read to him letter by letter.

5

The discovery, transmission and early publications of the fragments

The catalogue of the library of the dukes of Urbino at the end of the fifteenth century had, as one of its items, 'twelve fragments of bronze inscribed with Latin letters'. The *Inventarium Vetus*, now in the Vatican library, states that they were subsequently given as a gift to Pietro Bembo (Vat. Urb. lat. 1761, fo. 119v).[1] This probably happened shortly after the Borgia capture of Urbino in 1502.[2] We have no sure evidence of their being seen by any other scholar before Bembo's death in 1547, but a copy of the A fragment found its way into the *Epigrammata Antiquae Urbis* (fo. 180r–v) produced by Jacopo Mazzochi, bookseller to the Roman Academy, in 1521. This may be explained by the fact that Bembo was Secretary of the Briefs in the Curia from 1513 to 1521 and associated with the Roman Academy. It is likely that he had the fragments with him.

After Bembo's death the fragments at first remained in the *studio* of his *palazzo* at Padua, purchased in 1527, but gradually were dispersed. Paolo Manuzio had seen the E fragment some time before 1557; by 1564 it had reached the French royal library at Fontainebleau.[3] At least three fragments were sold to the Hungarian, J. Sambucus, a classical scholar with a post at the imperial court at Vienna. Two fragments, one of them via Sambucus, reached the von Montfort family in Swabia and thence passed as a legacy to their relatives by marriage, the Fugger of Augsburg – the formidable family of mine-owners and financiers with a strong interest in classical scholarship and good contacts with Italian humanists. These fragments (C and Dd) were loaned to Orsini for a short period in or before 1581.[4] They would have become imperial property in the seventeenth century and are now in Vienna, after being transferred there from Schloss Ambras at Innsbruck about 1820 (they are still recorded as there in 1819.[5] Two of Sambucus' fragments at least (these would

[1] Printed in C. Stornajolo, *Codices Urbinates Graeci*, Rome, 1895, clviii.

[2] Lintott, 1983, 203–4.

[3] P. Manuzio, *De Legibus Romanorum*, Venice, 1557, ch. XIII; Lintott, 1983, 205–6.

[4] P. de Nolhac, 'Lettere inedite del card. de Granvelle a Fulvio Orsini e al card. Sirleto', *Studi e documenti di storia e diritto* 5 (1884), 247–73, esp. 257–9; cf. Lintott, 1983, 210.

[5] A. Primisser, *Ubersicht der k. k. Ambraser-Sammlung*. 2nd edn. Vienna, 1819, Saal V, Schranke VII, nos. 257–8. Cf. Lintott, 1983, 212.

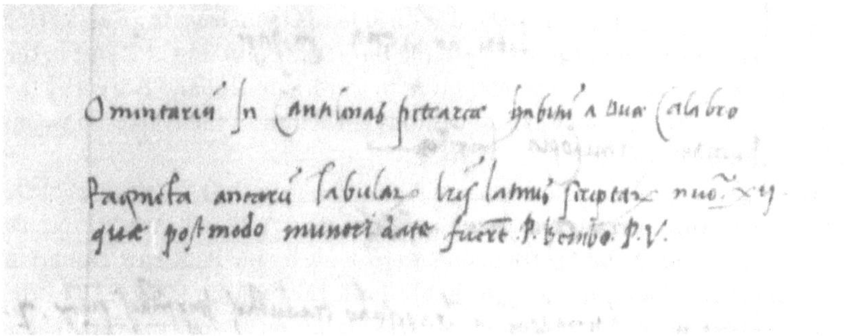

Fig. 2 Codex (Vaticanus) Urbinatis Latinus 1761 (the *Indice Vecchio* of the Urbino library), fo. 119v. The last two lines read, 'Fragmenta aenearum tabularum litteris latinis scriptarum numero xii, quae postmodo muneri datae fuerunt P. Bembo P(atricio) V(eneto).' *Photo:* Biblioteca Vaticana.

have been Dbc, which were also known to Pighius, see below) were sent by him to Fulvio Orsini in December 1575.[6]

In July of the same year Orsini bought the fragments that remained in Padua from Torquato Bembo, apparently five in number – in that case probably Aa, Ba-b, Bc and Da – and soon communicated the texts available to him to his friends Antonio Agustin and Piero Vettori.[7] On Orsini's death they were left to the Farnese family and, after some time at Parma, were taken to Naples in the eighteenth century, where they formed part of the Bourbon royal collection and hence are still to be found in the collection of the Museo Nazionale there. They were probably removed from Naples for a time *c.*1800 and certainly suffered from exposure to the elements and neglect.[8] The E fragment became lost in France in the early seventeenth century, its last known possessor being the painter Daniel du Moustier.[9] A very small fragment (F) was discovered in Italy, according to one story at Fossombrone near Urbino, in the late nineteenth century: after being copied and assigned as another fragment of this bronze, it was believed to be lost, but it has now been rediscovered in the Museo Nazionale at Naples, where it has apparently been since 1882, a gift from its previous owner R. Garrucci.[10] A good bronze facsimile of C was made in Italy,

[6] H. Gerstinger, *Die Briefe des Iohannes Sambucus 1554–84* (*Osterreich. Akad. d. Wiss. phil.-hist. Kl. Sitzungsberichte*, 255). Vienna, 1968, nos. xcii, xcv, cxxxv, clxviii; cf. P. de Nolhac, 'Piero Vettori et Carolo Sigonio – Correspondance avec Fulvio Orsini', *Studi e documenti di storia e diritto* 10 (1889), 91–152, at 117–21.

[7] London, British Museum 10270, fos. 9 and 33; de Nolhac (cited in note 6); A. Agustin, *Opera Omnia* (Luca, 1772), VI, nos. 49–52; F. Miguel Rosell, 'Epistolario de Antonio Agustin', *Analecta Sacra Tarraconensia* 13 (1937–40), 113–202, no. 30.

[8] Rudorff, 1839, 4ff.

[9] *Lettres de Peiresc*, ed. P. Tamizey de Larroque, Paris, 1888–96, VI, 172, 283.

[10] Bormann, 1905, 432; A. Ruesch, *Guida Illustrata del Museo Nazionale di Napoli* (Naples, 1908), inv. 112521.

presumably when the fragment itself was on loan to Orsini from the Fugger (see above): it is recorded by Muratori as in the Barberini collection at Rome in the early eighteenth century. It was later given to Cardinal Stephano Borgia by the republic of San Marino and passed with his collection to the Naples museum under the rule of Murat.[11]

Carlo Sigonio published both faces of Aab and Bab in the 1574 editions of *De antiquo iure Italiae* (II, ch. 2) and *De Iudiciis* (II, ch. 27). Good early minuscule copies of the A, Ba–b and Da fragments were made by the Paduan antiquarian Gian Vincenzo Pinelli in 1567, probably both through direct access to the bronze and knowledge of Sigonio's work (Vat. lat. 6531, fos. 174–84). These were apparently made for Aldo Manuzio the younger, since they do not belong with the main material (of Latino Latini) in their binder but are connected by their numeration with Manuzio's sylloge in Vat. lat. 5234. A good copy of Dbc, obtained by S.V. Pighius from Sambucus in Vienna in early 1575 and preserving readings not seen later by Orsini, was published in Pighius' *Annales Romanorum* in 1615.[12]

The E fragment was published three times in France, in each case badly: twice by J.-J. Boissard, in a manuscript dated 1559, but incorporating at least one later supplement (*Inscriptionum Antiquarum Descriptio* – Stockholm Royal Library, S.60, fos. 143v–144r) and in his subsequent printed collection[13] and once by B. Brisson.[14] These three editions have a common ancestor in a defective text. For they share a number of disastrous errors. First, in lines E5–14 of the *repetundae* face from QVOTIENS QVOMQVE AMPLIVS BIS IN VNO IV onwards they ignore the alignment of the inscription and the consecutive text of one line spills over on to the next, with the result that at the point where the text should break off at the edge of the fragment, it runs immediately and incoherently into what should be the beginning of a new line (e.g. in line E5, IN VNO IVREIS QVOMODO IVDICETVR). Secondly, on the same face a section from CVNDA CAVSA to DEVEXAM POPVL is repeated in their lines 10–11 and 13–14. Thirdly, lower down the copyist jumped from one VTEI QVOD RECTE FACTVM ESSE VOLET to another two lines lower down (E21–3). However, the Boissard MS and his printed edition show common errors in the text of the agrarian face, which are not in Brisson, jumping from the NEIVE in E6 to that in E8 and from the AGRI LOCEI in E14 to that in E15. Further, the Boissard MS alone omits the end of one line and the beginning of the next after QVAE VECTIGALIA IN AFRICA in E36.

However, the archetype copy of the bronze, presumably made at Fontainebleau, from which these editions ultimately derive, is represented by far more important and reliable manuscript sources. The first is Vat. lat. 6531, fos. 175–6

11 L.A. Muratori, *Novus Thesaurus Inscriptionum*, Milan, 1739–42, II.574.1; G. Fiorelli, *Catalogo del Museo Nazionale di Napoli: Iscrizioni Latine*, Naples, 1867–8, II.2054.

12 S.V. Pighius, *Annales Romanorum*, Antwerp, 1615, Tom. III, lib. xii, pp. 136–8.

13 *Inscriptionum Antiquarum Descriptio* – Stockholm Royal Library, S.60, fos. 143v–144r; *Romanae Urbis Topographiae et Antiquitatum*, Frankfurt, 1597–1602, III, fos. 104–5.

14 *De Formulis et Sollemnibus Populi Romani Verbis*, Paris, 1583, II, 173–6.

(also marked as 154 and 149 respectively). These pages, like those with the Pinelli copies, have nothing to do with their current binder: they belong with the text of the dedication of the Narbo altar, sent by J.J. Scaliger to Aldo Manuzio the younger in 1567 (now part of Vat. lat. 5234). The Scaliger copies of E portray the shape of the bronze, as do those of Boissard, but without the blatant errors in transcription, and many readings are common to Scaliger and either Boissard or Brisson. The second is the sylloge of inscriptions produced by P. Dupuy in 1643,[15] based on the material of Claude Dupuy, friend of Scaliger and Orsini. The *repetundae* face of E is reproduced in capitals in a text made to slant across the page, thus roughly reproducing the shape of the fragment, and texts of both faces are given in minuscule. The provenance of the Dupuy texts is said to be the bronze in the French royal library. They share some unusual readings with Vat. lat. 6531, Boissard or Brisson (notably the reading VERO ∧ R at the beginning of *lex rep.* 65, where ∧ may be a MS caret mark) and must ultimately derive from the same source as them. The indication in Dupuy that a space should be inserted between lines 76 and 77 must be an error and derive from an earlier MS copy (it is not found in other copies and would make an otherwise coherent text disjointed).

There is a further, independent, French source for fragment E. N.-C. Fabri de Peiresc made a careful copy of the top of the agrarian face and copies of the line-endings of the *repetundae* face and much of the agrarian face – in the *repetundae* face he included letters from a new top line.[16] He stated that he derived these from an 'ecmagma plumbeum' of Henri de Mesmes, which he had collated with the texts in Gruter's *Inscriptiones Antiquae Totius Orbis* (i.e. Orsini's) and those of Boissard and Brisson. The 'ecmagma' had been found in de Mesmes' cabinet of antiquities and manuscripts after his death by Peiresc's brother, in 1606, and had thus become known to Peiresc himself. Although in his copy he seems to have followed Boissard in believing that the original was on the Capitol at Rome, we find him in 1625 pursuing it unsuccessfully in France.[17]

The most important early publication was by Orsini in *Sylloge legum et senatus consultorum in lapide vel aere servatorum* (nos. I-XIV), provided as a supplement to Antonio Agustin's *De Legibus et Senatus consultis Liber* (Rome 1583, Paris 1584). We can see his work in progress, in particular his realisation that Da joined Dbc, in the manuscript pages now divided between Vat. lat. 6040, fos. 34r–37r, and 6037, fos. 52r–54r. His knowledge of C and Dd eventually derived from the fragments themselves loaned by the Fugger family. For E he probably used a copy sent from France, quite distinct from the Scaliger-Dupuy tradition, perhaps obtained through Piero Vettori, who left a nearly identical but better manuscript copy of the same fragment. Mommsen argued that he used the edition of Sigonio for Ab (since, like him, he omitted the

15 Paris, BN, Dupuy 461, fos. 88–9. 16 Paris, BN, Lat. 8958, fos. 167v–168r, 177–8.

17 Paris, BN, Dupuy 667, fo. 164r. Cf. *Lettres de Peiresc*, II, 358, n1; VI.172, 283.

line *lex rep.* A 36), but there is evidence in Vat. lat. 6037, fo. 54r for another source, probably the copy in Mazzochi. It seems in any case probable that Ab does not survive today because it never reached Orsini in the first place (this explains why he was assiduously pursuing another fragment which had belonged to the von Montfort family in 1581).[18]

No real progress was made in the edition of the fragments after Orsini's work until the early nineteenth century, when W.A. Klenze fitted C, Bc and D in their places and arranged (almost correctly) the fragments in the vertical plane, in order to publish the *repetundae* face. Then A.A. Rudorff developed these conclusions in relation to the agrarian face.[19] Their work formed the basis of Th. Mommsen's comprehensive and thorough edition in *CIL* I.[20] This edition, updated in the second edition of *CIL* and reproduced both in the *Fontes Iuris Romani* of C.G. Bruns and S. Riccobono and in P.F. Girard's *Textes de droit romain*, has remained the standard text till now, although it was problematic in some important ways, which will shortly be discussed. The present edition would probably never have been undertaken without the stimulus provided by the criticisms of Mommsen's text by G. Tibiletti (1953) and H.B. Mattingly (1969).

[18] De Nolhac, 1884, 257, 259. [19] Klenze, 1825, Rudorff, 1839.

[20] Nos. 198 and 200. The commentaries were reprinted in Mommsen, *Ges. Schr.* I.

1 Vienna, Kunsthistorisches Museum, Antikensammlung inv. III, no. 172. C fragment, *repetundae* face, containing the initial surviving section of lines 66–83. Note the traces of letters at the base of the fragment. *Photo:* Kunsthistorisches Museum.

2 Naples, Museo Nazionale, inv. no. 4611. The copy of the C fragment first documented in the Barberini collection at Rome in the early eighteenth century. *Photo:* Soprintendenza Archeologica delle Province di Napoli e Caserta.

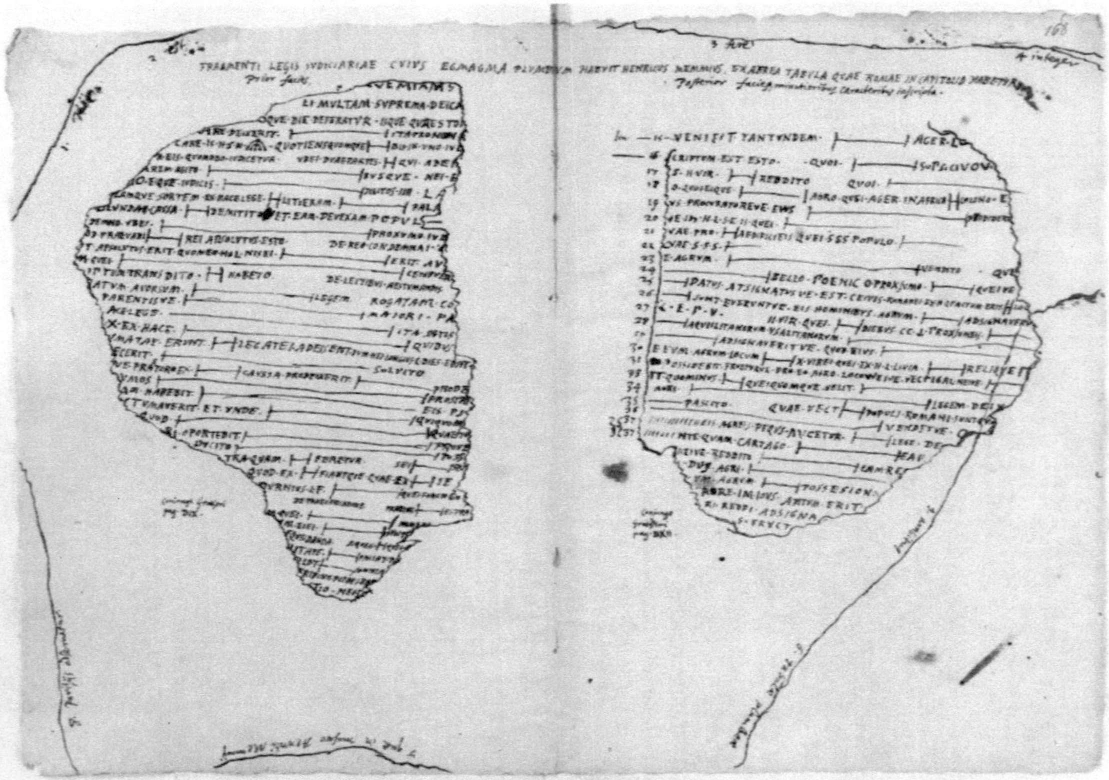

3 Paris, Bibliothèque Nationale, Latin 8958, fos. 167v–168. Peiresc's copy of the *ecmagma* of Henri de Mesmes – on the left the *repetundae* face of E, on the right the agrarian face. The width of the faces has been drastically compressed, as may be seen, for example, from the next illustration. Note the otherwise unattested first line on the *repetundae* face. The outline round the two pages seems to be intended to give an idea of the shape of *one* face of the lead plate, probably the agrarian face. The title indicates the belief that the original was on the capitol at Rome. *Photo:* Bibliothèque Nationale

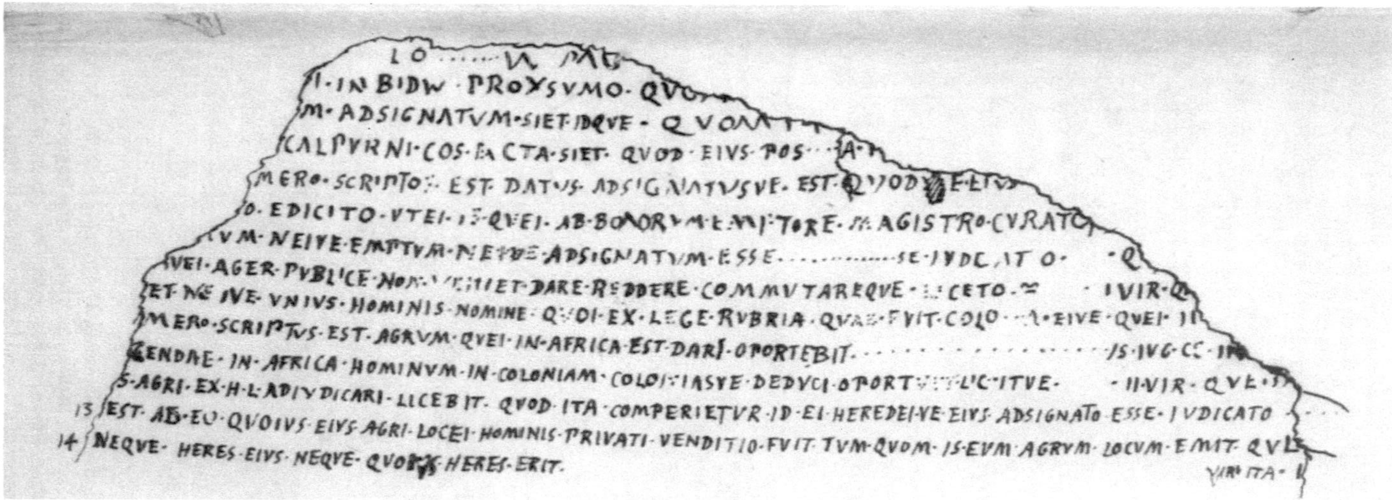

4 Paris, Bibliothèque Nationale, Latin 8958, fo. 178r. Peiresc's copy of the *ecmagma* of Henri de Mesmes. The top of the agrarian face of E recorded almost complete in what should be the correct outline. *Photo:* Bibliothèque Nationale.

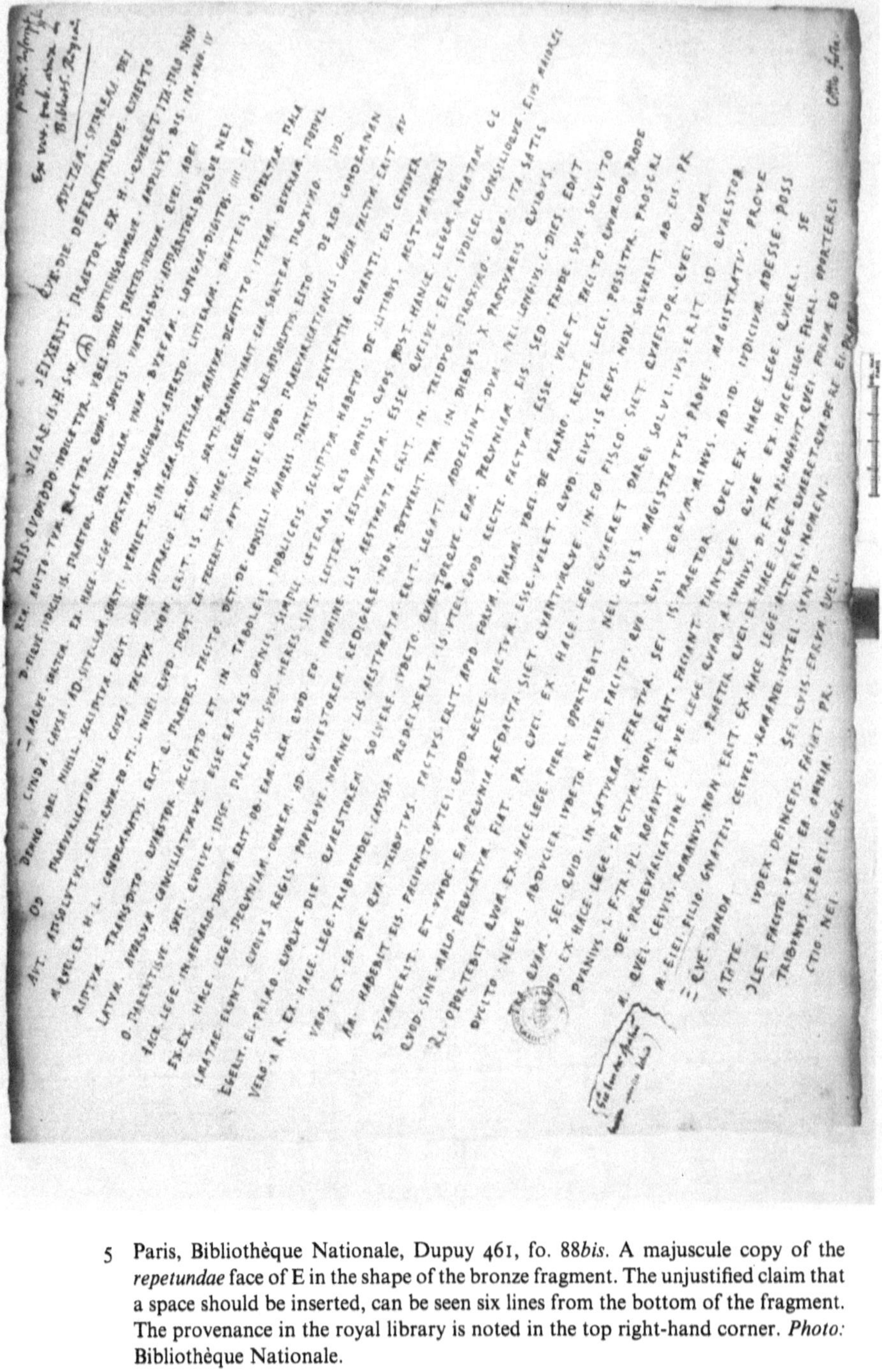

5 Paris, Bibliothèque Nationale, Dupuy 461, fo. 88*bis*. A majuscule copy of the *repetundae* face of E in the shape of the bronze fragment. The unjustified claim that a space should be inserted, can be seen six lines from the bottom of the fragment. The provenance in the royal library is noted in the top right-hand corner. *Photo:* Bibliothèque Nationale.

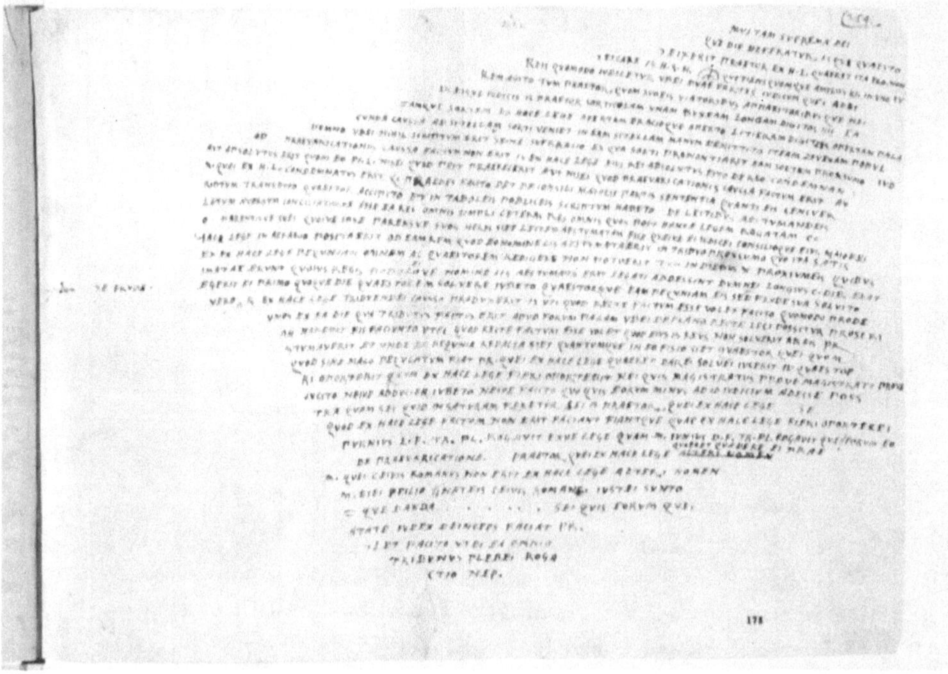

6 Codex Vaticanus Latinus 6531, fo. 175. Another majuscule copy of the *repetundae* face of the E fragment. The page number in the top right-hand corner is that of the manuscript sylloge of the younger Aldo Manuzio, corresponding to those otherwise found in Vat. lat. 5234. For material in the same hand deriving from J.J. Scaliger, cf. fos. 144–6 of that manuscript. *Photo:* Biblioteca Vaticana.

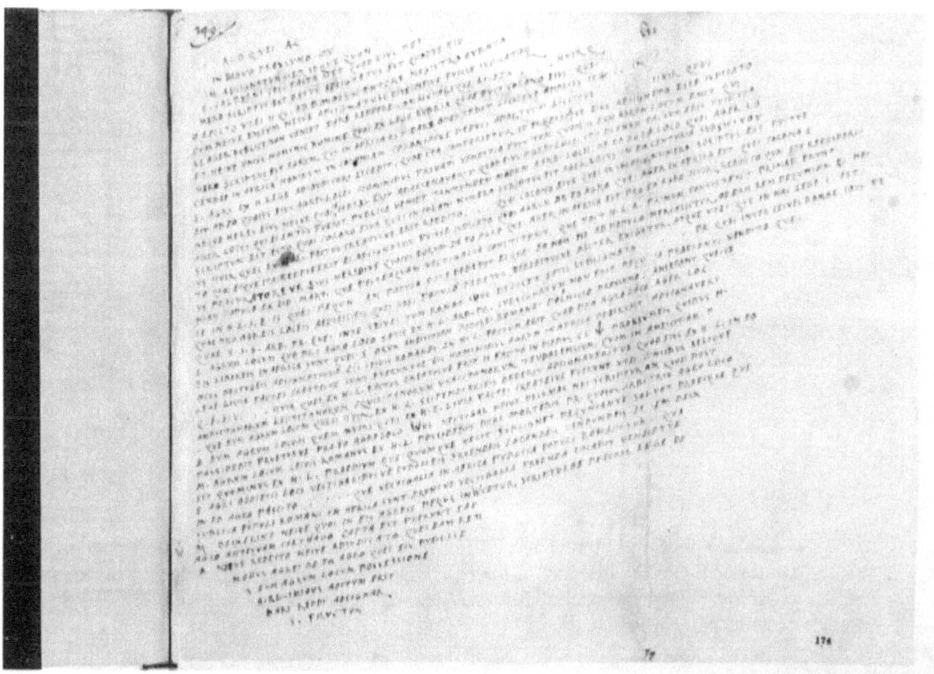

7 Codex Vaticanus Latinus 6531, fo. 176. The agrarian face of the same fragment. See note on plate 6. *Photo:* Biblioteca Vaticana.

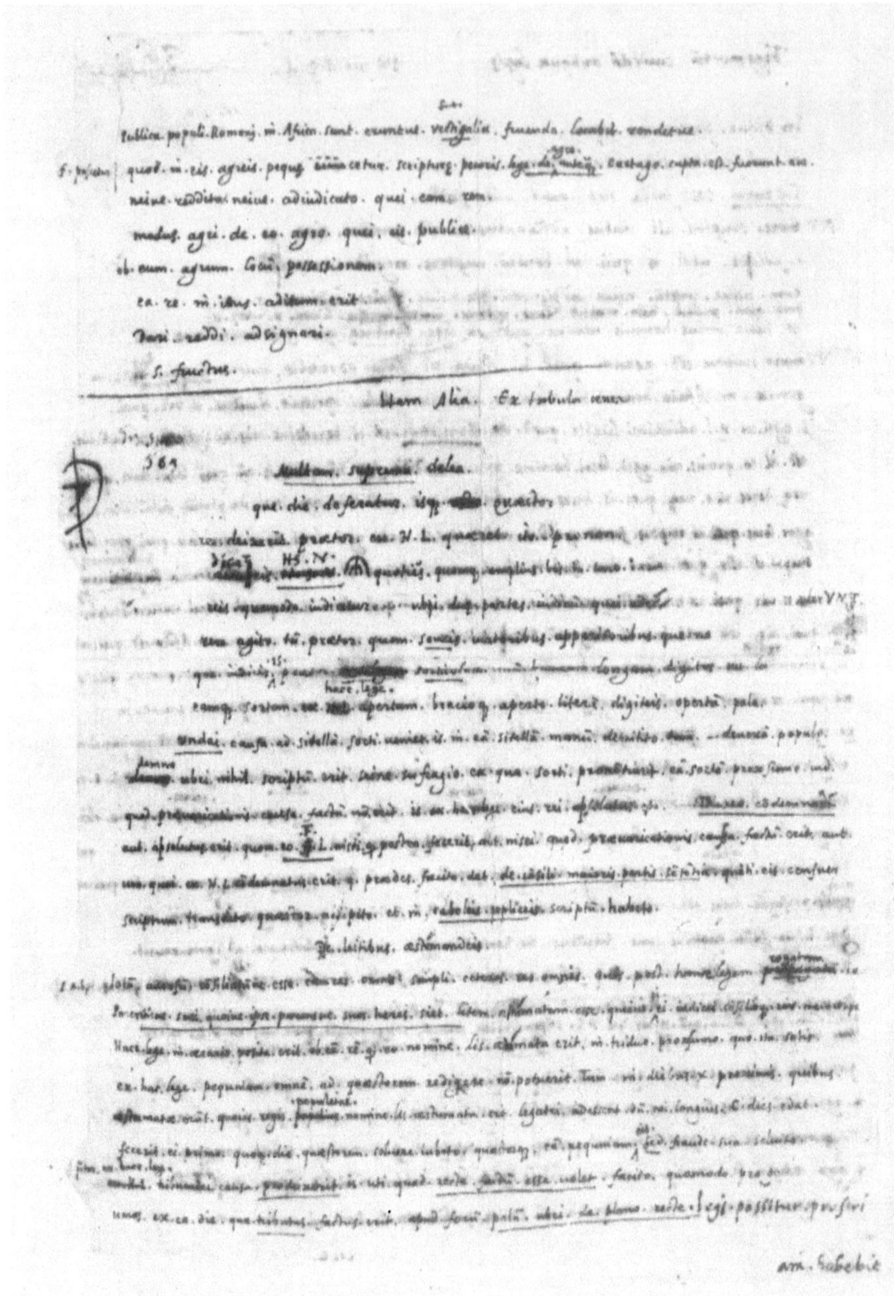

8 Codex Vaticanus Latinus 6040, fo. 36v. It contains the lower section of the agrarian face of E and the first half of the *repetundae* face. This appears to be a working version of Orsini's text. Supplements are indicated in majuscule. *Photo:* Biblioteca Vaticana.

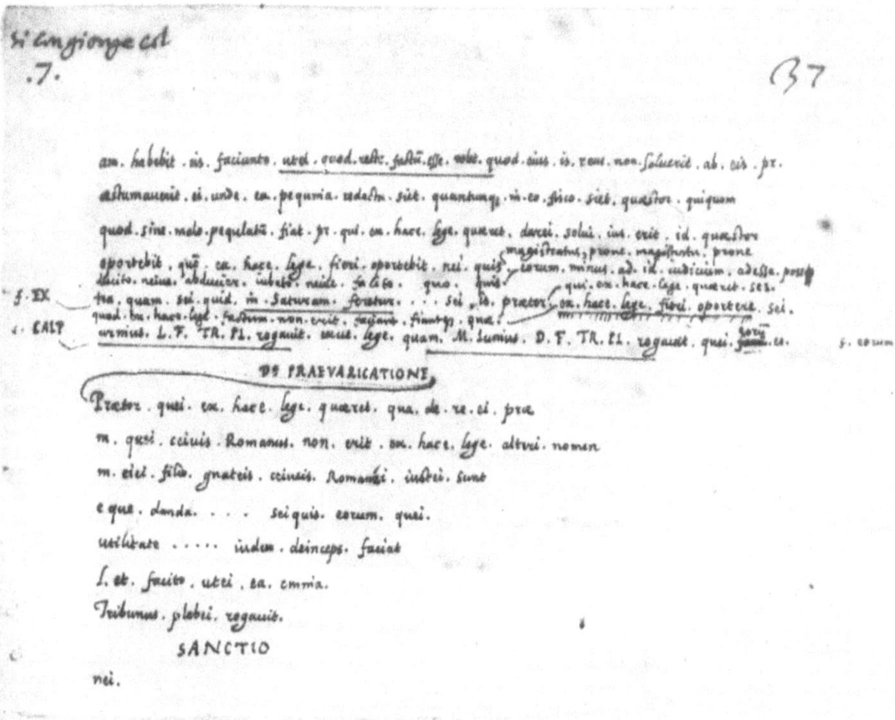

DE PRAEVARICATIONE

Praetor . quei . ex . hace . lege . quaeret . qua . de . re . ei . prae

m . quei . ceivis . Romanus . non . erit . ex . hace . lege . altrei . nomen

m . eiei . filio . gnateis . ceiveis . Romanei . iudicei . sunt

e qua . danda . . . . sei quis . eorum . quei .

utilitate . . . . . iudem . deinceps . faciat

l . et . faciet . utei . ea . omnia .

Tribunus . plebei . rogauit .

SANCTIO

nei .

9 Codex Vaticanus Latinus 6040, fo. 37r. The remainder of the *repetundae* face of the E fragment, where both DE PRAEVARICATIONE and SANCTIO have been placed as rubrics on separate lines. *Photo:* Biblioteca Vaticana.

10 Naples, Museo Nazionale, inv. 112521, cf. *CIL* XI, 364a. 'F' fragment: (a) *repetundae* face, (b) agrarian face. *Photo:* Soprintendenza Archeologica delle Province di Napoli e Caserta.

PART TWO

THE TEXTS

I

Lex Repetundarum

Introduction to the Text

Since Klenze's edition (prol. ix) the *lex repetundarum* has been treated as the obverse inscription. This was not originally because of the identification of the law engraved there (which Klenze, like Sigonio and Orsini, thought was the *lex Servilia* of Glaucia), but because it was held that this face was smoother and better prepared for engraving, while the writing on the agrarian side suffered through the use of a second-hand bronze. I originally accepted this view (e.g. in Lintott, 1981). However, close examination of the well-preserved Vienna fragments, C and Dd, and the top of fragments A and B has convinced me that originally both faces were equally smooth. As will be discussed later, the engraving of the agrarian face is shallower and cruder, but this in itself does not mean that the corresponding text was the later of the two. The roughness and illegibility of parts of the agrarian face (especially Bc, D and the bottom of Bb) seem, like the warping of the upper fragments, to be the result of poor conservation after their discovery (Rudorff, 1839, 5–6). The wear has rendered the shallow cuts in the agrarian face less legible, except where the original incision was sufficiently forceful for the edges of the cuts to stand out in relief. We cannot say, therefore, on formal grounds that one face is the obverse, although on the grounds of its content and identification I continue to think that the *lex repetundarum* is the earlier law. Furthermore, in view of the uncertainties about the way the texts were exhibited, we cannot rule out the possibility that the bronze was so mounted that both sides were visible at once.

The bronze is some 3.5–4 mm thick, like others on which late Republican laws, e.g. the *leges Bantinae* and the *lex Antonia*, were engraved. The fragments are thus very heavy. The C fragment, *c.* 200 sq.cm in area, weighs just over 700 g. On my reconstruction of the whole inscription, if it was engraved on a single bronze plate *c.* 2.2 m wide and 1 m high, this would be over 20,000 sq.cm in area and thus weigh over 70 kg. Even a tablet of reduced width, such as proposed by Mattingly (1969), would have weighed over 55 kg. It seems likely, therefore, that the inscription was on two plates, each about a metre square and weighing *c.* 35 kg – a solution possible on my reconstruction but not on those of Mommsen and Mattingly. It would have been difficult to support even plates of this weight by pegs alone, and so we should probably assume that they were fitted into some sort of frame.

On the surviving fragments of the *lex repetundarum* the letters are *c.* 1 cm high in the top line; 0.5–0.6 cm high in subsequent lines. Laterally, in the top line 10 cm contain on average 12 letters, in subsequent lines *c.* 18–21 letters. Although the space occupied by individual letters varies – M for example takes twice the space of any other letter; V, N and Q more than the average, while I, E, S and T less – the variations compensate for one another in a long text and the space taken by the same number of letters is very similar. The consistency of the letter-spacing is apparent from a comparison of two parallel sections of *repetundae* text in lines 13–14 and lines 16–17. In the former '*quei*[ve merc ...' stands above 'cognomen *ioudice*⟨t⟩{s}' on the A fragment. In lines 16–17 on Bb '*ioudice*sque' is not directly underneath '*queive*' but is only about 6 letter-spaces to the left of it – a small discrepancy in two pieces of text each over 400 letters long.

Individual words, whether abbreviated or spelt in full, are consistently separated by points. Gaps of four letter-spaces or more are left between the end of one chapter and the beginning of the next and also between any rubric at the beginning of a chapter and the text of the chapter itself. The chapters are not numbered or assigned fresh lines. In line 22 of the *lex repetundarum* a gap of eight letter-spaces is left for no obvious reason before 'l(ege) Rubr[ia'. This is much greater than the other meaningless gaps before 'hace' in line 74 and 'praetor' in line 82 noted by Mommsen, nor can it be accounted for by the poor quality of the bronze at this point (the bronze may have been originally poor immediately beneath this lacuna, as it is now, but this area was covered by letters).

The relation of the fragments to each other in the vertical plane, established by Mommsen, has not been challenged since and is accepted here, although the argument which appeared to clinch it – the join postulated between the base of the lost Ab fragment and the apex of the lost E fragment – is unsound and should be rejected (see below, p. 80). The fragments certainly cannot be brought any closer together in the vertical plane without jumbling the reconstruction of the text, nor can the A complex be moved nearer the top of the bronze without destroying an alignment with the B fragment which is convincing on both sides of the bronze. As for increasing the vertical distance between the fragments in the top half of the bronze (the A and B complexes) on the one hand and C, E and Dabc on the other, this is not completely unthinkable, but the displacement could hardly be increased by more than one line, given the connection in sense between the texts at the bottom of the upper fragments and the top of the lower fragments, and even this is not very plausible.

The upper part of the bronze

In the first forty lines of the *lex repetundarum* the fragments in question are A and Ba-b. The bottom half of A, Ab, is known to us only through the manuscripts of Orsini, Dupuy and Pinelli and the copies published by Mazzochi, Sigonio and Orsini. Mommsen's belief that both the latter two texts were derivatives of Mazzochi's cannot be justified, even though Sigonio and Orsini omitted the same line on the *repetundae* face. Orsini's MS copy of the agrarian face of Ab (Vat. lat. 6037, 54v) seems in fact to be collated from Sigonio and another source, probably Mazzochi (see e.g. *lex agr.* line 53), while Sigonio is independent of Mazzochi. The B complex is also known from the early printed texts of Orsini and Sigonio and from the MSS of Orsini, Pinelli and Vettori. Bc, the lowest portion, is recorded only by Orsini and Vettori, neither of whom realised its connection with Ba. The upper parts of Ba and Bb join; indeed the connection was much more complete in the sixteenth century. Sigonio and Orsini do not record any lacunae between the fragments until *lex rep.* 22, *lex agr.* 26, although the break now begins at *lex rep.* 16. Orsini, like Sigonio, was on the whole careful not to include obvious supplements to the surviving text as part of the text itself, to judge from line-endings, and in my view what both these editors record should be treated as a certain addition to the epigraphic text.

When viewed today, the left-hand side of Bb (as seen from the *repetundae* face) has warped inwards as well as wearing away, so that the gap between the fragments appears 1–2 cm more than it should. This can be judged not merely from the bronze itself, but from the letters inserted in the lacunae by Sigonio and Orsini, some of which were almost certainly visible to them and others indisputably correct.

The relationship of the fragments in the horizontal plane

Mommsen originally made three plausible hypotheses, on which his reconstruction hinged:

(i) that both laws had full prescripts, identifying and dating them and certifying their validity, which followed the standard formula attested elsewhere (cf. commentary on *lex agr.* 1)

(ii) that a formula regularly found at the beginning of the early chapters of *lex agr.* should be restored in line 16 of that law

(iii) that the parallel clauses in *lex rep.* 12–15 and 15–19 occupied roughly the same extent of bronze (as one pair of them has been shown to have done on any assumption about the relative position of the A and B fragments, *see* p. 74 above)

For the prescript of the *lex agraria* we must assume 55 certain letters and 25–35 more (to cover the names and filiation of the proposer, date and location of the legislation and the name of the first tribe to vote, *principium*) between the existing text and the margin of the *tabula*. Given the spacing of 17–18 letters to 10 cm in this line this implies a lacuna of *c.* 50 cm. When this lacuna is transferred to the right-hand side of the *repetundae* face, this becomes in line 1 (at 12 letters to 10 cm) *c.* 60 letter-spaces, and in subsequent lines (at 19–20 letters to 10 cm) *c.* 95–100 letter-spaces.

On the left-hand side of the *repetundae* face we must find space for at least 12 letters at the beginning of the law itself and a prescript. This prescript contains

73 certain letters and upwards of 45 letters more (names and filiation of both proposer and first voter, date and location of legislation and *principium*). A minimum lacuna of *c.* 130 larger or *c.* 215 smaller letter-spaces must be postulated.

In line 16 of the *lex agraria* between the B and A fragments an introductory formula – 'ager publicus populi Romanei ... prove vet]ere ...' – must be restored and two more letter-spaces to complete the gap between chapters (these gaps average 4 spaces on the *lex agraria* side). This cannot be reduced to less than 93 letters in all and is probably more. On the assumption that we should reproduce the initial formula of line 15, while inserting the 'quod' omitted there and retaining 'ex lege plebeive scito' (omitted in Mommsen's restoration), at the same time taking 'possessionem' in the surviving text to be an error for 'possessore', it will be 113 letter-spaces, namely: 2 spaces 'ager publicus populi Romanei, quei in Italia P.Mucio L.Calpurnio cos. fuit, quod eius agri IIIvir a.d.a. ex lege plebeive sc. vetere prove vet]'. This at the current letter-spacing of 22–3 letters to 10 cm requires 51 cm.

A lacuna of 51 cm in line 15 on the *repetundae* face is *c.* 97 letters at the frequency of 19 letters to 10 cm prevailing in that line. When the space occupied by the clause extending over the A–B lacuna in line 15 is transferred to the parallel clause in lines 18–19, the total B–A lacuna (at the end of line 18 and the beginning of line 19) is *c.* 171 letter-spaces. From this it follows that the lacuna to the left of the A fragment at the beginning of line 19 is *c.* 70–5 letter-spaces. The resulting line-length is *c.* 440 letter-spaces in the upper part of this face, which tends to increase to *c.* 450 in the middle and lower parts of the face – somewhat larger than that postulated by Mommsen. This implies an introductory lacuna in line 1 greater than the minimum required, *c.* 148 larger letters = *c.*235 smaller letters, but this may be an advantage since Mommsen's restoration, 'quoi socium', for the opening words of the law may well be too laconic.

The following are the equations between the parallel clauses in lines 12–19, that result from these assumptions and calculations (for the purposes of this table restored letters should be understood to include assumed but unfilled letter-spaces):

(i) Lines 12–13 (B–A), *quei in hac ceivit[ate – trium vi]rum a.d.a.*:
18 preserved + *c.* 163 restored letters inclusive = 181
Line 16 (A–B), *quei ha[c – trium vir a.d.a.*:
80 preserved + *c.* 98 restored letters inclusive = 178

(ii) Line 13 (A–B), *quei[ve – annos LX gnatus siet*:
93 preserved + *c.* 102 restored letters inclusive = 195
Lines 16–17 (B–A), *queive merc[ede – a]nnos LX gnatus siet*:
26 preserved + *c.* 169 restored letters inclusive = 195

(iii) Lines 13–14 (B–A), *queive in urbem Romam – trans mar]e erit*:
33 preserved + *c.* 174 restored letters inclusive = 207
Line 17 (A–B), *queive in urbe Romae – trans mare erit*:
111 preserved + *c.* 95 restored letters inclusive = 206

(iv) Line 14 (A–B), *ioudice{s}⟨s⟩ q[uei – tribum co{c}⟨g⟩nomenque*:
107 preserved + *c.* 96 restored letters inclusive = 203
Lines 17–18 (B–A), *ioudices quei – tribu⟨m⟩ cognomenque*:
38 preserved + *c.* 169 restored letters inclusive = 207

(v) Lines 14–15 (B–A), *descriptos hab[eto – quos e]x h.l. CDL viros*:
24 preserved + *c.* 166 restored letters inclusive = 190
Line 18 (A–B), *discriptos habeto – quos ex h.l. CDL viros*:
98 preserved + *c.* 87 restored letters inclusive = 185

These equations work extremely well, especially when allowance is made for space left blank at the ends of lines because the engraver could not complete a word (in general early Roman engraved legal texts begin new lines with a complete word, and this is true on the C fragment of this law, where we possess the margin of the bronze). Moreover, the A–B lacuna fits closely highly probable supplements in lines 20, 25 and 26, apart from accommodating other more controversial restorations. The point, however, is that not only the equations are successful in the text, as I have reconstructed it, but that this reconstruction is reconcilable with the other basic assumptions affecting the location of the fragments.

To summarise the results of these calculations, the inscription itself would have had a minimum width of *c.* 440 of the smaller letters on the *repetundae* face, i.e. a minimum of 2.20 m; at the level of line 16 of the *lex agraria* the A and B complexes were *c.* 50 cm apart; in consequence, since, according to calculations from preserved letters, the lacunae extending over the end of each line between the B and A complexes in *lex rep.* 12–19 were some 70–5 letter-spaces (*c.* 38 cm) longer than the corresponding A–B lacunae in the centre of the lines, the B–A lacuna should have totalled *c.* 88 cm at this level. The space required to complete the full prescript of the agrarian law (of which the last nine and a half words survive) is *c.* 50 cm, and this also determines the size of the lacuna at the right-hand end of the *repetundae* text near the top of the bronze (the edge of Bb is effectively vertical here and parallel to the margin of the bronze). Therefore at the level of *lex agr.* 16 = *lex rep.* 15 the left-hand edge of A *lex rep.* must have been *c.* 38 (88 – 50) cm or 70–5 letter-spaces from the left-hand margin of the bronze. Such is the logical development of Mommsen's original and plausible assumptions.

The problem of Mommsen's reconstruction and the resulting controversy

Unfortunately, Mommsen also postulated a join between the lost lower extremity of Ab and the lost apex of E. On any plausible drawing of the fragments this would have pushed the position of A almost to the left-hand margin of the bronze and so drastically reduced the textual B–A lacuna in the upper part of the bronze that at least two of Mommsen's previous assumptions would have had to be abandoned. In practice Mommsen only reduced the lacuna by some 35 letters instead of the 60 required by his proposed join, nor did he make the consequential reduction in the length of the prescript required by the moving of the fragments towards the left-hand margin. His adjustment did, however, mean that the lacunae in the parallel clauses in *lex rep.* 12–19 became inconsistent. There was a further unrelated error in establishing the correct relationship between the size of letters in the two top lines of the *lex rep.* face and those lower down.

Some attempt was made to tidy up the inconsistencies in *CIL* 1^2 by adding to the lacuna on the right of the *lex rep.* face (and the initial lacuna of the *lex agr.* face), but the drawings of the fragments in particular produced bewilderingly discordant figures for letters lost in lacunae, and even the quantification of lacunae in the text, though reasonably consistent with itself, is neither in harmony with Mommsen's original assumptions nor with the drawing which sketches the relationship of Ab to E. Nevertheless, the reconstruction was accepted apparently without question until after the last world war.

Tibiletti attempted a minor adjustment in the parallel clauses in order to reduce the lacunae and create a more consecutive text while accepting Mommsen's assumption that the bronze was some 420 smaller letter-spaces wide. However, since he was working on the basis of Mommsen's figures, his efforts were doomed from the start, and indeed the attempt was theoretically unsound, since any reduction of both the A–B and B–A lacunae must considerably reduce the width of the bronze. This stimulated Mattingly to make a more radical suggestion. He proposed to reduce the lacunae in the parallel clauses by some 35 letters from Mommsen's figures and simultaneously to reduce the width of the bronze to *c.* 385 smaller letter-spaces. Here he failed to take into account the fact that a reduction of 35 letters in the A–B lacuna should involve an accompanying reduction of 35 letters in the parallel clause in the B–A lacuna, thus overall a reduction of 70 letters in the width of the bronze. His calculations were still based on Mommsen's inaccurate figures. Furthermore he located the B fragment on top of the D fragment in a way which violated surviving and recorded texts (cf. commentary on *lex rep.* 53 and 54).

In the text that follows I have taken Mommsen's first three principles as a starting-point and sought to work them out consistently. In the light of this and of my reconstruction of the shape of the E fragment by drawing the letters, I have been forced to reject the join Mommsen proposed between Ab and E. It may be noted that both Klenze and Rudorff, who printed plans of the fragments which included the letters of surviving text and restoration were not tempted to make this join because their plans rendered it impossible. The join is less convincing than it appeared to Mommsen, when we take into account the letters visible on the Peiresc copy. It is, however, worthwhile considering under what circumstances the join might be retained, since clearly the drastic reduction of the B–A lacuna on the *lex rep.* face, which would follow a move of the A fragment close to the margin of the bronze, might seem consistent with a reduction of the A–B and B–A lacunae, as proposed by Mattingly. If we position the A fragment in such a way that a join with the E fragment can be made (this would involve drawing the outline of Ab so that the tip of its base was well over to the left-hand side of the fragment, viewed from the *lex repetundarum* side), its extreme left-hand edge, viewed from the same side, would be only *c.* 5 letter-spaces from the margin of the bronze. Briefly, the consequences of this would be as follows. First, the parallelism of the clauses in *lex rep.* 12–19 can only be maintained if, at the same time as subtracting 30–5 letter-spaces from the A–B lacuna (no more is possible without making the base of B overlap the apex of D), we also add 30–5 to the lacuna between the right-hand edge of Bb and the margin of the bronze – to compensate for the loss of *c.* 65 letter-spaces from the B–A lacuna on the left-hand side of the bronze. This would imply adding some 25 letters to the prescript of the *lex agraria*, allowing for the letter-spacing in that line – something not impossible (it could have been proposed by a number of tribunes jointly), but improbable, when a further consequence will be a severely truncated prescript for the *lex repetundarum*. Secondly, the combined result of the move of the A fragment to near the margin of the bronze and the reduction of the A–B lacuna will be that the space available for the prescript of the *lex repetundarum* can be no more than *c.* 80 large letter-spaces (the equivalent of *c.* 130 small letter-spaces), less a minimum of 12 letters for the beginning of the text of the law, thus some 40 letter-spaces less than what is required. Thirdly, the restoration of the standard introductory formula in *lex agr.* 16 becomes impossible with the reduced central lacuna, as do other necessary supplements for that lacuna in *lex rep.* 23 and 26, *lex agr.* 18 and 27. Fourthly, the overall width of the tablet will be only *c.* 380 letters: this will cause difficulty in the restoration of *lex rep.* 78. Fifthly, if the apex of D is brought within a few letter-spaces of the base of B, there is a problem over the restoration of *lex rep.* 54, on the assumption that Orsini was right to read REO AP as the lowest surviving letters of B.

There is a further advantage in my present reconstruction over both Mommsen's and that considered in the previous paragraph: it allows the law to have been engraved on two pieces of bronze side by side (the lines running across from one bronze to the other), whereas the other solutions involve a vertical overlap between the surviving fragments and thus imply a single bronze. The problems of mounting a bronze of this weight – *c.* 55 kg with the size postulated by Mattingly, *c.* 70 kg with that postulated by Mommsen (see above, p. 73) would have been formidable.

The lower part of the bronze

The reconstruction of the remainder of the bronze is made more difficult by the loss of the Ab and E fragments and the quality of the copies that survive. Unfortunately Renaissance copies and editors of the texts usually did not reproduce accurately the physical shape of the inscriptions – one exception to the rule was the MS copy of E from which those of Vat. lat. 6531, and Boissard derive (see 'History of the Text', above, pp. 68–9), another partial exception is that of Peiresc – but the point may be made by a comparison of the textually accurate versions of Orsini with the original fragments. The only way of recovering the shape of the lost fragments is to write out the text as it would have been engraved, using an existing fragment as a base. For the top and bottom of E the shape delineated by Vat. lat. 6531, Boissard and Peiresc provides a further guide.

The shape of the lower half of A (Ab) can be determined down to line 34 (A30) by relating the text to the lowest part of Aa. After this the natural hypothesis from the surviving letters is that the fragment continued vertically downwards and gradually tapered to a fairly blunt point in line 47 (A43). This, on the basis of the previous calculations about the location of the A fragment would have been *c.* 29 cm from the left-hand margin of the bronze (120 to 130 letter-spaces). The subject-matter of the bottom of both A and B (which projects even lower), when compared with the top of the lost fragment E, led Mommsen to postulate that the top line of E belonged to line 45 of the tablet (A41, B45). Klenze placed A to the right of the top of E. Mommsen placed A to the left, where it appeared that a join could be made. Reconstruction of the E fragment, however, shows that such a join is impossible without discarding two of the assumptions on which the upper part of the tablet was reconstructed (see above, p. 77). For Mommsen's location of A relative to E would mean that the left-hand edge of A was within a few letters of the left-hand margin of the tablet. Furthermore, if we accept Peiresc's copy of the 'ecmagma' of H. de Mesmes as a valid testimony to the E fragment, then the join or near join postulated by Mommsen in lines 45–7 becomes less easy to accommodate.

The position and the shape of E can be determined fairly exactly in relation to two other surviving fragments. Klenze realised that from lines 66 to 77 on the *repetundae* face of the tablet there was either a near or an exact join between the right-hand edge of C and the left-hand edge of E. C itself was at the left-hand margin of the bronze. At the right-hand edge of E only a few letters of certain or near certain supplement separated it from the left-hand edge of the D complex (i.e. the three fragments Dabc, joined by Orsini, and Dd, one of the Vienna fragments, whose position at the bottom of the complex was first demonstrated by Klenze). For example, in line 67 we have (apart from two letters between C and E) a continuous text from 'eandem' at the margin in C to 'ab eis pr' at the right-hand edge of E, then a supplement '[aedibus primo quo]' before '-que die pecuniam ...' in D. In line 69 after a continuous text from the margin of the tablet the E–D supplement is 'quaestor [quei aerarium pro]vinciam ...' In general from line 55 to line 75 of the bronze satisfactory supplements for the E–D lacuna can be provided, which range from 6 to 34 letters in length and are consistent with the relation of E to C and the margin of the bronze.

It might be argued that all these E–D lacunas should be enlarged. For example, in line 72 the supplement could be extended from 'sei[ve quaestor quoi aerarium provin]cia obvenerit' to 'sei[ve quaestor quoi aerarium *vel urbana* provinc]ia obvenerit', to correspond with the supposed repeat in line 79.

Assuming that an addition to the lacunae of some 10 letter-spaces is envisaged, in some lines this is tolerable, but it is very difficult to postulate in lines 56, 58, 60, 61, 63, 64, 66, 73, 74 and 75 – especially in lines 58, 63, 64 and 66, where it is a matter either of disproportionally expanding the spaces left either side of a rubric or implausibly expanding the rubric itself. Another important criterion is the corresponding lines of the *lex agraria*: here from lines 66 to 80 a series of short supplements (the smallest being 9 letters) in the D–E lacunae are desirable and in some cases seem inevitable.

When the physical shape of the E fragment is drawn, another interesting point emerges. Mommsen had assumed that in line 65 (E 21) the E fragment extended to the margin of the bronze. In fact the lost fragment seems to have been within two letters of this margin from line 55 (E 11) to line 65 – actually reaching it at lines 56, 61 and 65. The shape of the whole fragment that results from the reconstruction is roughly that depicted in Vat. lat. 6531 (Scaliger) and Boissard's copies.

The small F fragment, discovered in the nineteenth century and first associated with the *lex repetundarum* by Garrucci, was given a plausible location by Mattingly (1969, 133–41) adjoining and above the top left-hand corner of the D fragment. This fits well with the reconstructed E fragment, though some alterations must be made to Mattingly's restorations nor can any argument be derived from the location of this fragment about the pattern of the fragments as a whole.

A final major problem is the text in *lex rep.* 72–84, which since Mommsen's discussion has been held to consist of clauses repeated through carelessness by the engraver. Even Mommsen's publication of the text left some grounds for doubt about this and more arise from the present reconstruction of the E fragment and the supplements in the E–D lacunae. Before the texts of the relevant chapters are compared, some preliminary points should be made. First, it is uncertain that the text breaks off and restarts in line 79, as Mommsen postulated. Faced with the reading, '*ceiv*]itate iudex deinceps faciat PR', on the E fragment (E35), Mommsen printed 'iudex deinceps faciat pr[*incipe cessante*' as a rubric, assuming that the end of the chapter after '*ceiv*]itate' had been omitted through an oversight by the engraver (the chapter would not have ended with a noun, but a verb). A small space before 'iudex' occurs in the Dupuy MS and in the copy of the fragment sent to Orsini (though Orsini did not put 'iudex faciat PR' in capitals like other rubrics in his MS). If we treat this space as a paragraph-space, this appears to justify Mommsen's view. However, there is no such space recorded in Vat. lat. 6531 (Scaliger) or Boissard. Even if we accept that Orsini's copy and the Dupuy MS are right about the space before 'iudex' in line 79, as I am inclined to do, this may well be not a paragraph-space but an inexplicable lacuna, such as are found on the bronze itself in line 74 (3 letter-spaces) and line 78 (2–3 letter-spaces). It should also be noted that no rubric exists at the beginning of the chapter in line 72 (which, on Mommsen's view, the engraver was carelessly reproducing in line 79): a paragraph-space is recorded here by Orsini and Peiresc, without doubt correctly, though not by the Dupuy MS nor by any of the others).

Secondly, apart from one bad section on the D fragment in line 74, the text is as regularly and carefully engraved as that of the upper part of the bronze: there is no other evidence of a loss of control or concentration by the engraver. Thirdly, it is not clear why the engraver went on engraving some 2,000 unnecessary letters, if the text was too faulty to be acceptable. Fourthly, if there is no evidence of an abrupt break but merely of the possible repetition of chapters, this may be ascribed to the legal draughtsman, rather than to the engraver. Indeed, the probable repeat of the chapter dealing with substitution for the praetor and quaestor originally involved (lines 72–3 and 79–80) seems to me best interpreted as a piece of fussiness by the draughtsman, who wished the provision re-emphasised in a new context.

It is preferable to restore line 79 on the assumption that there is no break in sense before 'iudex faciat PR' and that the chapter about *provocatio* was in fact brought to an end. Apart from the uncertainties about the significance of the space left in the two manuscripts, 'iudex faciat PR' cannot be the beginning of the next chapter nor can it be satisfactorily supplemented to provide a rubric describing that chapter. Not only is 'iudex faciat pr[*incipe cessante*]' obscure and unattractive as Latin ('iudex faciat pr[*aetoris vicem*' would have been perhaps more plausible, see the commentary on line 79), but in any case the following chapter is not about the substitution of a member of the jury for the president of the court, as Mommsen believed, but the substitution for the original praetor and quaestor concerned of a new praetor and quaestor.

This chapter about substitutions for magistrates in lines 79–80 can be restored as parallel to that in lines 72–3 with one significant discrepancy. We must restore in line 79 '*quaestor quoi aerarium*] vel urbana provincia', but in line 72 there is only room for '*quaestor quoi aerarium provinc*]ia', if consistency is maintained with a number of certain restorations on both faces of the tablet. There is also an unimportant 5-letter-space difference between the lacunae calculated to the right of the D fragment in the corresponding sections of the two chapters. The chapter in lines 79–80, therefore, could well be a repeat of that in lines 72–3 with one surviving variation in drafting – something of which there are similar examples in the parallel chapters in lines 12–18. The next chapter referring to condemnations under previous laws (lines 80–2) is similar to that in lines 73–5, as far as its preserved text is concerned. But the similar passages are differently distributed within the two chapters: if we compare the lacuna to the right of the D fragment in lines 73 and 80, the first chapter is 30 letter-spaces longer than the second; if we compare the lacuna to the right of D in lines 74 and 81, the second chapter is 25 spaces longer than the first. It is thus not easy to interpret these chapters as repetition, except on the hypothesis of major errors by the engraver or legislator, and it is better to regard them as in fact different. A hypothetical reconstruction of the second chapter, which would relate it specifically to the rewards for accusers mentioned in the chapters immediately preceding it, is given in the commentary to chapter L (lines 80–2).

The chapters in lines 75 and 82–3 share a similar stretch of text (*c.* 45 letters long) and cover roughly the same amount of bronze, on the assumption that the second extends as far as the beginning of line 83. But there is no textual evidence that the latter was about *praevaricatio*, nor, if one, restores the initial text of line 75 in line 82, is there room for a rubric at all, only a paragraph-space. Finally, in the preserved part of line 82, we find 'satis fecerit' without a subject, as opposed to 'satis factum erit' in line 75.

When the chapters in lines 76–7 and 83–4 are compared, there is an immediate divergence, as there is no room to restore the rubric 'De ceivitate danda' in the initial lacuna in line 83, and it is unattractive to suppose that a rubric was split between the end of one line and the beginning of the next. From 'seiquis' to 'aera' inclusive the text in lines 76–7 is one whole line less 20 letter-spaces + *c.* 190 more in the following line – *c.* 430 + 190 = *c.* 620, whereas the inclusive text between the same words in lines 83–4 is one whole line less 18 letter-spaces + *c.* 145 more in the following line – *c.* 432 + 145 = *c.* 577. This makes it extremely improbable that the second chapter is a repetition of the first, although it too almost certainly concerns citizenship. In fact the space in line 83 between 'seiquis' and 'ad praetorem, quoius e]*x hace lege*' is marginally smaller than the corresponding space in line 76, and so we should perhaps read here 'Seiq[*uis eorum, quei ceivis Romanus erit* ...' As for the last sections of text that can be compared, the interval between 'stipendiaque' in line 77 and 'ad praetorem' in line 78 is *c.* 405 letters (*c.* 250 + 156), that between 'stipendiaque' in line 84 and '*ad praetorem*', where it may be confidently restored in the initial lacuna in line 85 is *c.* 350 letters (*c.* 290 + *c.* 60). It should be noted that these arguments hold good *mutatis mutandis*, even if the overall assumptions about the width of the bronze are changed.

To summarise, chapter XLIX (lines 79–80), about the continuing execution of the law by substituted magistrates, may well be a repetition (with minor divergences) of chapter XLIV (lines 72–3). Chapter L (lines 80–2), forbidding trial of men condemned under the *leges Calpurnia* and *Iunia*, is to a considerable extent parallel to chapter XLV (lines 73–5) but nevertheless divergent to an extent that cannot be merely explained by engraving errors. Subsequently, there is no justification for postulating repeated chapters. In any case, if a chapter is repeated, this is highly unlikely to have been the sole responsibility of the engraver, but was more probably the result of a legal draughtsman redrafting certain chapters and incorporating both versions in the text submitted to the engraver.

Appendix Note on lacunae and supplements

The figures in lacunae represent the number of letters missing after account has been taken of supplements. Any large lacuna, or one whose calculation depends on hypothesis, has been represented in multiples of five as a warning to the reader of the approximation involved. I have been more cautious than Mommsen in incorporating supplements in the text, where these cannot be guaranteed by parallel texts on the bronze elsewhere, but I have allowed myself some latitude on occasions where the sense is certain and it is helpful to show the reader how the sense may be plausibly presented in Latin in the space available. I have not recorded as part of the text letters included by humanist copyists, which can be shown by comparison to have been disguised supplements, but where this is not certain I have given the copyists the benefit of the doubt. In fact disguised supplements are only a very small proportion of what was recorded. Letters no longer readable are in any case indicated by underlining.

Conventions

[ ] = lacunae and supplements to these (figures in lacunae indicate unfilled letter-spaces after account has been taken of supplements)
{ } = deletion of error in surviving text
⟨ ⟩ = supplement to surviving text after error by engraver
( ) = supplement to surviving text, where engraver has deliberately abbreviated
-- = indecipherable traces on bronze
* * = suprascript correction actually made to surviving text on bronze

Underlining in Latin shows letters on one of the surviving bronze fragments which can be no longer read, though an earlier editor or copyist claimed to have read them. If these are left inside square brackets, they are being regarded as supplements.

Italics are used in the Latin text and translation for restorations outside the limits of the fragments.

In apparatus

aes = bronze, as read by current editor
Borgh = V. Borghini, Florence, Bibl. Magl. II.x.70,2–3
B = consensus of the copies of the E fragment in Scaliger. Dupuy, Boissard and Brisson
Bo[1] = J.J. Boissard, *Inscriptionum antiquarum descriptio*, Stockholm Royal Library, S.68, 143v
Bo[2] = Boissard, *Romanae Urbis Topographiae et Antiquitatum*, III, 105.
Br = B. Brisson, *De formulis et sollemnibus populi Romani verbis*, Paris, 1583, II. 172–4.
D = P. Dupuy, *Inscriptiones*, Paris, BN, Dupuy 461, 69. 89–89bis
Scal = J.J. Scaliger, leaves bound in Vat. lat. 6531, 175 = 154
Ha = P. Hameaux, Paris, BN, Franc. 19116, 17r, 32r, and in J. Mabillon, *De re diplomatica*. p. 344–5, Paris, 1681
Maz = J. Mazzochi, *Epigrammata Antiquae Urbis Romae*, 180v
O[1] = F. Orsini, Vat. lat. 6037, 52r–54v + 6040, 34r–37r
O[2] = F. Orsini, *Sylloge legum et senatus consultorum*, nos. I-XIV (attached to A. Agustin, *De legibus et senatus consultis*)
Peir = N.-C. Fabri de Peiresc. Paris, BN, lat. 8958, 167v
Pigh = S.V. Pighius, *Annales Romanorum*, III, 137–8
Pin = J.V. Pinelli. Vat. lat. 6531, 165r–71r (= 178–84)
Sig = C. Sigonio, *De iudiciis*, 1574, II, 27
Vett = P. Vettori, Munich. lat. 743, 107–112

edd veter	= consensus of relevant editors and copyists from among the above
CIL	= CIL I[2] (Th. Mommsen and E. Lommatsch), effectively the text used in Bruns
Eder	= W. Eder. *Das vorsullanische repetundenverfahren*, Munich 1969
Kl	= C.A. Klenze, *Fragmenta legis Serviliae repetundarum*
Mo	= Th. Mommsen CIL I[1] = *Gesammelte Schriften*, I
Rud/Rudorff	= A.F. Rudorff, *Ad legem Aciliam* (Abh. d. kgl. Akad. d. Wiss. phil-hist. Kl. (Berlin, 1861), 411–554

LEX REPETUNDARUM

Text

1 [*. . . f. tr.pl. plebem rogavit plebesque ioure scivit in foro a.d. . . ., tribus . . . principium fuit, . . .* (60) *f. primus scivit. . . . quoi socio n̲o̲*]minisve Latini exterarumve nationum, quoive in arbitratu dicione potestate amicitiav[*e populi Romanei res suae repetundae erunt* .2̣5̣]

2 [1̣6̣0̣ *sei petet ab eo quei dic*(tator), *co*(n)*s*(ul), *pr*(aetor), *mag*(ister) *eq*(uitum), *cens*(or), *aid*(ilis), *tr*(ibunus) *pl*(ebei), *q*(uaestor), *III vir cap*(italis), *III vir a*(greis) *d*(andeis) *a*(dsignandeis), *tr*(ibunus) *mi*]l(itum) l(egionibus) IIII primis aliqua earum fuerit, queive filius eorum quoius erit, quoius pater senator siet, in annos singolos pequniae quod siet amp[*l̲ius HS* . . . *n*(ummum), .9̣0̣]

3 [1̣3̣5̣ *quod ipsei parenteive suo filiove suo, quo*]ive ipse{i} paren{te}⟨s⟩*ve* suos filiusve suos heres siet, ablatum captum coactum conciliatum aversumve siet, de ea re eius petitio nominisque delatio esto, [*pr*(aetoris) *quaestio esto, ioudicium ioudicatio leitisque aestumatio, quei quomque ioudices ex h*(ace) *l*(ege) *erunt, eorum h.l. esto* . .5̣]

4 [1̣7̣0̣ *Sei quis pr*(aetori) *satis fecerit a rege populove ceiveve suo se legatu*]m esse utei peteret, de ea re eius petit[*i*]o nominisque delatio esto, pr(aetoris) quaestio esto, ioudicium ioudicatio leitisque aestumatio, quei quomque ioudic[*es ex h.l. erunt, eorum h.l. esto.* .7̣5̣]

5 [.9̣5̣]ỌỊṾ[.9̣0̣ *quei postea contra h.l. fecisse deicetur quam ea res ioud*]icata erit, aut quoius nomen praevaricationis caussa delatum erit, aut quoius nomen ex h.l. ex reis exemptum erit, sei quis eius nomen a[*d praetorem, quei ex h.l. quaeret, detolerit, pr*(aetoris) *quaestio esto, ioudicium ioudicatio leitisque aestimatio, quei quomque*]

6 [*ioudices ex h.l. erunt, eorum h.l. esto.* (vac) .6̣0̣ *ali*]eno nomin[*e petet* .8̣0̣ *de ea re eius petitio nominisque delatio esto*,] quaestio eius pr. esto, ioudicium{ve} ioudicatio leitisque aestumatio, quei quomque ioudic{ium}⟨es⟩ ex h.l. erunt, eorum h.l. esto. Is eum unde petet in ious ed[*ucito ad pr*(aetorem), *quoius ex h.l. in eum annum quaestio erit, ante k. Sept., quae eo anno erunt, et nomen eius deferto.* .1̣0̣]

Translation

For the formula of the lost prescript see the beginning of the *lex agraria* translation.

(lines 1–3) ... any man from among the allies, either of the Latin name or of foreign nations, or within the sovereignty, dominion, power or friendship of the Roman people, *who needs to seek the return of what is his, ...* I

If he sues a man who has been dictator, consul, praetor, magister equitum, censor, aedile, tribune of the plebs, triumvir capitalis, triumvir for the allocation of lands, tribune of the soldiers for any of the first four legions, or the son of any of these, whose father is a senator, for a sum of money more than ... sestertii in any single year, ... in respect of property which has been stolen, seized, extorted, procured or diverted *from himself, his parent, his son*, or from a man, to whom he himself, his parent or his son is heir, *the investigation shall belong to the praetor; trial, judgement and the assessment of damages shall belong to whichever judges shall be appointed by this law. ...*

(line 4) *If anyone satisfies the praetor that he has been deputed by a king, a community or a fellow-citizen of his* to sue, he shall have the right to sue and denounce in that matter; investigation shall belong to the praetor; trial, judgement and the assessment of damages *shall belong to* whichever judges *shall be appointed by this law. ...* II

(line 5–6) If anyone denounces *to the praetor investigating under this law a man who is claimed to have acted against the law after that matter* has been decided, or who has been denounced collusively or who has been removed from the list of defendants under this law, *investigation shall belong to the praetor; trial, judgement and assessment of damages shall belong to whichever judges shall be appointed by this law.* III

(lines 6–8) *(If anyone) sues* on another's behalf ... investigation shall belong to that praetor; trial, judgement and the assessment of damages shall belong to whichever judges shall be appointed by this law. The man shall bring him whom he is suing to the seat of justice *of the praetor, who is in charge of the investigation that year, before 1 September in the year in question and denounce him. ...* IV

7 [..90..] deque eo homine DE[..35.. *quorum nomina post k. Sept. ex h.l. delata erunt, sei volet quis quei petet, de ea re pr. ... recuperatores dato. Qu*]oius eorum ita nomen ex h.l. post k. Sept., quae eo anno fuerint, delatum *erit*, quei eorum eo ioudicio condemnatus erit, quanti eius rei slis ae[*stumata erit, tanta pequnia ei, quei petet,* ..65..]

8 [..50.. *eaque pequnia, quei eam peteiverit, sed fraude sua*] eius esto. Pr., quei ex h.l. q[*uaeret, facito* ..90.. *quantum ita ioudicat*]um erit, id utei privato solvatur, quei eorum petet. (vac. 3) De heisce, dum mag(istratum) aut inperium habebunt, ioudicium non fiet. (vac. 2) Dic., cos., pr., mag.eq., [*cens., aid., tr.pl.* ..85..]

9 [..70.. *Quei eorum e*]x eo mag(istratu) inperiove abierit, quo min[*us de eo ioudicium fiat e*(ius) *h.l.* n(ihilum) *r*(ogatur). ..70.. *De patrono dando* (vac.) *Quei ex h.*]l. pequniam petet nomenque detulerit quoius eorum ex h.l. ante k. Sept. petitio erit, sei eis volet sibei patronos in eam rem darei, pr. ad quem [*nomen detolerit* ..85..]

10 [..60.. *patronos ei dato, dum*] nei quem eorum det sciens d(olo) m(alo) quoiei is, q[*uoius nomen delatum erit,* ..40.. *gener socer vitricus privignusve siet, queive ei sobrinus siet prop*]iusve eum ea cognatione at{i}⟨t⟩igat, queive eiei sodalis siet, queive in eodem conlegio siet, quoiave in fide is erit maioresve in maiorum fide fueri⟨n⟩t, [*queive in fide eius, quoius nomen delatum erit, maioresve in maiorum fide fuerint,* ..30..]

11 [..70.. *queive*] quaestione{m} ioudicio{o}ve puplico condemnatu[*s siet, quod circa eum in senatum legei non liceat,* ..60.. *neive eum que*]ị ex h.l. ioudex in eam rem erit, neive eum quei ex h.l. patronus datus erit. (vac. 3) De patrono repudiando (vac. 4) Quei ex h.l. patronus datus erit, sei is mor[*am faciet ei, quei petet, quo minus ioudicium ex h.l. fiat, ei eum repudiare liceto* ..35..]

12 [..70..]VM pr., quei ex h.l. quaeret, alium patronum eiei QVEỊ[..80.. *dato.* (vac.) *De CDL vireis in hunc an*]ṇum legundis (vac. 2) Pr., quei inter peregrinos ious deicet, is in diebus X proxum(eis), quibus h.l. populus plebesve iouserit, facito utei CDL viros le{c}⟨g⟩at, quei in hac ceivit[*ate ingenui gnatei erunt* ..70.. *dum*]

13 [*nei quem eorum legat, quei tr.pl., q., III vir cap., tr.mil.l. IIII. primis aliqua earum, trium vi*]rum a.d.a. siet fueritve, queive in senatu siet fueri{n}t{ei}⟨v⟩e, quei[*ve mercede* ..55.. *queive quaestione ioudiciove puplico conde*]mnatus siet quod circa eum in senatum legei non liceat, queive minor anneis XXX maiorve annos LX gnatus siet, queive in urbem Romam propiusve u[*rbem Romam ... m*(ilia) *p*(assuum) *domicilium non habeat,* ..30.. *queive eius mag*(istratus), *quei s*(upra) *s*(criptus) *e*(st), *pater frater filiusve*]

and about that man . . . *whoever has been denounced after 1 September, if the man suing wishes, the praetor shall appoint recuperatores to deal with that matter.* Anyone who has been denounced in this way after 1 September in the year in question and has been condemned in the trial, *shall be liable to the man suing for the amount of money* at which the damages in that matter have been assessed. . . .

That money shall belong to the man *who sued for it without penalty to himself.* The praetor *investigating* under this law *shall ensure that . . . the amount so assessed in the judgement* shall be paid to the private citizen who sues.

(lines 8–9) No trial shall be held of the following, while they hold a magistracy or imperium – dictator, consul, praetor, magister equitum, *censor, aedile, tribune of the plebs . . .* V

Nothing is enacted by this law forbidding *the trial* of anyone of the foregoing, who has left a magistracy or imperium.

(lines 9–11) *Concerning the grant of a patronus* – if a man, *who* is suing for money in accordance with this law and has made a denunciation and whose suit in accordance with this law shall take place before 1 September, wishes to be granted patroni for the case, the praetor, to whom *he has made the denunciation, . . .* VI

shall appoint as his patroni . . . provided that he does not knowingly with unlawful intent appoint anyone to whom *the accused is father-in-law, son-in-law, stepfather or stepson, or who is the accused's cousin* or a closer blood-relative or a member of the same sodalitas or collegium as he, or to whom the accused is a client or his ancestors were clients of his ancestors *or who is a client of the accused or his ancestors were clients of his ancestors* . . .*

or who has been condemned in a quaestio or iudicium publicum *with the consequence that it is illegal for him to be enrolled in the senate, . . .* or a man who is a judge in the case in accordance with this law or a man who has been appointed a patronus according to this law.

(lines 11–12) Concerning the repudiation of a patronus – if a man, who is appointed patronus according to this law, *obstructs the man who is suing, so as to prevent the trial taking place according to this law, it shall be lawful for him to repudiate him. . . .* VII

The praetor investigating under this law shall give another patronus to the man who (has repudiated a patronus).

(lines 12–15) *Concerning* the selection *of 450 men* for the current year – the praetor, who has jurisdiction for foreigners, shall within ten days of the ratification of this law by the populus or plebs take measures to select 450 men, who are *free-born* members of this citizen body, . . . VIII

provided that he does not choose anyone, who is or has been tribune of the plebs, quaestor, triumvir capitalis, tribune of the soldiers for any of the first four legions, triumvir for the allocation of lands, or who is or has been a member of the senate, or who *has hired himself . . ., or who* has been condemned *in a quaestio or iudicium publicum* with the consequence that it is illegal for him to be enrolled in the senate, or who is younger than 30 or older than 60, or who *has no residence* in the city of Rome or nearer the city *than . . . miles, . . . or who is the father, brother or son of any magistrate mentioned above,*

* literally 'or in whose *fides* the accused is, or his ancestors were in the *fides* of his ancestors, or who is in the *fides* of the accused, or his ancestors have been in the *fides* of his ancestors . . .'

14 [*siet, queive eius, quei in senatu siet fueritve, pater frater filiusve siet, queive trans mar*]e erit. Quos legerit, eos patrem tribu{nu}m cognomenque ioudice{t}⟨s⟩, q[*uei ex h.l. in eum annum erunt, edito* .[45] *Pr*(aetor), *quei legerit, eorum, quei ex*] h.l. CDL virei⟨s⟩ in eum annum lectei erunt, ea nomina omnia in tabula in albo, atramento script{e}⟨o⟩s, patrem tribum co{c}⟨g⟩nomenque tributimque descriptos hab[*eto, eosque propositos suo mag*(istratu) *habeto, eorumque, quei ex h.l. CDL virei in eum annum lectei erunt,* .[20]]

15 [.[10] *potestatemque scribundi, quei volet, facito. Pr., quei legerit, is eos quos e*]x h.l. CDL viros legerit, facito recitentur in contione, iuratoque sese [*eos ex h.l. legisse, de quibus sibei consultum siet,* .[30] *quosque diligentes futuros io*]udices exaestumaverit esse, eosque CDL viros, quos ex h.l. legerit, is pr. omnis in taboleis puplicis scriptos in perpetuo habeto. (vac 4) De CDL vireis quot annis [*legundis* (vac.) .[85]]

16 [..[5] *Pr., quei post hunc annum ex h.l. ioudex factus erit, is in diebus X proxumeis, quibus quis*]que eorum eum mag(istratum) coiperit, facito utei CDL viros ita legat, quei ha[*c civitate ingenui gnatei erunt* .[70] *d*]um ne quem eorum legat, quei tr.pl., q., III vir cap., tr.mil.l.IIII primis aliqua earum, trium vir. a.d.a. siet fueritve, queive in senatu siet fueritve, queive merc[*ede* .[55] *queive quaestione ioudiciove puplico condemnatus*]

17 [*siet quod circa eum in senatum legei non liceat, queive minor anneis XXX maiorve a*]nnos LX gnatus siet queive in urbe Romae propiusve urbem Roma[*m* ... *m*(ilia) *p*(assuum) *domicilium non habeat,* .[30] *queive eius mag*(istratus), *quei s*(upra) *s*(criptus) *e*(st), *pater frater filiusve siet*] queive eius, quei in senatu siet fueritve, pater frater filiusve siet, queive trans mare erit. Quos legerit, eos patrem tribum cognomenque ioudices, quei ex h.l. in eu[*m annum erunt, edito.* .[50] *Pr., quei legerit, eorum, quei ex h.l. CDL virei*]

18 [*in eum annum lectei erunt, ea nomina omnia in tabula in albo, atramento scriptos, patr*]em tribu⟨m⟩ cognomenque tributimque discriptos habeto, eosque propositos suo m[*ag*(istratu) *habeto, eorumque, quei ex h.l. CDL virei in eum annum lectei erunt,* .[25] *potestate*]mque scribundi, quei volet, facito. Pr., quei legerit, is eos, quos ex h.l. CDL viros legeri{n}t, facito in con{c}tione recite⟨n⟩tur, iouratoque sese ex h.l. legise, de quibus sibei consul[*tum siet,* .[30] *quosque diligentes futuros ioudices exaestumaverit esse, eosque CDL*]

19 [*viros, quos ex h.l. legerit, is pr. omnis in taboleis puplicis scriptos in perpetuo habeto.*] (vac. 3) De nomine deferundo iudicibusque legundeis (vac. 3) Quei ex h.l. pequniam ab a[*ltero petet, quoius eorum ex h.l. ante k. Sept. petitio erit, eum, unde petet, postquam CDL virei ex h.l. in e*]um annum lectei erunt, ad iudicem, in eum annum quei ex h.l. factus erit, in ious educito nomenque eius deferto. Sei deiuraverit calumniae causa non po[*stulare utei is, unde petet, adsiet, is pr. eius nomen recipito* .[35] *facitoque utei*]

or who is the father, brother or son of a man who is or has been a member of the senate, or who is *overseas.* He shall *declare* those whom he has chosen, naming them by their father, tribe and cognomen, the judges *for the year according to this law. . . . The praetor, who has chosen them,* shall have the names of those chosen to be the 450 men for the year all written in black on white on a board, distinguished by father, tribe and cognomen and listed tribe by tribe, *and keep them on display during his magistracy. The praetor shall grant anyone who wishes the . . .*
and the facility to write down the names of the 450 men chosen for the year. The praetor, who has chosen them, shall ensure that the names of the 450 men he has chosen according to this law are recited at a public assembly, and shall swear that *he has chosen according to this law men, about whom he has taken advice* . . . and who in his estimation will prove *conscientious* judges, and the praetor shall keep all the 450 men he has chosen according to this law recorded in the public records for ever.

(lines 15–19) Concerning *the selection* of 450 men in each following year – . . . IX
whichever praetor shall be appointed a judge according to this law in subsequent years, shall each *within ten days* of the commencement of his magistracy take measures to select 450 men in this way, who are *free-born members* of this *citizen body* . . . provided that he does not choose anyone, who is or has been tribune of the plebs, quaestor, triumvir capitalis, tribune of the soldiers for any of the first four legions, triumvir for the allocation of lands, or who is or has been a member of the senate, or who *has hired himself . . ., or who has been condemned in a quaestio or iudicium publicum*
with the consequence that it is illegal for him to be enrolled in the senate, or who is younger than 30 or older than 60, or *who has no residence* in the city of Rome or nearer the city than . . . *miles, . . . or who is the father, brother or son of any magistrate mentioned above,* or who is the father, brother or son of a man who is or has been a member of the senate, or who is overseas. He shall *declare* those whom he has chosen, naming them by their father, tribe and cognomen, the judges for the year according to this law. . . . *The praetor, who has chosen them, shall have the names of those chosen to be the 450 men for the year all written in black on white on a board,* distinguished by father, tribe and cognomen and listed tribe by tribe and *keep* them on display during his magistracy. *The praetor* shall grant anyone who wishes *the* . . . and *the facility* to write down *the names of the 450 men chosen for the year.* The praetor, who has chosen them, shall ensure that the names of the 450 men he has chosen according to this law are recited at a public assembly, and shall swear that he has chosen according to this law men, about whom he has taken advice . . . *and who in his estimation will prove conscientious judges, and the praetor shall keep all the 450*
men he has chosen according to this law recorded in the public records for ever.

(lines 19–26) Concerning denunciation and the choice of judges – any man, who sues for X
money from *another according to this law, and whose suit according to this law shall take place before September 1st*, shall *after 450 men* have been chosen for the year *according to this law*, bring *the man, whom he is suing*, before the seat of justice of the judge appointed for the year according to this law and denounce him. If he swears that he is not demanding *the appearance of the defendant* in order to make a malicious prosecution, *the praetor shall accept the charge and ensure that*

20 [*die . . 5 ex eo die, quo quoiusque quisque nomen detolerit, is quoius nomen delatum e*]rit de CDL vireis, quei in eum annum ex h.l. lectei erunt, arvorsario edat eos om[*nes, quei vivant, ioudices, quoi is, queive ei, quoius ex h.l. nomen delatum erit, gener socer vitricus pri*]vignusve seit, queive ei sobrinus siet propiusve eum ea cognatione{m} attingat, queive ei sodalis siet, queive in eodem conlegio siet, facitoque coram arv[*orsario apud se palam iouret, quos ex h.l. edere oporteat, eorum omnes se edidisse . 30*]

21 [*neque ioudicem reliquisse nisei eum, quei se earum aliqua necesitudine quae s*(upra) *s*(cripta) *s*(ient)] non attigeret, scientem d(olo) m(alo); itaque is edito {c}⟨i⟩ouratoque. Ubei is ita ediderit, tum in EA[. 50 *pr. eum, quei ita ex h.l. nomen alterius detole*]rit, facito utei is die vicensumo ex eo die quo quoiusque quis nomen detolerit, C viros ex eis, quei ex h.l. CDL virei in eum annum lectei erunt, quei viva⟨n⟩t, legat e[*datque arvorsario ioudices, quos volet, . 65*]

22 [. 45 *dum nei quem eorum legat, utei ioud*]ex siet, quoi is queive *ei*, quei petet, gener socer vitricus privignusve siet, queive ei sobrinu[*s siet propiusve eum ea cognatione attingat, . 10 queive in eodem conlegio siet, queive ei*] so[*d*]alis siet, queive tr.pl., q., III vir cap., III vir a.d.a., tribun{i}⟨us⟩ mil.l.IIII primis al[*iqua*]{ẹ} earum siet fueritve, queive {queive} in senatu siet fueritve, queive (vac. 8) l(ege) Rubr[*ia in Africam missus colonusve scriptus est erit . 55*]

23 [. 40 *queive ab urbe Roma rei puplicae caussa*] aberit queive trans mare erit, neive amplius de una familia unum neive eum [*quem ? censores furti captarumque pequniarum nomine notaverunt notaverint, quod de eo lege Calpu*]rnia aut lege Iunia sacramento actum siet, aut quod h.l. nomen de[*latum sie*]t. Quos is C viros ex h.l. ediderit, de eis facito iouret palam apud se coram [*arvorsario pr., quoius ex h.l. quaestio erit, eorum nullum se edidisse scientem d*(olo) *m*(alo) . 30]

24 [. 20 *quem ex h.l., utei s.s.s., ioudicare non liceat, queive se earum aliqua*] necesitudine atingat, quae supra scripta sient. Q(uaestor), unde petitum erit, quomi[*nus is eorum nomina ex taboleis puplicis scribat, moram nei facito. Ubei is, quei petet, ita C*] viros ediderit iuraritque, tum is pr. facito utei is, unde petetur, die Ḷ [*ex eo die quo*] eius nomen delatum erit, quos C is quei petet ex h.l. ediderit, de eis iudices, q̣[*uos volet, L legat edatque . 75*]

25 [. 40 *Quei ex h.l. nomen detolerit, sei is, quoius nom*]en ex h.l. delatum erit. L iudices ex h.l. non legerit edideritve, seive [*ex CDL vireis, quei in eum annum ex h.l. lectei erunt, eius nomen, quei se aliqua adfinitate cognation*]e sodalitate atingat, queive in eodem conlegio siet, ex h.l. non e[*diderit, ei pe*]ṛ eum pr(aetorem) arvorsariumve mora{m} non erit quominus legat edatv[*e quos volet L de eis CDL vireis, quei in eum annum ex h.l. lectei erunt . 45*]

on the ... day from that on which the charge was made, the man who was charged shall declare to his adversary all those from the 450 men chosen for that year, *to whom he, the man charged, is father-in-law, son-in-law, stepfather*, stepson (*or vice versa*), or who is a cousin or a closer blood-relative, or who is a member of the same sodalitas or collegium as he, and the praetor shall ensure *that he swears openly* before his adversary *in his own presence that he has declared all those whom he should declare according to this law*
and that he has not deliberately with unlawful intent *left as judge anyone but* those not related to him *in the ways described above*; he shall make his declaration and oath in this way. When he has made this declaration, then *the praetor*, ... in that ... shall ensure *that the man who has denounced another* shall, on the twentieth day from the day on which the relevant denunciation was made, select 100 men *of his own choice*, who are living, from those 450 men chosen for that year according to this law *and declare them to his adversary* ...
provided that he does not choose to be a judge anyone of those to whom the man suing is father-in-law, son-in-law, stepfather or stepson (or vice versa), or who is his cousin *or a nearer blood-relative* or a member of the same sodalitas *or collegium*, or who is or has been tribune of the plebs, quaestor, triumvir capitalis, triumvir for the distribution of lands, tribune of the soldiers for one of the first four legions, or who is or has been a member of the senate, or who *has or will have been sent to Africa or registered as a colonist in Africa* under the Rubrian law, ...
or who is absent *from the city of Rome on public business* or overseas, nor shall he choose more than one from a single family nor a man *whom the censors have or shall have stigmatised because of theft and the taking of money, because* of an action by a sacramentum under the Calpurnian or Iunian law or a denunciation under this law. *The praetor in charge of the quaestio according to this law* shall ensure that he takes an oath openly before *his adversary* in his own presence about the 100 men whom he has declared according to this law, *that he has declared no man deliberately with unlawful intent* ...
who is not allowed to be a judge under the aforementioned provisions of the law or who is related to him by any of the connections aforementioned. The quaestor *shall cause no hindrance to* the man sued, preventing him *from writing down the names of these men from the public records. When the man suing* has declared the 100 men *in this way* and taken the oath, then the praetor shall ensure that the man sued shall on the fiftieth day *from the day* on which he was denounced *choose and declare 50 men of his own choice* from the 100 men declared by the man suing according to this law ...
If the man who has been denounced has not chosen 50 judges according to this law or declared them, or if he has not declared *those of the 450 men, chosen for the year according to this law, who* are connected to him *by some blood-relation, marriage-relation* or sodalitas, or who are in the same collegium, *the prosecutor* shall not be prevented by the praetor or his adversary from choosing and declaring *from the 450 men, chosen for the year according to this law, 50 men of his own choice* ...

26 [.30 *dum nei quem eorum, quos ex h.l. legere non liceat, sciens d*(olo) *m*(alo) *ioudic*]em legat. Quei ita lectei erunt, eis in eam rem ioudices sunto, eorumque eiu[*s rei ex h.l. ioudicium ioudicatio litisque aestumatio esto.* (vac. 4) *Ioudicum patronorumque nomina*] utei scripta in taboleis habeantur (vac. 3) Pr., quei ex h.l. quaeret, facito[*eos L viros, qu*]os is quei petet et unde petetur ex h.l. legerint ediderint eosque patronos, [*quei in eam rem dati erunt, utei patrem tribum cognomenque scripti in taboleis puplicis habeantur* .15]

27 [.65 *eorumque nomina ei q*]uei petiverit et unde petitum erit, quei eorum volet, ex taboleis popli[*ceis describundi pr*(aetor) *q*(uaestor)*ve potestatem facito* .45] (vac. 3) Eisdem ioudices unius rei in perpetuom sient (vac. 2) Quei iudices [*ex h.l. lectei erunt*], quam in rem eis iudices lectei *erunt*,[*eis eius rei ioudices in perpetuom sunto* .95]

28 [.75 *ioudicem q*]uei pequniam ex [*h.l.*] capiet, eum ob eam rem, quod pequniam ex h.l. ceper[*it, nei quis in ious educito nomenve eius deferto, neive cens*(or) *aerarium facito neive tribu mo*]veto neive equom adimito neive quid *ei* {eius}⟨ob⟩ eam rem fraudei esto. (vac. 4) [*Nei falsa nomina*]scripta sient (vac. 2) Pr., quei ex h.l. q[*uaeret, is nei falsa nomina eorum iudicum, quei ex h.l. lectei erunt, eorumve patronorum, quei in eam rem datei erunt, in taboleis poplicis scripta habeto* .10]

29 [.60 *De ioudicio in eum quei mortuos e*]rit aut in exilium abierit. (vac. 4) Quoium nomen ex h.l. delatum eri[*t, quoium nomen ab eo pr*(aetore) *receptum erit,* .15 *sei is ante mortuos erit aut in exili*]um abierit quam ea res iudicata erit, pr(aetor), ad quem eius nomen d[*elatum erit, ea*]m rem ab eis item quaerito[*queive heres ei siet, queive pater frater filiusve siet* .90]

30 [70 *Pr*(aetor), *quei ex h.l. quaeret, de eo quo*]iu[*m ita*) nomen ex h.l. ad se delatum erit, facito utei ioudicium p[*rimo quoque die fiat, eisque ioudicibus diem prodeicito, quo eis Romam adesse oportebit, utei q*]uod recte factum esse volet, dum nei quid advorsus h(anc) l(egem) fiat, a[*nte horam*] secundam; neive post h(anc) [? *horam* 135]

31 [.90] conquaeri in terra Italia in oppedeis foreis conciliab[*oleis ubei ioure dicundo praesse solent, itemque* .20 *in oppedeis foreis con*]ciliaboleis, ubei ioure dicundo praesse solent, in quibus di[*ebus* ..5 *prae*]tor, quei ex h.l. quaere[*t, conquaeri iouserit* 120]

32 [.80 *Ubei is praetor*] audierit quod eius rei quaerundai censeant refere et c[*ausam probaverit, tum eum, quei petet, hominibus dumtaxat IIL* .15 *testumonium denuntia*]re iubeto, et, quom e{i}⟨a⟩ res agetur, quam in rem quisque testis er[*it, in eam facito*] omnes adsient testimo[*niumque deicant* 125]

provided that he does not choose as a judge *deliberately with unlawful intent anyone of those whom he is forbidden to choose according to this law*. The men so chosen shall be judges for that case and to them shall belong *trial, judgement and assessment of damages* in that *case according to this law*.

(lines 26–7) *The names of the judges and patroni* should be kept recorded – the praetor XI
investigating under this law shall ensure that *the 50 men*, chosen and declared by the man suing and the man sued, and the patroni *appointed for the case* should be kept recorded *according to their father, tribe and cognomen in the public records* ...
the praetor (or quaestor) should grant the man suing or the man sued, if either wishes, *the opportunity of writing down their names* from the public records ...

(lines 27–8) The same men shall be judges throughout in a single case – the judges *chosen* XII
according to this law shall be judges *throughout in that case* for which they were selected ...

any judge who receives money according to *this law* shall not on account of having received money according to this law *be charged or denounced* nor shall *the censor make him liable to the treasury* nor shall he expel him *from his tribe* nor shall he deprive him of his public horse, nor shall he be subject to any other penalty.

(line 28) *No false names* shall be recorded – the praetor investigating according to this law XIII
shall not keep recorded false names of the judges chosen according to this law or of the patroni appointed for the case ...

(line 29) *Concerning the trial of a man* who is *dead* or has gone into exile – if the man, who XIV
has been denounced according to this law and *whose case has been accepted by the praetor* ... *is dead* or has gone *into exile* before that case has been judged, the praetor, to whom he was denounced, shall in the same way pursue *that* matter from those *who are his heirs or father, brother or son* ...

(line 30) *The praetor investigating according to this law* shall ensure that the trial of a man XV
denounced to him *in this way* according to this law, *shall take place as soon as possible, and shall appoint in advance a day on which the judges shall appear at Rome*, using his discretion as to the correct procedure, provided that no infringement of this law occurs, *before* the second *hour*, nor after this (? *hour*) ...

(line 31) ... there should be a search in Italy in towns, fora and conciliabula (? *by* XVI
praefecti), *where they are accustomed to supervise jurisdiction, and likewise* ... (*by some other magistrates*) in towns, fora and conciliabula, where they are accustomed to supervise jurisdiction, within the period in which the praetor investigating *shall order the search* ...

(lines 32–3) ... *when the praetor* has heard what they think is relevant to the investigation XVII
of the matter and *approved their case*, then he shall instruct *the man suing to summon as witnesses not more than 48 persons*, and when the matter, for which each is a witness, comes to court, *he shall see* that all shall be present *for it and give* their evidence ...

33 [.15 *dum nei quem testimonium deicere iubeat, quoia in fide is, unde petetur, siet maioresve in maior*]um fide {quaerat}⟨fuerint⟩, queive in fide eius siet maioresv[*e in maiorum fide fuerint*, .25 *nisei patronum quei eius, unde petetur, c*]ausam deicet, dumtaxat unum, quei*ve* eius parentisve eius [*leibertus leiberta*]ve siet. (vac. 4) De C̣Ḍ 140]

34 [.50 *nomina eorum quos ad testimonium deicendum evocari*]t secumve duxerit dumtaxat homines IIL earum re[*rum causa, de quibus id ioudicium fiet* .40 *testimoni*]ạ, quai ita conquaesiverit, et seiqua tabulas libros leiterasve pop[*licas preivatasve pos*]cere proferrequ[*e volet, ad praetorem deferto* 150]

35 [.95]IVE de ea re volet apud pr., is praetor ei moram ne faci[*to quo minus* .65]RAT. (vac. 7) Praetor utei interroget (vac. 7) Praetor quei ex h.l. q[*uaeret* 165]

36 [.90 *quei in ea*]m rem ioudices erunt, antequam primum caussa d[*eicetur* .65 *iourent facit*]o. Iudices, quei in eam rem erunt, omnes pro rostreis in foru[*m vorsus iouranto* 160]

37 [.60 *se facturum, utei quod recte factum esse vo*]let utei testium, quei ⟨in⟩ eam rem erunt, verba audiat[.50 *neque quicquam se facturum quo*] eam rem minus ioudicet, nisei seiquae causa erit, quae eiei[175]

38 [.60 *ubei is praetor fecerit utei in contione r*]ecitentur, proscripta propositaque palam apud for[*um, ubei de plano recte legi possitur, habeto potestatemque scribundi facito eis, quei ex e*]is C ioudicis L lectei erunt. (vac. 8) Ioudex ne quis disputet [175]

39 [.95]E iudicium adesse possit, de ea re praetori quei ex hac [*lege quaeret* .55 *De profere*]ndo (vac. 5) Quam rem pr. ex h.l. egerit, sei eam rem proferet, quoị [170]

40 [.95]RE poterit, quoius deicet nomen referre [.75]RIT, ut⟨ei⟩{eius} ad sese adveniat aut adferatur coram eo quei postulaveri[*t* 170]

41 [c.100 *quei vo*]let, quoius ex h.l. {h}⟨n⟩ominis delatio erit, ei eius rei pe[*quniaeve petitio esto* .60 *de*]que ea re hace lege iudicium litisque aestumatio essto quasei sei ei[170]

42 [.95 *sei praetor q*]uei eam rem quaeret, ex h.l. causam non nover[*it, quam ob rem is, quei petet, non adfuerit*, .35 *is praetor c*]oram [*iudici*]buṣ in contione pro rostris sententia ita prononțiato, fec[*isse non videri* 155]

43 [110] iudicium fieri oportebit ter[*tio die* .85 *quom eam r*]em quaeret, ex h.l. causam non noverit, pr. quei ex h.l. q[*uaeret* 160]

44 [.60]QVEM IAM S[.20 *iudices in consilium an*]tequam ibunt, facito iurent sese [.85 *neque facturos esse q*]uo quis suae alterius sententiae certior siet, quod P̣[165]

provided that he shall not instruct to give evidence anyone to whom the accused is a client, or his ancestors were clients of his ancestors, or who is a client* of the accused, or his ancestors *were clients of his ancestors*, ... (?) *except for the patronus*, who is pleading the case *of the accused*, or someone who is a (?) *freedman or freedwoman* of him or his parent ...

(lines 33–5) Concerning ... – ... XVIII

he shall report to the praetor the names of those men whom he has called to give evidence or brought with him, being not more than 48 persons, on account of the matters, *with which the trial is concerned* ... *and the evidence*, which he has searched for in this manner, and any documents, books or letters, public *or private*, which he wishes to *demand* or produce ...

or, if he wishes to deal with this matter before the praetor, the praetor shall not obstruct him ...

(line 35) The praetor shall interrogate – the praetor investigating ... XIX

(lines 36–8) ... (*the praetor*) *shall cause* the judges appointed for that matter *to take an oath* XX
before the case *is pleaded* for the first time ... The judges appointed for that matter shall all *take their oath* in front of the rostra facing the forum ...

(? *each shall swear*) *that he will ensure* that he hears the words of the witnesses in that matter, *using his discretion as to the proper procedure*, ... nor will he act in such a way as to impair his judging of the matter, unless there is some reason, which ...

When the praetor has caused to be recited *in a public assembly* ..., *he shall keep the* ... openly advertised and displayed in the forum, *where they can be read correctly from ground level, and give* the 50 judges selected from the 100 *the opportunity of writing them down* ...

(lines 38–9) No judge shall (?) discuss – ... XXI
he can attend the trial, on this point the praetor investigating ...

(lines 39–40) *Concerning adjourn*ment – if the praetor adjourns any matter which he has XXII
been carrying out according to this law, to whom ...

(lines 40–1) ... XXIII

he shall be able to ..., the man whom he states he is bringing back to court, ... that he should come or be brought to him in the presence of the man who demanded (his appearance) ...

anyone who wishes, who has the right to denounce according to this law, *shall have the right to sue* for that property *or* money ... and there shall be trial and assessment of damages concerning that matter according to this law, as if to him ...

(lines 42–3) ... *if the praetor* investigating that matter has found no excuse according to XXIV
this law (?) *why the man suing has not appeared in court* ... *that praetor* in the presence of *the judges* shall declare a verdict as follows on the rostra: '*Not* guilty' ...

(?when) the trial should take place, on the third *day* ... (?if) *when* he investigates *that* matter, the praetor investigating under this law has found no excuse according to this law ...

(lines 44–5) ... whom now ... (the praetor), before *the judges* retire *to consider their* XXV
verdict, shall cause them to swear an oath that they ... *and that they will not act* in such a way that any of them may find out a verdict other than his own, as far as ...

* See note on chapter VI (lines 9–11) above.

45 [. 50] ei multam suprema⟨m⟩ deica[*t* . 15 *is praetor edicito se mult*]aturum esse iudice[*s* 110 *eam rem qu*]aeret, causam non noverit, quei eorum ioudex [145 *facito utei eius nomen ad*]

46 [*quaestorem quei aerarium provinciam optinebit primo qu*]oque die deferatur, isque quaestor [*recipito* . 25 *de ea excu*]satione primo quo[*que die* 105 *Iudices in co*]nsilium quomodo eant (vac. 3) Pr., quei ex h.l. IV[155 *Sei plus*]

47 [*tertia pars iudicum, quei aderunt, se non posse iudi*]care deixerit praetor ⟨quei⟩ ex h.l. quaeret, ita pronon[*tiato, amplius,* . 45] VR [125 *iudicu*]ṃ, quei quomque aderunt, iudicare [165]

48 [. 15 *eis iudicibus, quei ita negarint iu*]dicare, is HS n(ummum) CCIↃↃ, quotiens quomque amplius bis in uno iud[*icio iudicare negarint, multam deicito* 140]M quam ob rem et quantum pequ[*niae multam deixerit proscribito* 135]

49 [. 30 *De*] reis quomodo iudicetur (vac. ?4) Ubei duae partes iudicum, quei ader[*unt, sibei liquere deixerint* 120 *praetor, quei ex h.l. quaeret, utei eiei iudice*]ṣ, quei iudicare negarint, semovant[*ur, facito* 155]

50 [. 30]REM agito. Tum praetor quom soveis viatoribus apparitoribusque nei Ẹ [. 15]ẠM V [125 *sitellamque latam digitos ... altam digitos*] XX, quo ioudices sorticolas coniecianṭ,[*ante tribunal suum poni iubeto* 140]

51 [. 20]IO eique iudici{s} is praetor sorticolam unam buxeam longam digitos IIII la[*tam digitos ... scri*]ptam atṛ[*amento utrimque* . 90 *in qua sorticola scripta siet ex altera parti A, ex alte*]ra parti C, inmanu palam dato a[*lteramque, utram velit, litteram inducere iubeto* 125]

52 [. 15] eamque sortem ex hacce lege apertam bracioque aperto lit{i}⟨t⟩eram digiteis opertam pala[*m in eam sitellam*] coicito D[150 *i*]temque in eos ceteros singilatim ịụ[*dices* 150 *Quei iudex*]

53 [. . 5]OLVNDAI causa ad sitellam sorti veniet, is in eam sitellam manum demit⟨t⟩ito {i}⟨e⟩t eam devexam populo [*palam ostendito*], ṇei quid Ẹ[. 22] iudicium[100 *quam in eum r*]eum sententiaṃ [*ea sors hab*]uerit, is Ẹ[115 *ubei littera A scripta erit, absolvo, ubei littera C scripta*]

54 [*erit, con*]demno, ubei nihil scriptum erit, seine sufragio. Ex qua sorti pronontiarit, eam sortem proxsumo iud[*ici transdito, isq*]ụe deincẹ[*ps eam ei praetorei r*]ẹḍḍịṭo. (vac. 9) De Ṛ[115] reo ap[*solvendo* 105 *Quoius ex h.l. nomen delatum erit, nisei de eo sententiae ibei plurumae erunt, condemno,*]

55 [*qu*]od praevaricationis causa factum non erit, is ex hacce lege eius rei apsolutus esto. (vac.) De reo condemnan[*do* (vac.) *Sei de eo reo*] senten[*tia*]ẹ ibei plurumae erunt, condemno, pr., qu[*ei ex h.l. quaeret,* 280 *Quei ex h.l. condemnatus*]

(that/if) he can inflict the maximum fine … *that praetor shall proclaim* that he will *fine* the judge(s) …

(lines 45–6) … (if the praetor) investigating *that matter*, has found no excuse, any of the judges … *he shall ensure* that *his name* XXVI
is reported *to the quaestor in charge of the treasury* at the first possible opportunity, and this quaestor *shall enter his name … concerning that excuse* at the first possible opportunity …

(lines 46–7) *How the judges* shall retire to consider their verdict – the praetor, who according to this law … *if more than* XXVII
a third of the judges present have stated *that they cannot* make a judgement, the praetor investigating under this law shall declare as follows: '*a further hearing*' … *of the judges*, whoever shall be present (? he shall order) to judge …

(line 48) … *on those judges, who in this way have refused* to judge, he *shall impose a fine* of 10,000 sesterces, on every occasion *that they have refused to judge* more than twice in one trial … *he shall display* the reason and the amount of money *he has imposed as a fine* … XXVIII

(lines 49–52) How judgement shall be made *about* defendants – when two thirds of the judges present *shall have stated that they have reached a decision … the praetor investigating under this law shall ensure that those judges*, who have refused to judge, shall be taken aside … XXIX
(?) he shall handle the matter. Then the praetor with his attendants and messengers (shall ensure) that … not … *and shall order a jar (?) fingers broad*, twenty *fingers high, to be placed before his tribunal*, into which the judges should cast their voting-tablets … and for the judge in question the praetor (shall prepare) a single voting-tablet of boxwood, four fingers long, (?) *fingers* broad, written in ink *on both sides* … he shall give *the voting-tablet, on which on one side A has been written, on* the other C, publicly into the hand (of the judge) *and order him to cancel whichever letter he wishes* …
and (the judge) shall cast that tablet in accordance with this law, uncovered and with his arm uncovered (but) with the letter covered by his fingers, publicly *into the jar* … and likewise to the other judges one by one …

(lines 52–4) … *the judge who* XXX
is selected by lot to come to the jar in order to (? pick up the votes), he shall put his hand down into the jar and when he has brought it down out of the jar, *he shall show it openly* to the people, so that the judgement … may not be (?) *concealed* … the vote *which that tablet has had on that* defendant, he … *where the letter A is written, 'I acquit', where the letter C is written,*
'I condemn', where nothing is written, 'No vote'. The tablet from which he has declared the vote *he shall pass on* to the next judge *and he* in turn shall hand it over *to the praetor*.

(lines 54–5) Concerning … – … the acquittal of the defendant … *unless there shall be a majority of votes cast, 'I condemn', about the man denounced under this law,* XXXI
in so far as this has not been done in order to achieve praevaricatio,* that man shall be acquitted of that matter under this law.

(line 55) Concerning the condemnation of the defendant – if the majority of votes cast *about that defendant* shall be 'I condemn', the praetor *investigating under this law* … XXXII

(lines 55–6) … There shall be no action under this law with the man *who has been condemned* XXXIII

* deliberate miscarriage of the accusation

56 aut apsolutus erit, quom eo {f}⟨h⟩.l., nisei quod postea fecerit aut nisei quod praevaricationis caussa factum erit aut [*nisei de leitibus*] aestumandis aut nisei de sanctioni hoiusce legis, actio nei es[*to.* [280] *Praetor, quei ex h.l. quaeret*]

57 [*e*]um, quei ex h.l. condemnatus erit, q(uaestorei) praedes facito det de consili maioris partis sententia, quanti eis censuer[*int. Sei ita pr*]aedes datei non erunt, bona eius facito puplice possideantur, conq[*uaerendo* [285] *quaestorei*]

58 [*sc*]riptum transdito. Quaestor accipito et in taboleis pobliceis scriptum habeto. (vac.) De leitibus aestumandis [(vac.) *Quei ex ha*]ci lege condemnatus erit, ab eo, quod quisque petet, quoius ex hace lege pẹ[*titio erit,* [210] *aestumanto, ita utei aestument, quod ante hance legem rogatam conperietur captum coactum*]

59 [*ab*]latum avorsum conciliatumve esse, ea⟨s⟩ res omnis simpli, ceteras res omnis qu{o}⟨a⟩s post hance legem rogatam co[*nperietu*]r captum coactum ablatum avorsum conciliatumve esse dupli, idque ad qua[*estorem, quei aerarium provinciam optinebit, deferunto.* [185] *Quei eiei ioudicei, consilioque eius maiorei partei satis fecerit nomine*]

60 [*su*]o parentisve suei quoive ipse parensve suos heres siet leitem aestumatam esse, queive eiei iudicei consilioque eius maiorei pa[*rtei sa*]tis fecerit regis populeive ceivisve suei nomine litem aestumatam esse sibei, Q[[175] *iudex, quei eam rem quaesierit, queive iudex hace lege factus erit, is facito utei eiei, quoi ita lis aestumata erit, sei tanta pequnia quanta satis erit ex*]

61 hace lege in aerario posita erit, ob eam rem, quod eo nomine lis aestumata erit, in triduo proxsumo, quo ita satis [*factum erit*], ex hace lege solvatur, neive quis iudex neive quaestor facito sciens dolo [*malo, quo minus ea pequnia ita solvatur* [180] *Sei iudex quei eam rem quaesierit, queive iudex hace lege factus erit, quantei is reus condemnatus erit,*]

62 [e]x {ex} hace lege pequniam omnem ad quaestorem redigere non potuerit, tum in diebus X proxsumeis, quibus q[*uanta potue*]rit, redacta erit, iudex quei eam rem quaesierit, queive iudex ex hace lege fac[*tus erit, edeicito sese tributum facturum esse* [85] *diemque prodeicito, qua is, quoi nomine suo parentisve suei, quoive ipse parensve suos heres siet, ceivisve suei nomine lis aestumata erit, adessit quave a rege populove, sei quibus regis populeive nomine leites*]

63 [*aest*]umatae erunt, quoius regis populeive nomine lis aestumata erit, legatei adessint, dum ne longius C dies edat. [(vac.) *De trib*]uto servando (vac. 6) Ubei ea dies venerit, quo die iusei erunt adesse, iudex, quei e[*am rem quaesierit, queive iudex hace lege factus erit, quanta pequnia ex praedibus, quei de ea re datei erunt, exve bonis eius, quei ex h.l. condemnatus erit, possidendis vendundisque in aerarium redacta erit, tantam pequniam eis, quorum nomine leites aestumatae erunt, pro portioni tribuito, queique ei consilioque eius maiorei partei litem suo nomine aestumatam esse satis*]

or acquitted *under this law*, except if he has committed some offence afterwards or if anything has been done to achieve praevaricatio,* or except *concerning* the assessment of *damages* or concerning the enforcement of this law ...

(lines 56–8) ... *The praetor investigating under this law* XXXIV
shall ensure that the man condemned under this law shall give guarantors to the quaestor according to the majority decision of the jury for the amount which they have decided. *If* guarantors have not been given *in this way*, he shall ensure that the property of the man is publicly seized, *by* searching ...
he shall pass it on when it has been written down *to the quaestor*. The quaestor shall receive it and keep it entered in the public records.

(lines 58–9) Concerning the assessment of damages – what each man, who has the right to sue, is suing for from the man, *who* has been condemned under this law ... *they shall assess in such a way that they assess* everything *discovered* to have been *seized, extorted*, stolen, diverted or procured *before the passage of this law* at simple valuation, and everything else, discovered to have been seized, extorted, stolen, diverted or procured after the passage of this law, at double valuation and *they shall report* this to the quaestor, *who has the treasury as his province* ... XXXV

(lines 59–61) *Anyone who has satisfied that judge and the majority of his jury* that damages have been assessed *on his own account* XXXVI
or (on account) of his parent or (of a man) to whom he himself or his parent is principal heir, or who has satisfied that judge and the majority of his jury that damages have been assessed for him on account of his king, his community or a fellow-citizen of his ... *the judge, who has investigated that matter or the man appointed judge under this law shall ensure that, if sufficient money*
has been deposited in the treasury under this law, payment shall be made under this law *to the man for whom damages have been assessed in this way*, because of the fact that damages have been assessed on that account, within three days following the day on which (such) satisfaction *has been given*, nor shall any judge or quaestor act knowingly with *unlawful* intent *to prevent the payment of* that money in this way ...

(lines 61–3) ... *If the judge who has investigated that matter or the man appointed judge under this law*, has not been able to deliver to the quaestor according to this law all the money, *for which amount the defendant was condemned*, then in the ten days following the day on which *the amount which could be delivered*, was delivered, the judge who has investigated that matter or the man appointed judge under this law, *shall proclaim that he will make a distribution ... and shall fix in advance a date, on which the man for whom damages have been assessed on his own account or on account of his parent or of a man to whom he himself or his parent is principal heir or of a fellow-citizen of his, should appear or on which, if damages* XXXVII
have been assessed *for anyone in the name of a king or community*, ambassadors from the king or community in whose name damages have been assessed, should appear, provided that he does not declare a delay of more than 100 days.

(lines 63–4) *Concerning* the maintenance of the *distrib*ution – when the date has come, on which they have been ordered to appear, the judge who *has investigated the matter or the judge appointed under this law shall proportionately distribute the amount of money, delivered to the treasury from the guarantors given in this matter or from the seizure and sale of the property of the man condemned under this law, to those on whose account damages have been assessed,* XXXVIII

* deliberate miscarriage of the accusation

64 [*f*]ecerit, ei primo quoque die quaestorem solvere iubeto, quaestorque eam pequniam eis sed fraude sua solvito. [(vac.) *Pequnia*] in aerario siet (vac. 6) Quod eorum nomine, quei non aderit, tributus factus [*erit, quanta pequnia ei tributa erit, tantam in aerario quaestor servato* ...220... *Ubei diem is quaestor*

65 [*is*]ve {ro}pra⟨e⟩tor ex hace lege tribuendei causa prodeixerit, is, utei quod recte factum esse volet, facito, quomodo prode[*ixerit, utei tabula ma*]iore parte diei ad eam diem, donec solutum erit, apud forum palam ubei de plano r[*ecte legi possitur, proscripta propositaque siet* ...230... *quei eum tributum*]

66 fecerit, ḍịẹṣ[... *proxs*]umos, ex ea die, qua tributus factus erit, apud forum palam, ubei de plano recte legi possitur, proscri[*bito.* (vac.) *Pequnia*] post quinquenium populei fiet (vac. 5) Quae pequnia ex hace lege in aerarium posita erit, quod in anneis Q̣Ṿ[... *proxsumeis eius pequniae quaestor ex h.l. non solverit, populei esto* ...140... *Quaestor quei nunc aerarium provinciam habet, queive deinceps*]

67 eandem provin[*ci*]am habebit, eis faciunto, utei quod recte factum esse volet, quod eius is reus non solverit, ab eis pr[*aedibus primo quo*]que die pequnia exigatur. (vac. 7) Pequnia in fiscis opsignetur (vac. 4) Quaequomque pequnia ex hace lege ad q[*uaestorem in aerarium redacta erit, is quaestor facito utei ea pequnia in fiscum ponatur isque fiscus signo suo opsignetur* ...125... *quoque in fisco inscribatur*]

68 quis praetor litis aestumaverit et unde ea pequnia redacta siet quantumque in eo fisco siet. Quaestor, qui quom[*que erit, utei quod r*]ecte factum esse volet, facito in diebus V proxumeis quibus quomque eiei aerarium provincia obvenerit, [...250... *Quoi*]

69 pequniam ex hace lege, quod sine malo pequlatu{m} fiat. pr. quei ex hace lege quaeret, darei solvi iuserit, id quaestor, [*quei aerarium pro*]vinciam optinebit, sed fraude sua extra ordinem dato solvitoque. (vac. 4) Quaestor moram nei facito (vac. 4) Q[...245... *Quod*]

70 ex hace lege iudicium fieri oportebit, quom ex hace lege fieri oportebit, nei quis magistratus prove magistratu prove [*inperio inpe*]di[*to quo*]minus setiusve fiat iudiceturve, neive quis eum, quei ex hace lege iudicium exercebit, neive eum, que[*i* ...220... *ab eo iudicio avocato neive*]

71 avocarier iubeto, neive abducito neive abducier iubeto, neive facito quo quis eorum minus ad id iudicium adesse poss[*it, quove quoi minus*] verba audeire, in consilium eire, iudicare liceat, neive iudicium dimitere iubeto, nisei quom senatus[...180... *quom centuriae aut*]

and he shall order the quaestor to pay the money on the first possible day to the man, *who has satisfied him and the majority of his jury that damages have been assessed on his account*, and the quaestor shall pay the money without prejudice to himself.

(lines 64–6) *The money* shall be in the treasury – regarding any distribution, which will have been made on account of a man who does not appear, *the quaestor shall preserve the amount of money distributed to him in the treasury* . . . XXXIX

when the quaestor or *the praet*or has appointed *a date* for distribution according to this law, he shall ensure, using his discretion as to the correct procedure, *that a notice-board* about the manner of this appointment *shall be made public and exhibited* for the greater part of the day, until the day on which payment is made, openly in the forum, where *it can be correctly read* from ground level . . .

the man who has made *that distribution* shall make this public for the next . . . days, following the date on which the distribution has been made, openly in the forum, where it can be correctly read from ground level.

(lines 66–7) *The money* will be made the property of the people after five years – any of the money deposited in the treasury according to this law, which in the *next* (?five) years *the quaestor has not paid out under this law shall belong to the people . . . the quaestor who now has the treasury as his province or who subsequently* XL

will have the same province shall ensure, using his discretion as to the correct procedure, that any part of the money which the defendant has not paid, shall be exacted from his guarantors *on the first* possible day.

(lines 67–9) The money shall be sealed in strong-boxes – whatever money *has been delivered* according to this law to the quaestor *at the treasury, the quaestor shall ensure that this money is placed in a strong-box and the strong-box is sealed with his seal . . . and that there is written on the strong-box*, XLI

which praetor assessed the damages and the source from which the money was delivered and how much is in that strong-box. Whoever *shall be* quaestor, shall ensure, using his discretion as to the correct procedure, that within five days of the treasury being allotted to him as a province . . .

to any man to whom the praetor investigating under this law shall have ordered money to be given and paid over under this law, in so far as it cannot involve fraudulent embezzlement, the quaestor holding the *treasury* as his province shall give and pay over that money outside the normal procedure without prejudice to himself.

(line 69) The quaestor shall cause no obstruction – . . . XLII

(lines 69–72) . . . XLIII

regarding any trial which is required to be held under this law, at the time when it is required to be held under this law no magistrate or promagistrate or substitute *for* (a holder of) *imperium* shall *cause obstruction* preventing this trial from taking place or delaying it, nor shall anyone *summon away from the trial* a man who is carrying out a trial under this law nor a man who . . .

nor shall (anyone) order him to be summoned away nor shall he abduct him nor order him to be abducted, nor shall he act so as to prevent anyone of them attending the trial *or to make it im*possible for anyone to hear what is said, consider his verdict or judge, nor shall he order the adjournment of the trial, except when the senate . . . *when the centuries or*

72 tribus intro vocabuntur, extra quam sei quid in saturam feretur. (vac.) Sei is praetor, quei ex hace lege quaeret, sei[*ve quaestor quoi aerarium provinc*]ia obvenerit, ioudiciove inperiove abierit abdicaverit mortuosve erit antequam omnia ioudica[*ta factave erunt, quae ex hace lege fieri oportebit* ...[55] *quei praetor deinceps ex hace lege quaeret, is facito utei ea omnia, quae non adhuc ioudicata erunt, ioudicentur, queique quaestor aerarium provinciam habebit, is, utei quod recte factum*]

73 esse volet, facito utei ea omnia, quod ex hace lege factum non erit, faciant fiantque quae ex hace lege fieri oporteret, sei [*apud eum ea res acta esset, eieique p*]raetori quaestorique omnium rerum, quod ex hace lege factum non erit, siremps lex esto qua[*sei apud eum ea res acta esset* ...[215] *quod iudicium*]

74 fuit fueritve ex lege quam L.Calpurnius L.f. tr.pl. rogavit exve lege quam M.Iunius D.f. tr.pl. rogavit, quei {f}⟨e⟩orum eo [*ioudicio condemnatus est eritve, quo*] magis de ea re eius nomen hace lege de{iu}⟨fe⟩ratur{um}, quove mag{istratus}is de ea re, quom [...[225] *antequam ea res ioudicata*]

75 erit, quom eis hace lege actio nei esto. (vac.) De praevaricatione (vac.) Praetor, quei ex hace lege quaeret, qua de re ei prae[*tori eisque ioudicibus, quei ad eam rem io*]udicandam adfuerint, quei vivent, eorum maiorei parti{s} satis factum erit, nomen, quod ex [*hace lege delatum siet, id praevaricationis caussa delatum esse* ...[200]]

76 (vac. 4) De ceivitate danda (vac. 6) Sei quis eor[*u*]m, quei ceivis Romanus non erit, ex hace lege alteri nomen [...[40] *ad praetor*]em, quoius ex hace lege quaestio erit, detolerit, et is{eo} eo iudicio hace lege condemnatus erit, tu[*m is, quei eius nomen detolerit, quoius eorum opera maxume is condemnatus erit, ipse ceivis Romanus iustus esto, et in ea tribu, qua is, quei ex h.l. condemnatus erit, fuerit, sufragium ferto, inque ea tribu censeto, militiaeque ei vocatio esto, aera stipendiaque ei omnia merita sunto, filieique eiei gnatei, quei*]

77 ceivis Romanus ex hace lege fiet, nepotesque [*t*]um eiei filio gnateis ceiveis Romanei iustei sunto, [*et in ea tribu, qua is, quei ex h.l. condemnatus erit, fuerit sufragiu*]m ferunto, inque ea tribu{m} censento, militiaeque eis vocatio esto, aera stipendiaque o[*mnia eis merita sunto.* ...[225] *eius h.l.*]

78 nihilum rogato. (vac. 7) De provocation[*e vocation*]eque danda (vac.) Sei quis eorum, quei [*ceiveis Romanei non erunt queive in ceivitate sua* ...[15]]TOR praetor aedilisve non fuerint, ad praetorem, quoius ex hace lege quaestio eri[*t, ex hace lege alteri nomen detolerit, et is eo iudicio hace lege condemnatus erit, tum, quei eius nomen detolerit, quoius eorum opera maxume is condemnatus erit, sei c*(eivis) *R*(omanus) *fieri nolet, eiei provocatio militiaeque munerisque poplici vocatio esto, neive mora esto quo minus provocatio vocatioque*]

tribes are summoned to vote, apart from occasions when proposals are made in saturam.*

(lines 72–3) If the praetor investigating under this law or *the quaestor, to whom the* XLIV
province of the treasury has been allotted, has demitted or abdicated that judicial office or *imperium*, or has died before everything has been judged *or performed, which is required to be judged or performed under this law ... the praetor subsequently investigating under this law shall ensure that everything not yet judged shall be judged, and the quaestor holding the treasury as his province,*
shall ensure, using his discretion *as to the correct procedure*, that, regarding what has not been done according to this law, they should do and there should be done everything, which would have been required to be done under this law, if *the matter had taken place under his supervision, and this* praetor and quaestor shall be in the same legal position in all matters, as to what has not been performed according to this law, as if *the matter had taken place under their supervision ...*

(lines 73–5) ... *regarding any trial* XLV
which has or will have been completed under the law proposed by Lucius Calpurnius, son of Lucius, tribune of the plebs, or the law proposed by Marcus Iunius, son of Decimus, tribune of the plebs, anyone among them who *has or will have been condemned* in that *trial*, (*let there be no provision under this law*) whereby he shall be denounced concerning that matter under this law or whereby concerning that matter when(?) ... *before that matter* has *been judged*,
there shall be no action with them under this law.

(line 75) Concerning praevaricatio – the praetor investigating under this law in any matter XLVI
concerning which the praetor *and the judges* who have attended to judge *that matter*, a majority of those surviving, shall be satisfied that a denunciation *made under this law has been made for the sake of praevaricatio ...*

(lines 76–8) Concerning the granting of citizenship – if anyone of those men, who is not a XLVII
Roman citizen, has denounced another man according to this law ... to the praetor in charge of investigation under this law, and that man has been condemned in that trial under this law, then *the man who has denounced him, whose efforts were most responsible for this condemnation, shall himself be a full Roman citizen and shall cast his vote in the same tribe as the man condemned under this law did, and shall register in that tribe, and shall have immunity from military service and his tribute-payments and years of military service shall be all counted as performed, and the sons born to the man who*
shall become a Roman citizen under this law, and the grandsons born subsequently to any son shall be full Roman citizens, *and* shall cast *their votes in the same tribe as the man condemned under this law did*, and shall register in that tribe, and shall have immunity from military service, and their tribute-payments and years of service *shall all be counted as performed*: ...
let there be no provision *to this effect under this law*.

(lines 78–9) Concerning the granting of provocatio† and *immunity* – any one of those XLVIII
men, who *are not Roman citizens or who* have not been ... praetor or aedile *in their own community, has denounced another man according to this law* to the praetor in charge of investigation under this law, *and that man has been condemned in that trial under this law, then the man who has denounced him, whose efforts were most responsible for his condemnation, if he does not wish to become a Roman citizen according to this law, shall have provocatio and immunity from military service and public duty nor shall there be any delay preventing*

* *en bloc* † Protection against flogging or execution without trial at the hands of a Roman magistrate.

79 eius militiae munerisque poplici, in su[*a quoique cei*]ỵitate iudex deinceps faciat pr[*onontietur*. (?vac.) *Sei is pr., quei ex h.l. quaeret, seive quaestor, quoi aerarium*] vel urbana provincia obvenerit, eo magistratu iudiciove inperiove abierit abdicaveritve [*mortuosve erit, antequam omnia ioudicata factave erunt, quae ex hace lege fieri oportebit* .50 *quei praetor deinceps ex hace lege quaeret, is facito utei ea omnia, quae non adhuc ioudicata erunt, ioudicentur, queique quaestor aerarium vel urbanam*]

80 provinciam habebit, is, utei qu[*od recte factum esse v*]olet, facito utei ea omnia, [*quod ex hace lege factum non erit, faciant, fiantque quae ex hace lege fieri oporteret sei a*]pud eum ea res acta esset, deque ea re eiei praetor⟨i⟩ quaestor⟨ique⟩ omnium rerum, quod ex [*hace lege factum non erit, siremps lex esto quasei apud eum ea res acta esset* 185 *quod*]

81 [*iud*]icium {e}⟨f⟩uit fueritve ex leg[*e quam L.Calpurnius L.f.*] tribunus plebei rogav[*it exve lege quam M.Iunius D.f. tr.pl. rogavit, quei eorum eo ioudicio condem*]natus est eritve, quo magis de ea re eius nomen hace lege de{e}⟨f⟩eratur quove magis de e[*a re* 250]

82 [..6]T, antequam ea res [*ioudicata erit, quom eis hace lege a*]ctio nei ẹṣ[*to*. (vac.) *Praetor, quei ex hace lege quaeret, qua de re ei praetori eisque ioudicibus, quei ad ea*]m rem ioudicandam adfueri[*nt*], quei vivent, eorum maiori{s} parti satis fecerit Ẹ[250]

83 [10-11] (vac. 7) Seiq[*uis* .85 *ad praetorem, quoius e*]x hace lege quaestio erit, detuler[*it et i*]s eo ioudicio hace lege condemnatus erit, tum eis, qu[*ei eius nomen detulerint* 230]

84 [.15 + + 100 *militiaeque ei*]s vocatio esto, aera stipendia[*que eis*] omnia merita sunt⟨o⟩. Neiqui magis[*t*]ratus pr[*ove magistratu* 240]

85 [.60 *ad praetorem, quoius ex hace lege quaestio erit, detolerit et is eo ioudicio condem*]natus erit, tum, quei eiu[*s nomen*] detolerit, quoius eorum opera ma[*xume is condemnatus erit,* 245]

86 [130]SI petetur, de ea re eius [*optio est*]o, utrum velit, vel in in sua ceivitat[*e* 270]

87 [130 *inh*]ibere liceto. (vac. 5) [(vac. 2) *Sei quis cei*]vis Romanus ex hace lege alte[*ri nomen detolerit et is eo ioudicio condemnatus erit* 225]

88 [130] (vac. 4) Quoi ex h[*ace lege militiae vo*]catio erit esseve oport[*ebit* 270]

89 [140 *praetor quei inter pe*]regrinos ious [*deicet* 280]

90 [155]ỊATEIỌỴ[290]

the judge from causing the *provocatio and immunity* from military service and public duty *to be declared* subsequently *for each man* in his own community.

(lines 79–80) *If the praetor investigating under this law or the quaestor, to whom* the province *of the treasury* or the urban province has been allotted, has demitted or abdicated that magistracy or judicial office or imperium *or has died, before everything has been judged or performed, which is required to be judged or performed under this law ... the praetor subsequently investigating under this law shall ensure that everything not yet judged shall be judged, and the quaestor holding the treasury or urban* XLIX

province shall ensure, using his discretion as to *the correct procedure*, that, *regarding what has not been done according to this law, they should do and there should be done* everything, *which would have been required to be done under this law, if* the matter had taken place under his supervision, and over that matter this praetor and quaestor *shall be in the same legal position* in all matters, as to what *has not been performed* according to *this law, as if the matter had taken place under their supervision ...*

(lines 80–2) ... *regarding any* L

trial *which* has or will have been completed under the law proposed by *Lucius Calpurnius, son of Lucius*, tribune of the plebs, *or the law proposed by Marcus Iunius, son of Decimus, tribune of the plebs, anyone among them who* has or will have been condemned *in that trial, (let there be no provision under this law)* whereby he shall be denounced concerning that matter under this law or whereby concerning *that matter* ... before that matter *has been judged, there shall be* no action *with them under this law.*

(lines 82–3) *The praetor investigating under this law, in any matter concerning which* (someone) shall have satisfied *that praetor and the judges who* have attended to judge *that* matter, a majority of those surviving, ... LI

(lines 83–4) If anyone ... has denounced *to the praetor in charge of* investigation under this law ... *and* that man has been condemned in that trial under this law, then those men who *have denounced* him ... LII

and they shall have immunity *from military service*, and their tribute-payments and years of military service shall be counted as performed. No magistrate *or* pro*magistrate* shall ...

(lines 85–7) ... *has denounced ... to the praetor in charge of investigation under this law and he* has been condemned in that trial, then the man who has denounced him, whose efforts were most responsible *for his condemnation ...* LIII

(?if) suit shall be made, in that matter he *shall have a choice*, whether he wishes either in his own community ...

it shall be lawful to restrain.

(lines 87–8) *If any* Roman citizen *has denounced* another man according to this law, *and he has been condemned in that trial ...* LIV

(lines 88–) LV

Any man who has or should be granted freedom from military service under this *law* ...

(line 89) ... *the praetor who has* jurisdiction *for* foreigners ...

(line 90) ... ? (the magistrate who has) jurisdiction (in each) community ...

Commentary

I (lines 1–3) Definition of suit that is permitted under the law in terms of accuser, accused and alleged offence.

1 (B1) On the calculations given above there is space in the initial lacuna for 60 large letters (= 100 small letters) more than those actually printed. The name of the proposer will require *c.* 10–12 of these (e.g. C. SEMPRONIVS C., or MN ACILIVS MN, where MN is written with five linked diagonal strokes), the remainder of the date *c.* 6–8 letters, the *principium* (i.e. the first tribe to vote) and the first voter perhaps no more than 20.

n]*ominis*: Sig: *Quoi socium no*]*minis*: Kl, Mo.

Rudorff (429), Venturini (1979, 52ff) and Meyer (1980) suggested that a reference to Roman citizens should occur at the start of the text of the law proper. Twenty more letter-spaces are available and it would thus be possible to restore 'Quoi *ceivei Romano* sociove no]minisve . . .' The *opinio communis* follows Mommsen on two main grounds. First, we do not hear of prosecutions for offences against Roman citizens under this law. Secondly, Cicero says in *Div.Caec.* 17–18: '*quasi vero dubium sit quin tota lex de pecuniis repetundis sociorum causa constituta sit? nam civibus cum sunt ereptae pecuniae, civili fere actione et privato iure repetuntur. Haec lex socialis est, hoc ius nationum exterarum est.*' However, in this text the strained introduction (*quasi dubium*) does suggest that even in Cicero's day some Roman citizens did get recompense under the current *lex rep.*, even if they did not promote such accusations alone. *Civili fere actione et privato iure* could describe the simplified private-law procedure which we find below in lines 7–8, still apparently available in the seventies BC (Asc.84C). If we put on one side Cicero's statement and concentrate on the law itself, line 87 seems to be concerned with rewards for Roman citizens who prosecuted under the main provisions of this law, and it is implied that they might prosecute in lines 22 and 76. However, such prosecutions may have been undertaken by them as a representative of a foreign community (cf. II, line 4).

[. . .res suae repetundae erunt]. If we are to account for the name of the *quaestio*, we must suppose that some phrase of this kind stood here.

For the language of the line, cf. Cic. *Div.Caec.* 66, '*ab exteris nationibus, quae in amicitiam populi Romani dicionemque essent, iniurias propulsare* (where the *in*+accusative for place where, unusual except in legal documents, suggests an allusion to a *repetundae* law known to Cicero).

Venturini (1979, 52ff) has argued from the fact that by itself '*socii nominisque Latini*' means the Latins and allies in Italy (e.g. in *lex agr.* 21), that '*exterarum nationum*' are Rome's provincial subjects, while '*quoive in arbitratu* . . .' are the other friends and subjects of Rome: hence on this view foreign allies are not referred to as *socii*, but *in arbitratu dicione potestate amicitia*. Sherwin-White (1982, 196, cf. his *Roman Foreign Policy in the East* (London, 1984), 58ff) has a similar interpretation of *socii nominisque Latini*, but regards *exterarum nationum* as complete foreigners, not *socii* or subjects at all, while for him those *in amicitia* are the allied free cities and kings generally, who are only unofficially called *socii et amici populi Romani*. Neither of these views can easily accommodate communities abroad with a treaty of alliance (*foedus*), e.g. Cibyra, Maroneia and Methymna (cf. p. 8, n14), who were as much *socii*, with their reciprocal treaties, as Italian allies were (interestingly, Sherwin-White holds that such treaty-allies were more common outside Italy than most other scholars would admit). In any case, it does not seem appropriate here to press the Latin to yield such precise distinctions. In fact, '*socii nominisque Latini*' has been adapted (. . .*nominisve Latini exterarumve nationum*) so that it clearly includes any ally of Rome, while the rest of the phrase (*quoive in arbitratu*. . .) covers any other foreigner with an established relationship to the *populus Romanus*, including individuals who were friends or subjects of Rome, even if their community was not a recognised ally. Cf. Ferrary (1983, 71) for other criticisms of Venturini's schematism, and see *lex de provinciis praetoriis* (Hassall, 1974), Cnidos III.31ff and Delphi B.6ff for attempts to render a similar formula into Greek.

For the general controversy over the meaning of friendship and alliance in Roman diplomatic language of this period, see Sherwin-White, *Roman Foreign Policy in the East*, ch. III; E.S. Gruen, *The Hellenistic World and the Coming of Rome* (Los Angeles, 1984), chs. I–II. The truth almost certainly lies between Sherwin-White's position, that *socius* only designates an ally with a *foedus*, and Gruen's, that the terms 'friendship' and 'alliance', when applied to communities outside Italy, are used for the most part loosely, and that the Romans, even when there were formal relations, were indifferent to their exact terms.

2 (B2) *quoius pater*: aes, Venturini, 1979, p. 91; ⟨*queive*⟩ *quoius*⟨*ve*⟩ *pater*: Kl, Mo; ⟨*queive ipse vel*⟩ *quoius pater*: CIL (citing Mommsen).

The alteration of the text by Klenze and Mommsen is unconvincing. In fact the subjunctive *siet* after *quoius* suggests not a parallel relative clause, but one qualifying the previous clause: as the text stands, sons of ex-magistrates are only included, if their fathers are senators, i.e. if they are scions of more distinguished fathers.

For the list of magistrates cf. Cic. *Rab.Post.* 14; *Clu.* 148; Guardia Vomana fragment (*CIL* I^2, 598), 5.

AMPL . . .: O, Sig, Vett.

Mommsen pointed out that the sum missing after *amp[lius* was not more than 4,000 HS (Vell. 2.81, recorded at double its value in Cic. *Verr.* 2.184, 4.22).

In the lacuna at the end of line 2 and the beginning of line 3 I suspect that a phrase like '*nisei quod ex legibus senatusve consultis ei capere liceret*' stood, in order that the legitimate exaction of taxes and corvées might be clearly excepted.

3 (B3) IPSEI PARENTE^VE SVOS: aes (reproduced by Pinelli); *Ipse parensve*: Kl, Mo. This engraver's mistake suggests that *ipsei parenteve* stood earlier in the line.

[. . . *pro inperio prove potestate ipsei regive populove ipsius parenteve ipsius, queive in potestate manu mancipio suo parentisve sui siet fuerit quo*]*ive* . . .: Mo, comparing Gai. 4.80 for *in potestate* . . .; [*pr. quaestio esto* . . .]: Mo; a more elaborate restoration in Kl, based on *Dig.* 48.11.1. [*ioudicium ioudicatio* . . .]: Sig. For the restoration of *ioudices*, not *ioudicium*, see line 4.

II (line 4) Provision for those who are neither themselves injured parties nor relatives of injured parties to sue.

4 (B4) [*sei quis . . . legatu*]*m esse*: adapted from Mattingly (1970, 167, n95) according to the reading of the bronze in line 60, cf. line 63 (contrast frag.Tar. 17, '*populo ceivitate regnove*' in a somewhat different context); [*sei quis deicet praetorem nomen ex h.l. ita non recepisse utei delatum esset, neque ioudicium ex h.l. datu*]*m esse*: Mo, unconvincingly, since the suit is then about the praetor's official misconduct, *de ea re*, before the praetor himself. For retaining *ceivisve suei* in line 60, see Venturini, 157; for the principle of the legal representative (*cognitor*) see Sherwin-White (1982, 20f).

quei quomque ioudic[*ium* . . ..: Pin, Sig, Kl, Mo, following text of bronze in line 6. It seems awkward to state that *ioudicium* should belong to those who are the *ioudicium*. In the rest of the text, apart from line 6, *ioudicium* is used for 'trial' and *ioudices* for 'jury-panel'.

III (lines 5–6) Special provisions for prosecution.

5 (A1, B5) OIV: scripsi; *eiu*]*s iu*[*dic*: Mo. The bottom curve of the first letter seems too broad for S. No interpunct is visible. Perhaps *qu*]*oiv*[*e. De quo ex h.l. ioudicatum erit, sei contra h.l. fecisse deicetur postquam ea res ioud*]*icata erit:* Mo, CIL.

Sigonio restored this line as permission to prosecute for someone whose property had been *abiud*]*icata*, which surely would have been covered earlier; Mommsen as permission for a *second* prosecution. It is at first sight difficult to see how permission could be given for the prosecution of someone whose name was *exemptum ex h.l.* However, this seems to refer to a special procedure employed for example when the prosecution failed to appear in circumstances which suggested corruption, cf. Asc. 60C. The complement to this provision is that in lines 55–6, where second prosecutions of those accused under the law are forbidden except in certain circumstances, such as *praevaricatio*. See also Florence frag. A (*CIL* I^2, 595) line 7 for *e]xemptus erit*, but the context is probably different.

IV (lines 6–8) Different procedure for those suing before 1st September and those suing after that date.

6 (A2, B6) NO NOMI: aes; NO NOMIN: O^2; *Sei quis ali]eno nomin*[*e*: Mo. Cf. Cyrene Edict (*FIRA* I, 68 = EJ 311) V, 98, δημοσίαι ἢ ἰδίαι.
IN IOUS ED: aes; *in ious ed[ucito*: Sig, Mo (cf. line 19); *in ious ei*: O, Vett.

The man suing on behalf of another here cannot be a *patronus*, who is still to be appointed (lines 9–11), but must be someone deputed to act by a community, king or fellow-citizen (cf. Rud. 440). Since Klenze, it has been recognised that there must have been a contrast in this clause between suits before 1 September, for which the full *quaestio* procedure was available, and those after 1 September, for which a form of private law process might be provided. Klenze thought that *peregrini* had to sue before 1 September, citizens after, but there seems no warrant in the text for this view. Mommsen in his commentary took 1 September as the final date for bringing new actions under normal Roman legal procedure (see now Behrends (1970), 174) and it is attractive to assume that this was a general rule applied here with some modification. It is significant that no plaintiff was allowed a *patronus* after 1 September (line 9). The emphasis on *eius praetoris* (line 6) and *eo anno* (line 7) suggests a contrast between the current year and a following one. One might restore in the second lacuna in line 6, *sei ante k. Sept ad praetorem, quei ex h.l. quaerit*. The implication will be that after 1 September the plaintiff will either have to wait till the next year or use a simple procedure.

7 (A3, B7) DEQVE EO HOMINE D: aes; -- D: edd veter; --. DE: Mo, CIL (noting the uncertainty of the last letter); [*ita uti i.s.est res agitor. Post k. Sept sei quod nomen deferetur, sei is quei petet volet, is praetor de ea re recuperatores dato. Qu*]*oius*: CIL following Mommsen (an earlier version on the same lines in Mo).

Sept: here and in the following lines down to and including line 21 all humanist editors and copyists recorded a continuous text with no letters lost at the join of Ba and Bb. This must have represented the actual state of the bronze at the time.

ae[stumata erit, tantam pecuniam quei eum condemnaverit dato: Mo, CIL; *ae[stumata erit, tanti reddere damnas esto*: Sig.

The man suing after 1 September could sue according to the forms of private law, as had occurred in 171 BC (Livy 43.2). Later, according to the *S.C. Calvisianum* (*FIRA* I, pp. 410ff), a special quasi-private procedure was available at any time, so long as no capital charge was involved. There is no reason to follow Serrao (1956, 490) in maintaining that the judges for the private procedure here had to be drawn from the panel of 450 (below, lines 12ff). Those selected in 171 and under the *S.C. Calvisianum* were *recuperatores*. By 122 BC these are likely to have been drawn from an album different to that prescribed for cases *de repetundis* (*lex agr.* 37 with commentary and above, p. 30). It is also appropriate to restore *recuperatores* here, because procedure before them was speedy and the praetor took a special interest in the execution of their judgements (cf. line 8). See Schmidlin (1963), 92ff, and above, pp. 13–14.

8 (A4, B8) [*eaque pequnia* . . .]*eius esto*: Mommsen saw half a downstroke before *eius*, not visible now or to earlier editors, and restored *quei eum condemnaveri*]*t*.
IM ERIT: aes; *um erit*: O[1]; m erit: O[2], Vett, Pin, Sig; *quidquid . . . iudicatu*]*m erit*: CIL (more elaborate restoration in Mo).

The point of the last provision seems to be that in cases begun after 1 September, even when conducted before *recuperatores*, execution of judgement was likely to take place after the praetor who had provided the trial had left office. His successor as president of the *quaestio* is therefore charged with assisting the plaintiff to obtain his damages.

V (lines 8–9) Certain magistrates not to be tried while in office.

8 Mommsen, following Sigonio, restored here a complete list of magistrates, including the minor officials listed in lines 13 and 16. Yet it is rash to assume that the latter were exempted from prosecution during their term of office unless *absentes rei publicae causa* (cf. Mommsen, *StR* I, 705ff). On the other hand censors are known to have been exempt (Livy 24.43.3), tribunes of the plebs were sacrosanct and, while aediles may have been liable in the third century BC (Val.Max. 6.1.7; Plut. *Marcell.* 2.5ff, cf. Gell. 13.13.4 for their original liability to summons by a *privatus*), the case of Clodius in 57 BC suggests that at least curule aediles were exempt then (Cic. *Att.* 4.3.4; *QF* 2.1.2; Dio 39.7.3–4; Ed. Meyer, *Caesars Monarchie*, 109). Promagistrates would have been certainly covered by this clause (*dum mag. aut inperium habebunt* implies this for consuls and praetors). So their titles need not have been listed.

9 (A5, B9) This passage is perhaps the best evidence that a dictator could be prosecuted when out of office, cf. Livy 9.26.17ff for an example of doubtful authenticity. For the general principle later see *Dig.* 48.2.12 (Venuleius), 48.5.39.10.

VI (lines 9–11) The appointment of patroni.

Patroni were only to be appointed by the praetor for those employing the new procedure established by the law, not for the alternative procedure used after 1 September. Similarly the *S.C. Calvisianum* allowed *patroni* to speak for plaintiffs in the senate (*FIRA* I, pp. 410ff, v, lines 100ff) but not apparently before *recuperatores*. Contrast their appointment in 171 for cases before *recuperatores* (Livy 43.2.3ff). For the procedure here cf. Cic. *de Or.* 2.280: *ut ille Siculus, cui praetor Scipio patronum causae dabat hospitem suum, hominem nobilem, sed admodum stultum, quaeso, inquit, praetor, adversario meo da istum patronum, deinde mihi neminem dederis.*

10 (A6, B10) IVSVE: aes, O[1], Pin, Sig; PIUSVE: O[2], Vett, Kl, Mo, CIL. The restoration of *gener socer* . . . (cf. line 22) goes back to Klenze. FVERIT: aes; FUERIN: O[2], Vett; FVERI: O[1], Pin.

Noteworthy are the importance of *collegia* and *sodalitates* (cf. Q.Cic. *Comm. Pet.* 30), also the fact that patron–client relationships were not necessarily transmissible from one generation to another but, after they had been broken off, some residual force was still thought to exist. For the multiplicity of patrons concerned with a single client in this period see P. Saller in Wallace-Hadrill (1989), 52ff.

11 (A7, B11) IOVDICIOOVE: aes; *ioudiciove*: Kl; *ioudicioque*: Maz, Mo, CIL. The latter is perhaps the easier correction of the text, but might suggest that the man in question had been condemned under both of two distinct procedures.

The restoration following *condemnatus* is based on line 13 and was first suggested by Klenze.

The term *quaestio* can cover any tribunal – whether permanent, like the present one, or temporary, such as that set up to deal with the Bacchanals (see above, p. 11), whether set up by *lex* or by *senatus consultum*, cf. Kunkel (1962), 51ff and (1963). *Iudicium publicum* under the Principate came to mean procedure under one of the laws establishing *quaestiones perpetuae* of the late Republic or Augustus' time. For the wider meaning of the term *iudicium publicum* in the Republic, namely any trial on a charge affecting the public interest, see Gell. *NA* 4.14.2ff; 10.6.2ff; Cic. *Acad.* 3.74; *lex lat.Bant.* (*FIRA* I, p. 82), 2, cf. Lintott (1978), 132–5; (1972b), 248.

For expulsion from the senate as the consequence of condemnation in a trial cf. *lex lat.Bant.* 1ff. and commentary on lines 13 and 23 below. There is no evidence that it was prescribed in the present law, as it was in *lex lat.Bant.* We should perhaps restore in the lacunae in this chapter the provisos about age, domicile and presence in Italy found in lines 13–14 and 17 (Hesky, 1903, 272ff).

VII (lines 11–12) The repudiation of patroni *offered.*

11 EX H L: aes; *quei ex h.l.*: O, Vett; *qu*]*ei ex h.l.*: Mo. SEI IS MOR: aes; MORI: Sig, Pin, Vett, Mo, CIL; hence *mori*[*etur*: Sig, Pin; *mori*[*bus suspectus erit*: Kl, Mo, CIL; *sei is mori* F(ortasse) morã fecerit: O[1], in my view rightly. The little that remains of a hasta on the bronze at the edge of Bb could as easily belong to an A as an I (the apparently clear mark visible in Degrassi, *Imagines*, p. 282, is a trick of the light).

Against Klenze's and Mommsen's restoration, accepted by Hesky, Brassloff (1904, 107–8) and Eder, 168, it may be argued that the suspect morals of a potential *patronus* should have been considered by the praetor first and a foreigner would have found it hard to contest the praetor's judgement on that point. A more concrete ground for repudiation must be sought. On the other hand one can hardly repudiate a man who is dead. For obstruction by *patroni* in 171, see Livy 43.2.11, *fama erat prohiberi a patronis nobiles ac potentes conpellare*; for the phrase *moram facere*, cf. lines 35, 69. Rudorff (537) wanted a reference excluding the defendant's quaestor from being *patronus* to the plaintiffs, but Cic. *Div.Caec.* 46 does not suggest that this was a legal rule.

12 (A8, B11) EIEI QVEI: aes; *eiei quem*: Maz, Sig, O, Kl; *eiei quei s[ibei darei petet*: Mo, CIL.

VIII (lines 12–15) The selection of jurors in this year.

12 *De CDL vireis in hunc an]num*: Kl. Mo, CIL; *De ... eum an]num*: Sig. *in hac ceivit[ate*: Pin; *civit[ate iudices, dum*: Sig; *ceivit[ate ... iudicent*: Kl; *ceivit[ate sestertium quadringentorum milium n(ummum) plurisve census siet*: Mo, Rud; *ceivit[ate equom publicum habebit habuerit*: CIL (Nicolet (1972), 203, compares *finitores ex equestri loco* in Cic. *Leg.Agr.* II.32); *ceivit[ate ex lege quam C.Sempronius Ti.f. tr.pl. tulit, iudicet iudicaturusve sit*: Mommsen, *StR* III³, 531, n1; *ceivit[ate liber natus siet*: Mattingly (1970), 168, comparing *lex de prov. praet.* C 23, ὅστις ἐ[ν] ταύτηι τῆι πολιτείαι γ[ε]γενήμενος ἐστὶν ἐλεύθερος.

In hac ceivitate suggests a definition involving Roman citizenship but more restricted than *ceivis Romanus*. I would prefer *ingenuus* to Mattingly's *liber* because it is used by Pliny, *HN* 33.32 in a later definition of the *equester ordo*. Since Mommsen's reconstructions there has been little doubt that we have here a positive definition of equestrian status which is further limited in what follows. The reference to a prior *lex Sempronia iudiciaria*, suggested by Mommsen, is too brief for the space available, even if we accept the existence of such a general law (see above, p. 26). There is ample room for a clause about the holding of the *equus publicus* or one about a census qualification or indeed both. Unfortunately, this very fact means that the law can be no help in defining the meaning of the word *eques* in the context of the courts and the political struggle over them in the late Republic (see above, pp. 27–9).

13 (A9, B13) FVERIT EIE QVEI: aes; em. Kl; *quei[ve mercede*: see under line 16.

quaestione ioudiciove puplico conde[mnatus siet ... liceat: see under line 11 and cf. *Tab.Heracl.* (*FIRA* I, pp. 140ff) 117–8 on banning from local senates *queive iudicio publico Romae condemnatus est, quo circa eum in Italia esse non liceat*. See also *Dig.* 1.9.2: *Cassius Longinus non putat ei permittendum, qui propter turpitudinem senatu motus nec restitutus est, iudicare vel testimonium dicere, quia lex Iulia repetundarum hoc fieri vetat.*

PROPIUSVE V: aes, O, Vett; *propiusve V [milia passuum urbem Romam non habitet*: Kl; *propiusve u[rbem Romam p(assus) M domicilium non habeat*: Mo,

CIL (presumably with reference to the extension of the city-boundary to the first milestone beyond the *pomoerium*).

I would assume that the figure here represented the distance a man might be reasonably required to travel to attend the court, for example twenty miles – the distance within which senatorial jurors were expected to live according to the *S.C. Calvisianum* (*FIRA* I, pp. 410ff, V, line 409, cf. Brunt, 1988, 147,n6). Note the evidence in *lex rep.* 30 for the time by which jurors were required to arrive on the first day. For the phrase *domicilium habere*, cf. *lex Ursonensis*, cap. XCVIII (FIRA I, p. 189) and *domi[cilium*? in Nicotera frag. A (*CIL* I² (1986), 2925a), line 5.

The list of minor magistrates at the beginning of the line was perhaps inserted before the reference to senators, because the former would most readily spring to mind after the mention of equestrian status. For the significance of the exclusion of the higher echelons of the *ordo equester*, see Sherwin-White (1982, 19) and pp. 21, 27 above. Examples of such men from the Ciceronian period are listed in Nicolet (1966, I, 270ff). The text shows that an ex-tribune did not automatically have a seat in the senate at the time of the passing of the law: the *lex Atinia* (Gell. *NA* 14.8.2), which ordered that ex-tribunes should be enrolled in the senate, must therefore have been subsequent to it. The legislator excludes from the jury men condemned on a non-capital charge who might otherwise have been senators – thus doubly undesirable from his point of view. The exact significance of *quod circa . . . non liceat* is very problematic. It is in my view too clear-cut to refer to the censor operating at his own discretion. C.T. Zumpt (1845, I.13) and Sherwin-White (1949, 7) believe that it implied a general law regarding non-capital condemnations already in existence, but this is unlikely in view of the passing later (in 104) of the *lex Cassia* regarding those who were condemned or had their *imperium* abrogated by the people (Asc. 78C). I prefer to think that it refers to specific provisions in laws about individual crimes, such as that in *lex lat.Bant*, (*FIRA* I, p. 82), 1ff, cf. Lintott (1978), 132–5.

14 (A10, B14) QVOS LEGERIT . . . TRIBVNVM COGNOMENQVE IOVDICET Q: aes; *tribum*: Kl, Mo, CIL; *indicet*: Mo, CIL, showing *quos . . . indicet* as a rubric with spaces before and after, although there are none on the bronze. Given the correction to *tribum*, the alteration of one more letter, T to S, produces the same text as on the B fragment in line 17 and this must be a securer emendation.

15 (A11, B15) *potestatemque scribundi* and *consultum siet*: see notes on l.18. VDICES: aes; *iudicaturos ex animi sententia i]udices*: Kl; *optumos eos futuros esse quosque oetiles io]udices*: Mo, CIL. *Diligentes* is *exempli gratia*. Other possible adjectives are *integros* and *severos* (Cic. *Verr.* I 30).

For the copying of legal texts cf. *Frag.Tar.* 15. *q]uei id consoluerit quique ad id scribendum aderit*; for recitations, *ibid.* 13. *in c]ontione et apud senatum*, and *S.C. de Bacchanalibus* (*FIRA* I, p. 240), 22–3, *haec utei in coventionid exdeicatis ne minus trinum noundinum*; for the permanent registration of jurors, as Mo. saw, Cic. *Phil.* 5.15 (the phrase here is *deferre ad aerarium*).

IX (lines 15–19) The selection of jurors in each following year.

15 [*legundis* vac. *Pr., quei post h.l. rogatam ex h.l. ioudex factus erit* . . .: Mo, CIL, cf. Kl, 28, Rud, 442.]

I take the B–A lacuna over the end of line 15 and the beginning of 16 to have contained a reference to the method of selection (probably by lot) of a praetor other than the *praetor peregrinus* to preside over the court in subsequent years. This man is called *iudicem in eum annum quei ex h.l. factus erit* in line 19 (cf. 63), *praetor, praetor quei ex h.l. quaeret* (lines 31, 35, 39, etc.) and *praetor, quoius ex h.l. quaestio erit* (lines 76, 78, 83). The use of *iudex* in place of *praetor* may result from adoption or adaptation of formulae in the preceding *leges Calpurnia* and *Iunia* (cf. line 23). C.Claudius Pulcher (*cos.* 92) is attested as *pr. repetundis* (*ILS*, 45).

16 (A12, B16) QVE EORVM: aes, Maz, Sig, Pin; *quei eorum*: O². *Queive merc[ator siet fueritve*: Sig, Pin; *queive merc[ede conductus depugnavit depugnaverit artemve ludicram fecit fecerit*: Mo (abbreviated in CIL) cf. Rud; *queive merc[aturam quaestumve sordidum faxit*: Tibiletti, 1953, 29ff; *queive merc[aturam vel argentariam exercet exercueritve lege Rubria (?Acilia)*: Carcopino, 1928, 223; *queive merc[ede vel aliquo pretio corruptus erit*: Nicolet, 1966, I, 507.

We have no right to suppose that *mercatura* was a legal disqualification. It is not in the same class as *corpore quaestum facere, lanistatura, ars ludicra, lenocinium* (cf. *Tab.Heracl.* 122–3) or the trade of *libitinarius* (cf. S.C. from Larinum, Malavolta. *Sesta misc. gr. rom.* 1978, 347ff = Levick, 1983, lines 15–16). Cicero (*Off.* I.150–1) does not suggest that *mercatura* itself is *sordida* but only that on a small scale and this moral judgement is too ill-defined to be the basis of a legal distinction. The Larinum S.C. shows that it was quite possible in the early principate for men even of the senatorial order to turn themselves into gladiators. Here we are dealing with the less prestigious members of the equestrian order. Caesar forbad senators to become gladiators but allowed *equites* to do so (Dio 43.23.5). Mommsen was in principle right, but I suspect that the text may have brought in the word *auctoratus*. Cf. *Tab.Heracl.* (*FIRA* I, pp. 140ff), 112–13, *queive depugnandei caussa auctoratus est erit*.

17 (A13, B17) VRBEM ROMA: Maz; ROM: aes. *quei ex h.l. in eum*: O.

erit. Quos legerit . . .: Mo and *CIL* insert rubric spaces both between *erit* and *quos* and between *ioudices* and *quei* to match the spaces they have previously inserted in line 14. They also emend *ioudices* to *indicet* to match their previous emendation in line 14. Further comment is superfluous.

18 (A14, B18) QVE: aes; MQVE: O; *ious potestate]mque*: Sig; *sei quis describere volet, is praetor permittito potestate]mque scribundi*: Mo, CIL, Pin, and Vett, record in what is now Ba–b lacuna *CDLviros* (*CBLviros* – O) with the form of D with central bar used earlier on the bronze in abbreviations.

CONSV: aes; *consul*: Sig, O, Pin, Vett; *consul[uerit*: Kl; *consul[tum siet optimos*

. . .: Mo, CIL. I have taken the construction of *consultum siet* as absolute (see the translation) but there is space for an *oratio obliqua* construction dependent on it.

X (lines 19–26) Procedure for accusation and selection of a jury for a trial.

19 (A15, B19) *Ab a[liquo*: Kl; *Ab a[ltero*: Mo (cf. *alteri nomen deferre* in lines 76, 87); *Ab a[rvorsario*: CIL (cf. line 20).

quoius eorum . . . petitio erit. Cf. line 9. Something of this kind is required to distinguish this procedure from the civil procedure in lines 7–8. Hesky (1903, 272ff) would have restored *sei quis alieno nomine* . . . here, cf. Eder, 176, but the civil procedure in lines 7–8 must be an option for the man suing *suo nomine*, not compulsory, since permission for the bringing of a suit by the injured party himself before the new court is one of the main provisions of the law (cf. line 3).

Note that it is the man suing, whether in his own or another's name, who performs *nominis delatio*, not the *patronus*, who may only be appointed after this has taken place (cf. line 9). Venturini's belief (1979, 137ff) that one did not initially have to bring one's opponent *in ius* is in the light of lines 6 and 19 baffling.

non po[stulare: Sig, Kl, Mo, CIL. Cf. Guardia Vomana fragment (*CIL* I², 598), 6 – *kalum]niae {r}⟨c⟩aussa non post[ulare*; Cic. *Fam.* 8.8.3, Asc. 64C – *calumniam iurare*; Oratio Claudii, col. III, 8–9, as restored in *FIRA* I, 44. It is not clear whether the *lex Remmia* (Cic. *Rosc.Am.* 55; *Schol.Gronov.* 309St) about *calumnia* was already in existence.

20 (A16, B20) *quei vivant*: cf. lines 21, 75, 82. *quoi is – pri]vignus*: Mo, CIL (cf. line 22); *om[nes quos edere velit. Iudex recipito, dum nei quem recipiat quei eius unde petetur gener socer vitricus pri]vignus*: Kl (a little too long).

For the formula of relationships cf. *lex Iulia de vi* (*Coll.* 9.2.3) and *lex Urs.* ch. XCV, col. II, lines 15ff. For its clumsiness, by comparison with a parallel Greek formulation see above, p. 63.

ARV: aes; *arv[orsario*: Kl, Mo, CIL; *ap[ud se*: Pin; APV: O; *apu[d se iuret palam se calumniae caussa nomen eius non deferre*: Sig; *arv[orsario apud se palam*: scripsi cf. line 23. *arv[orsario . . . is quei ita ediderit iouret in CDLvireis, quei in eum annum ex h.l. lectei erunt, non reliquisse nisei*. . .: CIL; other similar restorations in Kl and Mo.

21 (A17, B21) COVRATOQVE: aes, edd veter; *iouratoque*: Mo, CIL. *tum in ea[m quaestionem quei quoiusque ita nomen detolerit, is praetor, quoius ex h.l. quaestio e]rit*: Mo, CIL. *nomen deferre in quaestionem* seems a little odd as Latin, the supplement does not fill the space available and there is room for something which is not redundant in meaning.

CDL VIREI aes, edd. veter., Mo; *CDL vire(i)*: CIL. LEGAT F/: aes; legat e: O, Pin. Vett; *legat [edatve*: Sig.

22 (A18, B22) The suprascript addition of EI on the A fragment was missed by editors before Klenze.

SOBRINV: aes; *sobrinu*: edd veter, Kl; *sobrinus*[: Mo, CIL.

]SODALIS: aes; *queive e*]*i sodalis*: Sig, Pin, CIL;]*ei sodalis*: O, Mo; PRIM[ ]E EARVM: aes; *primis al ... earum*: O[2]; *primis* [*aliqua ea*]*rum*: Sig, Pin, O[1]; *prim[ ]ae earum*: Mo, CIL apparatus.

QVEIVE (vac. 8) L. RUBR: aes; *queive l.Rubr*[*ia IIIvir coloniae deducendae creatus siet fueritve*: Mo, CIL.

At the right-hand edge of B, Sigonio's text is completely corrupt – *queive mercator siet fuer*[*itve*, while Vettori has *queive cassat* (?*cessat*)*l. Rubr*. Sigonio's error seems to have prompted Carcopino to propose a restoration similar to that which he proposed for lines 13 and 16, see under line 16. The vacant space before *l. Rubr* cannot be explained by any flaw in the surface for engraving. A space may have been left for a subsequent insertion by the engraver, which was then only partially filled. The one *lex Rubria* of which we know in this period is the law devised by C. Gracchus for founding a colony on the territory of Carthage. It would be appropriate to exclude from the jury-panel both those who were to settle in Africa and those involved in founding the colony (for *finitores* of equestrian rank see Cic. *Leg.Agr.* 2.32 and cf. Gelzer, 1929, 655), though any IIIvir, as Carcopino pointed out (1928), was surely covered by the references to IIIvir a.d.a. earlier. There is room for the restoration in lines 13 and 17 of a similar clause relating to the *lex Rubria* (cf. Tibiletti, 1953, 20–1, and Eder, 180).

It may seem redundant for the legislator to list the minor magistrates and senators in this line, since they should have been excluded from the panel in the first place. However, the responsibility for providing properly qualified *iudices* as a basis for rejection lay as much with the prosecutor as with the praetor, as the oath in lines 23–4 shows. It is likely that in the lacunae in lines 21–2 and 22–3 other exclusions found in lines 12–19 are repeated.

23 (A19, B23) *eum* [*quem ... Calpu*]*rnia*: *scripsi*, cf. Cic. *Clu.* 120 and see *Hermes* 1978, 134 for an earlier similar suggestion; *eum* [*legat edatve, quei pecuniae captae condemnatus est erit aut quod cum eo lege Calpu*]*rnia*: Mo, CIL (improving on Kl); [*legat edatve quei ioudicio aliquo alieno nomine egerit aut quod ab eo lege Calpu*]*rnia*: Venturini, 169ff.

NOMEN [...]T QVOS: aes; *nomen de ... t quos*: O[2], Vett; *nomen* [*delatum siet*] *quos*: Sig.

apud se cor[*am se*: Sig; *apud se coram* [*arvorsario nullum se edidisse dolo malo, quem ob earum causarum aliquam de ea re ioudicare...*: Mo, similarly CIL.

It is impossible to find room for a clause of this length in the earlier provisions about the selection of the jury-panel by the praetor. So we seem to be dealing with an afterthought of the legislator. Those condemned under previous *leges repetundarum* are likely to have been senators, their sons or former minor magistrates, as under this law, thus men excluded from the jury-panel in the first place. Thus both Mommsen's suggestion and my proposal in *Hermes* 1978, referring to censorial expulsion from the senate are improbable. There is a further objection to Mommsen's solution. There is no trace in the rest of the text that this law imposed *infamia*, official disgrace and disqualification, on those condemned under it. So an additional penalty would have been imposed casually in passing. If there had been such a penalty those condemned would have fallen under the *queive quaestione ioudiciove puplico* clauses in lines 13 and 16–17 and so this clause would have been unnecessary. Venturini's restoration avoids these problems, which is why it was accepted by Ferrary (1983, 73) with understandable reservations about *alieno nomine egerit*. It is not clear to me, however, why the legislator should want to eliminate past prosecutors from the juries, especially as the ethos of the law is to reward accusers handsomely (line 76ff). I take the clause to refer to men not themselves liable under the *repetundae* law who were branded with infamy because they were involved as accomplices in such a case. I do not take Cicero's claim (*Clu.* 120) that no such clause had ever existed in any law to be decisive about a law of 123/2, whose text was unknown to his listeners. For the leges *Calpurnia* and *Iunia*, see below lines 74 and 81 and on the *legis actio sacramento*, above pp. 14–16.

24 (A20, B24) Q. VNDE PETITVM ERIT: aes, Sig, O (Maz omits Q), Kl, CIL. Mo. emended Q to *is*. The only explanation for the intervention of a quaestor seems to be his function as keeper of public records.

QVOM: aes, O², Sig; QVOMI: Maz, Kl, Mo, CIL. For *moram facere* cf. line 69. (*Is*) . . . *quomi*[*nus ex h.l. ex reis eximatur, per eum pr. advorsariumve mora non erit, nisei is quei petet ita C*]*viros*: Mo;. . . *Sei is quei petet ita C*]*viros*: CIL. DIE L: aes; *die*[*XX postquam*] *eius*: Sig; *die L*[*X postquam*]: Mo, CIL.

On the bronze DIE is followed by an inclined horizontal stroke, which, as Mommsen saw, can only be the left-hand part of an anchor-shaped L (the form used when L is an abbreviation in this text). There seems no reason to restore LX rather than L. For *ex eo die quo* cf. line 21.

25 (A21, B25) E[. . .]Ṛ EVM: aes (the R being partially hidden by the warp of the bronze); *e. . . eum*: edd veter; *e*[*diderit tum ei pe*]*r eum*: Mo, CIL; *e*[*diderit sei*(or *et*) *ei pe*]*r eum: Ancient Roman Statutes* ad loc. MORAM NON ER[. . .]MINVS: aes; *moram non erit quo minus*: edd veter; *edatur*: O¹; . . .*edatu*[*r*: Pin; [*legantur edanturve*: Sig; *legat edatve*: O².

Mo's restoration in the Ba–b lacuna was challenged by Daube (*Forms of Roman Legislation*, 54) followed by the editors of *Ancient Roman Statutes*, on the ground that a command should be expressed by an imperative, *esto*, not a future indicative, and that *erit* must therefore be construed as part of a conditional clause. However, there does not appear to be space for either Mo's *tum* or the *sei* or *et* postulated by his critics. A conditional clause is not attractive, since the tense expected would be the future perfect, *fuerit*. *Et . . . non* is equally awkward: we would have anticipated *neque* or *dum nei*. The future indicative is unusual in a jussive sense, but note *Pequnia*] *post quinquennium populi fiet* in the rubric in line 66 and see Kühner/Stegmann's Lexikon, I, 144 for its occurrence in less formal Latin. Here, if the future is unacceptable, the best solution is to assume that *erit* is an error for *fiat*.

XI (lines 26–7) The recording of the names of judges and patroni.

26 (B26) FAC[. . .]OS: aes; *facito. . . os*: Vett, Pin; *facito utei Lviros quos*: Sig; *fac[ito eos Lviros qu]os*: Mo, CIL.

ediderint eosque patronos: edd veter, Kl; *eosque pat[ronos, quos ei quei petet ex h.l. dederit*: Mo; *eosque . . . quos quei petet ex h.l. acceperit*: CIL.

The record of *patroni* and trial-jury would no doubt have been provided, like that of the jury-panel, on a white board (*in albo atramento scripta*, cf. line 14), but a more permanent record would have been kept in note-books or on tablets. For the permanent recording of the jury and the details of the trial in *tabulae publicae* see Cic. *Verr*. 2.1.96, 157–8; *Clu*. 62, 86; *Fam*. 8.8.3; *Frag.Tar*. 16–17, as restored in *ZPE* 45·(1982), 131. Cf. Cic. *Phil*. 5.15 – '*hos ille demens iudices legisset, horum nomina ad aerarium detulisset?*'

XII (lines 27–8) The jury not to be changed during a case.

27 (B27) LECTEI: aes; *lectei erunt*: edd veter, Kl; *lectei erunt e[ius rei iudices in perpetuom sunto]*: Mo, CIL.

The task of the *iudices* might extend into the following year beyond the term of the presiding praetor or treasury quaestor (lines 72 and 79). The legislator anticipated some diminution in their ranks during the trial – *ubei duae partes iudicum quei ader[unt]* (line 49), cf. *quei ad eam rem ioudicandam adfuerint, quei vivent* (lines 75, 82). Some reference to permitted excuses for absence may have appeared at the end of line 27. For the situation after Sulla's *lex Cornelia*, see *Verr*. 1.29–31. Jurors were then expected to continue in post unless called away by public office, in which case there was a *subsortitio* (supplementary selection by lot). The Gracchan jurors would not be undertaking any but the lowest public offices and and the size of the jury – 50 compared with *c*. 30 after Sulla (Cic. *Clu*. 74) or even less – would have made supplementary selection less necessary.

28 (A24, B28) PEQVNIAM EX̣[. . .]Ṭ EUM: aes; *pequniam ex. . .eum*: O, Sig, Pin; *pequniam . . . capiet eum*: Maz; *pequniam ex [h.l.] capiet eum*: Mo, CIL.

censor neive tribu mov]eto: Sig; *neive senatu mo]veto*: Pin; *neive tribu mo]veto*: CIL.

ei – suprascript correction after *eius* was erroneously engraved, recorded as such by Pin.

There is not much space in the B–A lacuna to complete one chapter and start a new one on a fresh topic. So it is likely that line 28 is still dealing with *ioudices*.

Klenze laconically restored a clause about giving security (*vades*) for appearance. However, after *nominis delatio* the problem of the non-appearance of the defendant was dealt with in another way (line 29). Mommsen supposed that the man receiving money *ex [h.l.]* had informed on some offence committed by a *ioudex*, but did not try to see how much could be restored to this effect in the space available. Rudorff (454–5) thought the clause referred to any informer or accuser. Nicolet (1972, 205–7), accepting that the clause still related to *ioudices*, argued that it exempted them from the charge of receiving bribes. Yet it is hard to see how *pecuniam ex h.l. capere* could refer to the illegal receipt of bribes (cf. Rudorff, 454). The same objection applies to Sherwin-White's view (1982, 24) that the clause referred to a defendant who had taken less than the minimum sum in line 2. Brassloff (1904, 110–11) suggested that *patroni* were hereby permitted to receive honoraria. My own view is that the text may refer to a *ioudex* receiving money according to the statute as grant or compensation in respect of his duties. For this meaning of *pecuniam capere*, cf. *lex Corn XX quaest.* (*FIRA* I, pp. 132ff), 5–6; *olleisque hominibus eam pecuniam capere liceto*; *lex Ursonensis* (*FIRA* I, pp. 179ff), cap. 63, 65, 71 and 81; *lex Irnitana* (J. Gonzalez, 1986, 147ff), VIIIB, lines 45ff. A *ioudex* receiving money in this way would have thus been assimilated to a scribe, for example (*lex Corn XX quaest.*, *loc. cit.*) or to a member of the staff of the land-commission (Cic. *Leg.Agr.* 2.36).

Expulsion from a tribe and relegation to the ranks of the so-called *aerarii* was, like the removal of the public horse, one of the original forms of public disgrace, which could be inflicted by the censors (see e.g. Livy 4,24.7; 24.18.6–8 and 43.3; 27.11.14; 29.37.9–15; 44.16.8; 45.25.8, and cf. Mommsen, *Staatsr.* II.1.402).

XIII (line 28) (?) No false names to be recorded.

28 (B28) RIPTA: aes; *scripta*: edd veter: *sc]ripta*: Mo, CIL; *nomina publice sc]ripta*: Rud (thus repeating the provision in line 26). The lacuna between Ba and Bb here is 15–16 letters, of which NOMINA SC are certain. We should also allow for the presence of either NEI or VTEI (though the law is not consistent in inserting VTEI, cf. lines 26 and 27).

EX H.L.Q: aes; *ex h.l.[quaeret*: Pin, Mo; *ex h.l.n[omen receperit*: Kl.

XIV (line 29) Trials of those dead or in exile.

29 (A25, B29) For the text of A we must now chiefly rely on humanist copies of Ab.

De ioudicio . . . mortuos e]rit . . . abierit: Mo, CIL, recognising that this, not the following clause as Kl thought, must be a rubric.

um abierit: edd veter; *prius urbe cesserit aut in exili]um abierit*: Sig. *iudicata*: the N taken by Mo and CIL as the reading of the bronze at the start of this word is in fact a slightly carelessly engraved IV (the apparatus to Bruns[7] wrongly states the reading to be *indicata*).

REM: aes; *m rem*; edd veter, Kl; QVAERIT: aes; *quaerito*: edd veter;

quaerito [quei vadimonium susceperint: Kl; *d[elatum erit, ea]m ... quaerito [quei ioudicium ex h.l. erunt, quasei sei is, quoium nomen ex h.l. delatum erit, viveret inve ceivitate esset*: Mo, CIL.

The *vadimonium*, suggested by Klenze, seems inappropriate in a *quaestio* – contrast the civil procedure in 171 BC (Livy 43.2) – and the *vades* are not necessarily those who needed investigation. Mommsen took *ab eis* to refer to the jurors, who he thought were being asked questions by the praetor, but it seems more likely to refer to the source of evidence about the money – either those closely related to the defendant or witnesses for the prosecution. Venturini (1979, 147) argued on the basis of Mommsen's restoration that there was a fiction of the life and presence at Rome of the accused and this excluded transmission of the case to heirs. However, the restoration is not automatic. Nor is it easy to see how heirs could be kept out of the case (even if their *nomina* were not *delata*), if the suit for the money continued after the death or exile of the accused. See Rudorff, 457ff, who cited the case of Caecilius Classicus (Pliny, *Ep*. 3.9.6): *Baetica etiam in defuncti accusatione perstabat. Provisum hoc legibus, intermissum tamen et post longam intercapedinem tunc reductum*. For the transmission of *repetundae* cases to heirs see *Dig*. 48.2.20; 11.2. The story that Licinius Macer saved his property by suicide (Val.Max. 9.12.7), if true, may indicate that the *lex Cornelia* was more generous than either the *lex Iulia* or the Gracchan law.

XV (line 30) The timing of the trial.

30 (A26, B30) IV: aes; *quo]iu[s*: CIL (Mo originally read N, earlier editors recorded nothing); *quo]iu[m ita*: scripsi (a few more letter-spaces are available than allowed for by Mo and CIL). *ex h ... delatum*: Maz. *ioudicium p[erficiatur eumque, quei ex h.l. nomen detolerit, eius iudici causa admittat utei q]uod*: Mo; *p[rimo quoque die fiat eique, quei ex h.l. nomen detolerit, dies quot sibi videbitur det utei q]uod*: CIL. Both restorations are on my reconstruction of the bronze too short and depend on the incorrect Ba–b restoration discussed below.

FIAT[...]VNDAM: aes; *fiat ... secundam*: O, Vett, Pin; *fiat aut [actionem] secundam*: Sig; *fiat [aut ... sec]undam*: Kl; *fiat [ante horam sec]undam*: scripsi; *fiat [ad inquisitionem fac]iundam*: Mo, CIL. Where the latter have recorded an I, no downstroke is visible, only the edge of the bronze catching the light.

The lacuna between Ba and Bb, as it now exists, cannot be more than 8 cm (15–16 letters), if we allow for the warp at the edge of Bb (see Introduction, p. 75), and may be less. Hence Mommsen's restoration is too long. Nor should *secundam*, the unanimous testimony of humanist editors and copyists, have been rejected. Sigonio's *aut* I take to have been a misreading of ANT[e: it does not seem a natural conjecture. *Secundam* suggests a time for starting the trial, cf. *Tabulae Herculanenses*, XIII–XIV (Pugliese-Carratelli, *PP* 3 (1948), 168–9) for the appearance of the second hour in a *vadimonium* of a civil suit. For *post h.[l.r.]* (Kl, Mo, CIL) we should perhaps consider *post h[oram secundam*.

Inquisitio, investigation by the prosecutor in the relevant province, is first securely attested under Servilius Glaucia's law (Asc. 21C, Cic. *Scaur.* 23) and it would have been appropriate in the light of the increasing importance given to Roman accusers appointed through *divinatio* under that law (see above, pp. 28–9 and Lintott, 1981, 196–7). Under the present law witnesses and evidence could be brought from Italy (below), but a claimant from abroad would have been expected to bring his witnesses with him. For pressure on jurors to attend cf. Cic. *Att.* 2.2.3: '*iudices cogi? Nam ita ad me mittunt, Nigidium minari in contione se iudicem qui non adfuerit compellaturum.*'

XVI (line 31) The search for witnesses and evidence in Italy.

31 (A27, B31) *. . . aut in provinciis extra Italiam in oppedeis foreis con]ciliaboleis*: Mo, CIL.

It is hazardous to assume that the Romans were talking of *fora* and *conciliabola* in the provinces in this period (they later form part of the abbreviated catalogue of communities of Cisalpine Gaul in *lex Rubr.*, cap. XXI, 1–2; XXII, 26; XXIII, 54ff). It is better to imagine operations by two different kinds of magistrate in the centres of communes in Italy. Cf. the S.C. de Bacchanalibus of 186 BC reported in Livy 39.14.7: '*sacerdotes eorum sacrorum, seu viri seu feminae essent, non Romae modo sed per omnia fora et conciliabula conquiri*', and 25.5.6; 40.37.3; 43.14.10 for the use of *fora* and *conciliabula* in prayers and recruiting, also C.Gracchus' speech *de Popilio circum conciliabula* (*ORF*, no. 48, frags. 34–7). For agents called *conquistores* see Varro. *L.L.* 6.79; Plaut. *Amph.* 64–74, 81–5; and especially Plaut. *Merc.* 664–5: '*post ad praetorem ibo, orabo ut conquistores det mihi in vicis omnibus*', discussed by Mantovani (1990, 40ff). Such would have been the men detailed to arrest Marius, Sulpicius and their friends in 88 BC (App. *BCiv.* 1.61.272).

Even though the law did not provide for an *inquisitio* in the provinces (commentary on XV, line 30), the fact that it ordered local magistrates to assist in searches in Italy – presumably for documents, witnesses and stolen property shows the difference between this *quaestio* and a normal civil suit. Even in cases before *recuperatores* we only hear of the 'subpoenaing' of already identified witnesses (see above, p. 30).

XVII (lines 32–3) The summoning of witnesses – testimonii denuntiatio.

32 (A28, B32) *in singulas res testimonium denuntia]re iubeto*: Sig; *c[ausam probaverit, quibus is qui petet denuntiaverit, eos homines dumtaxat IIL testimonium deic]ere iubeto*: Mo, CIL.

TESTIS ER: *aes*, Sig; *testis ei*: O, Vett, Pin (the last indicating doubts about the 'i'); *er[it, in eam rem facito eis*: Mo, CIL (but this is too long).

MNES ... TESTIM: aes; *o]mnes*: Kl; *omnes adsient testimo*: edd veter; *testimo[niumque deicant*: Mo, CIL.

The maximum number of witnesses is restored from line 34. It was increased by later laws to at least 120 (Val.Max. 8.1.damn.10). On summoning in general, see also Cic. *Verr.* 2.2.64; *Flacc.* 14, 18, 36 (cf. Eder, 191, 194). The defendant was not allowed to *evocare testes* by this or later *repetundae* laws (Pliny, *Ep.* 5.20.2; 6.5.1–2).

33 (A29, B33) *fide quaerat*: edd. veter.

... *queive eius, quoius ex h.l. nomen delatum erit c]ausam deicet*: Mo, CIL. The suprascript VE after QVEI was noted by Pinelli.

[leibertus leiberta]ve: Mo, CIL, comparing *lex Iulia de vi* (*Coll.* 9.2.2; cf. *Dig.* 22.5.3.5): '*qui se ab eo parenteve eius ... liberavit*'. See also *lex Gen. Urs.*, cap. XCV, 18. In the B–A lacuna between lines 32 and 33 there would also have been references to relatives (*gener, socer, vitricus*, etc.) as in lines 20–2 and in *lex Urs.*, cap. XCV, 18.

The clause clearly refers to the exclusion of persons from giving evidence because testimony hostile to the defendant would involve a breach of *fides*, while favourable testimony could not be trusted by the court. *Dumtaxat unum* must refer to the immediately preceding clause, not the previously enumerated *fides* relationships. It would read oddly if in a clause still dependent on *dum nei*: 'provided that he does not instruct to give evidence ... a man pleading the case of the defendant, not more than one'. Hence I have restored the text so as to make *dumtaxat unum* part of an exception clause: one of the defendant's advocates may be called as a prosecution witness. Eder (193) keeps the Mo/CIL text but translates *dumtaxat* as if it was *nisei*, thus obtaining the probable sense with some forcing of the Latin. For the later exclusion of advocates from giving evidence, see Cic. *Verr.* 2.2.24: for the exclusion of *patroni* in general from testifying against clients see Plut. *Mar.* 5.4 (an incident in a *quaestio de ambitu* a few years after this law): '*ἐπὶ δὲ τὸν Μάριον καὶ Γαίος Ἑρέννιος μάρτυς εἰσαχθεὶς οὐκ ἔφη πάτριον εἶναι καταμαρτυρεῖν πελατῶν ἀλλὰ τὸν νόμον ἀφιέναι ταύτης τῆς ἀνάγκης τοὺς πάτρωνας*'. It is not clear whether the '*νόμος*' here refers to an old general regulation, perhaps the Twelve Tables, or the *lex de ambitu* under which Marius was tried. However, our present text shows that this was neither an archaic rule, fallen into disuse, nor a quaint anachronism, as both Saller and Wallace-Hadrill argue (Wallace-Hadrill, 1989, 50, n4 and 66–7).

XVIII (lines 33–5) The registration of witnesses and documents.

33 (B33) DE ÇḌ: aes (CD faintly engraved and followed by further faint traces now confused by the crumpled edge of the bronze); DE T: Sig, Pin, O²; DE Ṭ: O¹; DE ... TABO: Vett: DE NO: Kl; *de inro[ganda multa*: Mo, CIL (Mo at one point read DE TIRO).

No restoration can be attempted with any certainty, but Mommsen's final conclusion about what survived is in conflict with all other testimony. What I read as an angular C may in fact be a T with its left-hand cross bar missing and the incomplete D may be an A. So the reading of Vettori should be taken seriously and we may suppose a rubric beginning *de taboleis*.

34 (A30, B34) [*De testibus tabulisque custodiendis* (vac) *Is quei petet, sei quis ad testumonium deicendum evocari]t*: Mo, CIL. *e]a quai*: Mo, CIL; *pop* or *pop[licas*: edd veter, Kl; *popl[icas preivatasve*: Mo, CIL. *proferriq*: edd veter; *produ]cere proferrequ[e*: Kl, Mo, CIL – but Klenze's *producere* is a little too long for the lacuna.

Something similar was laid down in the Florence fragment (*CIL* I², 595), A, 6: '*literaive testium*'. There is no sign in the preserved text of the more rigorous procedure in Cic. *Flacc.* 21 (probably in Sulla's *lex Cornelia*, under which Flaccus was charged, as well as Caesar's *lex Iulia*): '*Triduo lex (litteras) ad praetorem deferri, iudicum signis obsignari iubet*', and we should not, like Mommsen, assume its existence here.

35 (A31, B35) *Praetor ei*: Maz; *praetori*: Sig, O², D. *Moram ne fa*: Maz; *facito*: Sig, O²; *faci[to*: Pin; *fa[cito*: D.

It is hard to tell whether the early copyists and editors read the last letters of this line off the bottom of Aa (where it is no longer visible) or the top of the now lost Ab. The surviving traces in the bottom right hand corner of Aa are consistent with either FA or CI. Huelsen claimed in the apparatus of *CIL* to have read traces of CI. Pinelli, as elsewhere, seems to have taken his reading from the bronze itself.

ṚAT: aes; *at*: edd. veter; *]rat*: Mo. The lower right of the R remains.

I take the text before the new rubric still to relate to testimony or documents, possibly permission for a specific search (*quae]rat* or *conqui]rat*).

XIX (lines 35–?36) Questioning by the praetor.

35 (B35) The nature of this clause remains uncertain. Rudorff (462–3) thought that it was a preliminary investigation during the trial itself of witnesses' evidence – not implausibly. *Interrogo* is certainly used of questioning witnesses (Asc. 40C; Cic. *Flacc.* 22; *Dom.* 77; Pliny *Ep.* 1.5.6; cf. Sherwin-White, (1982, 16), though he presses the point too far in concluding that this was the exclusive right of the praetor in cases under this law). Mommsen (1899, 387) associated the text with the questioning of defendants in the preliminaries before the trial itself (Livy 38.50.8; 45.37.4; Sall. *Cat.* 18.2; 31.4.). Earlier in *CIL* I¹ he had discounted both these explanations and thought it referred to arranging the date for the trial.

XX (lines 36–8) Oath by the judges.

36 (A32, B36) FORV: aes, edd veter, Kl; *in foru[m pronuntiantur*: Sig; *in forum [vorsus iouranto*: Mo, CIL, cf. *lex lat.Bant.* 17.

37 (A33, B37) *facturumque se, utei quod recte factum esse vo]let*: Mo, CIL; *testium quei eam rem erunt*: Maz, O, Sig; *quei eam rem* (erasure): D; *quei eam* (caret mark) *erunt*: Pin. EIE: aes, Sig, Pin; *eis*: O, Vett; *eiei*: Mo; *eie[i ex h.l. quo rem minus ioudicet permittat*: CIL.

Valid excuses for the non-appearance of a member of a jury (*morbus sonticus, vadimonium, iudicium, sacrificium, funus familiare, feriae*) are found in *lex Gen.Urs.*, cap. XCV. 21ff. For an invalid excuse cf. Cic. *Phil.* 5.14: '*Quaero igitur, si Lysiades citatus iudex non responderit excuseturque Areopagites esse nec debere eodem tempore Romae et Athenis res iudicare, accipietne excusationem is quei quaestioni praeerit...?*' Such excuses may be in question in line 38 below.

38 (A34, B38) *for*: Maz; *fo[rum*: D; *forum*: O[2], Sig, Pin; *for[um habeto; neive quemquam ioudicare sinito, nisei quei ita iourarit eorum, quei ex e]is*: Mo (perhaps rightly); ... *neive, nisei ita iourarit, de ea re considere sinito quemquam eorum quei ex e]is*: CIL. For my *ubei ... possitur*, cf. lines 65–6.

For the recording of names of those who have taken an oath, cf. *lex lat.Bant.* 20–1; *frag.Tar.* 22. Alternatively, instead of *iudicum nomina* being *proscripta* we might suppose *verba iurisiurandi* or something similar and take the clause to be an injunction to publicise the text of the oath.

XXI (lines 38–9) A ban on argument/discussion.

38 (B38) *E iudicium*: edd veter, Kl; *sei... causam sibi esse deicat, quominus ad id] iudicium*: Mo, CIL.

Mommsen considered this chapter to be a ban on *iudices* making their own contribution to the case. However, the evidence he cited does not seem very relevant – Asc. 39C; Tac. *Ann.* 1.74; Pliny *Ep.* 2.11.9. The chapter might have concerned direct confrontations between members of the jury and the prosecutor or defendant. On the other hand, since at the end it seems to be dealing with attendance at the trial, *disputet* may refer to arguments by the judges that they were wrongly chosen and should not attend.

XXII (lines 39–40) Adjournment of the trial.

39 (B39) NDO: aes, O[2]; *inlo*: Vett; *nio*: Sig, O[1].
De iudicio proferendo vel refere]ndo: Mo, CIL. QVOI: aes; *quoi*: Mo, CIL; *quo*: edd veter.

From now on Orsini's and Vettori's versions of the lower portion of B are vitiated by their failure to realise that Bc, whose text they knew, joined Ba. Sigonio and Pinelli did not know of Bc at the time when they made their copies.

Mommsen compared *Dig.* 4.8.33, where it is argued that an *arbiter ex compromisso* can *proferre* (delay or adjourn) the case, not *referre* (bring it forward), but it is hard to see how the question of bringing cases forward can arise here since the praetor is already expected to hold the case as soon as possible (line 30, cf. Hesky, 1903, 281; Eder, 196). Adjournment is another matter. There seem already to have been at Rome adjournments of legal business for public holidays. See *frag. Tar.* 24: '*quom res prolatae [erunt*', cf. Cic. *QF.* 3.6.4; *Att.* 14.5.2; *Mur.* 28 for the legal recesses of the late Republic and *lex Irnitana*, VC, 24ff for procedure under the Principate.

XXIII (lines 40–1) ?Resumption of the trial.

40 (A36, B40) A36 was omitted by Sig, O[2], Pin, D. Hence the text rests solely on Maz. *Sei refer]re poterit*: Mo, CIL. For *referre* one might conjecture *deferre*, but see below.

IT: aes, edd veter, Kl, CIL; ṚIT: Mo. VT EIUS: aes; *utei*: Mo, CIL. POSTULAVER: aes; *postulaver[it*: O, Mo, CIL; *postulaveri*: Vett, Borgh.

41 (A37, B41) *vo]let*: Mo, CIL. *hominis*: Maz; *nominis*: O, Sig, D. I have followed Mommsen in assuming that *hominis* was the original incorrect reading of the bronze, later corrected.

rei pe[titio esto: Mo, CIL; for *rei pe[quniaeve* cf. *frag.Atest.* 17.

This clause is very obscure. It may deal with the resumption of an accusation after an adjournment. In this case *nomen referre*, if the engraving was accurate, might have the sense of 'to bring back a person's name, renew an accusation'. *Referre* is used with *causam* or *rem* and absolutely in this sense, cf. Cic. *Dom.* 78: '*hoc in genere solo rem iudicatam referri posse voluerunt*'; *Fam.* 8.8.3: '*postulante rursus Appio cum L. Lollio (Luterensis) transegit et se relaturum dixit*' (see Rudorff, 543).

XXIV (lines 42–3) ?Case to be dismissed, if prosecutor fails to appear.

42 (A38, B42) *uei*: Maz; *quei*: Sig, O; *qu]ei*: D; *sei ioudex q]uei*: Mo, CIL.

ORAM. . .S: aes; *ram. . .bus*: O[2]; *bus*; Vett; *die]bus*: Sig; *dam. . .bus*: Kl; *c]oram [iudici]bus*: Mo; *iudicib]us*: CIL. *fec[isse videri*: O, Mo, CIL.

For *causam noscere* Mommsen compared Cic. *Leg.* 1.11; *Fam.* 4.4.1. See also *Att.* 11.7.5. and on tolerable excuses, commentary on line 37. I cannot follow Mommsen in believing that the praetor passes sentence here on a delinquent judge, as more space would be required for the provision of a formal hearing. Nor do I find it convincing that a member of the panel should be appointed to hear the excuses of other delinquent judges. Misbehaviour by a *iudex* is later punishable by a fine pronounced by the praetor (lines 45, 48). A recalcitrant offender would normally be heard by *recuperatores* or the assembly, as in *lex lat.Bant.* 7ff. Here I suggest that the law provided for the formal acquittal of the defendant, if the prosecutor failed to appear on a due day without adequate excuse. For a similar provision, applying to private prosecutions, cf. *lex Gen.Urs.*, cap. XCV, col. ii, lines 28ff.

An emperor, usually believed to be Claudius, was dealing with the non-appearance of prosecutors in his speech about the law-courts. His proposal to give powers of summary judgement on the delinquent prosecutor to the praetor (*FIRA* I, 44 = *BGU* 611, col. iii, lines 5ff) – '*ut pot]est[atem] faciam[u]s praetori pr[aeteriti]s inquisition[is] di[e]bus c[i]tandi acc[usatorem], et si neq[ue a]der[it] neque excusa[bitur, pro]nuntiet c[alumniae] caussa negotium f[raude fec]isse videri* (or *negotium r[eliqu]isse videri*)' – might encourage us to adapt Mommsen's view so that *fecisse videri* applied to the prosecutor, not to a *iudex*: as in Claudius' proposal, the praetor would have been permitted to condemn the prosecutor on the spot, without further hearing for *calumnia*.

However, apart from the uncertainties in the text of Claudius' speech, it seems that the emperor was devising new remedies (col. ii, 9ff). So we should not necessarily expect to find the praetor undertaking such action himself here. *Calumnia* may have been dealt with in the next line (it is of course not certain that the *lex Remmia* had already been passed, cf. note on line 19). Hesky (1903, 282) thought that the line referred to the condemnation of an absent defendant. However, provision for trying such a man in his absence had already been made in line 29.

43 (A39, B43) *sei de ea re] iudicium ... ter[tio die facito iudicium fiat*: Mo, CIL. M QUAERET: aes; *quaeret*: edd veter; *sei ioudex quei eam r]em quaeret*: Mo, CIL.

Mommsen thought once again that there was a reference to a member of the jury-panel investigating a particular matter, but this does not seem a certain inference from what survives.

Here again we may have a reference to a trial for *calumnia*. This is in my view more plausible in that a formal trial is mentioned. Cf. Asc. 29C: '*Cato praetor... cessit imperitae multitudini ac postero die in consilium de calumnia accusatorum misit.*'

XXV (lines 44–5) Further oath by judges that they will deliver an unbiased verdict.

44 (Ela, A40, B44) (The numeration of the first line of E is designed to maintain consistency with Mommsen's numbering later.)
QVEM IAM S: Peir, CIL apparatus. *[Ioudices utei iourent in consilium antequam eant – Pr., quei ex h.l. quaeret, ioudices, quei ex h.l. in eam rem erunt, in consilium an]te quam*: CIL, on the same lines as Mo, but more simply. Klenze made what was for him the apex of the E fragment, MVLTAM SUPREMA, appear in this line to the left of A.

Facit iurent: Maz; *Facito*: Sig, O, D. QVOD P̣: aes; *quod* D: O, Vett; *quod*: Kl; *quod* P: Mo; *quod p[er dolum malum fiat*: CIL.

45 (El, A41, B45) EI MVLTAM SVPREMA DEICA: Peir; *multam suprema dei*: D. Bo[1], Br, Scal; *mutam...*: Bo[2]; *multam suprema delea*: O, Vett, Borgh. *]aturum esse*(vac) *Iudice[s] multam suprema(m) de⟨l⟩(b)eant*: Mo, CIL.

Mommsen's restoration depended on the assumption of a join between the lowest point of A and the apex of E, such that on the *lex rep.* face A frag. was to the left of E. I have argued earlier ('Introduction to the Text', p. 80) that this is in conflict with other reasonable postulates which he made. Klenze's diagram by contrast gave a fair, though rough, impression of the pattern of the fragments. Moreover, we should take seriously the text taken by Peiresc from the *ecmagma plumbeum* of Henri de Mesmes (the latter seems to have been a lead copy of E made on the basis of a wax impression). Peiresc's text preserves not only more letters than other MSS, but more plausible ones, and there is no reason to think that these were casually forged, as the meaningless letters at the bottom of Bo[2] probably were – by the illustrator de Bry. The reading DEICA has partial support from the B group of MSS and the reading of Orsini's group, *delea*, is an easy corruption of *deịca* in minuscule. The legal phrase, *multam deicere*, describes an action by a magistrate, not by *iudices*. *Ei* will therefore be the indirect object of the verb, presumably the delinquent *iudex*. Mommsen used a gap signalled by a comma in Mazocchi to justify his printing of a rubric-space between esse and *iudices* but this need only represent a space of one letter, as it does in A26 (line 30).

The requirement that jurors should not ascertain the voting-intentions of their colleagues is likely to have been an innovation, although one consistent with the secrecy of the vote itself later (line 52) and with the recent trend towards secrecy in voting in assemblies brought about by the *lex Gabinia* of 139 BC and other ballot laws. Traditionally, when a magistrate or civil *iudex* was being advised by a *consilium*, the advice was given orally and openly (Cic. 2 *Verr.* 1.73; *lex lat.Bant.* 2; Gell. *NA* 14.2.9; Pliny *Ep.* 6.22.3–5; 6.31.12; cf. Suet. *Nero* 15.1; Dio 52.33.4 for opposition to this tradition, and Kunkel, *ZSS* 85 (1968), 252–329, esp. 304ff). In *quaestiones perpetuae* the principle of complete secrecy seems to have been generally maintained from this time onwards, though Sulla's *lex Cornelia de sicariis et veneficis* at least permitted a defendant to require an open vote (Cic. *Clu.* 75). On the ballot-laws see especially Cic. *Leg.* 3.34–9; *Amic.* 41; *Brut.* 97 and 106; Asc. 78C. They seem to have been primarily concerned with the actual delivery of the ballot and the subsequent count. However, some laws, if not the *lex Gabinia* itself, may have forbidden examination of a ballot by any other person, before it was delivered (Cic. *Leg.* 3.38).

Like Crawford (1985; 19–20), I am suspicious about the reports of early laws concerning the *multa maxima* or *suprema* – *lex Aterneia Tarpeia* (454), *Menenia*

Sestia (452) and *Iulia Papiria* (430), see Cic. *Rep.* 2.60; Livy 4.30.3; Dion.Hal. 10.50.2; Festus 220, 268–70L; Gell, *NA* 11.1.2. At all events the tradition about assessing fines in numbers of animals does not help us to define the amount of the *multa* here. More contemporary parallels suggest that the maximum fine was relative to the property of the man fined: *lex Silia* (Festus 288L), *dum minore parti familias taxat*; *lex lat.Bant.* 12, [*dum minoris*] *partus familiae taxsat*; *lex osca Bant.*, new frag. 2–3. Note also Cato, *ORF*, frag. 167, *mille minus dimidium familiae multa esto*, which must mean 'a thousand, provided that it is less than half his property'.

XXVI (lines 45–6) Reporting an offender to the treasury.

45 (B45) *quaeret*: Vett.; *sei ioudex quei eam rem qu]aeret*: Kl, Mo, CIL.

46 (E2, A42, B46) OQVE DIE DEFERATUR ISQVE QVAESTOR: Peir. Other edd veter omit initial O; B group omit final R. . . .*excu]satione primo quo/que die deferatur*. . .: Mo, CIL.

Apart from the general grounds for rejecting Mommsens's reconstruction (above, p. 80) it would involve here the assumption that both Peiresc on E and the copyists of A recorded two halves of the same letter as O.

The offender in question is presumably a *iudex* who has failed to obey the provisions of the law.

XXVII (lines 46–7) Consideration of the verdict and opportunities for a rehearing.

46 (B46) ISILIVM: aes; *nsilium*: edd veter; *Iudices in co]nsilium quomodo eant*: Mo, CIL. PR.QVEI EX H.L.IV: aes, O[2], Vett, Borgh; *quei ex h.l. in*: O[1]; . . .*n[omen receperit*: Kl; *iu[dicabit*: Mo; *iu[dicium exercebit*: CIL. Perhaps *iu[dices in consilium vocarit* or something similar. For *ire in consilium* cf. Cic. *Quinct.* 34, referring to a civil judge.

47 (E3, A43, B47) ÇARE DEIXERIT: Peir; RE DEIXERIT: O, Vett, Borgh; ḌEIXERIT: B. All MSS omit *quei* after *praetor*. VR (A43): Maz only. *nondum pl]ur[imis lique]re deixerit*: Mo; *iudex, quei ad id delectus erit, sei rem de qua agitur, plus tertiae parti iudicum qui aderunt quom ea res aget]ur[non lique]re deixerit*: CIL; *iudex*. . .*sei plus tertiam partem iudicum quei aderunt quum ea res aget]ur [amplius deice]re deixerit*: Mattingly (1970, 159).

pronon[tiato et ad rem denuo agendam alium diem dato: CIL.

Ṃ QVEI QVOMQVE: aes; M *queiquomque*: Vett, Borgh; *eoru]m, quei quomque*: Mo; *eoque die eorum iudicu]m, quei quomque aderunt iudicare [iubeto*: CIL.

The position of VR in the Mo/CIL restoration of the beginning of the line depends on Mommsen's postulated join (on which see above, p. 80). My own restoration is based on the fact that Peiresc has recorded half an A and perhaps the lower part of a C, though the latter is blurred by the edge of the fragment (the account in *CIL* I^2, p. 445 is misleading). Peiresc's reading reinforces the argument against Mommsen's join, since it is hard to find a sensible context for VR immediately before CARE. Against Mattingly's text it may also be argued that other evidence shows that *iudices* said *non liquet* at this point (Cic. *Clu.* 76; cf. PsAsc. 193St for tablets marked NL later): it was only the presiding magistrate who had the authority to pronounce *amplius*, cf. Eder, 203. For the phraseology, cf. *lex Gen.Urs.*, cap. LXIV: '*cum non minus duae partes aderunt... decurionum maior pars aderunt*'; *lex Malac.* LXIV, 45ff; *lex Irnit.* VIIIC, 13ff; and see line 49 below.

For the procedure, cf. Cicero's charge (*pro Caec.* 29): '*venisse in consilium publicae quaestionis, cum eius consilii iudex non esset, et in eo consilio cum causam non audisset et potestas esset ampliandi, dixisse sibi liquere*', cited by Hesky (1903, 283ff). For *amplius pronuntiare*, see Cic. *Verr.* 2.1.26 and 74; *Brut.* 86 (performed by magistrates), and for *ampliatio* in general Livy 43.2.6–10; *Rhet. Ad Herenn.* 4.48; Val.Max. 8.1.11.

XXVIII (lines 48–9) Penalty for excessive demands for rehearings.

48 (E4, B48) CARE IS HS N ↀ – IVD: Peir; ḌEICARE IS HS N ↀ – IV: Scal, Bo^2; ḌICARE IS HS N ↀ – IV: D, Bo^1, Br, Ha, O^1; *dicat eis*: correction in O^1, O^2; *dicabeis*: Vett; *iudicabeis*: Borgh. (Scal has RIS for BIS *in uno iu.* Borgh omits N after HS. The numeral was misrepresented by O^2 as CIↃ and by Br as Ψ.) At this point the misalignment and consequent corruption of the text by omission in Bo and Br commences, on which see above, p. 68. I have not recorded the variants produced by this corruption but rather the correspondence of the basic text with the rest of the B group.

Iudices maior pars eorum sei ita noluerint iu]dicare: Mo; *ad quem praetorem ita relatum erit iudicum plus tertiam partem negare iu]dicare*: CIL. Mattingly (1970, 159) replaces *ita* with *iterum*.

iu[dicio pronontiatum erit, singulis multa esto: Mo; *iu[dicare negarint ... singulis, quei iudicare negarint, multam dicito*: CIL; *iu[dicio, qui iudex deixerit, multam deicito*: Mattingly, (1970, 159).

Mattingly understood *amplius* in quotation marks – as what the *iudex* said, but in fact he seems to have said '*non liquet*' (see note on line 47 above). In any case the drafting on that view becomes confusing, viz, 'on every occasion in one trial a *iudex* has said *amplius* twice'. Suppose he said '*amplius*' three times, is that any worse than twice or is a second fine only applicable when he has said '*amplius*' four times? It is better to take *amplius bis* to mean 'more than twice', in spite of the apparent relevance of *amplius pronuntiare*. For large numbers of *ampliationes* cf. Livy 43.2.6; Cic. *Brut.* 86; Val.Max. 8.1.11.

quantum pequ[niae: Kl, Mo, CIL; *pequ[niae dixerit publice proscribito*: CIL.

XXIX (lines 49–52) Procedure for casting votes.

49 (E5, B49) R EIS: Peir, REIS: B, O, Vett, Borgh. VBEI: Peir, D, Scal, Br, O[1]; VBI: O[2], Vett, Borgh, Ha, Bo. ADEI: Peir, B; ADER: O, Borgh; APER; Vett.

De] reis -- ader[unt, causam sibi liquere dixerint: Mo, CIL.

Ṣ QVEI: aes. Only the top right corner of the S is now visible. The letter was, however, read by O and Vett. *praetor...iudice]s -- semovant[ur facito*: Mo, CIL. Kl had an elaborate restoration including those *iudices* previously rejected by the *patroni* in the case.

It is a little puzzling that, although those *iudices* who said '*non liquet*' are apparently here being kept apart from the vote on the verdict, we find later the legislator envisaging ballots *seine sufragio* (lines 54ff). A *iudex* of course may have been reluctant to cast a vote for public or private reasons but unwilling to prolong the trial, when nothing was going to make him decide one way or the other. Why then are those who said '*non liquet*' prevented from casting a blank vote? This is perhaps because the majority of any kind of ballot would determine the verdict (on the significance of *plurumae* in line 55 see Venturini (1979), 203ff) and the legislator, although he was prepared to accept some *seine sufragio*, did not want a majority with no vote.

50 (E6, F1, B50) Ṃ REM AGITO: Peir; *rem*: edd veter; ?*ea]m rem*. NEI Ẹ: Peir; NEI: B, O[2], Vett, Borgh; NE: O[1]; *nei de i[udicio iudex discedat curato*: Mo, CIL (erroneously incorporating letters in Bo and Br, which in fact belong to the following line). ẠM·V: aes (F1). The apex of F (in the position assigned by Mattingly (1969, 133–4) would have been located on my calculations about fifteen letter-spaces from the right-hand edge of E.

Pr. quei ex h.l. quaeret sitellam afferri iubeto longam digitos . . . latam digitos] XX: Kl; *sitellamque latam digitos...altam digitos] XX*: Mo, CIL.

1¼ Roman feet seems more likely to be the height of the water-jar used for allotment than its diameter.

CONIECIAN: aes, Vett, Borgh, O[2]; CONIECTAN: O[1]; *conieciant*: Kl, Mo, CIL; *apponi facito*: Mo, CIL.

For *ante tribunal suum poni*, cf. *Tabula Hebana* (EJ 94a), 18 and note Florence fragment B (*CIL* I[2], 596), 8, *in eo tribun[ali* in a context of allotment.

51 (E7, F2, B51) IO EIQVE IVDICIS: Peir; D EIQVE IVDICIS: B; QVE IVDICIS: O, Vett, Borgh; *eius]que iudicis*: Mo; *quoius]que iudicis*: CIL. Peir's IO seems likely to be TO ending a third person imperative.

III LA: Peir, O, Vett, Scal; IIII ea: D. P̣TAM ATI: aes (F2) (the bronze has broken along the curve of the initial P). *la[tam digitos ... ab utraque parte ceratam*: Mo, CIL (in a similar sense, Kl); *utrimque scri]ptam atr[amento ex altera parti leitera A, ex alte]ra parti C*: Mattingly (1969, 134), using F2 and compressing the bronze; *in qua sorticola ex altera parti littera A (scripta) siet, ex alte]ra parti C*: Mo, CIL.

dato a[lteramque, utram velit, litteram eum iudicem inducere iubeto: Mo,

CIL; . . .*delere, eamque sortem palam in eam sitellam conicere iubeto*: Mattingly, (1969, 134). *Delere* is perhaps better for erasure, cf. Florence fragment B (*CIL* I², 596), 9.

It is clear from the text of the B fragment that A and C were already on the *sorticola* when it was given to each judge, cf. the tablet used for trials in the assembly on the denarii of C.Coelius Caldus (Crawford, *RRC*, 437) with *L(ibero) D(amno)*. It is also evident from line 54 that the tablet could in the end be left without a vote. Mommsen, therefore, concluded that the tablets were wax, from which any letter could be easily removed, cf. Cic. *Div.Caec.* 24. However, Mattingly's restoration of the F fragment is attractive and it would be possible to blot out the unwanted letter, if written in ink.

52 (E8, F3, B52) EAMQVE: Peir, O, Vett, Borgh, Bo, Br; ẸAMQVE: Scal, D. LITIERAM: Peir, B; LITERAM: O, Vett, Borgh. COICITO D: aes (F3). *pala[m ad eam sitellam deferto, eamque sortem in populum. . .*: CIL (sim. Mo); *pala[m in eam sitellam] coicito D[*: Mattingly, 1969, 134, line 51.

SINGILATIM ỊV: aes; *singilatim*: O; *singilatim i*: Vett, Borgh; *singilatim iu[dices versus ostendito itaque eam sortem in eam sitellam coniecito*: Mo (sim. CIL); *iu[dices is praetor facito*: Mattingly.

Mommsen's restoration at the end of the B fragment is no longer attractive, if the tablet has already been cast into the jar. It is possible that the text here is dealing with the selection by lot of a *iudex* to draw the ballots from the jar. If so, it should probably be regarded as part of the following section.

On secret ballot in assemblies, also introduced in this period, see commentary on line 44.

XXX (lines 52–4) Procedure for examining votes.

52 (end of line) *[Sententiae quomodo pronontientur – quei iudex pronontiationis*: Mo, CIL (cf. their restoration in the next line).

53 (E9, F4, D1, B53) OLVNDAI CAVSA: Peir; CVNDA CAVSSA: Scal; CVNDA CAVSA: D, Bo, B; VNDAI CAVSA: O; VNDAE CAVSA: Vett, Borgh; *fac]iundae causa*: Mo, CIL. DEMITITO: Peir, D, Bo, O¹; DEMITTITO: O², Vett, Borgh, Scal; DEMITTO: Br. ẸT EAM: Peir (in fact the first E is an upright followed by the remains of two crossbars); ITEAM: B; TAM: O, Vett, Borgh. POPVL: Peir, B; POPVLO: O, Vett, Borgh, Kl; *popul[o ostendito*: Mo, CIL.

Since the reading CVNDA(I) could result from the misreading of a slanted L, there is no reason to doubt Peir's text. It seems most likely to represent *t]ol(l)undai*, though *s]olv(e)ndai* or *v]olv(e)ndai* are also possible. Cf. e.g. Lucilius 313M = 343W for *tolutim* and generally for single L where double L might be expected *ILLRP*, 511, 2 and 29, *ILLRP*, 517, 8 and 17. The noun with which *t]olundai* agreed is probably the *sors* with the vote of the *iudex*. There is room for SORTIS T] at the beginning of the line. The final O of *populo* probably stood in the texts from which, O, Vett, Borgh derive, to judge from their methods elsewhere.

VEI QVID Ẹ: aes (F4). ỴDICIV: aes (D1); *iudicium*: O, Vett, Borgh; Br, *i]udiciu[m*: Mo, CIL; VM SENTENTIA [. . .] VERIT IS EI: aes (B53); *m sententia . . .uerit in*: O[1]; *m sententia . . .uerit iu*: O[2], Vett; *eum sententiam*; Mo, CIL (with some doubt over the initial E). Hence *Tum ad id i]udicium [se convertito et ex ea sitella sortem unam educito quamque in eum r]eum sententiam [ea sors hab]uerit*: Mo, CIL; *ne quid l[ateat occultum quamque in id]iudicium sententia[m ea sors hab]uerit is ei [praetori*: Mattingly (1969).

Apart from his following Garrucci's reading of I, in place of E, at the right hand edge of F4, Mattingly's restoration depended on his compression of the tablet (on which see above, pp. 78–9) and on a combination of the text of the apex of D with that on the base of Bc. This involved conflating the last V on D with the first V on Bc.

[. . . palam pronontiato, ubei A littera scripta erit, 'absolvo', ubei C littera scripta erit con]: Mo, CIL in the lacuna at the right of the face.

54 (E10, F5, D2) DEMNO: edd veter (except miniscule version in D: *denuo*); *con]demno*: Kl, Mo, CIL. SVFRACIO: Scal, D, Br.
VE DEINCẸ: aes (F5); hence *iud[ici iudex]ve deinc[eps praetori] transdito*: Mattingly, 1969; *iud[ici . . .]u. transdito*: Mo; *iud[ici. . . in man]um transdito*: CIL. However the traces on the bronze in D2 are more consistent with *reddito* than *transdito*.

XXXI (lines 54–5) Acquittal of the defendant.

54 (D2, B54) DE I: aes, Mo, CIL apparatus; DE R: O, Vett, Borgh, Br; *De n[umerandis sententiis*: Mo, CIL. REO AP (B54): O, Vett, Borgh – hardly to be explained by the corrupt transfer of the text of B62 *lex agr.* to the *lex rep.* face, as Mo thought. *De reo ap[solvendo*: Mattingly, joining D2 and B54.

[De reo apsolvendo. (vac) Nisei eae sententiae ibei plurumae erunt 'condemno', pr. quei ex h.l. quaeret eum reum pronontiato non fecisse videri. Quem reum ita non fecisse pronontiatum erit (De quo reo pr. ita pronontiaverit), quod postea non fecerit: Mo, CIL; *Sei eae sententiae ibei plurumae erunt 'absolvo'*: Mattingly.

Mommsen's formulation must be preferred, since line 55 shows that a tie secured an acquittal, cf. Cic. *Clu.* 74; Sen. *Controv.* 3.7; Plut. *Cato mi.* 16.8, also Cic. *Fam.* 8.8.3 (where the praetor followed usual practice and was caught out by a special provision for the *litis aestumatio*).

Rudorff, 490 interpreted Asc. 55C as showing that under the *lex Pompeia* of 52 BC a majority was needed for acquittal, but the numbers in that text are insecure.

55 (E11) OD PRAEVARI. . .: Peir; QUOD PRAEVARICATIONIS: O, Vett, Borgh. EX omitted by D minuscule. EIVS: Scal, D maius, O, Vett, Borgh, Br, Bo. CVIVS: D minus. EIS: Bo[2]. APSOLVTVS: Peir, D, O, Vett, Borgh, Br, Bo; ABSOLVTVS: Scal. Rubric space noted by Peir, O, Vett, Borgh, D maius.

XXXII (line 55) Condemnation of the defendant.

55 (E11, F6, D3) CONDEMNANDO: Vett, Borgh; CONDEMNAN: Peir, O, B. SENTEN: aes (F6); ẸỊḄEI PLVRVMAE: aes (D3); *sei plurumae*: edd veter; *ex iudicum sententiis] sei plurumae*: Kl; *sei eae sententia]e ibei plurumae*: Mo, CIL; *sei eae] senten[tia]e ibei plurumae*: Mattingly. PR.Q: aes; *pr. qu*: O, Vett, Borgh; *pr. quei*: Br; *pr. qu[ei*: Kl; *pr. qu[ei ex hace lege quaeret eum reum pronontiato fecisse videri*: Mo, CIL.

Venturini (1979, 203ff) emphasises that *plurumae*, as opposed to *plures*, should mean more than either of the other two types of vote. Hence if twenty voted 'C', eighteen 'A' and twelve 'no vote', the defendant is condemned. The elimination of those who had claimed '*non liquet*' should have ensured that those *seine sufragio* would not be the largest group (see commentary on line 49 above).

XXXIII (lines 55–6) Restriction on further prosecutions of the same man for the same offence.

55 [*Quei ex h.l. condemnatus*]: Mo; [*De eadem re ne bis agatur* (vac) *Quei*, etc.]: CIL. Venturini (1979, 214) preferred *De eadem causa* but this seems inferior to Mommsen's suggestion, as it might allow prosecution for the same offence by someone else.

56 (E12, D4) /T APSOLVTVS: Peir; AVT APSOLVTVS: O, Vett, B; /VT APSOLVTVS: Borgh. H.L.: Peir, FI.L; Scal, D, Vett, Borgh; F.L.: O; EI.L: Br; FL.L: Bo.
POST PRAEFECERIT: Scal; CAVSSA: Scal, O, Vett, Borgh; CAVSA: D, Bo, Br.
AV: Peir, B; AVT: O, Vett, Borgh. [*nisei de leitibus*]: Kl, Mo, CIL.
NEI E: aes, Kl; *nei ex*: O, Vett, Borgh, Br; *nei es[to*: Mo, CIL. Perhaps in fact a redundant *ex h.l.* preceded *esto*.

A *sanctio* was an enforcement clause penalising disobedience to the law in question (cf. *Dig.* 48.19.41), such as we find in *frag.Tar.* 25–6: *Hoic legei fraudem nei quis [facito*; *lex de Delo* (*CIL* I[2],2500), 34–5; *lex Irnitana* (Gonzalez, 1986), XC, 11ff, and, most elaborately, in *lex prov.praet.* Delphi C15ff. The *sanctio* of the present law does not seem to have been preserved. A chapter occurs in lines 70–1 forbidding interference with, or delay to the procedure, but no penalty seems to have been attached at this point. Sherwin-White (1982, 24–5) has rightly argued that the elaborate penalties in the *sanctio* of *lex prov.praet.*, including loss of senatorial status, would not have found a place in this law. The *sanctio* would have more probably resembled the provision of *lex lat.Bant.* 7–13, which prescribes the imposition of a fine for infractions of procedure, which may be imposed by a magistrate or sued for in a civil action before *recuperatores*.

The reference in this line to *litis aestumatio* is surely to the *l.a.* of the case in question, which might otherwise have been regarded as a second action. Venturini's view (1979, 214), that a *l.a.* could be held more than once, if faulty, receives no support from the text in the following lines about the *l.a.* nor is it plausible in itself. The exception for *praevaricatio* (collusive prosecution) also occurs, in texts dealing with prosecutions before *recuperatores*, in *lex agr.* 38; *lex prov.praet.* Cnidos V.38; *lex genet.Urs.* cap. 123. Notice also *Tab.Heracl.* 120 for the ignominy of *quemve k(alumniae) praevaricationis caussa accusasse fecisseve quod iudicatum est erit*. For the present law's handling of *praevaricatio* see line 75 with commentary.

This chapter, strictly interpreted, forbids second actions against a defendant about any alleged offence(s) against the law committed up to the time of the trial, apart from the *litis aestumatio* and except where the first action was vitiated by *praevaricatio*. This strict interpretation has been strongly urged by Alexander (1982) and H.D. Meyer (1978) independently. They have consequently argued that Mommsen's suggestion of a rubric, *De eadem re ne bis agatur*, was unsound. There is no space for *de eadem re* at the appropriate point in the chapter itself; instead, the definition of charges which cannot be brought, is derived from the phrases *h.l.* and *nisei quod postea fecerit*: that is, a man could not be sued under the *repetundae* law for any relevant actions which had taken place before a previous trial for *repetundae*. Trials under this law would tend to cover a range of offences against various victims. The present provision should not be seen as the outcome of a sudden burst of sympathy in the legislator for the senatorial defendant, but as an attempt to encourage the accumulation of complaints against the same defendant in a single trial. This would have prevented the time of the court being wasted by repetitive hearings of parallel or related complaints and avoided possible objections by defendants that the *praeiudicium* of one trial was being carried over to the next.

There was in 51 BC, under the *lex Iulia* of 59, the curious case of M.Servilius, accused of *praevaricatio* in a *repetundae* case and subsequently accused as a principal offender in the same court (Cic. *Fam.* 8.8.3). Shackleton Bailey's explanation of this (commentary on *Ad Familiares, ad loc.*), that in the first case he was accused of receipt of money from a defendant and in the second of direct extortion itself, will not work, if the formulation of the relevant chapter of the *lex Iulia* was based on this one. It may be precisely because Servilius was regarded, in Caelius' words, as *neque damnatus neque absolutus* that he was retried. We may contrast the present provision with those in lines 73–5 and 79–82, where it appears from the size of the lacunae available for supplement that second actions against men accused under the previous *lex Calpurnia* and *lex Iunia* were only forbidden if the accused had been condemned. It is likely that the same rule applied to those condemned in a trial before an assembly but not to those acquitted there. We may compare the situation in reverse in 70 BC, when Cicero proposed to bring before an assembly during his aedileship, should Verres be acquitted, corrupt executions which he had already made part of the case *de repetundis* (*Verr.* 2.1.14).

Liebs (1967, 104ff), followed by Eder, 206 and Meyer (1978) has argued strongly that there was no general legal rule against trying a man twice for the same offence, whose formulation our present law was repeating. Alexander (1982), by contrast, sees some indirect evidence for the operation of such a rule in the late Republic. The earliest references apart from those in the present text, are in a papyrus of 10 BC (*P.Lond.*, 354), which may reflect Greco-Egyptian practice. From Quint. 7.6.4: *solet et illud quaeri, quo referatur, quod scriptum est: bis de eadem re ne sit actio: id est, hoc 'bis' ad actorem an ad actionem*, it can be inferred that there was a written text of some sort at the time – perhaps from the *lex Iulia de iudiciis privatis*, cf. *Dig*. 48.2.7.2; 43.29.3.13. In the private law of Gaius' day one could not sue twice on the same matter *in personam*, according to the *ius legitimum*: other limitations had to be created by an *exceptio* produced by the praetor (Gai. 4.98 and 100ff). However, Gaius thinks that a general ban on second actions was part of the old regime of the *legis actiones*, and this may be correct.

The safest conclusion is that, although second actions on the same issue were prevented by one means or another in private actions at the time of the *lex rep.*, there was not yet any general rule of this kind regarding crimes or delicts against administrative regulations. The vital concepts here are *praevaricatio* and *calumnia*. The existence of the concept of *praevaricatio* shows that a prior acquittal did furnish worthwhile protection to the defendant, but this may have been simply *de facto*, because it would have been a powerful argument in any subsequent case, provided that the collusion itself was not revealed. In practice an accuser charging a man with an offence of which he had already been acquitted might have found it expedient to allege *praevaricatio*, even if this was not a legal requirement for the re-opening of the case. On the other hand, the man acquitted already could threaten his accuser with the charge of *calumnia*, vexatious accusation, even if second accusations were not formally forbidden.

XXXIV (Lines 56–8) Taking security from a condemned man.

57 (E13, D5) M QVEI: Peir, B; EVM QVEI: O, Vett, Borgh.

AEDES: aes; *praedes*: O, Vett, Borgh, Br; *cens[uerint sei ita p]raedes*: Mo, CIL.

CONO: aes; *conq*: O, Vett, Borgh, Br; *conq[uaerantur veneant*: Mo, CIL.

[*Sei ea bona venierint, quantae pequniae venierint, tantam pequniam ab eo emptore . . . ioudex, quei eam rem quaesierit, exigito quaestorique eam pequniam et quanta fuerit*]: Mo, CIL. This gives the right general sense and fills about half the space available.

58 (E14) IPTVM: Peir; RIPTVM: Scal, D, Br; SCRIPTVM: O, Vett, Borgh, Bo. TRANSPITO: Bo, Br. QVASTOR: Br; QVESTOR: Bo[2]. POBLICEIS: B; POPLICEIS: O, Borgh, Vett.

For *praedes* given by condemned men see Clusium fragment A (*CIL* I[2], 597), 3; Cic. *Rab.Post.* 8: *sunt lites aestumatae A. Gabinio, nec praedes dati nec ex bonis populo universae [lites solutae]*, cf. Cic. *Rab.Post.* 37: *si aut praedes dedisset Gabinius aut tantum ex eius bonis quanta summa litium populus recepisset.* and *lex lat.Bant.* 11: *Sei condemnatus [erit, quanti condemnatus erit, praedes] ad quaestorem urbanum det, aut bona eius poplice possideantur*, for the alternative of seizure and sale of property.

For the use of majority decisions to decide on valuation in the *litis aestumatio* cf. Cic. *Fam.* 8.8.3: *quod eorum iudicum maior pars iudicarit, id ius ratumque esto* (the clause in chapter 101 of the *lex Iulia* which confused Iuventius Laterensis).

Contra Sherwin-White (1982, 26), there is no reason to think the present chapter misplaced. Once a defendant was convicted, it was essential to secure guarantors or property, in case he absconded. The threat of seizure would have led most convicted men to have provided guarantors, if they could. When seizure occurred, only sufficient property to cover twice the maximum damages alleged may have been sold, not the entire estate. The active role of the magistrate in taking sureties and distributing money obtained makes a contrast with normal civil procedure, but seems to be paralleled in some civil suits on public matters heard by *recuperatores* (see above, p. 30).

XXXV (lines 58–9) The assessment of damages

58 (E14, D6) LEITIBUS: Peir, Scal, O, Vett, Borgh; LITIBUS: D, Bo, Br. *Aestimandeis*: D minus. CI LEGE: aes; ACI *f(ortasse) hace*: O[1]; ACI: O[2], Br; ACE: Vett, Borgh; IACI: Mo; *si quis ex*] *hace*: Kl; *quei ex*] *hace*: Mo, CIL.

LEGẸP̣Ẹ: aes (a truncated downstroke and the lower right-angle are all that survive of the last two letters); *lege*: edd veter; *lege pe[qunia capta coacta ablata avorsave reddenda erit*: Kl; *lege peti*[*tio erit, ad eundem praetorem, quei ex hace lege de ea re quaesiverit, deferto, isque praetor eosdem ioudices, quei eam rem ioudicaverit, eas leites aestumare iubeto*: Mo; *peti[tio erit, id praetor, quei eam rem quaesierit, eos iudices, quei eam rem iudicaverint, aestumare iubeto*: CIL.

It is not clear how Mommsen managed to see traces of the first TI in *petitio*. However, on balance his restoration seems more convincing than Klenze's.

[*id, leitibus singulis aestumatis, iudices quei ex hace lege lectei erunt, in certam summam redigunto, ita tamen utei aestumetur quod ante hanc legem rogatam convincitur captum coactum*]; Kl; [*quod ante h.l. rogatam consilio probabitur captum coactum*]: Mo, CIL.

59 (E15, D7) ATVM: Peir; LATVM: Scal, D, Bo, O, Vett, Borgh; ABLATVM: Br. EA RES: edd veter (except O[1] – *eas*). SIMILI: Vett; SIMPLICI: D minus. CAETERAS: Bo.

QVOS: edd veter. CO: Peir, Scal, D, O, Vett, Borgh; CE: Bo, Br. R CAPTVM: aes; edd veteṛ. *co[nvincitu]r*: Kl; *co[nsilio probabit]ur*: Mo, CIL.

I find it hard to imagine how a V was visible at the left-hand edge of D7 in the nineteenth century, as only half the R is preserved now. Mommsen's restoration is a little too long for the lacuna, which in this section can be calculated with near certainty, as we can determine the position of the margin of the bronze and the left-hand edge of D is fixed relative to this in view of some inescapable restorations below on this face and on the agrarian face.

QVẠ (the bottom of the left-hand stroke of the A survives): aes; *qu*: edd veter; *qu[aestorem, quoi aerarium provincia obvenerit, redigunto*: Kl; *qua[estorem, quantum siet, quoiusque nomine ea lis aestumata siet, facito deferatur*: CIL (sim. Mo).

The distinction in the rates of restoration required for offences committed before and after this law is generally thought to imply that the *leges Calpurnia* and *Iunia* only prescribed simple restoration and the present legislator did not wish to increase penalties retrospectively. It is the only good evidence for the penalties under the previous *repetundae* laws. *Legis actiones sacramento* (cf. line 23) could be in principle *dupli* or *quadrupli*. The argument based on conflating the *lex Calp. de repetundis* with the *lex Calp. de condictione* (Gaius 4.19) is unsound. See Mommsen, *Strafr.* 727–8; Strachan-Davidson, 1912, II.5; Sherwin-White, 1949, 6. Note, however, that in other respects *lex rep.* was retrospectively applicable to offences committed before it was passed, provided that they had not led to a condemnation under the previous laws (lines 73–5, 80–2).

XXXVI (lines 59–61) Payment of damages to injured parties or their representatives, when adequate funds are available.

59 [*De pequnia ex aerario solvenda.* (vac) *Quei iudici, quei eam rem quaesierit, consilioque eius maiorei parti satis fecerit nomine*]: Mo, CIL, refining a suggestion of Klenze.

60 (E16, D8) O PARENTISVE: B; PARENTISVE: Peir, O, Vett; PARETISVE: Borgh. LEITEM: B; LITEM: O, Vett, Borgh. EIEI IVDICEI: D maius, Br, O, Vett, Borgh; EI IVDICEI: Scal, Bo; *iudiciei*: D minus. CONCILIOQ: Bo².

MAIOREI: Scal, D, O, Vett; MAIORI: Peir, Borgh, Br, Bo. PA: Peir, O, Vett, Borgh (not in B). TIS FECERIT: aes, Br; VIS FECERIT; O, Vett, Borgh; *pa[rti sa]tis fecerit*: Kl; *pa[rti eorum sa]tis fecerit*; Mo, CIL (but the gap seems too small for this).

I have not emended *ceivisve* to *ceivitatisve*, as Mommsen did, since *populus* can cover cities and other communities and the possibility of an individual acting as a representative of a fellow-citizen is likely to have been envisaged by a legislator, see also commentary on line 4. Cf. Clusium fragment A (*CIL* I², 597), 7–8 for what may be part of a similar clause, including *quoi*]*ve ipse parens sit*.

Q[uom eo amplius de ea re actio ne esto: Kl; *q[uanta ea pequnia erit, is iudex facito ... sei de ea re praedes datae erunt, seive quantae pequniae eae lites aestumatae erunt, tanta pequnia ex*]: Mo, CIL. For my *iudex quei eam rem quaesierit, queive iudex ex hace lege factus erit*, cf. line 62.

Given that the money had to be paid to the victims in three days, one must assume that it had already been collected, either from *praedes* or the sale of property. There is room in the lacuna here for a restoration similar to that proposed in line 63, referring to this. So the distinction in Mommsen's restoration between *praedes* and money in the treasury seems inappropriate. He argued that the provision of *praedes* counted legally as payment. Yet this would not necessarily have meant that money was available.

61 (E17, D9) ACE LEGE: Peir; IACE LEGE: Bo; HACE LEGE: O, Vett, Borgh, Scal, D (in the last two the left-hand upright of the H is missing).

PROXSVMO: Scal, Bo, O, Vett, Borgh; PROXVMO: D, Br.

satis [fecerit]: Kl; *satis [factum erit*]: Mo, CIL; perhaps *satis [pequnia erit*]; *satis [datum erit*] is less likely as that would only entail sufficient security, not ready cash.

DOLO: aes; DOLO M: O, Vett, Borgh (O[1] has ALO in margin); *dolo malo*: Br; *dolo m[alo, quo minus in triduo proxsumo, quo ita satis fecerit, solvatur*: Kl; *dolo m[alo, quo minus ita satis fiat itaque solvatur*: Mo, CIL.

The *iudex* in this line must be the same man as the *iudex quei eam rem quaesierit queive iudex ex hace lege fac[tus erit*, found in line 62 (D10) and therefore restored by me in line 60 and later in this line. Since he is named before the quaestor and supervises payments, he must be the magistrate presiding over the court and not a member of the jury delegated to handle the *litis aestumatio*. *Iudex ... quaesierit* is the magistrate who actually investigated the case in question, *queive ... factus erit* is any magistrate who takes over the presidency of the court and has to handle the compensation of injured parties.

XXXVIII (lines 61–3) Announcement of a distribution in cases where funds are inadequate for complete payment.

61 *[De tributo indicendo.* (vac) *Quanti iudex quei eam rem quaesierit lites aestumaverit, sei is iudex]* : Mo, CIL.

The supplement was made presumably on the basis of line 68, '*quis praetor litis aestumaverit*'. However, this last phrase seems to be equivalent to 'who presided over the *litis aestumatio*'. More precisely, it is the jury with the president who estimate damages by a majority vote, not the president himself, cf. lines 57 and 60 above, Cic. *Clu.* 116; *Fam.* 8.8.3; *Rab.Post. passim*.

62 (E18, D10) EX EX HACE: Scal, D maius, Br; X EX HACE: Peir; EX HACE: O[1], Vett, Borgh, Bo, D minus; EX HAC: O[2]. POSTVERIT: Bo[2]. PROXSVMEIS: Scal, O[2], Bo; PROXVMEIS: D, Br, O[1], Vett, Borgh. QVIBVS O: Vett; QVIBVS: Peir, B, O, Borgh; *quibus [si potu]erit*: Kl; *quibus [quae potu]erit*: Mo, CIL.

Mommsen's restoration of *iud]ex* before *ex hace* is attractive at first sight. However, when the fragment is drawn, there does not seem to be room enough for the word *iudex* at the beginning of the line and, as can be judged from the C fragment below, new lines of the inscription begin with a complete word. EX EX may therefore have been a dittography. Another possibility is that the first letter E in Scal, D and Br is a conjecture or a misreading of a poorly preserved letter and that what stood on the bronze was a numeral, e.g. LX, qualifying a putative *diebus* at the end of the previous line: in this case the legislator would have been providing a time-limit for attempts by the president of the court to assemble the sum required to pay the injured parties in full.

> FAC: aes, edd veter; *fac[tus erit, tributum indeicito ... diemque edito, qua is, quoius parentisve quoius eiusve, quoi ipse parensve suos heres siet, lites*: Mo, CIL.

This restoration is not easily intelligible and it is preferable to include a phrase anticipating the reference to the *legati* of a king or people in the next line. Mommsen avoided this by assuming that *aut* had been omitted after *erunt* at the beginning of line 63, thus making the clause ending *aest]umatae erunt* parallel to that ending *aestumata erit*, but this is a dubious assumption. The distribution (*tributus*) must be restored, since the following chapters (XXXVIII–XXXIX), which mention it, develop the provisions of this chapter. The word itself first appears complete in line 66. In the Latin of this period *tributus* appears elsewhere only in its usual sense of a contribution or tribute in money (Cato, ap. Nonius 229; Plaut. *Epid.* 22). It appears in the present sense in *Dig.* 14.4, where through the *actio tributoria* the *peculium* of a slave is distributed among creditors. Note also the *fru]me[ntarios et n]umma[rio]s t[ributus]* in Augustus' *Res Gestae* 18 (the restoration is guaranteed by the Greek), where *tributus* does seem to mean distribution, although it was translated into Greek as σύνταξις.

63 (E19) VMATAE: Peir; IMATAE: Scal, D, Bo; AESTVMATAE: O, Vett, Borgh; AESTIMATAE: Br. Peir shows an oblique stroke at the edge of the fragment, recorded as I by copyists of the B group. *Aestumatae* must be a restoration.

QVO SVI REGIS: Bo. POPVLEIVE: O, Vett, Borgh, Bo², suprascript correction in Scal; POPVLOVE: Scal, D, Br; POPVLIVE: Bo; O¹ *in rasura. Populove* may in fact have been erroneously engraved on the bronze.

LEGATEI: Peir, O, Vett, Borgh; LEGATI: B. ADESSENT: Peir, O, Vett, Borgh; ADDESSINT: Scal, D; ADESSINT: Bo, Br, accepted by Mo, CIL.

Mommsen argued that the old form of the future is appropriate here, not the imperfect subjunctive. This should be what the legislator wrote, though not necessarily what the engraver inscribed.

XXVIII (lines 63–4) The distribution of the sum realised.

63 (D11) VTO: aes, edd veter; *sol]uto*: Kl; *De tempore a iudice stat]uto*: Rud (mistakenly trying to expand rubric to fill larger lacuna); *De trib]uto*: Mo, CIL.

Tributus has the sense of a proper allocation, hence it is something to be preserved (*servando*).

QVEI E: aes (last E not visible in photograph); *quei*: edd veter; *que[i*: Kl; *quei e[am rem quaesierit queive iudex ex hace lege factus erit, quanta pequnia de eius, quei ex hace lege condemnatus est, bonis redacta erit, tantam pequniam in eas lites, quae aestumatae erunt, pro portioni tribuito. Queique ei iudici consilioque eius maiori parti eam litem aestumatam esse sibi satis] fecerit*: Mo, CIL.

Mommsen's restoration, partly based on lines 60 and 62, is clearly right in essentials and my own is merely an expansion, which takes account of the two alternative sources of money. Proportionate sharing is *a priori* probable and found in the *actio tributoria*. For the phrase *pro portioni*, cf. *Tab.Heracl.* 38 (attribution of cost of building a road); Gaius 2.155; Cic. *Verr.* 5.55; *Flacc.* 32 (also demands for money). Another possibility is *pro rata (portioni)*, see *Dig.* 14.4.5.10 and 19; 36.1.77; 38.2.34.

64 (E20) ECERIT: Peir; EGERIT: B; FECERIT: O, Vett, Borgh. The difference between C and G on the bronze is often minimal and the fact that EGERIT is a Latin word no doubt influenced the source of the B group.

QVOQVE DEI: Bo[2]. D minus omits *eis*. FRVDE: Scal, D, Br; FRAVDE: O, Vett, Bo; FRADE: Borgh; *fraude*: Kl, Mo; *fr⟨a⟩ude*: CIL.

XXXIX (lines 64–6) The retention of money for injured parties not present at the distribution. Publicity for the distribution.

64 (D12) *quantum] in aerario*: Kl; *quei aberit, eius portio]*: Rud, expanding the rubric to fill a supposedly greater lacuna; *reliquom]*: Mo, CIL; *pequnia*: scripsi (this is how the sum is referred to in lines 66 and 67).

Quod eorum nomine tributus factus [erit, quaestor in aerario servato: Mo, CIL.

Mommsen apparently made a suppressed antecedent to *quod* the object of *servato*, but this involves a false concord between *quod* and *tributus*. Alternatively *quod* may be understood absolutely, in the sense of 'as far as'.

Mommsen supplied a new rubric, *De tributo proscribendo*, at the end of this line. He clearly believed that the provisions for publicity in lines 64–6 applied to the distributions of money by *tributus* in lines 63–4. On this point he was very probably right. However, it seems to me likely that in the long lacuna over the second half of this line provision was made for supplementary distributions to plaintiffs originally absent. In that case the clauses in lines 65–6 would have applied to all distributions by *tributus*, whether primary or supplementary.

65 (E21, D13) VE PRAETOR EX (the E of PRAETOR suprascript): Peir; 'ERO caret mark R EX: Scal, D; VERO A.R.: Bo; VERO REX: Br; PRAETOR EX: O[2], second hand in O[1].

It seems that VE PRATOR was visible, when the *ecmagma plumbeum* of E was made for Henri de Mesmes, at the left edge of the fragment, where it almost joins C. The deterioration of the bronze then produced the reading RO and a caret mark, which was in turn corrupted into an A in Bo. O's *praetor* seems to have been a pure restoration. It is significant that O[1]'s text began originally *ex h.l.*, while Vett, who was perhaps the source of O's copy, recorded nothing before *ex hace lege*. It is likely that, once the money for absent plaintiffs was deposited in the treasury, either the quaestor in charge there or the praetor presiding over the *quaestio* was permitted to initiate supplementary distributions at suitable intervals. Hence my restoration in lines 64–5.

CAVSSA PRODEIXERIT: Peir, D; CAVSSA PRODVXERIT: Scal; CAVSA PRODEIXERIT: Bo, Br, O, Vett, Borgh. PRODE: edd veter; IORE: aes, edd veter, AIORE: Mo; *prode[ixerit ma]iore*: Kl; *prode[ixerit eodem modo eam diem m]aiore*: Rud; *prode[ixerit ea omnia m]aiore*: Mo, CIL.

Mo's restoration is a little too short and we need a reference to the means of publication in conjunction with *ubei de plano* . . ., cf. *frag.Tar.* 14 and see below.

In D14 the E of ERIT has a very short bottom crossbar and there is a scar at the base of the F of FORVM. Hence CIL read the bronze as FRIT and EORVM.

At the end of this line begins the lower half of D (Dbc), of which we have a good copy by Pighius as well as those of Orsini and Vettori to supplement the worn bronze.

PLANO R: aes, Mo, CIL; PLANO: Pigh; PLAN: O, Vett. *plano l[egi recte possitur*: Kl (but the final trace cannot be of an L). *proscriptum propositumque habeto*: Kl; *proscripta propositaque habeat*: Mo, CIL. [. . . *praetor, quei eum tributum*]: Mo, CIL.

Cf. *Tab.Heracl.* 15ff for an *album in tabula propositum* and the provision, *idque (album) aput forum . . . maiorem partem diei propositum habeto*, combined with *unde de plano*, etc. For *proscripta propositaque apud forum*, cf. line 38 and *frag.Tar.* 24.

66 (C1, E22) FECERIT ḌỊẸṢ: aes (C) (only the bottom corner of this E and a trace of the bottom of S are preserved); FECERIT DI: O[2]; FECERIT LH: O[1]. VMOS: edd veter; *fecerit di[es . . . prox]umos*: Kl; *die[s*: Mo, CIL.

LECI: Scal. *proscri[bito]*: Mo, CIL.

In this chapter the law provides for prior advertisement of a distribution in line 65 (*ad eam diem, donec solutum erit*) and subsequent publication of the money actually paid out in line 66 (*ex ea die, qua tributus factus erit*). Both were measures against corruption (whether in private interest or that of the treasury) but also an insurance for the praetor and quaestor concerned against possible charges that they had dealt improperly with the sums realised from the condemnation. Prior advertisement suggests perhaps that it is not only a matter of distributing a preserved portion to a plaintiff who has at last come to Rome, but other recently collected money to any plaintiff who had not received his full share.

XL (lines 66–7) Unclaimed money to become public property after five years.

66 (D14) *(vac) Pequnia] post*: Mo, CIL (Kl did not restore this as a rubric).
ANNEIS QY: aes (the left-hand stroke of V is just visible); *anneis*: O; *annis*: Vett; ANN F: Pigh; *anneis* Q: Kl; *anneis qu[inque proxumeis ex ea die, qua tributus factus erit, eius pequniae quaestor ex hace lege non solverit, populei esto. (vac)*: Mo, CIL.

My reservation about restoring *quinque* is that apart from *unus* the law tends to use Roman numerals for cardinal numbers. What may have stood here is *in anneis qu[ibus posita erit V proxsumeis* (cf. line 68).

For the mood of *fiet* see commentary on line 25.

[De pequnia a praedibus a praedibus exigenda. (vac) *Sei ex h.l. praedes datei erunt, quaestor, quei eos praedes acceperit, queive deinceps]*: Mo, CIL; *Quei ex h.l. praedes datei erunt, q.quoi aerarium provincia obvenerit, queique deinceps]*: Rud.

67 (C2, E23, D15) EANDEM PROVIN: aes; *eandem provin*: O; AM HABEBIT: edd veter; *provinciam*: Kl, Mo, CIL.
AB EIS PR: edd veter (P.R.: Bo); QVE DIE: aes, edd veter; *ab eis pr.[quei ex h.l. quaeret facito utei primo quo]que die*: Kl (too long and nonsensical after *faciunto*); *ab eis pr[aedibus primo quo]que die*: Mo, CIL.

For the selling of *praedes* see Cic. *Phil.* 2.78 (cf. Rud, 508). Mommsen took the clause in lines 66–7 to be a general instruction to the quaestors in charge of the treasury to ensure that money was collected from *praedes* – one which, like that in the following chapter, applied however the money was later distributed. Money should normally have been secured from *praedes* within a comparatively short period after the conclusion of the *litis aestumatio*. If they did not voluntarily provide the money necessary, then the quaestor would have had recourse to *bonorum possessio* against them. This action may indeed have been provided for in the last two-thirds of line 57. (Mommsen pointed out that technically the condemned man was no longer bound to pay himself, after *praedes* had been given.) However, the question remains, why the legislator returned to this point here. In my view the present clause relating to *praedes* may have followed an instruction that not only the money actually collected by the quaestors but also any money due, but as yet uncollected, was now the property of the *populus Romanus* and attempts to exact it should not cease (cf. Plut. *Cato mi.* 17.2 for the pursuit of long-standing public debts). Mommsen also thought that under this law the *populus* was made liable for payment to plaintiffs, even when the appropriate sums had not been collected, and that this clause was an attempt to ensure that public losses would be recouped. However, the whole point of the *tributus* procedure was to deal with cases where inadequate sums had been collected. It would have been odd if this only applied after the sale of property and not when money was being collected from guarantors. Nor is there anything in the text (see especially lines 61–3) to suggest that the treasury was expected to cover the failure of *praedes*.

XLI (lines 67–9) The sealing of receipts in strong-boxes.

67 (D15) F̣ISCIS: aes; *fiscis*: O; *tiscis*: Pigh.

AD O: aes; AI: O[1]; AD: O[2], Vett; AD Q: Pigh; *ad q[uaestorem redacta erit*: Kl, Mo, CIL; *is quaestor ea pequnia facito in fiscis siet ... fiscique signo suo opsignentur singulisque fiscis inscribatur*]: Mo, CIL.

It appears from the following line that we are dealing with the identification of moneys extracted from different sources in differing years of magistracy. *Fisci* must not contain sums collected from different sources or by different magistrates. A reference to the defendant in question should probably be supplied in the lacuna in this line, since the actual source of the money (mentioned in line 68) might have been a *praes*. The attempt to see the money mentioned here as that produced by the procedure *quo ea pequnia pervenerit* (Mattingly, 1970, 162–3) must be rejected (see Sherwin-White, 1972, 90–1). There is no contrast with money deposited in the *aerarium*, merely an instruction about how that money should be handled. Nor is there room for provisions for the *quo ea pequnia pervenerit* procedure, which was a further hearing, in the lacunae in lines 59–61.

68 (C3, E24, D16) Aes (C3) has QVIS PRAETOR LITIS AE followed by the lowest stroke of an S: Peir shows the top of an S followed by TVMAVERIT; STVMAVERIT: B; *aestumaverit*: O, Vett, Borgh (O did not realise the join between C and E here. The text he received probably contained already the restoration *aestumaverit*.) REDACTE: Bo.

QVI QVOM: Peir, O, Vett, Borgh; QVEI QVOM: B; ECTE FACTVM: aes, O, Vett, Borgh; *recte*: Br, Kl, Mo, CIL. *Quei quom[que aerarium provinciam optinebit utei quod] recte*: Kl (too long for the lacuna); *quei quom[que erit, utei quod]*: Mo, CIL.

obvenerit, [fisci resignentur et, sei ea pequnia, quam in eo fisco esse inscriptum erit, ibei inventa erit, denuo opsignentur. (vac) Quaestor utei solvat. (vac) Quod]: Mo, CIL.

This is the first time in the surviving text that the quaestor involved is identified as being in charge of the treasury, though it is implicit from line 57 onwards. For the phrase describing this, cf. lines 69, 72, 79–80, and *lex agr.* 46. For actions required (in these cases oaths) within five or ten days of entering office, cf. *lex prov.praet. Delphi* C12; *lex lat.Bant.* 23.

Any treasury quaestor is presumably required here to take over custody of the *fisci* and check that their contents tally with the amount written on them. So far, then, Mommsen's restoration in the second half of the line gives the right sense. There follows in lines 68–9 a provision about payment *extra ordinem* where the quaestor is bound by instructions from the praetor. Mommsen restored a new rubric, *Quaestor utei solvat*, and thus seems to have understood the clause as a general instruction, which would have overlapped the orders to pay in lines 61 and 64. However, the phrase *extra ordinem* implies a procedure apart from the regular payments made either as soon as the correct sum became available (line 61) or after the *tributus* (line 64). Rudorff (p. 510), thought that the clause allowed payment before the regular time, but that would have contradicted lines 61–4. One may perhaps conjecture that, while the praetor in charge of the court and the treasury quaestor were required to hold from time to time further distributions, if money remained uncollected or became newly available after a *tributus*, those to whom their full damages were due but who had simply failed to collect them, could apply to the president of the court for the money at any time within the five-year limit and he would instruct the quaestor to make payment.

69 (C4, E25, D17) PEQVLATVM: edd veter, corrected by Kl. P.R.: Bo, Br. QVEI: B, Vett; QVI: O, Borgh. DAREI: Scal, D, O, Vett, Borgh; DARET: Bo, Br. SOLVEI: Scal. IVSERIT: Scal, Vett, Borgh; IVS ERIT: D, Bo, Br, O.
QVAESTO: Peir; QVAESTOP: Scal, Br; QVAESTOR: D, Bo, O, Vett, Borgh. VINCIAM: aes, O, Vett, Borgh; *provinciam*: Br; *quaestor[qui quomque aerarium vel urbanam pro]vinciam*: Kl; *[qui aerarium pro]vinciam*: Mo, CIL, correctly in view of the size of the lacuna.

If we read *ius erit* with Orsini and some MSS of the B group, the clause will mean that the quaestor is required to pay to the praetor money which it is lawful to pay him, presumably a grant for expenses. This is not impossible and in some ways attractive in view of *sine malo pequlatu*, but it is out of context here and would require a clause justifying the praetor in claiming these expenses, for which there is not enough space in line 68.

For *sine malo pequlatu*, cf. *lex Corn. XX quaest.* 1.4–5. For payments *extra ordinem*, cf. Cic. *Font.* 4: '*Quibus in terris gestum negotium est? Illo, illo, inquam, loco, quem videtis. Extra ordinemne pecunia est data? Immo vero nummus nullus sine litteris multis commotus est*' (referring to Fonteius' conduct as *quaestor urbanus*).

XLII (line 69) No delay by the quaestor.

(D17) Q: aes (not seen by edd veter). There is apparently a space following this, but the bronze is very rough. Q[uaestor: Kl, Mo, CIL. Perhaps Q(uaestor).

This chapter may be connected with the payments mentioned in the immediately preceding chapters. Alternatively, it may be more general and associated with the chapter forbidding other kinds of obstruction which follows.

XLIII (lines 69–72) No obstruction to the trial by magistrates or promagistrates.

69 [*Ne quis iudicio inpedimentum faciat.* (vac) Quod]: Kl; [*Iudicium ne quis inpediat.* (vac) *Quod*]: Mo, CIL.

70 (C5, E26, D18) The first I and V of IVDICIUM have been merged on the bronze into N, the third I is very faint.

FIEI: aes; FIET: O[1]; FIER: O[2]; RI OPORTEBIT: Peir, B; OPORTEBIT: O, Vett, Borgh. For QVOM Scal has Q crossed out followed by CVM.

ḌỊ: aes(Da); EE: Kl; ẸỊY with an interpunct between E and I: Mo (but he made no attempt to incorporate this in his restoration).

MINVS SETIVSVE: aes, O[1], Pigh; MIIIVS SEIIVSVE: O[2]; *ve setiusve*: Vett. *prove[quo inperio potestatev]e e[rit facito quo] minus*: Kl, Mo, CIL, following *lex Rubr.Gall.* XX, 50, but there is no room for either *potestate* or *facito*.

A variety of similar phrases are found elsewhere: *lex agr.* 10, *neive pro magistratu inpe]riove sententia(m) deicito neive ferto*; *ibid.* 87, *mag prove mag queive pro eo inperio iudicio [potestate erit*; *lex genet.Urs.*, cap. 94, *neive quis pro eo inper(io) potestat(e)ve facito*. See also *lex agr.* 30, *lex Corn. XX quaest.* II, 32 for *mag prove mag* and for the whole phrase *lex prov.praet.* Delphi C24ff: *μήτε τις ἄρχων μήτε ἀντάρχων ποιείτω, ὧι ἔλασσον κριθῇ, μήτε κωλυέτω, ὧι ἔλασσον ταῦτα τὰ χρήματα εἰς ἀμφισβήτησιν γένηται κὰι ἀπαιτηθῇ καὶ κριτήριον γένη[ται καὶ] ἀποκατασταθῇ τὰ χρήματα.*

EVM QVE: aes, Pigh; EVM QVI: O, Vett; *eum que[i iudex eam rem quaeret, neive eos quei iudices patronive testesve in eam rem ex h.l. erunt, neive eum quei ex h.l. petet eumve unde petetur, quo die in iudicium adesse iussi erunt avocato neive]*: Kl; *eum que[i ex hace lege iudicabit neive eum quei petet neive eum unde petetur(neive eum quei in eam rem patronus testisve erit) ... ab eo iudicio avocato neive]*: Mo, CIL, rephrasing the supplement of Kl.

These proposals must give the right sense. The effect of this clause is to prevent not only obstruction and delay to the proceedings but also the use of appeal to the tribunes against alleged defects in the procedure. Rudorff (511–12) argued that it was not directed against tribunes because there is no specific mention of *intercessio* in the preserved part of the text, but the actions of tribunes are covered by the phraseology there and there is no sign of an exception clause. The example of tribunician intervention cited by Rudorff, Cic. *Clu.* 74, shows a tribune stopping a private case in order to get Staienus, who was either the defendant or his *patronus* there, to join the jury in a *quaestio*. This is consistent with a ban on similar intervention in the *quaestio* itself.

In general, appeal to the tribunes or *provocatio* seem to have been impossible in trials before *quaestiones perpetuae*, cf. Cic. *Phil.* 1.21ff for M.Antonius' proposal to permit *provocatio ad populum* to those condemned *de vi* or *de maiestate* and see Cic. *Vat.* 33–4 for the one known occasion of appeal to tribunes in a *quaestio* – Vatinius' unsuccessful attempt to block his trial under the *lex Licinia Iunia*, where he may have tried to exploit a loophole in the drafting of this law, which was not primarily judiciary. A general clause forbidding magistrates and judges impeding the judicial procedure laid down by the law is found in *lex lat.Bant.* 7ff, cf. *lex prov.praet.* quoted above for a similar clause preventing intervention to stop trials before *recuperatores* which that law used as a sanction. It is interesting that there is no evidence for a penal sanction against intervention here as in *lex lat.Bant.* However, there must have been a general *sanctio* or enforcement clause later in the law, see line 56 and the commentary on it.

71 (C6, E27, D19) AVOCARIER IVBETO NEIVE AB: aes (C) (only the bottom left hand corner of the B is preserved); ≃ AL: O; DVCITO: Peir, O, Vett, Borgh, D, Bo; OVCITO: Scal, Br; *abducito*: Kl, Mo, CIL. ADDUCIER: Scal.

VERBA: aes, O, Pigh, Kl; O VERBA: Mo, CIL. *poss[it quove quoi eorum minus in eo iudicio verba deicere]*: Kl; *poss[it quove quoi eorum minus in eo iudici]o*: Mo, CIL. I could see no trace of Mommsen's O on the bronze. Nor is there room for his supplement. He may have seen the upper part of the s of *minus*.

SENATV: aes; *senatus*: O, Pigh (Vett has *neive eum quei* here in error); *nisei quom senatu[s ioure vocabitur ... aut nisei quom centuriae (intro vocabuntur) aut (nisei quom)]*: Mo, CIL, simplifying a much more elaborate but unconvincing restoration by Kl.

This chapter provides that no magistrate shall obstruct or delay the proceedings of the *quaestio*, except as a result of meetings of the senate (cf. Cic. *Fam.* 8.8.5; Dio 55.3.2), which, in this period at least, the president of the court was required to attend, formal meetings of the centuriate and tribal assemblies and perhaps other public occasions, whose description does not survive. For the phrase *intro vocare*, cf. Livy 10.13.11: '*populus nihilo minus suffragia inibat et, ut quaeque intro vocata erat centuria, consulem haud dubie Fabium dicebat*'. In the case of the tribal assemblies the phrase would have originally meant 'summon to the *comitium*', but by now, probably since 145 BC, the tribes' voting took place in the open space of the forum itself, probably near the temple of Castor (Varro, *RR* 1.2.9; Cic. *Amic.* 96; cf. the oath in *lex lat.Bant.* 17 and see Coarelli, 1985, 11ff and 163ff; and Taylor, 1966, 21ff).

The rules regarding *avocatio* were set out by Valerius Messala (*cos.* 53 BC) (Gell. 13.16.1) in his book on auspices. A consul could normally call away either a *comitiatus* (formal assembly) or a *contio* (public meeting) from any other magistrate, a praetor could do the same from any other magistrate but a consul. When other magistrates competed to hold a *comitiatus*, the first to begin prevailed, but they could hold competing *contiones*. Furthermore, we know that tribunes complained of infringement of their rights, if a *contio* was called away from them (Livy 43.16.9 and 11; *De Vir.Ill.* 65.5), even when a praetor did so to carry out jurisdiction (*De Vir.Ill.* 73.2). This chapter, then, seems to have given proceedings before the *quaestio* a privileged position, perhaps against a magistrate summoning a *contio* (the evidence for this is lost in the large lacuna at the end of the line).

72 (C7, E28) TRIBVS INTRO VOCABVNTVR EX: aes (C); EX: O; TRA QVAM: edd veter. *Staturam*: D minus.

Per saturam legislation, i.e. the tacking together of unrelated measures in order to force the voters, and tribunes contemplating a veto, to accept or reject the package as a whole, was only formally outlawed by the *lex Caecilia Didia* of 98

BC (Cic. *Dom.* 53, cf. 50; *Schol.Bob.* 140 St). It was, however, a debated issue in 133 BC, see *ORF*, no. 17, frag. 5 = Festus 416L – a remark in T.Annius Luscus' attack on Ti.Gracchus: '*imperium quod plebes per saturam dederat, id abrogatum est*' (cited by Rudorff, 503). It is not clear why the legislator should have singled out this kind of questionable legislative procedure. One possible reason is that it would have tended to be much lengthier than usual.

XLIV (lines 72–3) The transfer of obligations and authority to a succeding praetor or treasury-quaestor, when a case is not completed within the term of office of either of the original magistrates concerned.

72 (E28, D20) (vac) SEI: Peir, O, followed by Kl; no indication of new chapter: B, Vett, Borgh.

Mo and CIL supply, in my view improperly, a rubric created from the text of line 79, where a parallel clause begins, see commentary there. In any case the supplement of a complete rubric is highly questionable. We seem to have another instance of a chapter beginning without a rubric in line 82.

QVI: O, Borgh; QVEI: B, Vett. . . .SEI: Peir, QVAERET SEI: O, Vett, Borgh; QVAERI SE: D, Bo, Br; ( )SE: Scal; *sei[ve is quaestor quoi aerarium vel urbana provinc]ia*: Mo, CIL (too long for the lacuna available, as is the restoration of Kl, which has *queiquomque quaestor* for *is quaestor*).

ioudica[ta soluta factave erunt, quae eum praetorem eumve quaestorem ex hac lege ioudicare solvere facere oportet: queiquomque deinceps praetor ex hace lege quaeret quaestorve aerarium vel urbanam provinciam habebit, is, utei quod recte factum]: Mo, CIL, improving the suggestion of Kl (cf. line 80 for *provinciam habebit*, etc.).

This chapter provides for the continuing administration of the cases being heard in the *quaestio* and of the procedures for financial recovery associated with each of them, when the praetor in charge of the court or the treasury-quaestor dies or leaves office for any reason. Mommsen's restoration of a rubric beginning *iudex* might be interpreted as suggesting that, if the praetor was unavailable, a member of the jury should take over as his deputy, but this is impossible, since in line 73 it is only the new praetor or quaestor who are mentioned as being given the same rights and duties as their predecessors. A clause in *lex prov.praet.* (Cnidos IV.32ff, cf. Delphi C2ff) provides a rough parallel. There provision is made for the death or departure from office of a provincial governor or his quaestor and the powers of jurisdiction or financial management appropriate to these magistrates are conferred on deputies succeding them.

73 (C8, E29, D21) OMNIA̦: aes (C); OMNIA: O; QVOD EX: edd veter (QVD: O[2]). Bo[2] omits QVAE after FIANTQVE; *fiantque que*: D minus.

. . .SE: Peir; OPORTERE SEI: O, Vett; OPORTERES: Scal, D, Br; OPORTERET: Bo;

OPORTEBIT SEI: Borgh. It must be doubtful whether the T of *oporteret* or I of *sei* were actually visible to early copiers. RAETORI: aes; *praetori*: O, Pigh, Vett; *Sei [quod ex h.l. fieri oportet, factum non erit, de ea re]praetori*: Kl; *sei [apud eum ea res acta esset; deque ea re eiei] praetori*: Mo, CIL, comparing the text of line 80. However, here there does not seem to be room for *de ea re* nor is it necessary for the sense.

LEX ESTO QVA: aes; *lex eset qua*: O, Pigh (perhaps confused by a flaw in the bronze running through TO); *qua[sei apud eum ea res acta esset*: Kl, Mo, CIL.

XLV (lines 73–5) No trial on the same charge of men condemned under the leges Calpurnia *and* Iunia.

73 [*De rebus ante iudicatis factisve* (vac) *Queibus quom iudicium*]: Mo; [*De rebus ex lege Calpurniave iudicatis* (vac) . . . *iudicium*]: CIL.

The form of any rubric is quite uncertain.

74 (C9, E30, D22) CAL: aes (C) (with a trace of an upright following L); CAL: O; P̣VRNIVS: Peir (the top half of the P survives); PVRNIVS: Scal, D, Br, Bo[1]; VRNIVS: O, Vett, Borgh; DVRNIVS: Bo[2]. M. IVNIVS P.F.: Bo[1]; M. IVNIVS F.: Bo[2]; QVEI FORVM EO: Scal, D, Br, O *in rasura*; QVEI EORVM O: O[1] correction, O[2], Vett, Borgh, Bo[1]; RVEI EORVM EO: Bo[2]. MAGIS: aes, O, Vett; AGIS: Pigh. *[ioudicio condemnatus est eritve quo*] *magis*: Kl; *[ioudicio ex earum aliqua lege condemnatus . . . quo*] *magis*: Rud; *[ioudicio apsolutus vel condemnatus . . . quo] magis*: Mo, CIL.

Only *condemnatus* is indicated by the parallel clause in line 81. There is not enough space for *apsolutus vel*, nor is there any *a priori* ground for believing that it stood either here or in line 81, see commentary on line 56 and cf. Meyer, 1978, 150. Indeed, it was alleged that C.Gracchus introduced his legislation about misconduct in the provinces because of improper acquittals in the past (App. *BCiv*. 1.22.92).

DEIVRATVRVM: aes, O, Pigh; *deferatur*: Kl, Mo, CIL. MAGISTRATVS IS: aes, O, Pigh; *magis*: Kl, Mo, CIL. The engraver seems to have taken the letters MAG as the abbreviation for *magistratus*.

QVOM: aes (half of M preserved), Pigh; QVOI: O; *quom [eo ex hace lege ioudicium ioudicatio litisque aestumatio seit*: Kl; *quom [eo ex h.l. agatur, eius h.l. nihilum rogato . . . queique contra h.l. fecisse dicentur, nisei lex rogata erit ante quam ea res facta]*: Mo, CIL; *[. . . quei eorum eo iudicio apsoluti sunt eruntve, nisei sei haec lex rogata fuerit antequam ea res iudicata]*: Rud; *quom [eo lege Calpurnia aut lege Iunia sacramento agatur. . .]*: Meyer, 1978, 150.

For *antequam ea res iudicata*, cf. line 82 and see the commentary on line 75 for the context in which, in my view, it may have appeared in the text.

I have not inserted *eius h.l. nihilum rogato* as a supplement in the long lacuna, because of uncertainty about where it would have stood, but there can be little doubt that it did stand at the end of the clause forming the first part of this chapter. This clause, therefore, is excluding something which otherwise would be consistent with its previous provisions. Meyer's suggestion (*quom [eo lege Calpurnia* etc) is in some ways attractive, since it introduces a new element, which follows naturally from the word *quom*. Meyer assumes the concurrence of our present law with the *leges Calpurnia* and *Iunia*, on which see the commentary on line 75. According to his text this particular clause would have ensured that there were no second trials under those two laws of men previously condemned under them. However, it is highly unlikely that that was permitted in relation to the same charge under their provisions in the first place. If by any chance it was, and the present legislator desired to abolish such second trials, he should have amended the *leges Calpurnia* and *Iunia* directly. Instead, according to Meyer, we have an exclusion clause whereby there is no provision under the present law for certain actions under the procedure of the two previous laws: this does not, however, exclude actions of the same kind being taken according to the authority of the previous laws (it should be noted that this argument still applies, if we are working from Mommsen's text, where the issue is second trials after either condemnation or acquittal). Meyer realised the implausibility of our present law specifically excluding second trials of condemned men on the same issue under the same earlier laws and argued that *de ea re* meant 'concerning the same (general) matter', i.e. *de repetundis*. Hence, on his interpretation, this chapter was excluding any further trial *de repetundis* under any currently valid law of a man who had been condemned under either the *lex Calpurnia* or *Iunia*. Yet it is very doubtful if we can allow *ea res* to have this general sense. We need only consider *quasei/sei apud eum ea res acta esset* (line 73, supplemented from line 80) or *antequam ea res ioudicata erit* in this line (74, supplemented from line 82), where *ea res* must mean that specific matter or case.

75 (C10) About two letter-spaces of lacuna before the following rubric are visible at the edge of the C fragment after ESTO.

The first half of this chapter excepts those condemned under previous *leges de repetundis* from action under this law. The sense of Mommsen's restoration of the second half is that the law was not to be in any way retrospective. If we accept that the first half of the chapter allowed prosecutions of those previously acquitted under previous *leges de repetundis*, this restoration becomes inappropriate. Moreover, it is clear that in any case the law was retrospective, since it drew a distinction in damages between offences committed before and after it was passed (line 59). Mommsen attempted to evade this difficulty by arguing that, when offences committed before the passage of this law were actionable under the procedure of this law with the penalty fixed by the *leges Calpurnia* and *Iunia*, this counted as action under the *leges C.* and *I.* Yet the implication of his restoration here is that action according to the procedure of this law (*hace lege*) would in fact be outlawed for offences before its enactment. Moreover, Hesky (1903, 285ff) pointed out that action under the *leges C.* and *I.* is characterised in line 23 as being *sacramento* and not by the procedure of this law. Eder's riposte to this (222–3) – that an action could begin *sacramento* but continue according to this law – is highly unlikely both in principle and because there is no trace of such an eventuality being considered in the early chapters of this law. There we only hear of *nominis delatio* even when private law procedure is provided (lines 7–8). Rudorff's restoration avoids these problems, but it seems odd merely to allow trial of those acquitted under previous laws, when this law had been passed before the verdict, since the alleged offences did in any case precede this law.

Mommsen's restoration of *facta* is not required epigraphically, since there is room for *iudicata* in the parallel clause in line 82. We should, therefore, consider restoring here *[queive in exilium abierit antequam ea res iudicata] erit* (cf. line 29) or something similar. The law would then have exempted from prosecution under this law those who had gone voluntarily into exile when faced with a condemnation under previous *leges de repetundis*, but those who went into exile when threatened under this law were liable by contrast to be prosecuted in their absence (see line 29). Meyer (1978, 152, n24) also wished to restore *iudicata*, but as part of a general interpretation of this chapter, which is insecure (see above).

We should also consider in the light of this chapter how far the *leges Calpurnia* and *Iunia* were concurrent with this law. Mommsen believed that allowance was made for new trials under the *leges C.* and *I.* but only according to his special interpretation of this, i.e. that the procedure laid down by these laws was obsolete. Rudorff (517) believed that no new trials under them were permitted. The future perfects (*quod iudicium] fuit fueritve, ... condemnatus est eritve*) may have merely allowed for trials begun but not yet completed. It is at least clear, as Mommsen saw, that the *lex Iunia* had been concurrent with the *lex Calpurnia*, since both laws were regarded as being in force up to the point at which this law was passed, if not longer. A clear-cut decision cannot be made in the absence of a full text, but we should not rule out the possibility that actions on certain charges not covered by this law (that is, breaches of rules in provincial administration) were still possible under the preceding laws (Lintott, 1981, 176; Meyer, 1978, 147). The *saeva lege Pisonis* appeared in Lucilius' account of the trial of Q.Scaevola in 119 BC (607–8W = 573–4M).

The identity of M.Iunius is uncertain. Crawford, *RRC* I.259, has argued for the Iunius Silanus who was a *monetalis c.* 145 BC, but the man might alternatively be a Brutus, perhaps even the famous jurisconsult (Cic. *Brut.* 130; *de Or.* 2.142, 223–4), see Lintott, 1981, 172.

XLVI (line 75) Action to be taken when the court has decided that praevaricatio *has taken place.*

75 (E31, D23) PREVARICATIONE: Bo[1]. A lacuna is recorded by all copyists after DE PRAEVARICATIONE; Peir and Scal also record one before these words; O[1] originally recorded them on a separate line but then indicated that they should be moved to the beginning of the line following.

PRAETOR QVI: Borgh, D minus. EI PRA: Peir; EI PRAE: cett edd veter; *ei prae[varic*: Kl. VDICANDAM: aes (the right hand stroke of the v is visible), O[2], Vett; IDICANDAM: O[1]; DICANDAM: Pigh; *ei prae[tori eisque iudicibus quei ex h.l. ad eam rem i]udicandam*: Mo, sim. CIL (cf. line 82 for *ea]m rem*).

For the acceptance of diminution in the jury (*quei. . .]adfuerint, quei vivent*) cf. line 49 – *quei aderunt*.

quod ex [hac lege quis detolerit, praevaricationis causa eum detulisse: CIL (sim. Mo); *quod ex [h.l. praevaricationis causa delatum exve reis exemptum fuisse, quo minus de ea re denuo quaeret, eamque rem ab eis iudicibus, quei ad rem iudicandam adfuerint, iudicari litesque aestumari iubeat eius hace lege nihil rogato*: Rud (518).

It is not clear why there should be restored here a reference to defendants whose names were removed from the list of trials. For the investigation of *praevaricatio* by the *repetundae* court itself cf. Cic. *Fam.* 8.8.3, where the same panel of iudices that judged the *litis aestumatio* were employed. The praetor then treated a tied vote at first as an acquittal, which could have been correct if the provisions of this present law were still valid, but was then confused by a reference to a majority decision in chapter 101 of the *lex Iulia*, which may not have been relevant in that situation. For a definition of *praevaricatio* (corruption on the part of the accuser, so that he failed to perform his proper task) see Cic. *Part.Or.* 124–6. The function of this chapter is uncertain. It does not seem to be providing for prosecutions for *praevaricatio* for the first time in the law (in fact this may well have been dealt with in lines 42–3): instead it assumes that *praevaricatio* has been proved to the court and seems to be laying down the legal consequences of this. Rudorff's supplement involves the repetition of part of the content of lines 55–6 in a slightly different way and seems redundant. This chapter cannot be a special provision regarding prosecutions under the *leges Calpurnia* and *Iunia* on account of the reference to *nominis delatio*, since those laws required the use of the *legis actio sacramento* (line 23 and commentary) rather than denunciation to the praetor, as prescribed by this law.

XLVII (lines 76–8) The granting of citizenship as a reward for successful prosecution.

76 (C11, E32, D24) SEI QUIS EOR: aes (C), O. M QVEI: edd veter. *Sei quis eor[u]m quei*: Kl, Mo, CIL. ALTEREI: O.

nomen [de pequnia capta coacta ablata conciliata avorsave ad praetor]em: Kl (too long for lacuna). EO EO: aes.

Tu[m eis quei ex hace lege alterei nomen de pequnia capta coacta conciliata avorsave detulerit, quom uxore leiberisque, sei eis ceiveis Romanei non erunt]: Kl; *tu[m eis quei eius nomen detolerit, quoius eorum opera maxime unius eum condemnatum esse (ei iudicio) constiterit, sei volet, ipse filieique, quei eiei gnatei erunt quom]*: Mo, CIL.

My own restoration is more extensive than Mommsen's, exploiting the greater length of line on which it is based. Mommsen's restoration of *quom* before *ceivis Romanus ex hace lege fiet* implied (given the absence of *factusve erit*) that the grant of citizenship to sons was restricted to those already born at the time the father became a Roman citizen, but there is no evidence that this was the legislator's intention. Sons born to the new Roman citizen created by virtue of this law would only have been automatically Roman citizens themselves, if their birth was the outcome of a *matrimonium iustum* with a woman who was herself a citizen or had been granted *conubium* with Romans. This law, unlike many later grants of citizenship, seems to have made no reference to citizenship for wives. It seems improbable that the legislator intended to draw a distinction between sons born before and after the grant of citizenship. Rather, the general grant to sons and grandsons seems to have been a way round the absence of provisions for *conubium* or citizenship for women.

For *tu[m eis ... opera maxume*, cf. line 85; *frag.Tar.* 2; Clusium fragment A (*CIL* I², 597), 5; *lex Iulia agraria* (=*Mamilia Roscia*), cap. 55; *S.C. de Aquaeductibus* (Front. *de aquis* 127; *FIRA* I, p. 280); *lex genet.Urs.*, cap. 66. See also Asc. 54C: '*damnatum autem opera maxime Appi Claudi pronuntiatum est*' and, for a paraphrase of a clause in the *lex Cornelia, Dig.* 29.5.25.2. For the restoration following this phrase, cf. line 77.

77 (C12, E33, D25) NEPOTESQVE: aes (C), O; YM EIEI: Peir (the break of the bronze is along the left-hand stroke of the V; M EIEI: Scal. D. O, Vett, Borgh; M EI EI: Br; M EI: Bo. GRATEIS: D minus. CEIVIS: Scal. IVSTI: Bo².

SVNTO: Peir, B; SVNT: O, Vett, Borgh; *sunt[o, quom eis commercium et conubium ex iure Quiritium esto, munerisque poplicei capiendi ious esto, sufragium in tribu]m*: Kl; *sunto [et in qua tribu (quam tribum), quoius is nomen ex h.l. detolerit, sufragium tulerit, in ea tribu (eam tribum) sufragiu]m*: Mo, CIL.

Mommsen rightly saw that a relative clause was required defining the tribe in which the new citizen was to exercise his rights but his supplement is a little too long for the lacuna.

STIPENDIAQVE: aes, edd veter (Mommsen claimed also to have read an O at the right-hand edge of D); *stipendiaque o[mnia merita sunto. Nequi magistratus prove magistratu ...*]: Mo, CIL, following the text in line 84.

For *aera militaria stipendiaque* cf. *frag.Tar.*, 4, 9 and on *militiae vocatio = vacatio* Cic. *ND* 2.6; Livy 39.19.4. For the provisions in general contrast *Ed. Oct. de priv. veter.* (FIRA I, p. 316), 9ff: '*utique optimo iure optumaq[u]e leg⟨e⟩{is} cives Romani sint, immunes sunto, liberi s[unto mi]litiae, muneribus publicis fu[ngend]i vocat[i]o, item in [quavi]s tribu s(upra) s(cripta) suffragium [fe]rendi c[e]nsendi[que] potestas esto, et si a[b]sentes voluerint, [c]enseri detur. Quod[cum]que iis, qui s.s.sun[t i]psis parent{es}⟨ibus⟩ [co]niug{es}⟨ibus⟩ liberisq[ue] eorum ...*', where the provisions are adapted to Roman citizens living in non-Roman communities.

In the clause relating to the tribe of the new citizens here and in line 76, Mommsen's supplement has been adopted, as it still seems the most plausible. However, it has been recently argued by Alexander (1985, 23) that the parallels cited by Mommsen for this were inadequate – viz. Cic. *Balb.* 57 (Balbus' change to the Clustumina tribe as a result of an *ambitus* prosecution); Dio 46.49.3–4 (the extraordinary rewards under the *lex Pedia*; Dio 36.40.3–4 and Memnon *FGH*, 434, F59.3–4 (Carbo's prosecution of M.Cotta); *lex genet.Urs.* cap. 123 (the rewards for procuring the expulsion of unworthy decurions). It is certainly possible that successful prosecutors here were allowed to enrol in a tribe of their choice, like the beneficiaries of Octavian's edict (see above), though it should be noted that even there the choice was restricted.

78 (C13) *eius h.l.] nihil rogato.* Mommsen noted that in this standard formula, frequently abbreviated into a series of capital letters, the verbal form *rogato* is found also in *lex Quinctia ad fin.* (Front. *de aquis* 129), while *rogatur* appears in *lex Ant.Term.* II.30 and Valerius Probus 3.13. Badian (1988) has argued that in fact the latter is more correct grammatically, adducing further Cic. *Caec.* 95, *eius ea lege nihilum rogatum. Rogatur* is certainly more intelligible to us, but *rogato*, a third person imperative which must be understood in a passive sense, may still have been equally authentic, in the sense of having textual precedent.

This famous chapter offers Roman citizenship to any man not already a Roman citizen, who is judged most responsible for the condemnation of the man on whom he himself has performed *nominis delatio*. It thus might apply to any non-Roman prosecuting *suo nomine* or one prosecuting *alieno nomine* as a representative of fellow-citizen, community or king (cf. line 60), but not to *patroni*, who did not perform *nominis delatio* (see commentary on line 19), Cicero comments on this privilege for successful accusers in *pro Balbo* 53–4, where L.Cossinius and T.Coponius from Tibur are cited as examples of men becoming Roman citizens in this way (perhaps under this law, perhaps under one of the *leges Serviliae*). Mattingly (1970, 163) argued that the Cicero passage in question implies that only Latins could profit from the offer of citizenship under the *lex Servilia* mentioned there (for arguments against this view see Sherwin-White, 1972, 96–7; Lintott, 1981, 186ff with further bibliography), and then that only Latins could profit under the present clause, in spite of what the text plainly says. He believed that this chapter rewarded *patroni* – wrongly, see above and cf. Sherwin-White, 1972, 93–4 – and that only Romans and Latins were allowed to be *patroni*, which may have been true *de facto* but is irrelevant. More recently, Sherwin-White has argued that the privileges of the present clause only make practical sense if they apply to Latin and Italian allies who, because resident in Italy, could enjoy membership of a Roman tribe and also would normally perform military service with the Romans (1982, 29–31).

Whereas Mattingly holds that a restriction in this clause was omitted because of tact by the legislator, Sherwin-White appeals to the theory that the text of the law is faultily engraved (see above, Introduction, pp. 81–3 and commentary on line 79 below). The basis of this theory is questionable and in any case it should not be a justification for an arbitrary approach to the text. Nor is it true that the clause only makes sense as a benefit offered to residents of Italy. In this era it was impossible, from the Roman point of view, to hold two citizenships simultaneously (cf. Cic. *Balb.* 30; Sherwin-White, 1973, 300ff). Anyone, Italian or non-Italian, who was eligible for the privilege of citizenship under this law, would not have accepted it, unless he was prepared to abandon his old identity. He had to acquire a new legal personality by registering at the census (in person, unlike Octavian's veterans); the *suffragium* was an important part of his new status; the freedom from military service was valuable, wherever he lived, since Roman citizens could be conscripted in the provinces. In fact he might well have decided to move into Roman territory, since as a Roman citizen he was no longer liable to civic obligations at home and it might be embarrassing to remain in his local *patria* in these circumstances. Certainly, in practice, citizenship may have been more attractive to Latins and Italians who had a closer relationship to the Romans already, but that is no reason for discounting the preserved text of the law and the vision of the legislator. I assume that a successful prosecutor was not forced to take Roman citizenship. That seems to be implicit in what follows and provision for this may have been made explicitly in the missing half of line 77.

The general topic of rewards for accusers (and informers) at Rome still awaits a comprehensive study (on Republican history, see Alexander, 1985; L.R. Taylor, *Party Politics in the Age of Caesar* (1961), 112–16). That such rewards were offered was to be expected in a city without a police-force or a prosecution service, such as are characteristic of current European societies. However, the major stimuli towards prosecution were private injuries, actually sustained by the prosecutor or a relative, or personal hostility, which sought an outlet in a case, in which the prosecutor's interests were not directly concerned. Prosecutors under this law were pursuing grievances of their own or of those connected with them. The offer of further reward by the legislator was probably intended to be a counterweight to the deterrent effect of the sheer labour involved in a *repetundae* prosecution and the fear of offending powerful Romans. In the field of electoral bribery (cf. Alexander, 1985) rewards may have been offered to accusers in order to overcome their fear of reprisals by counter-prosecutions and their fellow feeling for those indulging in practices only marginally different from their own.

XLVIII (lines 78–9) The granting of provocatio, *freedom from military service and other privileges to non-citizens who do not wish to change their status.*

78 (C13, E34, D26) DE PROVOCATION: aes, O (a trace of a horizontal bar is visible to the right of the N on the bronze); EQVE DANDA: Peir, O, Vett, Borgh, Br, D maius (the latter with the upright of the E missing); = QVE DANDA: Scal; Ẹ (as in

D maius) QVAE DANDA: D minus, Bo. All MSS leave a large space after this rubric. *De provocation[e immunitat]eque danda*: Rud; *De provocation[e vocation]eque danda*: CIL, following a suggestion of Mommsen's.

There is little to choose between the two supplements and I have printed Mommsen's merely because it is more familiar.

SI QVEIS: Peir (probably an error in copying); SEI QVIS: Scal, D, Br, O, Vett, Borgh; SEI QVEIS: Bo. OR: aes; TOR: O, Pigh, Vett. *quei [nominis Latini sunt . . . quei eorum in sua quisque civitate dicta]tor*: Mo, CIL; *quei [in amicitia dicione potestate p.R.sient, socium nominisve Latini exve XII coloniis, quei eorum dicta]tor*; Strachan-Davidson, 1912, I.147ff; . . . *quaes]tor*: Mattingly, 1987, 71.

The second Vienna fragment (Dd) now enters into the text of D26.

QVAESTIO ERI: aes; ER: edd veter; ERIT: Kl, Mo, CIL.

It is clear from line 79 that this chapter deals with members of another community than Rome. I have therefore restored *quei [ceiveis Romanei non erunt*, following the model of line 76, since it is likely that the cautious and pedantic draughtsman would repeat this in any chapter dealing with privileges for non-citizens. It is not, however, certain that the chapter only refers to members of the *nomen Latinum*, as Mommsen's restoration implies. Sherwin-White (1972, 95) pointed out that this clause could be restored so as to provide a summary in Latin of every type of civic magistracy existing in Italian communities, whether Latin, Oscan, Etruscan or Greek – though he then went on to assume that the clause was limited to Latins, on the ground that there is no outside evidence for non-Latin Italic peoples benefiting in this way (see also 1982, 29–31). *Praetor* could certainly represent the Oscan *meddix tuticus* or the Etruscan *zilath*, while *aediles* appear in a second-century inscription from the territory of the Vestini (*Arch. Class.* 16 (1964), 296–7). Strachan-Davidson's restoration is too long and raises other problems, e.g. the position of *socium nominisve Latini* in the clause and the mention of the twelve *coloniae* but his instinct to make the clause refer to *peregrini* in general seems sound. Another conceivable supplement is *[ceiveis Romanei non erunt, queive in ceivitate Latina IIvir dicta]tor*, so that the clause applies to all *peregrini* with the exception of a group of Latins, though it is questionable whether *Latina* is acceptable as shorthand for *nominis Latini* in a legal text such as this.

One reason for Mommsen's restoration was that he believed that the point of the clause was to exclude Latins who had already received Roman citizenship by virtue of having held a local magistracy – a privilege which, Asconius (3C) implies, was granted them before 89 BC. But those who had already taken up Roman citizenship would surely have been more precisely excluded by *quei ceives Romanei non erunt*. Moreover, Mommsen's text could, at most, warrant the conclusion that Latin ex-magistrates had already been granted *provocatio*, freedom from military service and from performing local *munera* (Rosenberg, 1920, 347–8; Bradeen, 1958/9, 221ff; Mattingly, 1970, 167, though Mattingly now thinks (1987, 71) that this line implies a choice for such men between citizenship and *provocatio*). Is it certain, however, that the exception clause with the titles of magistrates is excluding people from a privilege that they have already got? An alternative suggestion has been made by Gabba (1989, 241–2), that, when it came to privileges for those who did not want to change their citizenship, the Roman legislator did not want to stop some of the most important members of the liturgical class from performing such public services in allied communities. The chapter, then, admits no inferences about the chronology of the grant of citizenship to Latin ex-magistrates: it might imply that they already had *provocatio*, freedom from military service and local *munera*, if they had not taken up (or were not yet allowed to take up) Roman citizenship, but there is another possible reason for the denial of the last two privileges. Moreover, as we have seen, there is no good reason to assign the privileges conferred by this chapter to Latins alone.

My restoration of the second half of the line follows Mommsen as far as *maxume*. Then Mommsen continued, *unius eum condemnatum esse ei iudicio constiterit, sei ceivis Romanus ex h.l. fierei nolet, ei deinceps ad p.R. provocare liceto tamquam sei c.R. esset. Quodque]*; CIL omits *ei iudicio*, has *postea* for *deinceps* and in place of *quodque* at the end *ipsei filiisque nepotibusque ex filio*. We should not necessarily assume that *provocatio* was granted here to the descendants of a person who was not admitted to the privileges of full citizenship, as it was to the descendants of the Greek sea-captains in 78 BC (*FIRA* I, 35, Greek 12ff), cf. *FIRA* I, 55 and 56 and *frag.Tar.* 7–9 for privileges granted to the children of newly admitted Roman citizens. For freedom from *munera*, cf. *frag.Tar.* 10, '*neive facito utei] munus faciat neive imperato*'; *Tab.Heracl.* 93; *S.C. de Asclepiade* (*FIRA* I, 35), Greek 12; *FIRA* I, 55, 20ff; *ibid.* 56, 5ff. (in the last three examples dealing with people outside Italy it is associated with freedom from tribute).

79 (C14, E35) INSV (with no interpunct after N): aes (C), O; *in su[a quoiusque ceiv]itate*; Mo, CIL; IITATE (dash indicating omission of text) DEINCEPS PR: Peir; ATATE IVDEX DEINCEPS FACIAT PR: Scal; ITATE IVDEX DEINCEPS FACIAT lacuna P.R.: Bo; ATATE lacuna IVDEX DEINCEPS FACIAT PR: D; VTILITATE lacuna IVDEX DEINCEPS FACIAT: O; VTILITATE IVDEX DEINCEPS FACIAT: Vett, Borgh; VTATE IVDEX DEINCEPS FACIAT PR: Br; *ceiv]itate* (vac) *Iudex deinceps faciat pr*: Mo; *ceiv]itate* (vac) *iudex deinceps faciat pr[incipe cessante itemque quaestor* (vac): CIL; *sei is praetor, quei ex h.l. quaeret, seive is quaestor. quoi aerarium]*: CIL.

E35 surely began as Peiresc reported from the *ecmagma plumbeum*. This was misread as LITATE by the source of O. Vett and Borgh and restored by him as *utilitate* without the restoration being indicated as such. It is most unfortunate that the copyists of E then give variant records at the point in the text, which was crucial to Mommsen's view that the engraver broke off one chapter in error and started repeating earlier chapters. Certainly, the next is closely parallel to that in lines 72–3, and the next but one (lines 80–2) has similarities to that in lines 73–5 though it is of a different length. However, even if there was an unintended and erroneous repetition on the bronze, it does not follow that this was the fault of the engraver, unless a break in sense in the received text can be established.

Ceiv]itate cannot have been the last word recorded in a chapter in the original text of the law: we need a verb. Mommsen took the lacuna indicated after this word by Orsini (also, unknown to him by the Dupuy manuscript) to indicate that IVDEX ... PR was the rubric to a new chapter. However, other copies closely related to O and D give no sign of this. The text surviving on the bronze nearby occasionally shows lacunae for no reason whatsoever – after *nomen* in line 74 (3 spaces), before *praetor* in line 78 (2–3 spaces) – and it may be that a lacuna was left here, but small enough for some copyists to discount it and thus unlikely to have indicated the beginning of a rubric. If, with Mommsen, we suppose *iudex*, etc. to have been a rubric referring to the content of the following clause, we encounter the following problems: (i) Such a rubric does not exist before the corresponding clause in line 72 (which on this view should be practically identical). (ii) Although the term *iudex*, with or without an accompanying relative clause may be used for the praetor in charge of the court (lines 19, 60ff), this is inconsistent with the specific references later to the praetor and quaestor (line 80, cf. 73 and see also commentary on line 72). (iii) Mommsen's rubric is quite unconvincing. *Cesso*, when it appears in later legal Latin, is used of a participant in a case failing to appear, not of a magistrate leaving office (*Dig*. 47.10.17.20; 49.14.2.4), while the contrast between *princeps* and *deinceps* is not found outside Festus (71, 75M = 62, 65L). Nor will a phrase in which PR is part of *praetor* do, e.g. *iudex faciat pr[aetoris vicem*, since this would suggest the substitution of a juryman for the praetor, which the chapter clearly does not provide (*eiei praetori quaestorique* – line 80). Hence I believe that the gap before *iudex* recorded by Orsini and the Dupuy MS does not justify us treating *iudex deinceps faciat pr* as a rubric and have restored it as part of the preceding chapter.

Once this is done, the case for a gross error by the engraver becomes very weak. Mommsen himself realised (Mo, p. 71) that his theory was open to dispute and in particular that there were considerable differences in length between clauses which on his view should have been parallel (for a full discussion of these variations see the 'Introduction to the Text', pp. 82–3). If Mommsen's theory is to stand, we would have to assume that the engraving of the last three allegedly repeated chapters was catastrophically wild (something quite out of character with the rest of the inscription). Furthermore, the engraver, in spite of the ruinous text he had produced, would have gone on engraving for at least three more chapters after those which on Mommsen's view were faulty.

As to my own restoration of the end of this chapter, the announcement of the privilege conferred in the recipient's own community would be an important corollary to the gift. It may seem an arrogant imposition on the community, but it was no more so than the unilateral decision by Rome to free a member of an allied community from his civic duties. This is certainly provided by this law, as by the *S.C. de Asclepiade* and probably also by the *fragmentum Tarentinum*.

XLIX (lines 78–9) The transfer of obligations and authority to a succeding praetor or treasury-quaestor.

79 (D27) VEL: aes; VEI: O; IEI; Pigh.

The horizontal bar of the L is minimal but sufficient to distinguish the letter from an I. The restoration after *abdicaveritv[e* follows the preserved text of line 72 as far as *ioudicata* and then the restoration there, except that *vel urbanam* is supplied after *aerarium* to correspond with *vel urbana* in the text of D27.

80 (C15, E36, D28) VTEIQV; aes (C); O. OLET: D, Scal; OLET: Bo; VOLET: Br; L.ET: O, Vett, Borgh. NOMINA for OMNIA: Bo.

PVD EVM: aes; O; *a]pud*: Pigh, Kl; *apud*; Mo, CIL.

PRAETOR QVAESTOR: aes (Dd); *praetor(i) quaestor (i)*: Kl; *praetor(i) quaestor(ique)*: Mo, CIL.

As far as *lex esto quasei* the restoration follows the preserved text of line 73.

There is apparently a discrepancy of about ten letter-spaces between the lengths of this chapter and that in lines 72–3, which may well be explained by variations in drafting and engraving, e.g. the insertion of *vel urbana/m* twice in the second chapter and the loss of five letters in line 80. It therefore appears probable that the two chapters (XLIV and XLIX) are in substance the same. In my view this is best explained either by careless repetition by the legal draughtsman or of a desire to emphasise that action in the sensitive matter of awarding *praemia* should not be delayed or impeded by the departure of one of the original magistrates from office, see the 'Introduction to the Text', p. 82.

L (lines 80–2) (?) No trial on the same charge for men condemned under the leges Calpurnia *and* Iunia.

81 (C16, E37, D29) ICIVM EVIT: aes; *iudicium fuit*: O. Only the upper left portion of the G of *leg[e* survives.

TRIBVNVS PLEBEI R (followed by two smudged letters): Peir; ROGA: Scal, D; ROGAC: Br; ROGAVIT: O, Vett, Borgh; ROGAT: Bo. Bo[2] also records AT separately at the end of the line. As Mommsen realised, this was a meaningless addition, probably by the illustrator de Bry, to fill up the outline of the fragment. The copyist from whom O, Vett, Borgh derive, cannot have seen more than ROGAV.

[exve . . . condem]natus: Kl; *[exve . . . apsolutus vel condem]natus*: Mo, CIL. There is not enough space available for *apsolutus* and no external justification for its insertion, see the commentary on line 74.

DEERATVR: aes; deferatur: O. *Quove magis de e[a re quom eo ex hace lege agatur, eius hace lege nihil rogato*: Mo, CIL.

Mommsen restored the rest of the chapter in the same way as in line 74, see the commentary on that line. There are about 25 letter-spaces more in the lacuna at the end of this chapter in lines 81–2 than in the lacuna in line 74. Furthermore, there are about 30 letter-spaces less in the lacuna at the end of line 80 than in that at the end of line 73. This suggests more than minor variations in phrasing, spelling and letter-spacing. Either the order of the clauses in the chapter has been recast (presumably by the man who drafted them, not the engraver) or, in spite of the close similarity of what survives, the contents of the two chapters are not identical. For example, it is conceivable that the current chapter began with a reference to prosecution by non-citizens under the *leges Calpurnia* and *Iunia* and went on in this line to prescribe that no further prosecutions could be made, if the offender had been previously condemned under either of these laws, nor could any reward be claimed: '*sei quis, quei ceiveis Romanus non fuit fueritve, pequniam ab altero petivit petiveritve, quod iud]icium fuit fueritve ex leg[e . . . quei eorum eo ioudicio condem]natus est eritve, quo magis de ea re eius nomen hace lege deferatur quove magis de e[a re is, quoius ex hace lege petitio erit, ceivis Romanus fiat eave praemia quae s.s.s. accipiat, ex hace lege nihil rogatur*'.

82 (C17, E38) ÇTIO NEI ẸṢ: Peir (the middle bar of the E is missing, only the top of the S survives); CTIO NEP; Scal; CTIO NEI: D, Br; SANCTIO NEI: Vett, Borgh (similarly O, but with SANCTIO as a rubric and NEI deferred to the next line); TIONEI: Bo (after this Bo[2] has ICVT and R – apparently meaningless stuffing, cf. commentary on line 81); *Sanctio*: Kl; *ea res [facta erit, quom eis hace lege a]ctio nei esto*: Mo, CIL.

There can be little doubt that the reading of O, Vett and Borgh results from a supplement by the copyist who was their ultimate source. This supplement might of course be correct, but, in view of the parallel between line 82 and line 75, this is unlikely. As in line 74, I would prefer to restore here *quelve (mortuos erit aut) in exilium / abieri]t, antequam ea res [ioudicata erit, quom eo hace lege a]ctio nei es[to.*

LI (lines 82–3) Subject matter uncertain

82 (D30) M REM IOVDICANDAM: aes, edd veter, Kl. *[De praevaricatione* (vac) *Praetor, quei ex h.l. quaeret. qua quis de ea re ei praetori eisque ioudicibus, quei ex h.l. ad ea]m rem ioudicandam*: Mo, CIL.

It may be that at this point in the chapter a similar text to that in line 75 should be restored, but it cannot be identical since the main verb is active here (*satis fecerit*), passive in line 75 (*satis factum erit*). In my restored text the subject of *satis fecerit* is missing. It may have been deferred or, with Mommsen, we should insert *quis*. The latter is in this context vague and unsatisfactory (is it really *quei volet* or anyone who has the right to accuse another of *praevaricatio* under this law?). If we do insert *quis*, it will be necessary to contract *praetor* to *pr* in order not to exceed the space available, unless the paragraph gap is eliminated. There is in any case no room for the rubric *De praevaricatione*, which Mommsen supplied from line 75, or indeed any other rubric.

ADFVERỊ: aes (the top of a *hasta* is just visible); ADFVER: O, Pigh, Vett, Borgh; *adfuer[int]*: Kl; *adfuerit*: Mo, CIL. I can find no trace of T on the Dd fragment. There is, however, a small gap between Db and Dd at this point, where NT can be inserted.

MAIORIS: aes, O[1]; *maiori*: O[2]. (The upper part of the S incorrectly added to MAIORI is now visible on Dc, the letter was also recorded by Orsini in his MS as visible on Dd.) SATIS FECERIT Ẹ: aes; *satis fecerit*; edd veter, Kl; *satis fecerit e[um, quei ex hace lege nomen detulerit, praevaricationis causa id detulisse*: Mo, CIL (the E surviving at the edge of Dc made it impossible to restore the same phrase that was used in line 75, *nomen, quod ex [hace lege delatum siet...*).

Given that the surviving text of this chapter is not identical in phrasing with that in line 75, it is far from certain that it is in fact a repeated clause about *praevaricatio*, even though the text completely lost in the lacuna in lines 82–3 is close in length to that largely lost after *satis factum erit* in line 75. The chapter might equally plausibly have given instructions about a non-Roman who had convinced the court that he deserved a *praemium* under the law, e.g.: '*Sei quis eorum, quei ceivis Romanus non erit, ei praetori eisque ioudicibus, quei ad ea]m rem ioudicandam adfueri[nt], quei vivent, eorum maiori(s) parti satis fecerit e[x hac lege se praemium meritum esse.*'

LII (lines 83–4) Rewards for Romans or non-Romans who have successfully prosecuted.

83 (C18, D31) SEIC: aes (C); SEIQ: O; *seiq[uis eorum, quei ceivis Romanus erit, ex hac lege alterei nomen ... ad praetorem quoius e]x*: Mo, CIL, following line 76.

The space available for the text before *quoius ex hace lege* is similar in the two lines, but this chapter might equally well begin *sei quis eorum, quei ceivis Romanus erit*. The mention of *aera militaria* is as appropriate to Roman as to non-Roman beneficiaries, cf. *frag.Tar.* 7–9. Moreover, there is not enough room for the rubric. *De ceivitate danda*, at the beginning of the line and it is unlikely that it was spread over the end of one line and the beginning of the next. The text between SEIQ here and AERA MILITARIA on the D fragment in line 84 is *c.* 595 letters, while the corresponding text in lines 76–7 is *c.* 640 – a discrepancy which would be difficult to explain if the texts of this chapter and XLVII were practically identical.

S EO IOVDICIO: aes (Dd); EO IOVDICIO: O.

detuler[it et is] eo: Kl; *detuler[it et i]s eo*; Mo, CIL. There is room for the plural *detulerint*. In the lacuna to the right of D Mommsen restored *tum eis, qu[ei eius nomen detolerit, quoius eorum opera* etc, as in line 76.

84 (C19, B32) At the bottom of the C fragment, I could see the tops of two *hastae* and two *apices*, which might represent VM. Mommsen saw VM and then the top of an o or s, which he nevertheless represented as *t]um ei[ei*. This was about ten letter-spaces to the left of where he would have expected it, if the clause had been identical with that in lines 76–7. He then restored *nepotesque t]um ei[ei filio gnatei ceiveis Romanei iustei sunto et, in qua tribu, quoius is nomen ex h.l. detolerit, sufragium tulerit, sufragium ferunto inque eam tribum censento militiaeque eils vocatio* – far too long for the space available. Even if my own restoration of line 77 is used instead, it is impossible to fit *tum eiei* where Mommsen wanted to place it.

> S . . . STIPENDIA: aes, Pigh; S . . . STIPENDIAQ: O, Vett, Borgh (but Vett has *vacatio* for *vocatio*). SVNT: aes. NE QVI MAGIṢ ṚATVS PR: aes (Dd, DC); NEQVI MAGI/ATVS PR: edd veter; *pr[ove magistratu prove quo inperio potestateve erit facito quominus ita siet*: Kl (following *lex agr.* 87).

A prohibition on magistrates disregarding privileges conferred by the law seems to occur in *frag.Tar.* 10–12, see also *lex Ant.Term.* II, 13ff; *ep. Oct. de Seleuco* (*FIRA* I, 55), 63ff.

LIII (lines 85–7) Successful foreign prosecutors are to have a choice of forum in which to conduct their law-suits.

85 (D33) Mommsen restored this clause as a reproduction of that in lines 78–9. This was obviously speculative and a comparison of the space covered by the text in lines 77–8 and 84–5 does not support this (see 'Introduction', p. 83). It seems more natural to connect the clause with the provisions in the line below.

86 (D34) PETETVR: aes; SI PETETVR: O, Pigh, Vett, Borgh; REPETETVR: Kl; I PETETVR: Mo, CIL; SI or TI PETETVR: CIL apparatus. SI is unlikely to be the conditional conjunction – normally SEI in this text: it may be the end of the dative or ablative of a noun or adjective.
Optio est]o: Mo, CIL.

Cf. *frag.Tar.* 5: '. . .*in] ioudicium, Romae certet, sei Romae velet*', see also *S.C. de Asclepiade* (*FIRA* I, 35), Latin 3ff, Greek 19ff; *ep. Oct. de Seleuco* (*FIRA* I, 55), 53ff. Whereas Asclepiades and Seleucus were offered a choice of venues in the empire – their own city, another free city or a Roman magistrate or judges – on the Tarentine fragment, as was appropriate with Italians as prospective beneficiaries, Rome was one of the options and it was probably so here too.

87 (D35) BERE LICETO: aes, Mo; IBERE LICETO: O, Vett, Borgh, Kl; ABERE LICETO: Pigh; *ha]bere liceto*: CIL; *inhi]bere liceto*: Mattingly (1969, 141), comparing *frag.Tar.* 7: '*s]ed fraude sua inperio inhiberi liceto*'.

As Mattingly saw, the run of the chapter must have been similar to that in *frag.Tar.* 5–7.

LIV (lines 87–8) Concerning rewards for Roman citizens.

87 (D35) LEGE ALT: aes; LEGE ALTE: O; *Sei quis cei]vis Romanus ex hace lege alte[rei nomen detolerit*: Kl, Mo, CIL.

This need not have been the first time that privileges for successful Roman prosecutors were mentioned. They may have been first conferred in LII (lines 83–4), where the benefits are freedom from military, and perhaps other public, service and from tribute-payment. Here, in addition, they may have been awarded privileges in the law-courts, as non-citizens were in the previous chapter. Rudorff (533) suggested the award of *ornamenta praetoria*. Acquisition of the *dignitas* of the condemned man was apparently a reward for accusers in Cicero's day (Cic. *Balb*. 57; *Sulla* 50; Dio 36.40.3–4, but cf. Alexander, 1985) and we do not know when it originated.

LV (line 88) ?Consequences of the grant of freedom from military service.

88 (D36) QVOI EX H: aes; QVOI EX HAC: Pigh; QVOI EX HA: O, Vett, Borgh; *Quoi ex h[ace lege provo]catio erit*: Mo, CIL.

The size of the lacuna is better suited to *militiae vocatio* (*vacatio*) and it is easy to imagine a clause forbidding commanders to override the privileges conferred by the law, except in extreme emergencies such as *tumultus Gallicus* or *Italicus*. It is precisely this which seems to be provided in *frag.Tar*. 11.

89 (D37) REGRINOS IOVS: aes, O²; REGRINOS IOVD: O¹.

In *frag.Tar*. 12 *praetor quei Romae inter peregrinos] ius deicat* has been restored in a clause which seems to be dealing with publicity for the law. We do not know whether only the *praetor peregrinus* is mentioned here or the praetor in charge of the *quaestio* is also instructed.

90 (D38) ẠTE IỌỴ: aes; ATL: O¹; ATEL: O²; ATEI: Kl; ATEIQ: Mo, CIL.

My own reading of the bronze here would allow a reference to a local magistrate – *quei in ea ceivi]tate iou[s deicet.*

Identity of the lex repetundarum

Sigonio and at one time Orsini identified the *lex rep.* with the *lex Servilia* of C.Servilius Glaucia, tribune in 104 or 101 BC. There were and are certain *prima facie* arguments in favour of this view: the *lex Servilia* was a known *repetundae* law with non-senatorial jurors passed close to 111 BC, the date of the law on the other face of the bronze (which Sigonio and Orsini identified with the *lex Thoria agraria*). Sigonio also used argument (a) below and the correspondence between *lex rep.* 8 and Cic. *Rab.Post*. 14. His view was retained by Klenze and has been more recently revived by Carcopino (1928, 211ff) and H.B. Mattingly

(1970 and 1979). The majority of modern scholars follow the interpretation first enunciated by Mommsen, that the *lex rep.* is a law of C.Gracchus, and many also share his opinion that it is the *lex Acilia* mentioned by Cicero in the Verrines (1.51; 2.1.26). Two formal arguments used to prove that the law is Gracchan, which I once accepted (Lintott, 1981, 182ff) now seem to me invalid. It is far from certain that the apparent duplication of material which commences in *lex rep.* 79 is an engraver's error and at the time rendered the copy of the law unsuitable for publication (see above pp. 81–3). Nor can one argue that the *lex rep.* face must be the obverse, because it was smoother and better prepared. This is not true of the Vienna fragments (see above, p. 73). The engraving of the *lex rep.* face is bolder and has more precise letter-forms but it is not more regularly spaced nor more accurate textually.

Nevertheless the arguments from the material in the text still give support to Mommsen rather than to his opponents:

(a) There are references in lines 23, 74 and 81 to the *leges Calpurnia* (of 149) and Iunia (of uncertain date) but to no other law. The law is therefore either itself the *lex Servilia Glauciae* or prior to it but subsequent to the other two laws.

(b) There is no trace of three features which, according to Cicero, were characteristic of Glaucia's law:

  (i) *Comperendinatio*, the double-hearing introduced by Glaucia and compulsory in Cicero's day (*Verr.* 2.1.36). We find instead in *lex rep.* 46–9 *ampliatio*, the possibility of any number of rehearings if more than a third of the jury say *non liquet*. The jurors are merely threatened with fines if they say *non liquet* more than twice (or, on Mattingly's view, twice, see commentary *ad loc.*). Such *ampliatio* Cicero says specifically was a feature of earlier procedure including *illam veterem ... Aciliam legem* (for other refs. to *ampliatio* see commentary *ad loc.*).

  (ii) Investigation *quo ea pecunia pervenerit*, introduced by Glaucia (Cic. *Rab.Post.* 8). The clause in *lex rep.* 67–8, suggested by Mattingly as an equivalent, simply deals with the correct labelling of money-boxes assigned by the treasury-officials to receipts from different condemnations.

  (iii) *Divinatio*, the procedure used in Cicero's time for deciding who should undertake the prosecution case, first attested at the end of the last decade of the second century BC (Cic. *Div.Caec.* 63) – thus either introduced by Glaucia or possibly by Q.Servilius Caepio in 106 (cf. Lintott, 1981, 188). The ethos of *lex rep.* is entirely different: the injured parties or their representatives have the right to conduct their own cases: they perform *nominis delatio* themselves and are only allocated *patroni* by the praetor, if they so wish (lines 2–4, 9–12, 19).

(iv) A further discrepancy may be added. Mommsen's restoration of a phrase including the word *inquisitio* in *lex rep.* 30 must be rejected on epigraphic grounds (see commentary *ad loc.*). Prosecutors under the *lex rep.* were certainly allowed to collect (*conquirere*) witnesses and documents in the towns of Italy (lines 31–4), but there is no trace of time being granted after nominis *delatio* for investigation abroad. However, the latter, termed *inquisitio*, is attested under Glaucia's law (Asc. 21C, cf. Cic. *Scaur.* 23). A fuller discussion of how Glaucia's law differed from earlier *repetundae* laws and indeed may have marked a turning-point in their history may be found in Lintott, 1981, 189–97. A rebuttal of Mattingly's case *seriatim* is provided by Sherwin-White, 1972.

(c) If then the *lex rep.* antedates Servilius Glaucia, it is tempting to associate it with C.Gracchus because:

(i) The elaborate provisions for a non-senatorial jury, especially *in hunc annum*, suggests that it was creating such a jury for the first time. Appian regarded acquittals in the *repetundae* court as the main reason for the introduction of *equites* by C.Gracchus to the courts (*BCiv.* I.22.92);

(ii) The reward of Roman citizenship for successful foreign prosecutors is in accord with Gracchan policies in so far as Gracchus proposed an extension of Roman citizenship to the Latins, at least, while his partner, Fulvius Flaccus, had proposed to give Roman citizenship to all Italians in 125.

(iii) The meticulous details and the penalties for incorrect procedure, found also in *lex prov. praet* (the so called 'pirate law'), are reminiscent of the methods of Athenian democracy and embody the principle of a control of the executive and the judiciary ultimately resting on the authority of the *populus Romanus* (on the political ideas implicit in the law see especially Sherwin-White, 1982).

(iv) The law cannot in any case antedate C.Gracchus because of the nature of the jury-provisions, nor for the same reason can it be the *lex Servilia Caepionis*, which brought back senators to the juries. (See below for the possibility of another *repetundae* law intervening between Gracchus' and Caepio's. In view of (i) our law is unlikely to be this.)

(d) If the law was devised by C.Gracchus, it belongs to either 123 or 122. It was passed after the allocation of praetorian provinces for that year (hence the temporary assignment of the court to the *praetor peregrinus*) but probably in the first half of the year (otherwise the special provision for a president and jurors *in hunc annum* might have seemed otiose), see Fraccaro, *Opuscula* II, 30.

It is not easy to reconcile the *lex rep.* with the accounts of a *lex*

Sempronia in Livy, *Per.* 60 and Plut. *C.Gr.* 5.2–3; *Compar.* 2.1. Plutarch talks of the creation of mixed juries of senators and *equites* (300 of each), Livy of enlarging the senate by adding 600 *equites* to the existing 300 senators. One solution, advocated by a number of scholars, is to deny these conflicting accounts any evidential value. Since they cannot be describing the jury-panel of the *lex rep.* and, in the view of these scholars, there are no other jury-panels to describe, they can only arise from the ancient authors' confusion (see e.g. Strachan-Davidson, 1912, II, 85ff; Fraccaro, *Opuscula* II, 273ff; Gruen, 1968, 86ff, 293ff; Griffin, 1973, 113ff). Another solution is to accept Plutarch's account as a true summary of a general judiciary law of 123, which was later modified in respect of *repetundae* cases by our law (see Kunkel, *RE* 24, 750, *s.v. quaestio*; Brunt, 1988, 194–239; variants of this view are in Last, *CAH* IX[1], 70–6; Jones, 1960; Badian, 1954). Some evidence for a jury-panel other than that laid down by the *lex rep.* may be found in *lex agr.* 37 and that is a warning against outright rejection of the possibility of a general *lex Sempronia iudiciaria*.

(e) There is nothing in the text of *lex rep.* inconsistent with Cicero's description of the *lex Acilia*. Nor is it historically implausible that M'.Acilius Glabrio, father of the praetor of 70, should have been associated with C.Gracchus (Badian, 1954, and *AJP* 96 (1975), 67ff). Nevertheless, we cannot rule out the possibility that the *lex Acilia* was a subsequent law on the same lines as C.Gracchus', whose significance Cicero has over-emphasised as a compliment to the praetor of 70 (Sherwin-White, 1972, 99). In that case *lex rep.* must be the earlier Gracchan law because otherwise there would be no need for special jury-provisions in the initial year. If, as I have argued above, *lex rep.* was *not* a faulty copy never posted, then we must take seriously the view that the bronze recording C.Gracchus' law was turned to the wall in 111 BC or a little later in order to receive the text of *lex agr.*, because by then it had been rendered obsolete by the *lex Acilia* (Fraccaro, *Opuscula* II, 283ff; Serrao, 1974, 215; Tibiletti, 1953, 66ff; Ferrary, 1979, 108ff). The alternative is to suppose that both faces were visible simultaneously. As Miss Rhoda Lee has pointed out, there is at least one fine example of a free-standing opisthographic bronze from Olympia (*Olympia* V, no. 39, cf. no. 38). Moreover, F.E. Brown claimed to have found the setting of a 'bulletin board' – a series of free-standing tablets – at the south-west end of the forum at Cosa (1980, pp. 41–2, with figs. 44 and 49).

II

Lex Agraria

Introduction to the Text

The *lex agraria* text begins higher on the bronze than that of the *lex repetundarum*, since the engraver left no blank space between the text and the top edge. On the surviving fragments of the *lex agraria* the letters are *c.* 0.8 cm high in the top line, *c.* 0.55 cm high in the immediately following lines, *c.* 0.45 cm high on average in the lower half of the bronze. They are thus between 0.05 and 0.15 cm less high than the letters on the *repetundae* face. This is the reason why the surviving fragments of the bronze contain 105 lines of agrarian text as opposed to 90 lines of *repetundae* text. Laterally, in the top two lines 10 cm contain on average 17–18 letters, in the lines immediately below 20–2 letters, from line 15 onwards 22–4 letters.

After allowance has been made for the above variations the spacing of the text is as regular as on the *repetundae* face when taken in sections of 20 letters or more. Indeed the spaces occupied by individual letters are more regular. Apart from M, which still tends to take double the space of any other letter, and Q, which takes more than the average, the remaining letters are allocated a similar area of bronze. This is because the engraver of the agrarian text has tended to space out his smaller letters more than the engraver of the *repetundae* text and this has diminished the effect of different sizes of letter. Individual words, whether abbreviated or spelt in full, are separated by points. There are no rubrics. However, paragraph-spaces are left between chapters, about four letter-spaces wide and indicated by extra points in the first quarter of the text.

The engraving contains fewer gross errors than that of the *repetundae* face (even on the assumption that the engraver of the latter text did not repeat chapters). However, the letters are more shallowly and narrowly cut and are also sometimes carelessly formed, e.g. Λ for A, Γ for T, ≡ for E. The lines frequently deviate from the horizontal. Rudorff argued in the first full edition of the text that a major reason for some of these faults was the use of a second-hand bronze: the engraver might have been trying to minimise the effect of the deeply indented lines of the *repetundae* face. Yet the bronze is 3.5–4.0 mm thick and it is only where it has been subsequently damaged that the agrarian text has really suffered. The shallower engraving means that, where the bronze is worn, the text is less easy to read than the *repetundae* text, especially at the edges of the fragments. This was probably true in the Renaissance, when the lost fragments were copied.

The length to be assigned to the prescript and the implications of the restoration of *lex agr.* 16 and of the parallel clauses in the *repetundae* text have been discussed in the introduction to that text. We must assume a lacuna of *c.* 50 cm between the left-hand margin of the bronze and the left-hand edge of Bb agr., allowing 80–5 letters. Between the right-hand edge of Ba and the right-hand margin of the bronze the space corresponding to the prescript of the *repetundae* text is *c.* 123 cm, allowing *c.* 215 letters in lines 1–2 and 250–70 in the following lines. The lacuna between the B and the A fragments in line 16 is taken to be 113 letter-spaces or 51 cm.

The principles on which the lower fragments are assembled have also been discussed in the introduction to the *repetundae* text. The lost E fragment not only adjoins on its right C, which includes the right-hand margin of the bronze, but must itself have extended almost to the right-hand margin of the bronze. The supplements between D and E (or between the F fragment in the position proposed by Mattingly and E) create no problem. Indeed from lines 65 to 88 uncontroversial restorations, 9 letters upwards in length, can be made, which are not easily expanded and support the length of the restorations on the *repetundae* side.

Conventions

[ ] = lacunae and supplements to these (figures in lacunae indicate unfilled letter-spaces after account has been taken of supplements)
{ } = deletion of error in surviving text
⟨ ⟩ = supplement to surviving text after error by engraver
( ) = supplement to surviving text, where engraver has deliberately abbreviated
+ + = indecipherable traces on bronze
* * = suprascript correction actually made to surviving text on bronze

Underlining in Latin shows letters on one of the surviving bronze fragments which can be no longer read, though an earlier editor or copyist claimed to have read them. If these are left inside square brackets, they are being regarded as supplements.

Italics are used in the Latin text and translation for restorations outside the limits of the fragments.

In apparatus

aes = bronze, as read by current editor
B = consensus of the copies of the E fragment in Scaliger, Dupuy, Boissard and Brisson
Bo[1] = J.J. Boissard, *Inscriptionum antiquarum descriptio*, Stockholm Royal Library, S.68, 144r
Bo[2] = Boissard, *Romanae Urbis Topographiae et Antiquitatum*, III, 104.
Br = B. Brisson, *De formulis et sollemnibus populi Romani verbis*, Paris, 1583, II, 172–6.

D	= P. Dupuy, *Inscriptiones*, Paris, BN, Dupuy 461, 68, 88
Scal	= J.J. Scaliger, leaves bound in Vat. lat. 6531, 176 = 149
Ha	= P. Hameaux, Paris, BN, Franc. 19116, 17r, 32r, and in J. Mabillon, *De re diplomatica*. p. 344–5, Paris, 1681
Hu	= P.E. Huschke, Review of Rudorff, *Ackergesetz – Krit. Jahrb. f. deutsch. Rechtswiss.* 5 (1841), 579–620
Maz	= J. Mazzochi, *Epigrammata Antiquae Urbis Romae*, 180v
O[1]	= F. Orsini, Vat. lat. 6037, 52r–54v + 6040, 34r–37r
O[2]	= F. Orsini, *Sylloge legum et senatus consultorum*, nos. I-XIV (attached to A. Agustin, *De legibus et senatus consultis*)
Peir	= N.-C. Fabri de Peiresc. Paris, BN, lat. 8958, 168r, 178r
Pigh	= S.V. Pighius, *Annales Romanorum*, III, 137
Pin	= J.V. Pinelli. Vat. lat. 6531, 165r–171r (= 178–84)
Sig	= C. Sigonio, *De antiquo iure Italiae*, 1574, II, 2
Vett	= P. Vettori, Munich. lat. 743, 129–30
edd veter	= consensus of relevant editors and copyists from among the above
CIL	= *CIL* I[2] (Th. Mommsen and E. Lommatsch), effectively the text used in Bruns, FIR[7]
Jo	= K. Johannsen, *Die lex agraria des Jahres 111 v.Chr*
Mo	= Th. Mommsen *CIL* I[1] = *Gesammelte Schriften*, I
Rud	= A.F. Rudorff, Das Ackergesetz des Spurius Thorius, *Zeitschr. f. geschichtl. Rechtswissenschaft* 10 (1839), 8ff

LEX AGRARIA

Text

1 [... *tr.pl. plebem rogavit plebesque ioure scivit in foro a.d.* ... (35), *tribus* ...*princi*]pium fuit. Pro tribu Q.Fabius Q.f. primus scivit. Quei ager poplicus populi Romanei in terram Italiam P.Muucio L.Calpur[*nio cos. fuit, extra eum agrum, quei ager ex lege plebeive scito, quod C.Sempronius Ti.f. tr.pl. rogavit, exceptum cavitumve est nei divideretur* 1̣0̣0̣]

2 [.3̣0̣ *quem quisque de eo agro loco ex lege plebeive sc. vetus possessor sibei a*]grum locum sumpsit reliquitve, quod non modus maior siet, quam quantum unum hominem ex lege plebeive sc. sibei sumer[*e relinquereve licuit* 1̣1̣5̣ *Quei ager publicus populi Romanei in terra Italia P.Muucio L.Calpurnio cos. fuit, extra eum agrum, quei*]

3 [*ager ex lege plebeive scito, quod C.Sempronius Ti.f. tr.pl. rogavit, exceptum cavitumve est nei divideretur, quem agrum locum*] quoieique de eo agro loco ex lege plebeive sc. III vir sortito ceivi Romano dedit adsignavit, quod non in eo agro loco est, quod ult[*ra* .7̣0̣ *Quei ager publicus populi Romanei in terra Italia P.Muucio L.Calpurnio cos. fuit, extra eum agrum, quei ager ex lege plebeive scito, quod C.Sempronius Ti.f. rogavit, exceptum cavitumve est nei divideretur, de eo agro loco*

4 *quei ager locus pro eo agro loco, quem de sua possessione vetus possessor dedit, a III viro datus adsignatus commutatus re*]dditus est. (vac. 4) Quei ager publicus populi Romanei in terra Italia P.M{n}⟨u⟩ucio L.Calpurnio cos. fuit, extra eum agrum, quei ager ex lege [*plebeive scito, quod C.Sempronius Ti.f. rogavit, exceptum cavitumve est nei divideretur,* 1̣7̣5̣]

5 [.8̣5̣ *quod eius quisq*]ụe agri locei publicei in terra Italia, quod eius extra urbem Roma⟨m⟩ est, quod eius in urbe{m} oppido vico est, quod eius III vir dedit adsignavit, quod [2̣4̣5̣]

6 [.1̣0̣ *Quei ager publicus populi Romanei in terra Italia P.Muucio L.Calpurnio cos. fuit, extra eum agrum, quei ager ex*] lege plebive scito, quod C.Sempronius Ti.f. tr.pl. rog., exceptum cavitumve est nei divideretur, quod quoieique de eo agro loco agri locei aedific[*iei* 1̣4̣0̣]VỊḄV[1̣0̣0̣]

Translation

Prescript: . . ., *tribune of the plebs, asked the plebs and the plebs lawfully resolved in the forum (date). The . . . tribe* was the first to vote. Quintus Fabius, son of Quintus voted first for the tribe.

(lines 1–2) Regarding the land which was the public property of the Roman people in the land of Italy in the consulship of P.Mucius and L.Calpurnius (133 BC), *apart from that land whose division was made the subject of an exception or forbidden according to the law or plebiscite of C.Sempronius, son of Tiberius, tribune of the plebs, . . .* I

any land or territory which *any prior possessor according to law or plebiscite* took for himself or kept for himself from that land or territory, provided that its size is no greater than the amount an individual *was allowed* to take *or keep for himself* according to law or plebiscite;

(lines 2–3) *Regarding the land - - - - tribune of the plebs.* . . . any land or territory, which* a triumvir according to law or plebiscite gave or assigned by lot from that land or territory to a Roman citizen, which is not in the land or territory beyond . . .: II

(lines 3–4) *Regarding the land - - - - tribune of the plebs,* any land which was given, assigned, exchanged or* duly delivered *by a triumvir from that land or territory in place of that land or territory which a prior possessor surrendered from his possession*; III

(lines 4–5) Regarding the land - - - - *tribune of the plebs,** . . . any part of that public land in Italy, which is in a city, town or village outside the city of Rome, which a triumvir has given or assigned . . .: IV

(lines 6–7) *Regarding the land* - - - - tribune of the plebs,* . . . any land, territory or building . . . from that land or territory to each man . . . to whom . . . V

* I do not repeat in full the introductory definition, given in full in I, which can be reconstructed with certainty from the chapters in combination.

7 [100 *i*]n terra Italia III vir dedit adsignavit reliquit inve formas tabulasve retulit referive iusit. (vac. 4) Ager locus aedificium omnis quei supra scriptu[*s est, quei publicus populi Romanei in terra Italia P.Mucio L.Calpurnio cos. fuit, extra eum agrum, quei ager ex lege plebeive sc., quod C.Sempronius Ti.f. tr.pl. rog., except*]um cavitu[*mve est nei divideretur, privatus esto* .70]

8 [.40 *eiusque locei agri aedificiei emptio venditi*]o ita, utei ceterorum locorum agrorum aedificiorum privatorum est, esto, censorque, quei quomque erit, facito utei is ager locus aedificium quei e[*x hac lege plebeive scito privatus factus est eritve, ita utei ceteri agri locei aedificia privati, in censum dedicetur referatur, deque eo agro loco aed*]ificio eum quoium [*is ager locus aedificium erit,* .70]

9 [100] est. Neive quis facito quo, quoius eum agrum locum aedificium possesionem ex lege plebeive scito esse oportet oportebitve, eum agrum l[*ocum aedificium possesionem minus oetatur fruatur habeat possideatque* .65 n]eive quis de ea re ad sen[*atum referto* .80]

10 [.60 *neive quis pro potestate inpe*]riove sententia⟨m⟩ deicito neive ferto, quo quis eorum, quoium eum agrum locum aedificium possesionem ex lege plebeive scito esse oport[*et oportebit,* .50 *eum agrum locum aedificium possesionem minus oetatur fruatur habeat possid*]eatque, quove possesio invito mo[*rtui eius heredei auferatur* .60]

11 [*Quei ager publicus populi Romanei in terra Italia P.Muucio L.Calpurnio cos. fuit, quod eius agri III virei viasiei*]s vicaneis, quei in terra Italia sunt, dederunt adsignaverunt reliquerunt, nei quis facito quo minus ei oetantur fruantur habeant po[*ssideantque* .90 *quei eum agrum locum aedifici*]um non ab alienaverit, extra {eum} eum [*agrum* .75]

12 [.95 *extra*]que eum agrum, quei ex h.l. venire dari reddive oportebit. (vac. 2) Quei ager locus aedificium ei, quem in viasieis vicanis ex s.c. esse oportet oportebitve, [*ita datus adsignatus relictusve est eritve* .65 *quo magis is ag*]er locus aedificium privatus siet, quove ma[*gis eius agrei locei aedificiei emptio venditio ita, utei ceterorum locorum agrorum aedificiorum*]

13 [*privatorum est, siet, quove magis is ager locus ab censore, quei quomque erit, in censum relatus aliter atque u*]tei est, siet, ex h.l.n.r. (vac. 3) Quei ager locus publicus populi Romanei in terra Italia P.Muucio L.Calpurnio cos. fuit, extra eum agrum, quei ager ex lege plebeive [*scito, quod C.Sempronius Ti.f. tr.pl. rog., exceptum cavitumve est, nei divideretur, extraque eum agrum, quei viasieis vicaneis adsignatus est erit, ex*]traque eum agrum, quem vetus possesor ex lege plebeive [*scito sibei sumpsit reliquitve quod non modus maior siet, quam quantum unum hominem ex lege pl.ve*]

in the land of Italy a triumvir has given, assigned or maintained in its former state, or entered on maps or records or ordered to be entered;

(lines 7–10) All land, territory or buildings mentioned above which were the public property of *the Roman people in the land of Italy in the consulship of P.Mucius and L.Calpurnius, ... apart from that land, whose division* was made the subject of an exception or forbidden *according to the law or plebiscite which C.Sempronius, son of Tiberius, passed as tribune of the plebs, shall be private ...* VI

and there shall be buying and selling *of that land, territory or building* on the same terms as that of other private land, territory or buildings ... and, whoever shall be censor, he shall ensure that the land, territory or building *made private by this law is recorded in the census and he shall ... about that land, territory or* building, the man, whose *land, territory or building it is ...*;

nor shall anyone act so as to impair *the use, enjoyment, tenure and possession* of any land, territory, building or possession by the man to whom the land, territory, building or possession should belong now or in the future according to law or plebiscite ... no one shall refer the question to the senate ...

nor shall any magistrate by virtue of a magistracy or imperium propose a motion or put it to the vote so as to impair *the use, enjoyment, tenure or possession* of any man to whom the land, territory, building or possession should belong now or in the future ... or so as to *remove* possession against his will from *any heir* of that man when he is dead ...

(lines 11–12) VII

Regarding the land ---- L.Calpurnius, any part of that land which the triumviri have given, assigned or kept in its former state for the benefit of the viasii vicani (villagers by the roads), who are in Italy, let no one act so as to impair their use, enjoyment, tenure and possession of it, ... *provided that the possessor* has not alienated the *land, territory or* building, apart from that land ...

and apart from that land which will be required to be sold, given or duly delivered according to this law.

(lines 12–13) Regarding any land, territory or building, which *has been or shall be so given, assigned or kept in its former state* for a man, who is or shall be required to be among the viasii vicani according to senatus consultum ... let there be no provision under this law whereby this land, territory or building shall become private, or that *there shall be buying and selling of that land, territory or building on the same terms as that of other private land, or that the land or territory* shall be *recorded by any future censor in the census in any other condition than* it is. VIII

(lines 13–14) Regarding the land ---- *tribune of the plebs, apart from any land assigned to the viasii vicani* and apart from any land which a prior possessor *has taken or kept for himself* according to law or plebiscite, *provided that its size is no greater than the amount an individual according to law or plebiscite* IX

14 [*sc. sibei sumere relinquereve licuit, extraque eum agrum quem III vir sortito ceivei R. dedit adsignavit, sei quis c.R. agri colendi cau*]sa in eum agrum agri iugra non amplius XXX possidebit habebitve ⟨i⟩s ager privatus esto. (vac. 4) Quei in agrum compascuom pequdes maiores non plus X pascet quaẹ[*que ex eis minus annum gnatae erunt* .50. *queique ibei pequdes minores non plus* . . .] pascet quaeque ex eis minus annum gnatae erunt, post ea qua[*m vectigalia consistent, quae post h.l.r. primum consistent*, .30.]

15 [.10. *is pro eo numero pequdum populo aut publicano pequniam scripturam vectigalve nei debeto neive satis de ea r*]e dato neive solvito. (vac. 3) Ager publicus populi Romanei, quei in Italia P.Mucio L.Calpurnio cos. fuit, eius agri III vir a.d.a. ex lege plebeive scito sortito quoi ceivi Roma[*no agrum dedit adsignavit, quoive ab eo is ager hereditate testamento deditioneve obvenit obveneritve* (?), *quod eius agri neque is abalie*]navit ab alienaveritve neque heres eius abalienavit abalienav[*eritve*.60. *quei eorum*]

16 [*de ea re ante eidus Martias primas in ious adierit ad eum, quem ex h.l. de eo agro ius deicere oportebit, is de ea re ita ius deicito d*]e̲c̲{r}⟨e⟩rnitoque utei possesionem secund{o}⟨um⟩ eum heredemve eius det, quoi sorti is ager datus adsignatusve fuerit, quod eius agri non ab alienatum erit ita utei s.s. est. (vac. 2+) [*Ager publicus populi Romanei, quei in Italia P.Mucio L.Calpurnio cos. fuit, quod eius agri III vir a.d.a. ex lege plebeive sc. vetere prove ve*]tere posses{ionem}⟨ore⟩ dedit adsignavit reddidit, quodque eius agri III [*vir a.d.a. in urbe oppido vico* (?) *eorum quoi dedit adsignavit, quoive ab eo hereditate testamento*]

17 [*deditioneve obvenit obveneritve, quod eius agri neque is abalienavit abalienaveritve*, .15. *neque heres eiu*]ṣ, queive ab eorum qu{ei}⟨o⟩ emit, quei eorum de ea re ante eidus Martias primas in ious adierit ad eum, quem ex h.l. de eo agro ius deicere oportebit, is de ea re ius deicito d[*ecernitoque utei possesionem secundum eum heredemve eius det, quod eius agri non ab eorum quo abalienatum erit ita utei s.s. est,*] quoi is ager vetere prove vetere possesore datus adsignatusve ⟨fuerit⟩, q*u*eive A[.75.]

18 [.80. *Sei quis eorum, quorum age*]r s.s. est, ex possesione vi eiectus est, quod eius is quei eiectus est possederit, quod neque vi neque clam neque precario possederit ab eo quei eum ea possesione{m} vi eiec[*erit, quem ex h.l. de ea re ious deicere oportebit, is sei quis, quei ex ea possesione vi eiectus est, ad eum de ea re in ious adierit ante eidus Mart̲*]ias, quae post h.l.rog. primae erunt, facito utei is, quei ita vi eiectus e[*st, in eam possesionem, unde vi eiectus est, restituatur*. (vac.) *Quei ager publicus populi*]

was allowed to take or keep for himself, and apart from any land assigned by lot to a Roman citizen by a triumvir, if any Roman citizen shall possess or hold for the purpose *of agriculture* not more than 30 iugera in that land, this land shall be private.

(lines 14–15) Anyone who grazes on common pasture-land not more than 10 larger beasts *and the offspring of these beasts less than a year old . . . and anyone who* grazes *not more than – smaller beasts* and the offspring of these beasts less than a year old *after the fixing of the taxes on the first occasion after the passage of this law . . .* X
he shall not owe to the people or tax-collector rent or pasture-tax (scriptura) for these beasts, nor shall he give security nor make payment.

(lines 15–16) Regarding the land which was public property of the Roman people in Italy in the consulship of P.Mucius and L.Calpurnius, any Roman citizen to whom any part of that land a triumvir for the assignation and grant of lands *has given or assigned* by lot according to law or plebiscite, *or anyone to whom that land has accrued or shall accrue by inheritance, will or cession, such land as he* has not alienated nor subsequently alienates and his heir has not alienated nor subsequently alienates . . . *if anyone of them approaches before the next Ides of March at his tribunal the man who shall be required to give judgement about that land according to this law, he shall give judgement about that matter* and decree so as to give possession to the man or his heir, to whom that land was given or assigned by lot, in relation to any part of that land not alienated in the manner described above. XI

(lines 16–17) *Regarding the land - - - - L.Calpurnius, any part of that land which a triumvir for the assignation and grant of lands* has given, assigned or given in return *according to law or plebiscite to a prior possessor or the equivalent of a* prior possessor, and any part of that land which a triumvir *has given or assigned to any such man, which is in a city, town or village outside the city of Rome, or anyone to whom that land has accrued or shall accrue by inheritance, will* XII
or cession, such land as he has not alienated nor subsequently alienates and his heir has not alienated nor subsequently alienates, or anyone who has bought it from any of the former, if anyone of them approaches before the next Ides of March at his tribunal the man who shall be required to give judgement about that land according to this law, he shall give judgement about that matter *and decree so as to give possession to the man or his heir, in relation to any part of that land not alienated in the manner described above*, to whom that land was given or assigned as a prior possessor or the equivalent of a prior possessor or who . . .

(line 18) XIII
If any of those, whose land is mentioned above, is ejected by violence from possession, in so far as he, who was ejected, was in possession of it, and he was in possession of it neither through violence nor by stealth nor on sufferance at the expense of the man who ejected him by violence from that possession, *if the man so ejected shall approach at his tribunal the man, who shall be required to give judgement about that land according to this law, before the Ides of* March which shall be next after the passage of this law, that man shall ensure that the man so ejected *shall be restored to that possession from which he was ejected by violence.*

(lines 18–19) *Regarding the land - - - -* XIV

19 [*Romanei in Italia P.Mucio L.Calpurnio cos. fuit, quei ex eo agro agrum locum aedificium possidebit, quod ex lege plebeive sc*]ito exve h.l. privatum factum est eritve, pro eo agro loco aedificio proque scriptura pecoris, quod in eo agro pascitur, post quam vectigalia constiterint, quae post h.l.[*rog. primum constiterint, is nei populo aut publicano pequniam scripturam vectigalve dare debeto, neive quis facito quo is populo aut p*]ublicano pequnia⟨m⟩ scripturam vec{p}⟨t⟩igalve det dareve debeat neive quis [*decernito* (vac.) *Quei ager publicus populi Romanei in Italia P.Mucio L.Calpurnio cos. fuit, quod eius*]

20 [*agri III virei viasieis vicaneis, quei in Italia sunt, adsignaverunt, nei quis mag. prove mag. facito quo ei agri vectigalis sie*]ṇṭ quove quid ob eam rem populo aut publicano detur exsigaturve, neive quis quid postea quam vectigalia consistent, quae post h.l.rog. primum constiterint, ob eos ag[*ros quid populo aut publicano dare debeto, neive quis facito quo quis pequniam pro eo agro prove scriptura pecoris, quod in eis ag*]reis pascetur populo aut publicano dare debeat. (vac. 3) Ager locus publicus popul[*i Romanei, quei* .70.]

21 [*extra eum agrum, quem* .80. *ex s.*]c. a.d. X⟨I⟩{E} K. Octobris oina quom agro, quei trans Curione est, locaverunt, quei in eo agro loco ceivis Romanus sociumve nominisve Latini, quibus ex formula togatorum [*milites in terra Italia inperare solent* .60. *agrum loc*]um populi Romanei de sua possesione vetus possesor prove vetere possesor[*e dedit, quo in agro loco oppidum coloniave ex lege plebeive sc. constitueretur deduceretur*]

22 [*conlocaretur,* .70. *quo in agro loco III vir i*]d oppidum coloniamve ex lege plebeive sc. constituit deduxitve conlocavitve, quem agrum locumve pro eo agro loc⟨o⟩{um}ve de eo agro loco, quei publicus populi Roman[*ei in terra Italia P.Muucio L.Calpurnio cos. fuit, III vir ei dedit reddidit adsignavit, ei sed fraude sua possidere liceto, extra eum a*]grum locum, quei ager locus ex lege plebeive sc., quod C.Sempron(ius) Ti.f. tr.pl. rog., exscep[*tum cavitumve est nei divideretur,* .40.]

23 [.20. *eique ceivei Romano nominisve Latini* (?), *quoi is ager locus a III viro datus redditus adsignatus erit*] quoive ab eo heredive eius is ager locus testamento hereditati deditionive obvenit obveneritve ⟨queive ab eo⟩ emit emeritve, queive ab emptore eius emit emeritve, is ager privatus esto QVE[.30. *Ager locus publicus populi Romanei, quem III vir de eo agro loco pro eo agro loco, qu*]ọ coloniam deduxsit ita utei s.s. est, agrum locum aedificium dedit reddidit adsignavit, quei [*de eo agro loco aedificio pr. consolve ex h.l. ious deicet,* .20. *quo de ea re*]

L.Calpurnius, anyone who holds land, territory or building in it, which has been made private *by law* or plebiscite or by this law, *shall not be obliged to pay money, scriptura or tax to the people or the tax-collector* for that land, territory or building or for the tax on the livestock, which graze in that land, after the fixing of the taxes *on the first occasion* after the passage of this law, *nor shall anyone cause him* to pay money, scriptura or tax *to the people or* the tax-collector nor shall anyone *so decree.* XIV

(lines 19–20) *Regarding the land - - - -* XV

L.Calpurnius, no magistrate or promagistrate shall cause any land assigned by the triumviri to the viasii vicani, who are in Italy, to become liable to tax or cause anything to be given to or exacted by the people or the tax-collector on that account, nor shall anyone after the fixing of taxes on the first occasion after the passage of this law *be obliged to pay* anything on account of those lands *to the people or the tax-collector, nor shall anyone cause a man* to be obliged to pay to the people or the tax-collector *money for that land or for the tax on the livestock which* graze on that land.

(lines 20–3) Regarding the land and territory which is public property of the Roman people, ... XVI

apart from that land which ... (magistrates' names) leased *according to senatus* consultum on September 20th in conjunction with the land which is beyond (the?) Curio, any Roman citizen or any ally or member of the Latin name, from whom *they are accustomed to demand troops in Italy* according to the schedule of togati (formula togatorum), who in that land or territory *gave* ... as a prior possessor or the equivalent of a prior possessor public *land* or territory of the Roman people from his possession, *so that a town or colony might be established, founded or settled in that land or territory according to law or plebiscite, ...*

land or territory, in which a triumvir established, founded or settled the town or colony in question according to law or plebiscite – any land or territory which *a triumvir gave, assigned or duly delivered to such a man* in return for the land or territory in question from the land or territory which was the public property of the Roman people *in the land of Italy in the consulship of P.Mucius and L.Calpurnius, that man shall lawfully possess it without prejudice to himself, apart from that* land or territory, whose *division* was made the subject of an exception *or forbidden*, according to the law or plebiscite of C.Sempronius, son of Tiberius, tribune of the plebs ...

and for that Roman citizen or (?) member of the Latin name, to whom this land or territory has been given, assigned or duly delivered by a triumvir or to whom this land or territory has accrued or shall accrue by inheritance, will or cession from him or his heir, or who has bought or shall buy it from him, or who has bought or shall buy it from its original purchaser, this land shall be private ...

(lines 23–4) *Regarding the land or territory which is the public property of the Roman people*, any land, territory or buildings, *which a triumvir* has given, assigned or duly delivered *from that land or territory in return for the land or territory* where he founded a colony in the manner described above, *the praetor or consul* who *gives judgement about that land, territory or building according to this law ...* XVII

24 [*ante eidus Martias preimas in ious aditum erit, is de ea re ita ious deicito decernitoque, utei possesionem secundum eum h*]eredemve eius det, quoi III vir eum agrum locum pro eo agro loco, quo coloniam deduxit, deddit reddidit adsignavitve, facitoque is pr. consolve, quo de ea re in ious aditu⟨m⟩{n} erit [. 80 . *Ager locus quei sup*]ra screiptus est, quod eius agrei locei post h.l.rog. publicum populei Romanei erit, extra eum ag[*rum locum, quei ager ex lege plebeive sc., quod C.Sempronius Ti.f. rog., exsceptum cavitumve est,*]

25 [*nei divideretur, extraque eum agrum quei publice locatus est,* . 55 .] NEIVE is ager compascuos esto, neive quis in eo agro agrum oqupatum habeto neive defendito quo minus quei velit compascere liceat. Sei quis faxsit, quotiens faxsit, in agri iugra singula L [*HS n*(ummos) *in publicum dare damnas esto* . 60 . *dar*]e debeto ei, queiquomque id publicum fruendum redemptu⟨m⟩{w} co⟨n⟩{w}ductu⟨m⟩{w}ve habebit. (vac. 3) Boves equ[*os* . 80 .]

26 [. 65 . *quei volet pascere ad eum numerum pecudum que*]i numerus pecudum in h.l. scriptus est, liceto, neive quid quoi ob eam rem vectigal neive scri[*pturam da*]re debeto. (vac. 3) Quod quisque pecudes in calleis viasve publicas iteneris causa indu[*xerit ibeique pastum inpulerit* . 40 . *pro eo pecore, quod eius in calli*]bus viei⟨s⟩{l}q⟨v⟩e publiceis pastum impulsum itineris causa erit, nei quid populo neive publicano d[*are debeto* . 55 . *Quei ager publicus*]

27 [*populi Romanei in terra Italia P.Muucio L.Calpurnio cos. fuit, de eo agro loco, quem agrum locum III vir ex publico in privatum co*]mmutavit, quo pro agro loco ex privato in publicum tantum modum agri locei commutav[*it, is ager locus do*]mneis privatus ita, utei qu⟨e⟩{o}i optuma lege privatus est, esto. (vac. 3) Quei ager ex priva[*to in publicum a III viro commutatus est, quo pro agro loco tantus modus agri locei publicei ex p*]ublico im privatum commutatus est, de eo agro siremps lex esto quansei is ager P.Mucio L. C[*alpurnio cos. publicus fuisset.* (vac.) . 55 .]

28 [. 60 . *quanti agrum patritum mancipes* (?) *L.Caecilio Cn.Dom*]itio cens. redemptum habe[*n*]t, censoribus, queiquomque post hace facteis erunt, ei faciunto [*mancipes*(?), *sei*] volent, tantidem pro patrito redemptum habeant p.p. supsignent. (vac. 2) II virum qu[*ei* . 60 . *quae viae publicae p*]er terram Italiam P.Mucio L. Calpurnio cos. {e}⟨f⟩uerint, eas faciunto pateant vacuaeque sie[*nt* . 80 .]

29 [. 80 . *Quod quoieique ex h.l. it*]a utei s.s. est, in agreis quei in Italia sunt, quei P.Mucio L.Calpurnio cos. publiceis populi Ro[*manei fuerunt*] Romano facere licebit, item Latino peregrinoque, quibus M.Livio L.Calpurnio cos. [*in eis agreis agrum locum aedificium possesionem oeti frui habere possidere ex lege pleb*]eive sc. exve {e}⟨f⟩oedere licuit, sed fraude sua {e}⟨f⟩acere liceto. (vac. 2) Quod ex h.l. ita, utei s.s. est, in agreis, que[*i* . 85 .]

who is approached about that matter at his tribunal before the Ides of March next, shall give judgement about this matter accordingly and decree so as to give *possession to that man* or his heir, to whom the triumvir gave, duly delivered or assigned that land or territory in return for the land or territory, where he founded a colony, and the praetor or consul in question, who is approached at his tribunal about that matter . . .

(lines 24–5) *Regarding the land or territory* mentioned above, any of that land or territory which is public property of the Roman people after the passage of this law, apart from that land *or territory, whose division was made the subject of an exception or forbidden according to the law – tribune of the plebs and (?)* XVIII

apart from that land which has been publicly leased, . . . and it shall (not) be common pasture-land, . . . nor shall anyone keep land under occupation in that land nor fence it off so as to prevent anyone who wishes from joining in pasturing. If anyone does so, *he shall be liable to pay* 50 *sesterces to the treasury* on each occasion for each iugerum of land . . . he shall be obliged *to give* to the man, who has bought or leased the exploitation of this public revenue.

(lines 25–6) Oxen, horses . . . XIX

anyone who wishes may lawfully *pasture up to that* number of beasts which is prescribed in this law, nor shall he owe anyone any rent or pasture-tax (scriptura) on that account.

(line 26) On each occasion that a man has led beasts on to drove-roads (calles) and public roads in order to make a journey *and here has driven them to graze* . . . he shall not *owe* anything to the people or the tax-collector *in respect of the beasts which* have been driven to graze on the drove-roads and the public roads while on a journey . . . XX

(lines 26–7) *Regarding the land* - - - - XXI

L.Calpurnius, any land or territory from that land or territory, which a triumvir has changed *from public into private land* in return for which he has changed a corresponding amount of land or territory from private into public land, *this land or territory* shall be the private land of its owners with as good title as any private land.

(line 27) Any land changed from private *into public land by a triumvir, in return for which a corresponding amount of public land or territory* was changed from public into private land, let the same law apply regarding this land, as if it *had been public in the consulship of* P.Mucius and L.Calpurnius. XXII

(lines 27–8) *Regarding any land belonging to ager patritus (ancestral land),* XXIII

at whatever value the contractors have bought a public contract in the censorship of *L.Caecilius and Cn.Domitius* (115 BC), in any subsequent censorship they (the censors) shall ensure that *the contractors, if* they wish, have their contract bought and give security at the corresponding value for land which is a substitute for ager patritus.

(line 28) The duumvir, who . . . they shall ensure that *any public roads*, which existed throughout Italy in the consulship of P.Mucius and L.Calpurnius, shall be open and free from obstruction . . . XXIV

(line 29) XXV

Whatever every Roman citizen has the right to do *according to this law*, as is prescribed above, in the lands in Italy which *were* public property of the Roman people in the consulship of P.Mucius and L.Calpurnius, any Latin and foreigner, who had the right by *law*, plebiscite or treaty *to use, enjoyment, tenure and possession of land, territory or building in those lands* in the consulship of M.Livius and L.Calpurnius (112 BC), shall likewise have the right to do so without prejudice to himself.

(lines 29–30) Whatever, according to this law, as is prescribed above, in the lands *which are mentioned above* . . . XXVI

30 [. 90 *de ea re, quod eoru*]m quis, quod eum ex h(ac) l(ege) facere oportuerit, non fecerit, quodve quis eorum ex h.l.[*fecerit, is mag.*] prove mag., quo d⟨e⟩ ea re in ious aditum erit, quod ex h.l. petetur, item iudicium iudi[*cem recuperatoresve ei et in eum, quei Latinus peregrinusve erit, dato* . 15 *ita utei ei*] et in eum iudicium iudicem recuperatoresve ex h.l. dare oporteret, sei quis de ea re iudiciu[*m peteret, quei ceivis Romanus esset, queive a ceive Romano peteret* . 40]

31 [100 *sei quibus colonieis seive moi*]nicipieis seive, quae pro moinicipieis colo[*nieisve sunt, ceivium R.*] nominisve Latini poplice deve senatus sententia ager fruendus datus [*est erit, seive quei in trientabuleis sunt*, . 25 *ei colonei moinicipesve queiv*]e pro colonia moinicipiove prove moinicipieis fruentur, quei⟨ve⟩ in trientabule[*is sunt* . 55 *quod eius agri colonei moinicipesve*]

32 [*habebunt, queive pro colonia moinicipiove prove moinicipieis fruentur, quodve eius agri eis, quei in trientabuleis sunt, testamento hereditate deditione ob*]venit obveneritve, quibus ante h.[*l.rog. agrum locum con*]ductum habere frui possidere defendere licuit, extra eum agrum locu[*m* . 90]MVE oportebit, id, utei quicquid quoieique ante h.l.r. licuit, ita ei habere [*conductum frui possidere defendere post h.l.rog. liceto* . 55]

33 [135] Quei ager locus publicus pop[*uli Romanei in t*]erra Italia P.Mucio L.Calpurnio cos. fuit, quod eius agri loci ex lege [*plebeive scito privatum factum est* . 55 *sei qu*]id de eo agro loco ambigetur, cos. pr., quei quomque erit, de ea re iuris[*dictio, iudici iudicis recuperatorum datio esto i.v.e.e.r.p.f.s.v.e.* . 55]

34 [. 90 *neive quis mag. prove mag. de eo agro loco ious deicito neive dec*]ernito neive iudicium neive[*iudicem neive*]recuperatores dato, nisei cos. pr.ve. Quod vadimonium eius rei c[*ausa promissum non erit, quo minus de eo, quei non promeiserit aut vindicem locupletem non dederit, cos. pr. eius r*]ei causa decernant, eius h.l.n.r. Quod iudicium iudex recuperator[*es datei erunt, sei quis de ea re mag. adpellatus erit, quoi id e r.p. non esse videbitur, quo minus is inpediat vel intercedat, e.h.l.n.r.* . 10]

35 [*Quei ager locus publicus populi Romanei in terra Italia P.Mucio L.Calpurnio cos. fuit, quod eius agrei locei post h.l.rog. publicum populei Romanei erit, sei quid de eo agro loco ambigetur,*] cos. pr. cens. queiquo[*mque erit, eius de ea re iu*]ris dictio iudici iudicis recuperatorum datio esto i(ta) v(tei) e(i) e r(e) p(ublica) f(ideque) s(ua) v(idebitur) [*e*(sse), . 50 *neive quis mag. prove mag. nisei cos. pr. cens. de e*]o agro loco ious deicito neive decernito neive iudicium [*ne*]ive iud[*icem neive recuperatores dato. Quod vadimonium eius rei causa promissum non erit, quo minus de eo, quei non promeiserit aut vindicem*]

concerning any action which anyone *of these* has not done which he should have done according to this law or which *he has done* according to this law, *the magistrate* or promagistrate, who is approached at his tribunal, when suit is made according to this law, shall grant a jury, a judge *or recuperatores both to the man and against the man who is a Latin or a foreigner*, ... in exactly the same way as he would be required by this law to grant a jury, a judge or recuperatores to the man and against the man, if anyone *was seeking* a trial in that matter, *who was a Roman citizen or was suing from a Roman citizen* ...

(lines 31–2) ... XXVII

in any case where the enjoyment of any land *has been* given *or is given in the future* by the people or a vote of the senate *to any colonies or* municipia or any equivalent of municipia or colonies, whether *Roman* or of the Latin name, *or where there are men in the trientabula ... those members of a colony or a municipium or those* who enjoy (land) on behalf of a colony, municipium or (?) the equivalents of municipia, or those who *are* in the trientabula ... *any of that land possessed by members of a colony or municipium or those who enjoy (land) on behalf of a colony, municipium or the equivalent of municipia, or any of that land which* has accrued or accrues in the future to those, who are in the trientabula, by inheritance, will or cession, who had the right before *the passage of this law* to hold, enjoy, possess and defend *land or territory* which had been leased, apart from that land or territory ... or shall be required to be ..., he *shall have the right to* hold, *enjoy, possess and defend* it to the extent that anyone had the right to do so before the passage of this law ...

(lines 33–4) XXVIII

Regarding the land or territory, which was the public property - - - - L.Calpurnius, any of that land or territory which *has been made private* according to law *or plebiscite ... if* there is any dispute about that land or territory, whoever *is* consul or praetor *at the time*, shall have jurisdiction *in that matter and the right to appoint a jury, a judge or recuperatores as he decides to be in the public interest and to cause no breach of his own good faith* ...

nor shall any magistrate or promagistrate give judgement about that land or territory or make a decree or appoint a jury *or judge or* recuperatores except a consul or praetor. If any surety *has not been promised* for that case, nothing is enacted in this law forbidding *a consul or praetor* making a decree *for that* case *concerning the man who has not promised or provided a vindex of sufficient wealth.* On any occasion when a jury, a judge or recuperatores *have been appointed, (?) if appeal is made to a magistrate on that count and he considers this not to be in the public interest, nothing is enacted by this law forbidding him using obstruction or veto* ...

(lines 35–6) XXIX

Regarding the land or territory, which - - - - L.Calpurnius, if there is any dispute about that part of that land or territory which is public property of the Roman people after the passage of this law, whoever *is* consul, praetor or censor *at the time*, shall have jurisdiction and the right to appoint a jury, a judge or recuperatores *in that matter*, as he decides to be in the public interest and to cause no breach of his own good faith ... *nor shall any magistrate or promagistrate* give judgement *about that* land or territory or make a decree *or appoint* a jury or judge *or recuperatores, except a consul, praetor or censor. If any surety has not been promised for that case, nothing is enacted in this law forbidding a consul, praetor or censor making a decree for that case concerning the man who has not promised or provided a vindex of sufficient*

36 [*locupletem non dederit, cos. pr. cens. eius rei causa decernant, e.h.l.n.r.* . 10 *Quod iudicium iudex recuperatores datei erunt, sei quis de ea re mag. adpellatus erit, quoi id e r.p.*] non esse videbitur, quo [*minus is inpediat ve*]l intercedat, e.h.l.n.r. Quoi publicano e.h.l. pequnia debebitur, [*nei quis* . 80]EM facito quo quis pro agro minus aliterve scripturam v[*ectigalve det, atque utei ex h.l. dare debet debebitve* . 70]

37 [100 *Sei quid publicanus eius rei causa a quo eorum sibi deberi*] darive oportere de[*icat, eis cos. prove co*]s. pr. prove pr., quo in ious adierint, in diebus X proxsumeis, qu[*ibus de ea re in ious adierint* . 65ṾIBVS L, quei classis primae sient, XI dato, inde alternos du[*mtaxat quaternos* (?) *is quei petet et is unde petetur, quos volent reiciant facito* . 55]

38 [130 *de ea re iudicare iubeto,*]quae res soluta no[*n siet inve iudici*]o non siet iudicatave non siet, quod eius praevaricationus [*causa* . 90]MVE factum non siet. Sei maior pars recuperatorum [120]

39 [145 *sed fr*]aude sententia [*pronontiato quod eius*] rei ioudicandae maxsume verum esse co{m}mperrit, facitoqu[*e* . 80 *quod ita ioudicatum e*]rit, se d{u}⟨o⟩lo m{n}⟨alo⟩ utei is, quei iudicatus erit dare oporteat [120]

40 [. 10 *Quas in leges pl.ve sc. de ea re is, quei iurare iubetur iubebitur, non iuraverit, quod eum, quei agrum publicum populi Romani ita habebit possidebit fruetur, utei ex h.l. licebit, earum q*]uaẹ ag[*rum, quem ex h.l. habebit, h*]abere possidere frui{e} vetet, quasve in leges pl.ve sc. de ea r[*e is, quei iurare iubetur iubebitur, non iuraverit, quod earum quae ei, quei agrum publicum populi Romani aliter habebit*] possidebit fruetur, quam ex h.l. licebit, eum agrum, quem [*contra h.l. habebit, habere possidere frui permittat, ei sed fraude sua ita non iurare liceto* . 40]

41 [150 *neive ei ob eam rem magistratum inperiumve q*]uem minus petere capere gerere habereque liceto, neive q[*uis minus eum in senatu sententiam deicere sinito, neive censor minus eum in senatum legito.* . 20] Si quae lex plebeive sc. est, quae ma{s}⟨g⟩. quem ex h.l. [*de aliqua re decernere oportet, de ea re decernere vetet, is mag. de ea re nihilo minus decernito* . 45]

42 [105 *quaeque ei eis legibus plebeive scitis facere vetitum est, quae eum ex h.l. facere oportebit, ea omnia ei sed f*]raude sua facere liceto, inque eas leges pl.sc. de ea re, quod ex [*h.l. aliter, quam in eis legibus plebeive scitis scriptum est* . 50] decernere oportebit, sed fraude sua nei iourato neive [*quid ei ob eam rem fraudei esto* 100]

43 [190] TVS est, dedit adsignavitve, quemve agrum locum de eo agro lo[*co* . 90 *ex lege*] pl.sc., quod M.Baebius tr.pl. III vir coloniae deducend[*ae rogavit* 115]

44 [185 *datu*]m adsignatum esse fuiseve ioudicaverit, utei in h.l. sc(riptum) est, quei L[100] extra eum agrum locum quei ager locus in ea cen[*turia supsicivove* 110]

wealth. On any occasion when a jury, a judge, or recuperatores have been appointed, if appeal is made to any magistrate on that count and he considers this not to be *in the public interest*, nothing is enacted by this law forbidding him *to use obstruction* or veto.

(lines 36–9) [A new chapter seems in fact to begin here, although there is no lacuna indicating this in the inscription.] Any tax-collector, who is owed money according to this law, ... no one shall cause anyone to pay in return for land pasture tax (scriptura) *or tax* of a lesser amount or in a different fashion *than he is or will be obliged to do according to this law* ... *If a tax-collector* claims that *anything is owed* or should be given *to him by any of these men on that account, the consul or proconsul* (*censor* ?), praetor or propraetor, whom they have approached at his tribunal, shall within the next ten days, from the time *they have approached him about this matter at his tribunal* ... provide *as recuperatores* 11 men from (the) 50, who are of the first class, and then *allow the man who is suing and the man who is being sued to reject* alternately not more than *four each (?) at their own discretion* ... XXX

He shall order them to judge about anything, which has not been paid or is not *subject to trial* or to a previous judicial decision, provided that nothing has been done *for the sake of* praevaricatio or ... If a majority of the recuperatores ...,

he shall declare without prejudice in his verdict what he has discovered to be most true for the judgement of *that* matter and ensure ... that the man, who according to the verdict shall be obliged to give *what is so judged*, shall without intent to frustrate justice ...

(lines 40–1) *Regarding any oaths to observe laws or plebiscites on this subject, which a man, who is ordered or shall be ordered to swear, has not sworn, on the ground that* any *of the laws* forbids *the man who holds, possesses and enjoys public land of the Roman people, as is permitted under this law*, to hold, possess and enjoy *the land, which he holds according to this law*, or any oaths to observe laws or plebiscites on this subject, *which the man, who is ordered or shall be ordered to swear, has not sworn to observe, on the ground that any of the laws allows the man, who holds, possesses and enjoys public land of the Roman people on other terms*, than is permitted under this law, *to hold, possess and enjoy* that land, *which he holds contrary to this law, it is lawful for him to refuse to swear these without prejudice to himself* ... XXXI

nor shall it be any the less lawful *for him* to seek, undertake, exercise and hold any *magistracy or imperium on that account* nor shall anyone *refuse to allow him to deliver his opinion in the senate nor shall the censor refuse to enrol him in the senate* ...

(lines 41–2) If there is any law or plebiscite, which *forbids* a magistrate, who *is required to decree about some matter* by this law, *this magistrate shall none the less decree about this matter* ... XXXII

and everything, which is forbidden by those laws and plebiscites, which he is required to do by this law, it shall be lawful *for him* to do without prejudice to himself, and regarding the laws and plebiscites about this matter, in so far as he shall be obliged to decree according to this law *in a different fashion to what is prescribed in these laws and plebiscites* ..., he shall be exempted from swearing without prejudice to himself, nor *shall he suffer in any way by this* ...

(line 43) ... gave or assigned, or any land or territory from that land or territory ... *according to the law* or plebiscite, which M.Baebius, tribune of the plebs and triumvir for the foundation of a colony, *has passed* ...

(line 44) ... has judged to be *given* and assigned or to have been given and assigned, as is prescribed in this law, ... apart from the land or territory, which is in that centuria *or subsecivum* ...

45 [1̣9̣0̣ *e*]um agrum locum, quem ex h.l. colonei, eive quei in colonei numero [*scriptei sunt, .*8̣0̣ *oportet*] oportebitve quod eius agri locei quoieique emptum est, [1̣2̣0̣]

46 [1̣9̣0̣ *m*]anceps praevides praediaque soluti sunto, eaque nomina mancup[*is, .*9̣0̣ *quaestor,*] quei aerarium provinciam optinebit, in tableis [*publiceis* 1̣1̣5̣]

47 [1̣8̣5̣] mag. Romano emit, is pro eo agro loco pequunia⟨m⟩ neive praevides nei[*ve praedia data .*6̣5̣ *neive de ea re quis ob eam*] rem, quod praes factus est, populo obligatus est[*o* 1̣2̣5̣]

48 [1̣7̣5̣ *quei ob eu*]m agrum locum manceps praesve factus est quodque [*pr*]aedium ob [*eam rem populo obligatum est .*7̣5̣ *q*]uei ager locus in Africa est, quei Romae publice [1̣2̣5̣]

49 [1̣8̣5̣] eius esto isque ager locus privatus vectigalisque Ṿ[1̣1̣0̣]TVS erit, quod eius agri locei extra terra Italia est [1̣2̣0̣]

50 [1̣4̣0̣ *socium nominisve Latini, quibus ex formula t*]ogatorum milites in terra Italia inperare solent, eis PO[1̣1̣5̣]VE agrum locum queiquomque habebit possidebit [*fruetur* 1̣1̣5̣]

51 [1̣8̣0̣]E rei procurandae causa erit, in eum agrum locum in [1̣1̣5̣ *Quei ag*]er locus in Africa est, quod eius agri [.3̣5̣ *facito se dolo m*]alo, quei ag[*er .*6̣5̣]

52 [1̣7̣0̣ *habeat poss*]ideat fruaturque item, utei sei is ager locus publi[*ce* 1̣1̣0̣ *II vir quei ex h.l.*] factus creatusve erit, EIICI [(*edicito*?) .4̣5̣] I in biduo proxsumo, quo [.6̣5̣]

53 [1̣7̣0̣ *in diebus*] XXV proxsumeis, quibus id edictum erit, P̣P̣Ṿ [1̣3̣0̣ p]rofitebitur, cognito[*rem .*4̣5̣ *dat*]um adsignatum siet, idque quom [.6̣0̣]

54 [1̣8̣0̣] MVM emptor siet ab eo, quoius homin[*is privati venditio fuerit* 1̣2̣5̣]IQVE ipse N[.2̣5̣ *quae venditio ante k. Ian. M.Livio L.*]Calpurni⟨o⟩ cos. facta siet, quod eius postea Ị[.5̣5̣]

55 [1̣8̣0̣ *p*]raefectus milesve in provinciam E[1̣5̣0̣] ag[*er locus ex lege Rubria, quae fuit, colono eive, quei in colonei nu*]mero scriptus est, datus adsignatusve est, quodve eius [.4̣5̣]

56 [1̣8̣0̣]utei curator eius profiteatur, item ute[*i* 2̣0̣5̣]O edicito utei is, quei ab bonorum emptore magistro curato[*reve emerit .*3̣0̣]

57 [1̣8̣0̣]IT, quod edicto II vir(ei) professus ex h.l. N[1̣9̣5̣ *ei eum agrum lo*]cum neive emptum neive adsignatum esse neive fuisse iudicato. (vac.) Q[..3̣]

58 [1̣8̣0̣]RO ei ceivi Romano tantundem modu[*m agrei locei* 1̣6̣5̣]ṾEI ẸIṾ[.2̣2̣] quei ager publice non venieit, dare reddere commutare liceto. (vac.) II vir, q[*uei ex h.l. factus creatusve erit*]

(line 45) . . . that land or territory, which according to this law colonists or those who *have been enrolled* as colonists . . . *is or* shall be required, regarding any portion of that land or territory which has been bought by each person . . .
(line 46) . . . the contractor (manceps), the guarantors and the property secured shall be free of obligation, and the names of the contractor *and guarantors* (?) . . . *the quaestor*, who has at the time the aerarium as his province, . . . in *public* records . . .
(line 47) . . . has bought (?from) a Roman magistrate, he shall *give* money and not guarantors nor *security in property* for that land or territory . . . *nor shall anyone in that matter on account of* the fact that he has been made a guarantor, be under obligation to the (Roman) people . . .
(line 48) . . . *the man* who has been made a contractor or guarantor *on account of that* land or territory and any security in property *pledged to the people on that account* . . .
. . . Any land or territory in Africa, which publicly at Rome . . .
(line 49) . . . shall belong to him and this land shall be private and subject to tax . . . shall be *given in security* (?), any of the land or territory outside Italy . . .
(line 50) . . . *allies or members of the Latin name, from whom* they are accustomed to demand soldiers in Italy *according to the schedule* of togati, these *peoples* (?) . . . whoever holds, possesses *or enjoys* land or territory . . .
(line 51) . . . is in the future, in order to handle business, into that land or territory . . . *Any land* or territory in Africa, regarding that portion . . . *let him act without intent* to frustrate justice so that the land which . . .
(line 52) . . . should *hold*, possess and enjoy, just as if the land or territory publicly . . . *the duumvir who* has been appointed or created *according to this law* . . . within two days from the time when . . .
(line 53) . . . in the next 25 days following this edict . . . he will declare, a legal representative (cognitor) . . . (it) may have been given and assigned and this, when . . .
(line 54) . . . may be a buyer from a man, whose . . . he himself . . . *any sale which* took place *before* the consulships of *M.Livius and* L.Calpurnius, in so far as subsequently . . .
(line 55) . . . as a praefectus or soldier to the province . . . any land *or territory which* was given or assigned *to a colonist under the repealed Rubrian law or to a man, who* was enrolled as if he were a *colonist*, or any part of it . . .
(line 56) . . . that his/its receiver (curator) should make a declaration, likewise that . . . he shall make an edict ordering anyone who *has bought* from the purchaser, administrator or receiver of a property . . .
(line 57) . . . what he has declared under the terms of this law according to the edict of the duumvir . . . he shall judge *that land* or territory to have been neither purchased *by him* nor assigned *to him* then or in the past. XLIII*
(line 58) . . . a corresponding amount *of land or territory* to that Roman citizen . . . he may give, duly deliver and exchange land, which has not been publicly sold. XLIV*
(lines 58–61) The duumvir *appointed or created under this law* . . . XLV*

59 [1̣8̣0̣ de] eis agreis ita rationem init{i}o itaque <u>H</u>[1̣6̣5̣ *quantum uni*] homini [*ex h.l. dari adsignari lic*]et, neive unius hominis nomine, quoi ex lege Rubria, quae fuit, colono eive quei in [*colonei numero scriptus*]

60 [*est, agrum, quei in Africa est, dare oportuit licuitve* 1̣2̣5̣ *data adsign*]ata fuise iudicato, neive unius hominus [*nomine* 1̣4̣5̣ *quoi ex lege Rubria, quae fuit,*] colono [*eive, quei in colonei nu*]mero scriptus est, agrum, quei in Africa est, dare oportebit licuitve, amplius iug(era) CC in [.2̣0̣]

61 [1̣1̣0̣ *neive maiorem numerum in Africa hominum in coloniam coloniasve deductum esse fu*]<u>is</u>eve iudicato q̣uam quantum numer[*um* 1̣7̣0̣]O QVAE E[..3̣ *ab III viro coloniae dedu*]cendae in Africa hominum in coloniam coloniasve deduci oportuit licuitve. (vac.) II vir, quei [*ex h.l. factus*]

62 [*creatusve erit* 1̣6̣5̣]TỴ[.1̣5̣]ṚỌṂ[1̣4̣5̣ *d*]atus a<u>ds</u>[*ignatus est,* .1̣5̣ *quod*]eius non [*venieit, quod eiu*]s agri ex h.l. adiudicari licebit, quod ita comperietur, id ei heredeive eius adsignato esse iudicato. [.1̣2̣]

63 [3̣3̣5̣ *quod* ...]OQVE eius agri loc<u>ei ante</u>[..4̣ *M.Livio L.Calpu*]rnio co[*s. quoique emptum*] est ab eo, quoius eius agri locei hominis privati venditio fuit tum, quom is eum agrum locum emit, quei [.1̣0̣]

64 [3̣4̣0̣]T, planum faciet feceritve emptum esse, q[*uod*] eius ne[*que is ipse postea*] neque heres eius neque quoi is heres erit abalienaverit, quod eius agri locei ita planum factum erit, II vir ita [..2̣]

65 [3̣3̣0̣ *dato re*<u>d</u>]dito, quod is emptor habuerit, quod eius publice non venie<u>r</u>[*it.* (vac.) *II vir, sei is*]ager locus quei ei emptus fuerit publice venieit, tantundem modum agri locei de eo agro loco, quei ager lo[*cus in*]

66 [*Africa est, quod eius publice non venieit, ei reddito* 2̣4̣0̣ *Quei ager locus ita ex h.l. datus redditus erit, ei, quoius ex h.l. f*]<u>a</u>ctus erit, HS n. I emptus esto, isque ager locus privatus vectigalisque, ịtạ [*utei infra*] scriptum est, esto. (vac.) Quoi colono eive, quei in colonei numero scriptus est, ager locus in ea centuria supsicivov[*e*]

67 [2̣9̣0̣ *tantundem modum agri locei pro eo agro loco de eo a*]<u>gr</u>o loco, quei ager locus in Africa est, quod eius publice non venieit, ei he[*redeive ei*]us II vir, quei ex h.l. factus creatusve erit, reddito. (vac.) Quoi colono eive, quei in colonei numero scriptus est, fuitve [..5̣]

68 [2̣8̣5̣ *tantundem modum agri locei ei, quem ita habuise possedi*]<u>s</u>eve comperietur, heredeive eius de agro, quei ager in Africa est, pro eo agro Ị[*I vir reddi*]to, quoieique ita reddiderit, adsignatum fuisse iudicato. (vac.) Quoi agrum de eo agro, quei ager in Africa est, quei colono e[*ive*]

shall make a computation *about* this territory in such a way, and in such a way ... (shall judge to have been assigned) *as much as may be given and assigned to one* individual *under this law* and no (more) on account of one individual, to whom, as a colonist under the repealed Rubrian law or as a man who *was enrolled as if he were a colonist, it was right or legitimate to give land in Africa* ... he shall judge (? ... iugera) to have been assigned and shall not *on account of* one individual ... *to whom*, as a colonist *under the repealed Rubrian law or as a man* who was enrolled as if he were *a colonist*, it was right and legitimate to give land in Africa, (assign) more than 200 iugera in ...
nor shall he judge a greater number of men to be or have been *settled in a colony or colonies in Africa* than the number of men, whose settlement in a colony or colonies in Africa *by a triumvir* for the founding of *a colony* was right or legitimate.

(lines 61–2) The duumvir *appointed* XLVI*
or created under this law ... was given *and assigned*, ... *in so far as* it was not *sold, in so far* as it will be legitimate for *this* land to be adjudicated under this law, shall assign any land discovered in this way and judge it to belong to that man or his heir.

(lines 63–5) ... *that part of* that land or territory which was *bought by each person* before ... the consulship of *M.Livius* and L.Calpurnius from any man, who had the right as a private citizen to sell that land at the time when he bought the land and territory, which ... XLVII*
(if the man ...) shall or shall have made it plain that it was bought, in so far as neither *he himself afterwards* nor his heir nor any man to whom he is heir, has alienated it, any part of that land or territory so made plain in the future, the duumvir in such a way ...
shall give and duly deliver, in so far as the buyer shall have kept it and it was not publicly sold.

(lines 65–6) *The duumvir, if the* land or territory, which has been purchased by this man, was publicly sold, *shall duly deliver to him* a corresponding amount of land or territory from the land or territory XLVIII*
in Africa, the part of it not publicly sold ... *Any land or territory which has been given and duly delivered according to this law in this way*, shall be bought for one sestertius *by the man, who* is made *its owner according to this law*, and this land or territory shall be private and liable to tax, *as* is described *below*.

(lines 66–7) Any colonist, or any man enrolled as if he were a colonist, to whom land or territory (? has been given) in any centuria or subsecivum ... XLIX*
the duumvir appointed or created according to this law shall duly deliver to him or his heir *a corresponding amount of land or territory in return for that land or territory from the* land or territory in Africa, the part of it not publicly sold.

(lines 67–8) Any man, to whom, as a colonist or as a man who was enrolled, as if he were a colonist, or was ... L*
the duumvir shall duly deliver in place of that land *a corresponding amount of land or territory to the man, who* is discovered to have *held* or *possessed* (it) in this way, or to his heir from the land in Africa, and he shall judge it to have been assigned to the man to whom he has duly delivered it.

(lines 68–70) A man, to whom land from the land or territory in Africa, which *was given or assigned* to a colonist or a man LI*

* These paragraph numbers are adopted for convenience. They are based on a calculation from the amount of text since the last paragraph which can be isolated.

69 [*quei in colonei numero scriptus est, datus adsignatus est,* 25 *ei, quei emit emerit,* ...]S adiudicaverit, tum tantundem modum agri ei, quoi ita emptum esse comperiet[*ur, sociove ei*]us procuratoreve eius heredive quoius eorum de eo agro, quei ager in Africa est, pro eo agro II vir reddito; quoi ita reddiderit,

70 [32 *quod eius p*]equniae adsignatum discriptum adsignatumve in tabuleis publiceis est eritv[*e, tantam pequ*]niam populo ex eid. Mart., quae, postea quam vectigalia consistent, quae post h.l.r. primum consistent, primae erunt, in

71 [*diebus ... dare debeto* 23 *neive quis, quei eo nomine ab populo mercassitur, ob eam rem pequniam propiore die exigito, atque*] uteique in h.l.s. est, neive quod pequniae ob eam rem propiore{m} die exactum er[*it atque uteiq*]ue in h.l.s.e., is, quei pequniam populo dare debebit, ei, quei eo nomine ab populo mercassitur, ob eam rem pequniam ei nei

72 [*propiore die solvito* 30]NVM fiat, neive quis mag. neive pro mag. facito neive quis senator decernito q[*uo ea pequnia,*] quae pro agreis loceis aedificieis quei s.s.s., populo debetur debebiturve, aliter exsigatur atque atque uteique in h.l.s. est.

73 [21 *sei ea pequnia, quae pro eo agro loco, quei ager locus in Africa est, populo debetur debebitur, quod is ager locus Romae publice venieit v*]enierit, populo non soluta erit, is pro eo agro loco in diebus CXX proxsumeis ea[*s eidus Martias*], quae s.s.s., arb(itratu) pr(aetoris), quei inte⟨r⟩ ceives tum Romae ious deicet, satis supsignato. (vac.) Pr., quei inter ceives Romae ious dei[*cet*]

74 [32 *nisei*] praedium ante ea ob eum agrum locum in publico obliga⟨t⟩{i}um erit in publicu[*mve praes datus erit* .. 3–4]E agrum locum, quo pro agro loco satis ex h.l. arb. pr. supsignatum non erit, pequnia praesenti vendito. (vac.) Que[*i*]

75 [32]A ager locus in Africa, quei Romae publice veniei⟨t⟩{i} venieritve, quod eius agri[*locei, quei popul*]eis libereis in Africa sunt, quei eorum ⟨in⟩ ameicitiam populi Romanei bello Poinicio proxsumo manserunt, queive ạ[*d*]

76 [*imperatorem populi Romanei bello Poinicio proxsumo perfugerunt, eis antea datum adsignatum est* 18 *pro eo agro loco II vir in diebus ... proxsumeis, qu*]ibus II vir ex[*h.l. fac*]tus creatusve erit, facito, quantum agri locei quoiusque in populei leiberei inve eo agr[*o loco, quei ager l*]ocus perfugeis datus adsignatusve est, ceivis Romanei ex h.l. factum erit, quo pro agro loco ager loc[*us ceivei Ro*]ṃano ex h.l.

77 [*redditus commutatusve non erit, tantusdem modus agri locei quoieique populo leibero perfugeisve reddatur adsignetur* 20 *II*] vir, quei ex h.l. factus creatusve erit, is in diebus CL proxsumeis, quibus factus creatusve erit, facito, quan[*tum X virei, quei ex*] lege Livia factei createive sunt fueruntve, eis hominibus agrum in Africa dederunt adsignaveru[*ntve*], quos stipendium

enrolled as if he were a colonist, . . . (if . . .) has *not* adjudicated (it) *to any man who has or will have purchased it,* then the duumvir shall duly deliver in return for that land a corresponding amount of land to the man who is discovered to have purchased it in this way, *or to his partner* or to his procurator or to the heir of any one of these, from the land in Africa; . . . to the man to whom he has duly delivered it in this way . . .

(lines 70–2) . . . LII*

in so far as that money has been or will have been assigned, apportioned or assigned in public records, *he shall be obliged to pay that amount* of money to the people within . . . *days* (?) from the first Ides of March following the first fixing of taxes after the passage of this law . . .

nor shall anyone, who has contracted with the people on that account (for the task of exacting the money), *exact money for that reason earlier than* is prescribed in this law, nor, in relation to any money which has been exacted for that reason earlier *than* is prescribed in this law, shall any man, who is obliged to pay money to the people, *pay earlier* the money for that reason to the man who has contracted with the people on that account . . .

(line 72) . . . should become . . . nor shall a magistrate or promagistrate act nor shall a senator make a decree *to the effect that the money,* which is or will be owed to the people in return for the lands territories and buildings described above, should be exacted differently from the manner prescribed by this law. LIII*

(line 73) . . . *if the money owed to the people in return for land and territory in Africa, because this land and territory has or* will have been sold *publicly at Rome,* has not at that time been paid to the people, the man shall give sufficient security for this land and territory at the discretion of the praetor, who then has jurisdiction for citizens at Rome, within the 120 days next following *the Ides of March* mentioned above. LIV*

(lines 73–4) The praetor who has jurisdiction for citizens at Rome . . . LV*

unless property has been pledged as security at the treasury beforehand on account of that land and territory *or a guarantor has been given* to the treasury, shall sell for cash the land and territory, for which sufficient security has not been given at the discretion of the praetor according to this law.

(lines 74–7) (Any) . . . which . . . LVI*

land and territory in Africa, which has or will have been sold publicly at Rome, that part of the land *and territory,* which *was previously given and assigned to those* members of the free *peoples* in Africa, who remained in the friendship of the Roman people in the last Punic War,

or *took refuge* with *a commander of the Roman people during the last Punic War . . . in return for that land and territory the duumvir within the next . . . days,* after he has been appointed or created under this law, shall ensure that, regarding the quantity of land and territory, which has been made the property of a Roman citizen according to this law, belonging to the land and territory of each free people or that given or assigned to refugees, in return for which land and territory was not *exchanged or duly delivered* by a Roman *citizen* according to this law,

a corresponding quantity of land and territory shall be duly delivered and assigned to each free people or to the refugees . . .

(lines 77–8) . . . The duumvir appointed or created under this law shall within the next 150 days following his creation or appointment ensure that, *regarding the quantity* of land in Africa *which the decemviri* appointed or created under the Livian law gave or assigned to those men, who *were obliged to pay* tribute LVII*

78 [*pro eo agro populo Romano pendere oportuit,* 1̣8̣0̣ *tantundem modum agri de eo agro, quei ager in Africa est, quantum ex lege Livia stipendiarieis popul*]i Romanei esse oportet oportebit, is stipendiariei⟨s⟩ det adsignetve idque in formas publicas facito utei[*referatur v.e.r.p.f.*] q.e.e.v. (vac.) II vir, quei ex h.l. factus creatusve erit, is facito in diebus CCL proxsumeis, quịbus h.[*l.*] populus plebesve iuserit,

79 [*utei, extra eum agrum locum, quei ex lege Rubria, quae fuit, colono eive, quei in colonei numero scriptus est, datus adsignatus est* 1̣6̣5̣ *quo pro agro loco ager locus com*]mutatus redditusve non erit, extraque eum agrum, quei ager intra finis populorum leiber{l}⟨o⟩rum Uticensium H[*adrumetinorum T*]ampsitanorum Leptitanorum Aquillitanorum Usalitanorụm Teudalensium, quom in ameicitiam populei Romanei proxumum

80 [*venerunt, fuit;* 1̣5̣5̣ *extraque eum agrum locum, quei ager locus eis hominibus, quei ad imperatorem populi Romanei bello Poinicio proxsumo perfugerunt, datus adsignatus est*] ex⟨t⟩{p}ra eum agrum, quei ager ex h.l. privatus factus erit, quo pro agro loco ager locus redditus commutatusve [*non erit, extr*]ạque eum agrum locum, quem II vir ex h.l. stipendiarieis dederit adsignaveritve, quod eius ex h.l. in {e}⟨f⟩ormam publicam relatum

81 [*erit* 2̣4̣0̣ *extraque eum agrum quem P.Cornelius imperator leib*]ereis regis Massinissae dedit habereve fruive iusi⟨t⟩{i}; extraque eum agrum locum, ubei oppodụm Çarṭ[*hago*] f̣uit qu[*ondam, extraqu*]e eum agrum locum, quem X virei, quei ex {h.}l. Livia factei createive fuerunt. Uticensibus reliquerunt adsignaverunt; ce⟨t⟩erum

82 [*agrum omnem quei in Africa est, in formas publicas referat adque aerarium deferat, isque ager publicus esto* 1̣5̣0̣ *queicumque de eo agro loco vectigal decumas scripturamve pr*]o pecore ex lege Sempronia dare non solitei sunt, quei ager eis ex h.l. datus redditus commutatus erit,[*quei eum agr*]ụ[*m locum ita*] possidebit frueturve, pro eo agro loco {W}⟨n⟩eive vectigal neive decumas nei⟨ve⟩ scripturam, quod post h.l.r. fruetur, dare debeto.

83 [1̣9̣5̣ *Quem agrum locum de eo agro loco Latinus peregrinusue* (?) *possidebit frueturve, is pro eo agro loco vectigal decumas*] scripturam populo aut publicano item dare debeto, utei pro eo agro loco, quem agrum locum populus [*Romanus ex h.l. locabit, que*]m agrum locum ceivis Romanus ex h.l. possidebit, dare oportebit. (?vac.) Pr., quoius arb(itratu) pro⟨eo⟩agro loco, quei Romae publice venierit, e.h.l.

84 [*satis supsignari oportebit* 2̣5̣5̣ *praedia* ...]RIS ter tanti, i{II}⟨n⟩vito eo quei dabit, accipito, facitoque, quei ex h.l. praedia dederit, utei ei satis supsig[*netur, neive quis quid fax*]sit quominus ex h.l. praedium, quei quomque velit, supsignet pequniamve solvat praesque, quei quomque ex h.l. fieri volet, fiat.

to the Roman people for that land ... any part of that land made the property of a Roman citizen ... he gives or assigns to the tribute-payers *the exact amount of land from the land and territory in Africa which* should now or in the future belong *to the tribute-payers* of the Roman *people* and ensure that this is recorded on the public maps as he decides *to be in the public interest* and to cause no breach of his own *good faith.*

(lines 78–82) The duumvir appointed or created under this law shall ensure that, within LVIII*
the next 250 days after the populus or plebs have ratified this law,
apart from any land and territory given and assigned under the repealed Rubrian law to a colonist or a man enrolled as if he were a colonist ... in return for which land and territory land and territory will not have been exchanged or duly delivered, and apart from the land which *was* within the boundaries of the free peoples of Utica, *Hadrumetum*, Thapsus, Leptis (minor), Acholla, Usalis and Teudalis, when last *they came* into the friendship of the Roman people,
and apart from the land and territory given and assigned to those who took refuge with a commander of the Roman people in the last Punic War ... apart from the land made private under this law, in return for which land and territory *no* land and territory has been duly delivered or exchanged, and apart from the land and territory which the duumvir has given or assigned to tribute-payers under this law, in so far as this has been recorded on a public map according to this law ...
and apart from the land which the commander P.Cornelius has given to the *children* of king Massinissa or ordered them to hold or enjoy, and apart from the land and territory, where the town of Carthage was formerly *and apart from* the land and territory which the *decemviri* appointed or created under the Livian law kept and assigned to the people of Utica, *he shall record all* the rest of
the land in Africa on public maps and deposit them in the treasury, and this land shall be public (?)

(line 82) ... *regarding all those who* were not accustomed to pay *tax, tithe or pasture tax* for LIX*
their livestock according to the Sempronian law *on that land and territory*, any man possessing or enjoying *land and territory in this way*, which has been given, duly delivered or granted in exchange to these people according to this law, shall not be liable to pay tax, tithe or pasture tax for that land and territory in relation to his enjoyment of it after the passage of this law.

(line 83) ... *regarding any land and territory possessed and enjoyed by a Latin or foreigner* LX*
(?) from that land and territory, he shall be liable to pay *tax, tithe* and pasture tax *for that land and territory* to the people or the tax-collector on the same terms as a Roman citizen is obliged to pay them for that land and territory, which the *Roman* people *lease* and a Roman citizen possesses according to this law.

(lines 83–4) The praetor, at whose discretion *sufficient guarantees should be given* LXI*
according to this law for the territory publicly sold at Rome
... shall accept *property in security* of three times the value ... *of the buyer* (*contractor*?), if the man who provides the guarantees is unwilling, and ensure that sufficient guarantees may be taken from the man who has provided property as security under this law, *and that no one should do anything* to prevent anyone who wishes providing security and paying money according to this law, and (to prevent) anyone who wishes to become a guarantor according to this law from so doing.

85 [*Quem quomque vectigal decumas scripturamve pro pecore* 2̣3̣5̣ *quei ager*] locus populorum leiberorum perfugarum non fuerit, pro eo agro aedi⟨f⟩{e}icio locoque e.l. dicta [*quam L.Caecilius Cn.Domitius cen*]s. agri aedificii loci vectigalibusve publiceis fruendeis locandeis vendundeis legem deixerunt, publicano dare oportuit,

86 [2̣3̣5̣ *is post h.l.rog. tantundem publicano vectigal decumas scriptura*]mque pecoris (vac. 4) dare debeto, neive amplius ea aliubeive aliterve dare debe⟨t⟩o, pequsque ne[*i aliubei aliterve aliisve legibus*] in eo agro pascito. (vac.) Quae vectigalia in Africa publica populi Romani sunt, quae L.Caecilius Cn.Domiti. cens. fruenda

87 [*locaverunt vendideruntve,* 1̣3̣5̣ *quo minus is publicanus ea lege siet pareatque, quam legem L.Caecilius Cn.Domitius cens. eis vectigalibus fruendeis locandeis vendundeis deixerunt, quove ampli*]us populo dare debeat (vac. 3) solvatque, e. (vac. 1) h.l. (vac. 1) n.r. (vac. 4) Mag. prove mag. queive pro eo inperio iudicio [*potestateve erit,* ..4̣ *quei, quae*] publica populi Romani in Africa sunt eruntve vectigalia, fruenda locabit vendetve, quom ea vectigalia fruenda locabit vendetve,

88 [*nei eis vectigalibus legem deicito, quo* 2̣5̣5̣]E ex lege dicta, quam L. (vac. 2) Caeci. Cn.Dom. cens., quom eorum agrorum vectigalia fruenda locaverunt[*vendideruntve, eis agreis lege*]m deixerunt, neive, quod in eis agreis pequs {INW} ⟨pas⟩cetur, scripturae pecoris lege⟨m⟩ de[*i*]cito quo, inviteis eis, quei eum agrum posidebunt,

89 [*aliubei aliterve pascatur, quam pastum est ex lege dicta, quam L.Caecilius Cn.Domitius cens., quom eorum agrorum vectigalia fruenda locaverunt vendideruntve, legem deixerunt* .5̣5̣ *quae vectigalia in Africa publica populi Romani sunt, quae Cn.Paperius cos. fruenda locavit vendiditve, qu*]ominus ea lege sient pareantque, quam legem Cn.Paperius cos. eis vendundeis ⟨locandeis deixit⟩, e.h.⟨l.⟩n.r. (vac. 4) Quei [*ager in Africa est, quae quomque viae* .1̣8̣ *in eo*] agro, antequam Cartago capta est, fuerunt, eae omnes publicae sunto limitesque inter centuria⟨s⟩

90 [2̣1̣0̣ *II vir, quei ex h.l. factus creatusve erit, sei apud eum is, quoi ager in Africa adsignatus est, quem a*]grum in eo numero agri professus erit, quo in numero eum agrum, quem is, quoi adsigna[*tus est, professus erit, profiteri non oportuerit, eum agrum ei nei dato*] neive reddito neive adiudicato. Quei eam rem [*ita*] indicio fuerit, ei eius agri, quod is indicio eius

91 [*rei fuerit, tantundem modum, quantum* ... *dato adsignato.* 2̣4̣5̣f̲actum est, utei bona, quae habuisent, agrumque, quei eis publice adsignatus esset, haberent [*possiderent fruerentur* .2̣7̣ *quantus*] modus agrei de eo agro, quei eis publice [*datus adsign*]ạtus fuit, publice venierit, tantundem modum

(lines 85–6) . . . *anyone who* was obliged to pay to a tax-collector *tax, tithe or pasture-tax for livestock* . . . on account of land, building and territory, which will not belong to the free peoples or refugees, according to the terms of the law laid down *by the censors L.Caecilius and Cn.Domitius* for the lease and sale of the exploitation of the public taxes on land, building and territory . . . LXII*
he shall be required to pay *after the passage of this law a corresponding amount of tax, tithe* and *pasture tax* for livestock, nor shall he be required to pay more than this or pay it in different places or in a different way, and he shall not pasture his livestock *elsewhere or in other ways or on other terms.*

(lines 86–7) Regarding the public taxes of the Roman people in Africa, whose exploitation the censors L.Caecilius and Cn.Domitius *leased or sold* . . . LXIII*
let there be no provision under this law *whereby the tax-collector should not conform with and obey the law laid down by the censors L.Caecilius and Cn.Domitius for the lease and sale of the exploitation of those taxes, or whereby* he should be obliged to pay and should deliver a greater amount to the people.

(lines 87–9) The magistrate or promagistrate or anyone discharging that authority (imperium), jurisdiction *or power, who* leases or sells in the future the exploitation of the public taxes of the Roman people in Africa, at the time when he leases or sells the exploitation of these taxes, LXIV*
shall not lay down a law for these taxes, whereby . . . (*otherwise than*) according to the law laid down by the censors L.Caecilius and Cn.Domitius *for these lands*, at the time when they leased *or sold* the exploitation of the taxes on these lands, nor shall he lay down a law for the pasture-tax on livestock, which are grazed on these lands, without the consent of those who possess the land, whereby
they *should be grazed elsewhere and in a different way from that in which they were grazed according to the law laid down by the censors L.Caecilius and Cn.Domitius, at the time when they leased or sold the exploitation of taxes on this land.*

(line 89) *Regarding* . . . *the public taxes of the Roman people, whose exploitation was leased or sold by the consul Cn.Papirius*, let there be no provision under this law whereby (these people) should not conform with and obey the law which the consul Cn.Papirius laid down for their sale and lease. LXV*

(lines 89–90) Regarding the *land in Africa, whatever roads* existed *in that* land, . . . before Carthage was captured, these shall all be public and the paths between the centuries . . . LXVI*

(lines 90–1) . . . LXVII*
the duumvir appointed or created according to this law, if a man, to whom land was assigned in Africa, shall have declared *before him any* land in a category of land, in which the land *declared* by the man to whom it was assigned *should not be declared, shall not give* nor duly deliver nor adjudicate *that land to him.* To the man who has *thus* laid information on that matter, because *he has laid* information on that *matter, he shall give and assign a corresponding amount* of that land . . .

(lines 91–2) . . . LXVIII*
(which) was made . . ., that they should hold, *possess and enjoy* the property which they had held and the land which had been publicly assigned to them, . . . a corresponding amount *of land from that land* to the amount of land publicly sold, which was part of the land publicly *given and* assigned to them . . .

92 [*agri de eo agro, quei* 210 *quei agrum possesionemve agrive possesionisve superficium habet possidetv*]e fruiturve, quem agrum possesionemve quoiusve agri possesionisve superficium q(uaestor) pr(aetor)ve pụ[*blice vendiderit* .45 *o*]b eum agrum locum possesione[*m agreive superfic*]ium scrip{i}⟨t⟩uram pecoris nei dato neive

93 [290] is ager ex s.c. datus ads[*i*]gnatus est, ei agrei quei s.s.s. possesionesque, ea omnia eorum h[*ominum sunto* .40 *magistratus, quo de e*]a re im ious aditum erit [*ita de ea re iudicium de*]ṭ, utei de ea re in h.l.s. est, neive

94 [290]OS comportent, quibus ex h.l. ager locus datus redditus commutatus adsignatus[*ve est* .50 *agrum locum ex h.l.*] dari reddi adsignar[*i* .20 *e*]um agrum locum ceivis R[*oman* ...]

95 [290 *q*]uodque in eo agro loco vinei oleive fiet, quae messis vindemiaque P.Cornelio L.Ca[*lpurnio cos. posteave fiet,* .55] S fructus [.25 *q*]uei eum agrum tum [.10]

96 [255 *Quei ex h.l. II vir factus creatusve erit, is in diebus ... proxsume*]is, quibus ex h.l. II vir factus creatusve {d}⟨e⟩rit, a[*gru*]m locum, quei Corinthiorum [*fuit* 120 *e*]x̣tra eum ag[*rum* ..8]

97 [295 *agrum locum*], quem ex h.l. venire oportebit, omnem me[*tiun*]dum terminosque statuẹ[*ndos curato* 120]ỌM Ạ[.14]

98 [290 *opu*]sque loc[*at*]o eique operei diem deicito, u[*bei inf*]ectum siet, facitoque [145]

99 [295]CRṾM[..6]S agri loci aedificiei quoieiqu[*e emptum*] erit, is eius pequniai, Q̣[145]

100 [305 *prae*]ṿidesque nei magis solutei su[*nto, eaque*] nomina mancupuṃ [145]

101 [... *praevi*]ḍibusque eorum persequtio e[*sto. Quei*] ager locus edifi[*cium* 140]

102 [310 *populo*] dare damnas esto P{Ṿ}⟨R⟩[*que, quo de ea*] re in ious adi[*tum erit* 140]

103 [320] Ị venierit, N[[.15 + + 150]

104 [320] POSSESI[170]

105 [325]OI I[170]

(lines 92–3) ... LXIX*

any man who holds, possesses or enjoys land or a possession or a building on land or a possession, which the quaestor *has* publicly *sold*, ... he shall not pay on account of that land, territory, possession *or building on land* pasture-tax for livestock nor ...

(lines 93–4) ... LXX*

that land was given and assigned by decree of the senate, those lands mentioned above and possessions shall all *belong* to those *men* ... (*to the effect that*) *a magistrate who* is approached at his tribunal about that matter, should *provide a trial about that matter* in the manner prescribed in this law, nor ...

(line 94) ...

(*those men*), to whom land and territory has been given, duly delivered, given in exchange *or* assigned, should gather together ... *land and territory* to be given, duly delivered *or* assigned *according to this law* ..., that land and territory a Roman citizen ...

(line 95) ... any wine or oil produced in this land and territory by the harvest or vintage in the consulship of P.Cornelius and L.*Calpurnius or subsequently*, ... the fruits ... any man who then ... that land ...

(line 96) ... *the duumvir appointed or created under this law within ... days* after his appointment or creation as duumvir, ... the land and territory, which *belonged to* the Corinthians ... apart from that land ...

(line 97) ... *he shall ensure that the land and territory*, which should be sold according to this law, is all measured and boundary-stones erected ...

(line 98) ... he shall put the *work* out to contract and fix a date for the work, where *it is in*complete, and shall take measures ...

(line 99) ... consisting of land, territory or building has been *bought* by each person, he ... of that money ...

(line 100) and the guarantors shall not be any the more released (on that account), *and the* names of the contractors ...

(line 101) ... and *there shall be* suit (for the money) from their *guarantors. Any* land, territory or building ...

(line 102) ... he shall be liable to pay damages *to the people*. And the praetor, *who* is approached at his tribunal *about that* matter ...

(line 103) ... *which* will have been sold ...

(line 104) ... possession ...

Commentary

Prescript (line 1)

1 (B1) PIVM: aes, O; *princi]pium*: Sig, Pin. Rud, Mo, CIL, Jo restore an outline prescript, Rud entering Sp.Thorius as proposer. For the form of a prescript see *lex Quinctia* (Front. *de aquis*, 129); *lex Corn. XX quaest.*; *lex Ant. Term.*; *lex de Delo* (*CIL* I², 2500); *lex convivalis* (Bruns, no. 26). Jo added *de s(ententia)* before *plebem* for reasons not clear to me.

We can infer from *pro tribu* that this law was passed before a tribal assembly. There is, however, no internal evidence that it was a plebiscite, only the evidence of Appian about agrarian legislation after C.Gracchus (see pp. 47–8 above). For the use of the *forum* as opposed to the *comitium* for legislation see Coarelli (1985), 156ff; Taylor (1966), 23ff. This apparently began in 145 BC.

Chapters I–VI (lines 1–10) deal with categories of land which are declared private by this law.

I (lines 1–2) Public land retained by prior possessors.

1 (B1) CALPVRN: aes; *Calpurnio*: O, Sig, Pin; *Calp[urnio cos. fuit ... divideretur*: Mo, CIL, Jo, cf. e.g. lines 4 and 13.

It is interesting that we find *terra Italia* here, but *Africa* unqualified in, e.g. line 51 and similarly *Gallia Cisalpina* in *lex Rubr.Gall.* This may imply that *Italia* by itself in 111 BC had a political sense as that part of Italy which was neither Roman nor Latin. *Terra Italia* may also exclude by implication the city of Rome, which was not the subject of agrarian legislation. It is true that Rome is explicitly excluded in line 5, but that may be because the chapter in question is dealing with urban public land.

The public land of the Roman people is a clearly defined legal category of land, which belongs to the people as a whole in the same way that private land belongs to a private individual. As in other ancient republics, the citizens might in theory legislate to change the status of any category of land within their territory – public or private – however repugnant to the land-owning classes attacks on private property might be, for example the confiscations and proscriptions of land by Sulla and by the triumvirate of Antony, Lepidus and

Octavian. On the other hand, the Roman people were actually the landlords of public land. Magistrates, who represented them – especially consuls and censors – regularly took action about this land (such as letting contracts and checking boundaries) without seeking specific authority for this from the people. Major actions, however, such as the disposal of such land to private individuals in perpetuity, required the people's consent through legislation.

The exception clause, *extra eum agrum*, etc., restored here on the basis of lines 4 and 6, has been generally interpreted since Mommsen as a reference to the *ager Campanus* in the light of Cic. *Leg.Agr.* 2.81: *qua de causa nec duo Gracchi, qui de plebis Romanae commodis plurimum cogitarent, nec L.Sulla, qui omnia sine ulla religione, quibus voluit, est dilargitus, agrum Campanum attingere ausus est* – a claim which goes somewhat further than *Leg.Agr.* 1.21 – *qui ager ipse per sese Sullanae dominationi et Gracchorum largitioni restitisset.* As far as Sulla is concerned, Cicero's assertion is of doubtful validity, cf. Greenidge and Clay (1960), 217–8, while on the Gracchan period there is a considerable difference between the statements, that the land resisted distribution, and that no one dared to distribute it. They are in themselves a dubious basis for interpreting this clause.

The *ager Campanus*, i.e. the greater part of Campania, was confiscated after the recovery of Capua and the seceding Campanian cities in the Hannibalic War (Livy 26.16.7). Some of it was sold (28.16.4; 32.7.2–3), some later devoted to the founding of the colonies of Puteoli, Liternum and Volturnum (32.9.3; 34.45ff), the rest was in theory to be rented (27.3.1 and 11.7–8). In fact, many private citizens seized land in this last category without paying and measures had to be taken in 172 and 165 to recover it (Livy 42.1.6; Gran. Lic. 9–10 Flem; Cic. *Leg.Agr.* 2.82). From then until 59 BC this major portion of the *ager Campanus* continued to be rented – largely, it seems, to peasant farmers (Cic. *Leg.Agr.* 2.84). It thus cannot have formed part of the Gracchan allotments which were made private by this law (see below). Cf. in general on this topic, Frederiksen (1984, chs. 11 and 12). The fact that the *ager Campanus* was not in fact redistributed in this period into long-term holdings, which eventually became private, is the strongest argument that it must have been specifically exempted by C.Gracchus and hence also by this law. However, if the laws of both the Gracchi had only been concerned with public land which was neither formally distributed nor rented by censorial contract – *agri occupatorii* in the language of the *gromatici* (Hyg. 78 Thul; Sic.Flacc. 102 Thul, cf. App. *BCiv.* 1.7.27–9) – then there would have been no need to exempt the *ager Campanus*, rented as it was by the censors (Livy 27.11.7–8; 42.19.1). Burdese (92–3) indeed believed that it was *ager censorius* and pasture land as a whole that was excepted in this clause, but in that case it is hard to see why the exception only began with Gaius' legislation. And there is nothing in the literary sources on Tiberius Gracchus about an outcry by censorial tenants expelled from their land.

Then there is the problem of the Gracchan *terminus* (*ILLRP*, 467) – *C.Sempronius Ti.f., Ap.Claudius C.f., P.Licinius P.f. IIIvir.A.I.A.* – found at S.

Angelo in Formis near the site of the temple of Diana Tifatina above ancient Capua. This means that Cicero's statements in *Leg.Agr.* I and II (above) can at best only be true with some qualification, cf. de Martino (1988), 172–4. Recently, Chouquer and his collaborators have detected a grid of centuriation in the *ager Campanus* earlier than that of the Caesarian period, which they associate with the Gracchi (1987, 199ff). Thus we may have reasonable doubts about Cicero's reliability and accept that settlement in the *ager Campanus* may have been disturbed in this period. Yet we do not thereby rule out the possibility that the exception clause refers to a proposal by Gaius Gracchus to exclude the *ager Campanus* from distribution. We may reconcile the *terminus* with the traditional interpretation of the exception clause by arguing, as Gohler (1939, 150), Bloch and Carcopino (I.142, n15) and Frederiksen (275) did, that Ti.Gracchus planned to redistribute the *ager Campanus*, but his brother deliberately excluded it from his own law – because he planned to found a colony there (Plut. *C.Gr.* 8.3). The difficulty with this is that the exception clause appears in a chapter of this law specifically referring to colonial foundations (lines 20–2), where on this view it would be self-defeating.

Another approach is that of Johannsen who suggested that the commissioners did not deal with the lands rented to tenants by the censors in Campania but only with the *ager occupatorius* in the neighbourhood. This may well have been what happened in fact, but it does not require us to believe that censorial tenants needed to be protected by a special proviso of C.Gracchus, whether, as Johannsen believed, this related to the *ager Campanus* in particular, or, as Burdese believed, to censorial tenants as a whole. It is perhaps significant, as Johannsen points out later (235ff), that the exception clause does not appear in the chapter concerned with the *viasiei vicanei* (line 11–12), since these are likely to have been placed on the *ager Campanus* and any exception for the land of censorial tenants would have been relevant in that chapter. More attractive, therefore, is the interpretation of Hinrichs (254ff) that the exception concerned land occupied by Italian allies, whom C.Gracchus did not wish to offend (cf. ch. XXV, line 29). In my view Ti.Gracchus' commission may have initially dealt with land which before 133 BC had been traditionally ceded to Italian communities for exploitation, perhaps land which originally had been confiscated from them, but such operations were ended by his brother's law. We also find a reference to the cession of *ager publicus* to *coloniae* and *municipia* in lines 31–2. This land may have been similarly protected by C.Gracchus.

2 (B2) GRVM: aes; AGRVM: edd veter, Rud, Mo, CIL, Jo; SVMER: aes, Rud, Mo, CIL, Jo; SVMERE: edd veter; *[quem quisque...sibei]*: Mo, CIL (cf. line 13); [...*possessor prove possessore sibei*]: Hin, Jo; *sumer[e relinquereve licuit]*: Mo, CIL; *[... licuit, quod eius agri quoique IIIvir a.d.a. dedit adsignavit reddidit]*: Jo, sim. Hin.

Burdese (76, n.13) wished to omit *ex lege plebeive scito* in the restoration at the beginning of the line, so that it might cover the situation existing at the time of

Ti.Gracchus' law, but his view that the phrase can only refer to C.Gracchus' agrarian law is unjustified: it refers to any law still valid. The standard restoration, moreover, does cover the behaviour of *possessores* in accordance with the law of 133. '*Vetus possessor*' does not necessarily mean someone with an ancestral right to the land, but rather the current occupier at the time of any redistribution (provided that this occupation was not illegal), cf. e.g. Hyg. 142, 165 Thul (*adsignatum per professiones veterum possessorum, reddita veteri possessori*). Mommsen restored *CIL* 1^2, 645, an apparently Gracchan *terminus* without the names of the commissioners, as *f(undus) p(ossessoris) vet(eris)*. In *Dig*. 43.16.28 the *v.p.* is the holder of the land recently expelled by violence.

I have not followed Johannsen in restoring here *prove vetere possesore*, since we can only be sure that such a man came into question when either the land was assigned (line 17) or there was an exchange (line 21). By contrast in line 13 *vetus possessor* is immediately followed by *ex lege plebeive scito*. The traditional view (Mommsen, *Ges. Schr*. 1.97; Johannsen, 201) is that, while the *vetus possessor* is the man established in possession at the time of the operations of the IIIvir, *pro vetere possessore* is someone who had held the land there improperly but for a long time. However, provided holdings were within the prescribed limits, the Gracchan legislation seems to have treated all kinds of existing possession alike. Nor would there have been much point in distinguishing in this way between those who seized the land and those who succeeded to this possession, as Burdese (77) suggested. Other explanations may be sought. One possibility is that *pro vetere possessore* was someone who should have been in possession but had recently been driven off the land and was treated by the IIIvir as if he had been in possession (the sense used in the *Digest* above). Another, in my view preferable, is that *p.v.p.* is someone who was persuaded by the commission during its reorganisation of holdings to exchange the land he originally possessed for a new holding, on condition that this was to be held on the same terms as if he possessed it before Ti.Gracchus' agrarian law.

For *relinquere* = 'maintain in a former state', cf. lines 7 and 81, *lex lat.Bant*. 6. Hardy (1912, 56) also compared Cic. *Att*. 5.21.12: *Scaptius rogat . . .ut rem sic relinquam*. Burdese (74ff) wished to translate 'leave as a legacy' but *relinquere* is a little too bald to describe a legacy without further qualification and the only dative available to which it can relate is *sibei*.

Hinrichs and Johannsen inserted in the lacuna at the end of the line a limiting relative clause referring to assignation by the *IIIvir a.d.a.* The implication of this is that any annexation of public land up to the legal limit, which took place after, or apart from, the work of the commissioners (especially the situation after the cessation of distribution under Appian's 'second law' – *BCiv*. 1.27.122), would not have been a title to private ownership under this law. They argued that in lines 16–17, where the issue is judicial confirmation of the holdings of *possessores* declared private by this law, we only find '*quod eius IIIvir a.d.a. . . .dedit adsignavit reddidit*' and '*quoi is ager vetere prove vetere possessore datus adsignatusve ⟨fuerit⟩*': there is no mention of land which a possessor '*sibei sumpsit reliquitve*'. However, that may be explained in another way, if we realise that the sort of mandatory judicial decisions described in lines 16–17 could only be made in favour of those who were recorded by the commission as holders of the land (or their heirs or, in some cases, purchasers from them). Where a man simply claimed to have taken land himself, the law could not instruct the magistrate to decide automatically in his favour. Land annexed in this way would only get recognition as private after the defeat of any competing claims and registration in the census.

Finally, we should note the significance of *quod non modus maior* etc. Contrary to the impression given by Appian (*BCiv*. 1.27.122), not all holdings of *veteres possessores* were recognised and legitimised when the activities of the land-commission ceased, but only those within the limits of the *leges Semproniae*, i.e. 500 *iugera* for each man with an additional 250 in respect of each child (App. *BCiv*. 1.9.37). (I follow Badian (1972), 702–3, in rejecting the inference sometimes made from the Livian report of 1,000 *iugera* as the upper limit (*Per*. 58; *De Vir.Ill*. 64.3), that only two children were allowed to count in claims to land.) Holdings above the limit remained *ager publicus* with no protection against resumption by the *populus Romanus* or occupation by another private citizen who did not possess *ager publicus* to excess.

II (lines 2–3) Land assigned by lot to a Roman citizen by a land-commissioner

2 The restoration here of the introductory formula found in the preceding chapter was first made by Rudorff.

3 (B3) *quod] quoieique*: Rud; *quem agrum locum]*: Mo, CIL, Jo. VLT: aes, edd veter; *ult[ra*: Pin; *ultr[a*: Mo, CIL, Jo (Mo claimed to have seen the downstroke of the R); *ult[ra fines eius agri loci est*: Sig; *ultr[a terram Italiam colonis datum adsignatum est* / *ultr[a terram Italiam situm est* / *ultr[a praescriptum legis datum adsignatum est*: Hin (260, n19).

The first two of Hinrichs' suggestions are inappropriate, given that the land is *in terra Italia* in the first place, the third is an awkward and unconvincing way of producing an equivalent to *quod non modus maior* ... in line 2. For *quod non* ... we might have expected *quod eius non* ..., but the sense must still be 'in so far as it is not'. The second *quod* can only be a relative referring to *ager locus*.

Mommsen believed that this line could only refer to assignments in a colony, since these were by lot – a view accepted recently by Kaser (1942), 11–12; Burdese, 78. However, after the measurement and centuriation of the land, lot would have been a perfectly appropriate method of making the Gracchan assignments to individuals. Moreover, the appearance of these assignments by lot in lines 15–16, where provision is made for their judicial confirmation in a chapter parallel to that following it, which concerns *veteres possessores*, suggests strongly that these are the allotments to new settlers first enacted by Ti.Gracchus; cf. Johannsen, 212ff.

III (lines 3–4) ?Land assigned in exchange for land surrendered to the commission

3 For the restoration see below.

4 (B4) DDITVS EST: aes (all of the chapter that survives); *[quei ager – re]dditus*: Jo (adding *a.d.a.* to *IIIvir*); Hin (omitting *commutatus*); *[quei... de eo agro loco, quei ager locus ei, quei agrum privatum in publicum commutavit, pro eo agro loco a IIIviro datus commutatus re]dditus*: Mo, CIL; *[quei in eo agro loco veteri possessori prove vetere possessore ager locus re]dditus*: Rud; *[quei ager locus veteri possessore prove vetere contra ius ademptus, deinde a IIIviro causa denuo cognita re]dditus*: Zancan (72).

This chapter clearly concerns land assigned in some way by an authority, since *redditus* in this law is associated with *datus adsignatus*. The notion of an exchange, first suggested by A.W. Zumpt (1850, I, 210–11) was developed by Mommsen in *CIL* I. Investigation of the holdings of prior possessors would have revealed many untidy and unclear boundaries, both between the holdings of the possessors themselves and between their land and as yet unsettled land (cf. App. *BCiv.* 1.19). It would have been natural for the commission to regularise these boundaries, especially as it would have helped them to judge which holdings were in excess of the limit. Hence would have arisen the need to remove some land from possessors, while compensating them with other land in exchange. Similar operations, necessitated by uncoordinated distribution and occupation, can be found in the African section of the law (lines 58ff).

Provision for exchange of land and buildings appear later in the Italian section of the law (lines 20–4 and 26–7), but in different contexts. The first section deals with the situation when the original possessor has given up land to a new colony, not when the surrender has been made to facilitate allotments to individuals by the land-commission. The dual provision in lines 26–7 concerning land becoming private by exchange and that becoming public by exchange seems to be related to the context of road-building (see commentary on chs. XXI–XXII). In any case the second part of this (ch. XXII) deals with land surrendered which had been fully private property, not a *possessio* on *ager publicus*. Neither of these chapters, therefore, makes a chapter about exchange here redundant and this is certainly more plausible than one referring to land taken away by a commissioner and then returned by him, as Zancan believed.

IV (lines 4–5) Land assigned in a city, town or village outside Rome

4 (B4) MNCIO: aes. EX LEGE: aes, O[2]; EX LEGE PLEBEIVE SC: Sig, Pin, O[1].

It is hard to see how the bronze can have projected at the level of this line, as far as three of the humanist copies imply, without other letters now lost having been visible in other lines.

5 (B5) IE: aes, O, Pin, Mo apparatus; VE: Sig; *[quod eius quisq]ue*: Mo, CIL; *[quod eius agri locei publicei in urbem Romam est quod]ve*: Rud; *[quod aedificii superficii areae (possessionisve) in terra Italia, quod eius extra urbem Romam est, quod eius in urbe appido vico est, quod eius IIIvir dedit adsignavit quod]ve*: Hu.

ROMA: aes; VRBEM: aes (*in urbem* seems to have been acceptable Latin for rest at a place in Republican legal texts, cf. e.g. *lex rep.* 13, but conflicts with *oppido vico*).

quod [non in eo agro loco est, quem vetus possessor prove vetere possessore sibei sumpsit reliquitve ita utei s.s.est]: Rud; *quod [...tum cum haec lex rogabitur habebit possidebitve*]: Mo, CIL; Jo combines the two supplements.

The subject of this chapter is again assignments by the Gracchan land-commission. We do not know for sure why the legislator has separated those made in towns and villages from the rest, but the lot is not mentioned here and the method was probably different to that used in the assignments of line 2–3. The idea that the assignments here could have extended to non-Romans, considered and rejected by Johannsen (221), is surely excluded by the fact that the land concerned is later to be registered with the Roman censor as private land (line 8), since non-Romans without *commercium* could not own Roman land. It is in any case interesting that cities, towns and villages might be in part or whole comprised within the *ager publicus populi Romani*. The home territory of a Roman colony or *municipium* (as opposed to land leased by it from the Roman people, as in lines 31ff) can hardly have remained public land of the Roman people, once it had been assigned (cf. App. *BCiv.* 1.7.26). The communities in question in this chapter are therefore likely to have been among those who defected in the Second Punic War. Their territory would have been confiscated and remained *ager publicus populi Romani* in 111 BC even if the communities themselves were allowed a precarious existence. *Agri locei publicei* seems to refer to land without building, such as might be found within the perimeter of a town or village, contrasting with *agri locei aedific[iei* in line 6.

V (lines 6–7) Other land assigned by the commission, including buildings

6 (B6, A1) AEDIFIC: aes, O; AEDIFICII: Sig; *aedific[ii*: Pin. IB̦ (with apparently the bottom angle of a letter on either side): aes(A1); *aedific[iei ...q]uibu[s*: CIL; *aedific[iei ... ex earum causa aliqua de q]uibu[s supra scriptum est]*: Mo; *aedific[ii, quo in agro loco oppidum coloniamve ex lege plebeive scito constituit deduxit conlocavitque, ceivi Romano nominisve Latini sociumve q]uibu[s ex formula togatorum milites in terra Italia imperare solent]*: Rud; *aedific[ii superficii areae in terra Italia, quod eius extra urbem Roma est, quod eius in urbe oppido vico est, quod eius IIIvir dedit adsignavit quodve agri loci*: Hu.

7 (B7) N TERRA: aes, O[2], Sig; IN TERRA: O[1]; *i]n terra*: Pin.

For *formas tabulasve* cf. lines 78 and 81 (*formae publicae, forma publica*). A *forma* was a stylised map representing Roman surveying and centuriation in relation to natural features; if *publica*, it was probably engraved on stone, bronze or wood and displayed in a public place, as the *formae* at Arausio were (Piganiol, 1962). See Siculus Flaccus (118 Thul = 154 Lach) – '*Ergo agrorum divisorum, qui institutis limitibus divisi sunt, formae varias appellationes accipiunt. quidam ⟨in⟩ arbore⟨i⟩s, alii in {v}⟨a⟩enis, alii in membr⟨an⟩is scripserunt, et quamvis una res sit forma, alii dicunt perticam, alii centuriationem, alii metationem, alii cancellationem, alii typon* ...' cf. 165 Thul = 202 Lach, '*omnes aeris significationes et formis et tabulis aeris inscribemus*'. Siculus Flaccus goes on to refer to the *commentarii*, which were in the *sanctuarium Caesaris* under the principate. *Formae tabulaeve* here probably comprise both engraved maps and other records not published. It is not clear why maps are mentioned here and not, for example in lines 3 and 5. For the *termini* left in Italy resulting from the centuriation carried out by the commission see *ILLRP*, 467–74, *AE* 1973, no. 222.

This may well be the first occasion that the assignment of buildings is mentioned in the law. Johannsen thought that it was a resumptive chapter which extended the previous definitions by the inclusion of buildings. However, it is possible that, whereas the previous chapter dealt with land without buildings in towns, the present one was concerned with built-up areas there. *Reliquit* (cf. line 2) means 'left alone, left in its former state' and suggests that the beneficiaries were prior possessors as well as new settlers.

VI (lines 7–10) All the above-mentioned categories of land to be private and recorded in the census as such

7 (B7, A2) VM CAVITV: aes, O (only the base-angles of the Vs at either end are now visible); CAVIT: Maz; *quo ⁽C.Sempronius Ti.f. tr.pl. rog. excep]tum cavit[um est nei dividerctur*: Sig, sim. Pin. Like Jo, I have restored the full introductory description of public land in Italy, for which there is space on my reconstruction of the fragments.

[. . .privatus esto]: Rud, Mo, CIL, Jo; *[. . .ita utei privatus est, esto]*: Zancan, 75.

It is certain that the law is declaring the various categories of land listed previously to be private, as editors since Rudorff have realised – first, because in line 8 we find *ita, utei ceterorum locorum agrorum aedificiorum privatorum est, esto*; secondly, because in line 14 a man may in the future make up to 30 *iugera* of public land private by occupation for the purpose of agriculture; thirdly, because a later chapter freeing land from tax refers to (line 19) *[. . .quod ex lege plebeive sci]to* <u>*exve h.l.*</u> *privatum factum est eritve*. Cf. Johannsen, 226–7).

Was this law the first to declare these categories to be private? As Johannsen has stressed (228ff; 72, n30), line 19 (see above) suggests that for some, but not all, types of land, this law was not the instrument by which they were made private. On the other hand, a comparison between lines 15–16 and lines 16–17 reveals that no recognition was given to the purchase of land assigned to new settlers by the commission, if this occurred before the passage of the law, whereas purchases of land from *veteres possessores* were ratified. It is, therefore, arguable that by the first post-Gracchan law, which allowed sale of land (App. *BCiv.* 1.27.121), only the land of *veteres possessores* became private and open to sale as well as bequest, while the allotments made to new settlers could be bequeathed but not sold.

The argument for believing that all the categories of land retailed in lines 1–7 were all already private before this law is a purely theoretical one, which rests on two propositions – first, that later Roman law recognised no half-way stage between public and private land, secondly, that private land might be subject to limitations in public law (such as the payment of tax) while remaining at the disposal of the owner in private law by bequest or sale (Kaser, 1942, 25–6; Johannsen, 229). However, although by the rules of classical jurisprudence land was either public or private, this is not to say that under the pressure of revolutionary legislation a legal anomaly, or what would have been later regarded as one, could not have arisen. Moreover, in so far as they were originally inalienable, the new Gracchan allotments were certainly not fully private in the sense of being disposable by the owner (App. *BCiv.* 1.10.38). As for the land of *veteres possessores*, it is uncertain whether the 'secure tenure for ever' they were allowed by Ti.Gracchus' law (App. *BCiv.* 1.11.96) was originally a guarantee of possession or a grant of ownership (see Burdese, 84, for the view that it was only the former). In fact, the importance accorded by the *lex agraria* to the listing of these various categories of land, before declaring them private and detailing the consequences, suggests that the status of the land had been previously subject to dispute. The *lex agraria* does not say that the land made private by recent laws should remain private, but that the land public in 133 BC, which has since then been disposed of in a number of different ways, should be private. This implies that a transformation begun in 133 has now, and only now, been completed and brought to a satisfactory conclusion.

8 (B8, A3) O ITA: aes, edd veter; *[eiusque locei agri aedificii privati possessi]o*: Rud; *[eiusque locei agri aedificii emptio venditi]o*: Mo, CIL, Jo; *[eiusque agri locei aedificii apud censum professi]o*: Hin.

F. . .ITO: aes; FACITO: edd veter; *fa[c]ito*: Mo, CIL, Jo.

e[x hac lege privatus (factus) est, ita utei ceteri loci agri aedificia privati, in censum referatur: Mo, CIL; *[– ita utei cetera loca agros aedificia referri oportet*: Rud; *e[x lege plebeive scito exve hac lege – referatur]*: Hin; *e[x lege plebeive scito – referatur]*: Jo; *e[x lege – in tabulas censorias referatur]*: Saumagne.

[. . .deque eo agro loco aed]ificii, eum quoium [is ager locus aedificium erit, eadem profiteri iubeto, quae de cetereis agreis loceis aedificieis privateis, quoius eorum quisque est, profiterei iusserit]: Mo, CIL, Jo.

In the initial lacuna the supplement, *possessi]o*, seems pointless without a definition of who was to possess it. Nor does there seem to be a reason to distinguish the *possessio* of private lands, *qua* possession, from that of public lands. Hinrichs' suggestion, *apud censum professi]o*, is in many ways attractive.

However, in view of the fact that it had been forbidden to alienate by sale the allotments to new settlers by the Gracchan land-commission (cf. line 16 with its commentary; App. *BCiv.* 1.10.38), it would have been particularly appropriate to stress the right to sell (cf. line 63 – *eius agri locei hominis privati venditio*).

Regarding the suggestions made to fill the central lacuna, the important difference is whether the land, whose registration in the census the law is here requiring, was declared private by this law itself (*ex h.l.*) or by any law (*lege plebeive scito*). Hinrichs and Johannsen cite in support of the latter the language of line 19. However, at this point it is natural for the legislator to be dealing with the land declared private earlier in the chapter. This may have included land which had already been declared private by previous legislators, provided that its status was being confirmed by this law. For my '*in censum dedicetur*' cf. Cic. *Flacc.* 79; Gell. 6.11.9 = *ORF*, no. 21, frag. 19.

In the final lacuna Rudorff restored a reference to the censor demanding *tributum*, which is not mentioned elsewhere in the Italian section of the law and, although Roman citizens were in theory still liable to pay this if required, was not currently being exacted. Hinrichs restored a reference to security of possession, which anticipates what follows in lines 9–10 and seems therefore redundant.

9 (B9, A4) SCIT. . . .E: aes; SCITO ESSE: edd veter. AGRVM L: aes, edd veter; *l[ocum – possideatque]*: Rud, Mo, CIL, Hin, Jo. *[neive tr.pl. de ea re legem scribito neve plebem rogato n]eive quis*: Hin; *[neive tr.pl. – scribito neive plebes de ea re scito n]eive*: Jo.

AD SEỊ: aes; AD SEN: edd veter; *ad sen[atum referto*: Sig, CIL, Jo (Mo adds *neive quom populo agito*); *sen[atum referto, neive in senatu sententiam deicito, neive ferto, quo minus is ager aedificium, quei ex h.l. privatus factus est, privatus siet]*: Rud.

The traditional restoration in the central lacuna is by analogy with line 11. *Vti frui habere possidere* does not seem to describe a particular legal status. It certainly is not a characteristic description of private land (note its conspicuous absence in lines 23 and 27) but may be used, where there is either full private ownership or possession, to describe the practical consequences of this legal status, which need protection against interference (cf. Kaser, 1942, 23).

10 (B10, A5) ṚIOVE; aes, Mo, ĈIL; IOVE: O, Pin; *n]eive*: Sig, Rud. *[neive pro magistratu impe]riove*: Mo, CIL, Jo. SENTENTIA: aes. POSS. . . .NEM: aes; POSSESSIONEM: edd veter; *posse[sio]nem*: Mo, CIL, Jo. OPORT: aes, O, Pin; *oportet[oportebitve eo agro aedificii possessione spolietur]*: Sig; *oport[et oportebitve . . . eum agrum locum – possid]eatque*: Mo, CIL, Jo. After *oportebitve* Rud adds *quei ager locus aedificium e lege plebeive scito datus est.*

INVITO MO: aes; INVITO MOR: Maz, Sig, Pin, O[1]; INVITO: O[2]; *invito mor[tuove eo heredibus eius inviteis auferatur]*: Mo, CIL, Jo; *invito mor[tuove eo auferatur]*: Rud.

For *pro potestate inpe]riove* cf. *lex Rubr.Gall.* XX.50: *neive quis mag. prove mag.neive quis pro quo imperio potestateve erit, intercedito*; *lex Gen.Urs.*, cap. 94:

neive quis pro eo imper(io) potestat⟨e⟩ve facito. I assume that a reference to *magistratus prove magistratu* came earlier in the line, cf. *lex rep*. 70, 77; *lex prov. praet*., Delphi C24–5. Whereas the previous line was dealing with political decisions by the senate and probably by the people, this line treats actions by a magistrate both in a judicial capacity and in a political capacity.

Mommsen's restoration at the end of the line is less bald than Rudorff's, but seems to require before *invito* either *ei* (dative of the person concerned) or *eo* (ablative creating an ablative absolute with *invito*). Otherwise the translation of his text would be 'should be taken away from his heirs, if they were unwilling and he was either unwilling or dead'.

Review of chapters I–VI (lines 1–10)

When dealing with each type of land detailed in these chapters, the law begins with its public status in 133 BC. In chapter VI it finally declares all the land mentioned private. No reference is made in the surviving text of these chapters to any previous enactment declaring the land private, though line 19 (see commentary on line 7 above) suggests that an earlier law than this may have done so. To judge from lines 16–17, the Gracchan allotments to new settlers cannot have been alienable by sale, and so fully private, before this law. The same may have applied to other categories of land in the foregoing chapters. However, the elaborate formulation of these early chapters suggests a further inference. Even if some land, most probably the land of *veteres possessores*, had been declared private by an earlier law, there was doubt and confusion about its status, which the present legislator aimed to clear up.

Although Roman civil law did draw a clear distinction between public and private land, recent legislation had tended to blur this by the assignation of public land to individuals under strict conditions, which fell short of conferring full private ownership – i.e. where possession could be bequeathed and ceded but not alienated by sale. These uncertainties were resolved by the present law. Moreover, the provisions concerning the census may well have been an innovation, either over-ruling or resolving doubts about earlier legislation. The Gracchi may have left it unclear whether the allotments of the commission could be registered in the census. More probably, they may have actually forbidden the registration of the land of settlers, both in order to prevent the previously landless from becoming liable to conscription until they had time to build up families and households, and to avoid the irrevocable cession of public land, especially to wealthy *possessores*, which would deprive public authorities of ultimate control.

A further point arises from the reference to the censor's operations. This must exclude the possibility that any class of land made private in chapters I–VI was assigned to non-Romans. *Censor, quei quomque erit*, without qualification, can only refer to the Roman magistrate – nor indeed could the law give instructions to magistrates of a foreign community – and the registration of the private property of non-Romans was not a matter for the censor in the Roman

Republic. I leave aside here the problem of how any non-Roman could become the owner of Roman land, unless he possessed *commercium* (cf. Richardson, 1980, 6–8). The stress on *ceivei Romano dedit adsignavit* in line 3, the chapter dealing with Gracchan allotments, implies that some allotments had been made to non-Romans, but these were not affected by the provisions of chapters I–VI of this law. Such land would have remained public land in the *possessio* of the non-Roman assignee without *commercium*. Land in this category, belonging to a particular group of non-Romans seems to be mentioned in lines 20–2.

VII (lines 11–12) Confirmation of the possession of public land given to viasiei vicanei *by the commission*

11 (B11, A6) Ṣ VICANEIS: aes; S VICANEIS: edd veter; *quei ager – quod eius IIIvirei a.d.a. viasiei]s*: Mo, CIL, Jo. (Rud. unaccountably introduced *Xvirei ex lege Livia*).
QVO ..VVS: aes; QUO I. .NVS: Mo apparatus; QVO MINVS: edd veter. VM: aes, Mo, CIL; M: edd veter; *po[ssideantque, quod eius possessor ... agrum locum aedifici]um*: Mo, CIL; *po[ssideantque, quove invito mortuove quo eorum possessio auferatur, quom ipse possessor heresve eius eum agrum*: Rud; *po[ssideantque, quod censor eum agrum locum aedificium in censum retulerit, quodque eius possessor eum agrum*: Jo.
EVM EVM: aes; EVM EVM Ạ: Mo, CIL.

This chapter, confirming the holdings of the *viasiei vicanei* which had been assigned by the land-commission, must be considered in the light of the related chapter (VIII) following. Mommsen's view that all the land of the *viasiei vicanei* remained public still seems to be fundamentally correct. It is hard to see why, if such land was to become private, it was not included in chapters I–V, which list types of land previously assigned which were to be declared private by this law. Furthermore, chapter VIII (lines 12–13) contains a ban on land given to members of the *viasiei vicanei* becoming private – *quo magis is ag]er locus aedificium privatus siet quove ma[gis* ... Against this Hinrichs (268ff) and Johannsen (237) have argued that the land assigned by the land-commission in lines 11–12 was private because the draughtsman in the second half of line 11 uses the word *abalienare*, which normally means transference by sale: if the chapter envisages that this land might be sold, they argue, then it must have been private. The term *abalienare* is used, however, in lines 15–16, of land which could not be legally sold. The legislator there seems to have been envisaging the ceding of property in what could not amount to a proper sale by *mancipatio*, and the same is probably true here. Johannsen's argument, that the legislator was awarding different statuses to land assigned by the commission to *v.v.* and to land held by them now and in the future on the senate's authority, because of the persistence of old antagonisms between the *populares* and the senate, has little value. If this law was to some degree *popularis*, why should it be vindictive to future *v.v.*? If it was not, then it would have had no interest in maintaining the supposed Gracchan antagonisms. In any case, the Gracchi were perfectly prepared to use the senate as a mechanism for certain kinds of administration, e.g. the allocation of consular provinces.

The distinction between the two clauses (VII, VIII) seems to be that the first confirmed the holdings of *v.v.* who had been specifically assigned land by the land-commission, according to the terms of the original assignation, while the second referred to anyone who had been granted a place among the *v.v.* by the senate now or in the future and similarly confirmed his holding, with the strict proviso that this was not to be regarded as private land.

The repair of the roads was normally during the Republic the responsibility of those whose property bordered them (Cato *RR.* 2.4; *Tab.Heracl.* 20–49). Similarly, by the triumviral period the Romans expected those neighbouring a road in Italy to provide essential supplies for travellers (Hor. *Sat.* 1.5.45–6) – the practice is of course much better attested in the provinces (e.g. Cic. *Att.* 5.10.2 and 16.5). I assume that, in order to ensure the maintenance of the roads and support of travellers, property and agricultural holdings by the roads were granted, perhaps without rent, on condition that the occupants performed these services. The Gracchan *IIIviri* would have made their own selection of *v.v.* Apart from this, magistrates may have been regularly entrusted by the senate with allocations of this kind in the course of road-building and maintenance. Furthermore, a *viasius vicanus* himself probably had the right and duty to ensure that he was replaced, if he decided to move through age, illness or other commitments. We have no other specific evidence of allotments to *viasiei vicanei*, but the famous monument from Polla (*ILLRP*, 454), where the road-builder claims, '*Eidem primus fecei ut de agro poplico aratoribus cederent paastores. Forum aedisque poplicas heic fecei*', may in fact be referring to such grants (cf. Hinrichs, 1967, 172).

12 (B12, A7) *extra]que*: Mo, CIL, Jo. Rud restored in the A–B lacuna at the end of line 11 and the beginning of line 12 *quei ager – cavitum est nei divideretur –* perhaps correctly. There is in fact room for both this and another exception clause.

Quei ex h.l. venire dari reddive oportebit implies that this law provided for the sale of certain land which was still public in 111 BC. The future sale of public land in Italy cannot be discerned elsewhere in what survives of the law, though we hear of the buying of contracts for the exploitation of *ager patritus* in lines 27–8 – something which perhaps might have been described as *venire*. It is just possible that there was a reference to sale in the lacunae in lines 5–7, but what survives, especially the verbs *dedit, adsignavit, reliquit* lends no support to this assumption.

VIII (lines 12–13) Present and future holdings of viasiei vicanei *dependent on a* senatus consultum *should not be made private*

12 (B12, A7) IN . . .SIEIS: aes; IN VIASIEIS: edd veter; OPORTEB.TY: aes; OPORTEB: Pin, O; OPORTEBIT: Sig; OPORTEBI VE III: Mo apparatus; *[ita – eritve]*: Mo, CIL, Jo (Burdese, 81, added *a IIIviro*); *[datus adsignatus relictusve erit, is ager locus* *aedificium privatus nei esto, neive quis ad senatum ferto]*: Rud. *[quo magis is ag]er*: Rud, Mo, CIL, Jo.

QVOVE MA: aes, edd veter; QVOVE MAQ: Mo, CIL; *quove mag[is eius agri locei emptio siet*: Mo; *quove mag[is censor, queiquomque erit, eum agrum locum in censum referat ita utei cetera loca agros aedificia privata referri oportet*: Hu; *quove – referat*: CIL; *quove mag[is eius agri loci aedificii professio apud censorem, quei quomque erit, fiat*: Hin, Jo.

Any *viasiei vicanei* appointed after the dissolution of the land-commission appear to have owed their appointment ultimately to a *senatus consultum*. It was envisaged that this would continue both in relation to roads already built and those to be built in the future. This chapter ensures that any land assigned them, whether it was the re-allocation of an old allotment or a new allotment from Roman public land, would not become private.

13 (B13) EI EST SIET: aes; TEI EST SIET: edd veter; *[quove magis eum agrum locum censor, queiquomque erit, in censum referat, quove magis de eo agro loco aliter atque u]tei est*: Mo, CIL; *[quove magis censor – quove magis eius agri locei possessio aliter atque u]tei est*: Hin, Jo; *[quem agrum ex h.l. venire dari reddive oportet, quo minus is ita u]tei est*: Rud.

It is common ground among editors since Mommsen that there was a reference to registration by the censors here and it seems to me attractive to connect this closely with *aliter atque u]tei est*. It would also have been appropriate to forbid any buying or selling of this land, as proposed in Mommsen's restoration.

IX (lines 13–14) Up to 30 iugera *of hitherto unassigned public land used by an individual for agriculture are to be private*

13 (B13, A8) PLEBẸỊ followed by the traces of two letters and an interpunct: aes; PLEBEIVE: edd veter; PLEBIVE: Mo, CIL. ṬRAQVE: aes (A8); XTRAQVE: O, Sig, Pin; RAQVE: Maz. – *divideretur, extraque eum agrum quei viasieis vicaneis datus adsignatus est ex]traque*: Jo; – *divideretur, extraque eum agrum, quem IIIvir sortito ceivi Romano dedit adsignavit, ex]traque*: Hin. PLEBEIVE: aes (only the lowest bar of the final E is preserved), O[1]; PLEBEIV: Sig, Pin, Maz, O[2]; *plebeive [scito – licuit*: Rud, Mo.

As Johannsen has pointed out (241), all categories of land in the countryside already listed and declared private must have been excluded from occupation and conversion into the private property of a new occupier under the provisions of this chapter, similarly also the special category of the land of the *viasiei vicanei*. Land and buildings in towns and villages discussed in lines 4–7 may be regarded as included in the clause referring to allocations by the land-commission. My restoration largely follows Johannsen but has greater freedom because the line-length of this reconstruction is greater than that in Mommsen's. However, Hinrichs' insertion of the clause referring to the Gracchan allotments in the central B–A lacuna of this line must be rejected because of insufficient space there. In the clause referring to the *vetus possessor* it is desirable that an explicit reference should be made to the legal limit on holdings, *quod non modus maior*, etc., as in the restorations of Rudorff and Mommsen.

14 (B14) *[– – quom quis ceivis Romanus agri colendi cau]sa*: Rud; *[– –sei quis tum cum haex lex rogabitur agri colendi cau]sa*: Mo, CIL, Hin, Jo. S AGER: aes; *⟨i⟩s ager*: Rud, Mo.

Although the detail of the restoration proposed by Rudorff is open to question, its general sense must be correct. The chapter must be dealing with occupation for agricultural rather than pastoral purposes in view of the contrast in formulation with what follows in lines 14–15. Cf. *Sententia Minuciorum* (*CIL* I^2, 584 = *ILLRP*, 517), line 31, *dum ne alium intro mitat . . . colendi causa*. It is just possible that there was a specific reference to the planting of trees (*arborum serendarum causa*) in view of the parallel of emphuteutic contracts in the Hellenistic world cf. *P.Teb.* 5.93ff = Mitteis, Wilcken, *GCP* I, 2, no. 339 – 118 BC).

Mommsen inserted *tum cum – rogabitur*, because he did not believe that this chapter could look forward to the future. However, if the chapter was only concerned with current occupation of *ager publicus*, it would have been more natural to have used the present tense rather than *possidebit habebitve*. Nor is there any reason why the legislator should have wished to exclude future occupiers from the benefits of this chapter. It would in any case have been difficult to prove occupation at the moment of the passage of the bill. Mommsen's view was a consequence of his belief that the occupation of public land after this bill was forbidden in lines 24–5. However, that chapter seems to be dealing specifically with public land left over after all previous dispositions, including occupation such as is described here. If this view is correct, it will follow that the law assumed that there still existed vacant public land suitable for agriculture. Some of this may well have been public land currently occupied by *veteres possesores* in excess of the legal limit. In so far as the holding of *ager Romanus* as private property was only open to Roman citizens or those with *commercium*, we should probably add *c(eivis) R(omanus)* in the conditional clause. These holdings will then be, as it were, a continuation of the Gracchan allotment scheme.

It is impossible to decide whether the 30 *iugera* upper limit mentioned here represents the standard module of land assigned by the commission. We have evidence of smaller allotments in the middle Republic – 7 *iugera* (Colum. I. praef. 14); 14 (*De Vir.Ill.* 33); Plut. *Crass.* 2.10); 5 and 8 (Livy 39.55.7–8); 10 (Livy 42.4.4) – and in the late Republic – 10–12 *iugera* in the *ager Campanus* and *Stellas* (Cic. *Leg.Agr.* 2.76–9, 88; *Att.* 2.16.1). The allotments in the triumviral period were on a much greater scale (66⅔ – Hyg. 163–4 Thul = 199–201 Lach), as were the allotments in Africa in this period (line 60, cf. *De Vir.Ill.* 73.1). Note also the odd figure of 51½ *iugera* at Luna in 177 BC (Livy 41.13.5), where the agricultural plot was probably 50 and the building plot in the town 1½ *iugera*. Much depended on the quality of the land in different regions and a *IIIvir* actually assigning land on the spot could take account of this, while a legislator could only prescribe in general terms, as here.

X (lines 14–15) A limited right of free grazing on ager compascuus

14 (B14, A9) X PASCET QVAI: aes, edd veter, Rud; QVAE: Mo, CIL, Jo (it is more likely that the final downstroke is what remains of an E); *quae[que eis minus annum gnatae erunt, posteaquam gnatae erunt, queive – non plus (L)...*: Rud, Mo, CIL, Jo – Rud alone adding *L* after *plus* in the light of the ratio of small to large beasts in the earlier *lex de modo agrorum* (App. *BCiv.* 1.8.33).

PASCET ... POSTEAQVA: aes, O, Sig, Pin; ASCET POSTEAQVE: Maz; *posteaqua[m vectigalia – primum constiterint*: Mattingly (1969, 131) comparing line 19. See also line 20.

15 (B15) DATO: aes; O DATO: O[1]; E DATO: Sig, Pin, O[2]; Ş DATO: Mo. Mommsen believed that he had seen the top semicircle of an S. This, however, may equally have been the top of an E.

[is pro eo numero pequdum, quae in eo agro pascentur, populo – nei debeto, neive eius pequniae nomine sati]s: Rud; *[is pro iis pequdibus populo – nei debeto, neive de ea re sati]s*: Mo, CIL; *[nei is pro eo numero pequdum, quae in eo agro pascentur, populo aut publicano vectigal scripturamve pecori]s*: Jo (sim. Hin); *[is pro eo pecore, quod in eo agro pascetur, scripturam vectigalve nei dare debeto neiv]e*: Mattingly, 1969, 131. For these restorations, cf. lines 19–20. Huschke accepted Rudorff's restoration but added before it *[eius ita utei in agro privato ius compascendi esto...]*. For the theory behind this see below.

Ager compascuus (common pasture land) is understood by the *agrimensores* to be pasture land specifically assigned to neighbouring farmers: '*Compascua, quod est genus quasi subsecivorum sive loca quae proximi quique vicini, id est qui ea contingunt, pascua (?pascunt)*' (Sic.Flacc. 121 Thul = 157 Lach); '*cum plus terrae quam datum erat, superesset, proximis possessoribus datum est in commune nomine pascuorum*' (Hyg. 164 Thul = 201 Lach, cf. Front. 6 Thul = 15 Lach). The second-century AD jurist Scaevola also refers to the buying of a private common pasture, *ut ius compascendi haberent* (*Dig.* 8.5.26.1).

Since Huschke (590, cf. Mommsen, *CIL* I, p. 91), it has been assumed that the *ager compascuus* here is pasture land assigned to a specified number of neighbours by a Roman official as described by the *agrimensores*. Huschke's supplement was an attempt to refer to this explicitly in the text – far too brief to be clear and dependent on the assumption that privately owned *ager compascuus* already existed. However, the near-contemporary *Sententia Minuciorum* of 117 BC (*CIL* I², 584 = *ILLRP*, 517, 32ff), quoted below in the commentary on chapter XVIII, suggests that then *ager compascuus* described the public pasture land of the whole community. The land referred to in the present chapter is clearly public, not private land, since tax is payable to the *populus*, if beasts in excess of a small upper limit are grazed. Moreover, it seems to be open to the community as a whole, since there is no clause in this chapter restricting grazing to a limited number of landowners nearby, as envisaged in the *Digest* and *agrimensores* texts above. The situation described by Frontinus (above) in Campania, where the *silvae* appropriate to cultivated land were more than four or five neighbours distant, was also probably the outcome of original general areas of pasture land common to all the farmers in a wide area. It should be emphasised that here, although it is implied that tax or *scriptura* is payable on animals exceeding the number mentioned, there is no mention in the surviving text of any other legal restriction on the exploitation of this pasture. It is assumed that it will be used by anyone for whom it is convenient. However, the man with but a few beasts, who may well be a local, with be able to use it without payment.

(See further commentary on chapter XVIII, lines 24–5.)

XI (lines 15–16) Granting of possession by a magistrate to recipients of allotments from the land-commission and their heirs

15 (B15, A10) *Roma[no agrum locum dedit adsignavit, quo eius agri loci neque ipse possessor abalie]navit*: Rud, *Roma[no agrum dedit adsignavit, quod eius agri neque is . . .abalie]navit*: Mo, CIL; *Roma[no agrum dedit adsignavit, quod eius agri IIIvir in formas tabulasve retulit referive iusit, quod eius agri neque is* –: Hin, Jo. *abalienav[eritve, de eo agro consul praetorve, quo* (*de ea re*): Rud; *abalienav[eritve, quoive ab eo hereditate testamento deditioneve obvenit, queive ab eorum quo emit, quei eorum*: Mo, CIL; *abalienav[eritve, queive ab eorum quo emit, quei eorum*: Hin, Jo.

Like Mommsen, I have assumed in the text and translation that the line was accurately engraved, so that *quoi (ceivi Romano)* is a deferred relative pronoun, while *eius agri* is a partitive genitive depending on the restored *agrum*. It is of course possible that *quod* has slipped out of the text before *eius agri*.

For *hereditate – obveneritve* cf. line 23. A reference to the heir of the assignee in an elaborate clause should logically either appear before *quod – neque heres eius abalienaverit* or not at all. Hinrichs and Johannsen took the latter course; I have tentatively preferred the former. On the other hand, *queive ab eorum quo emit* should not be restored at all, as it has been by editors since Mommsen. The end of the chapter in line 16, *utei possessionem secundum eum heredemve eius det, quoi sorti is ager datus adsignatusve fuerit*, excludes any grant of possession to a buyer (only the assignee and his heir are mentioned). This implies that the assignees of new allotments had not been allowed to sell them before the passage of this law. It follows that the statement about the first agrarian law after the death of C.Gracchus in App. *BCiv*. 1.27.121 is misleading: only the *veteres possessores* were allowed to sell their land (see below).

16 (B16) ECRRNITOQVE: aes, Pin, Mo, CIL; ECERNITOQVE: O, Sig. SECVNDO: aes; em. Rud. *de ea re – deicito d]ecernitoque*: Mo, CIL, Jo. cf. line 17.

XII (lines 16–17) Granting of possession by a magistrate to prior possessors of public land, their heirs and buyers from them

16 (A11) ṬERE POSSESIONEM: aes (only the bottom of the initial T is visible); ERE: O, Pin; ERET: Maz, Sig. *Ager publicus – eius agri IIIvir a.d.a. veteri prove ve]tere possesionem*: Mo, CIL; *ager publicus – quod eius agri IIIvir a.d.a. veteri possesori prove ve]tere possesore*: Hin, Jo; *quoi ceivi Romano eius agri. quei supra scriptus est, IIIvir a.d.a. veteri possesori prove vetere possesso]re*: Rud. *III[vir a.d.a. possesionem reliquit*: Rud; *III[vir a.d.a. in urbe oppido vico dedit adsignavit reddidit*: Mo, CIL; *III[vir in formas tabulasve rettulit referive iusit*: Hin; *III[virei a.d.a. viasieis vicaneis dederunt adsignaverunt reliquerunt*: Jo.

In the B–A lacuna we must restore the standard introductory formula, which begins the parallel chapter in lines 15–16. In this *quod eius agri* is necessitated by *quodque eius agri* preserved on the A fragment and *ex lege plebeive sc(ito)* seems also required in view of the parallels in lines 13 and 15. Only assignments in accordance with previous legislation could receive legal recognition now. The length of the ensuing restoration is one of the considerations which determines the distance between the B and A complexes of fragments (see *Lex Repetundarum*, 'Introduction to the Text', pp. 75–6).

For *prove vetere possesore* see commentary on lines 3–4. It would be appropriate here if the term referred to men who had received land from the commission in exchange for a prior possession. The *viasiei vicanei* cannot have appeared in this line if their land remained public (*contra* Johannsen, cf. commentary on lines 11–13), since they would not have had the right to sell. A reference to land assigned in towns or villages should have appeared either in this chapter or the preceding one.

17 (B17, A12) S QVEIVE: aes (S only visible on photograph), O, Sig, Pin; T QVEIVE: Mo (with no indication of uncertainty), CIL, Hin, Jo; *[quod eius agri neque is abalienavit abalienaverit neque heres eius, quoive ab eo obveni]t*: CIL (sim. Mo, Hin, Jo). QVEI: aes; *quo*: Rud, Mo, etc.

d[ecernitoque utei eius agri locei possesionem secundum eum heredemve eius det: Rud; *d[eque eo agro decernito utei possesionem secundum eum heredemve eius det*: Mattingly, 1969, 131. Like Mommsen and Johannsen, I have followed the formulation in line 16, inserting *ab eorum quo* to complete the lacuna.

ADSIGNATVSVE QEIVE A (with V added suprascript between Q and E): aes; *queive*: edd veter (only Pin shows the V as suprascript); *adsignatusve ⟨fuerit⟩*: Rud; *adsignatusve ⟨redditusve fuerit⟩*: Mo, CIL, Jo. *queive a[grum ab eorum quo emit emerit, quod eius agri non abalienatum est, ita utei s.s.est*: Rud (plausible, but perhaps the simpler *queive a[b eorum quo emit* is better); *queive a[grum in urbe oppido vico acceperit*: Mo, CIL; *queive a[grum in eo agro acceperit, quem III virei viasieis vicaneis dederunt adsignaverunt reliquerunt*: Jo;

queive a[ger redditus fuerit pro eo agro quem quisque de sua possesione vetus possessor dedit, quod – s.s.est: Hin.

A reference to a buyer of the land in question is to be expected after the clause beginning *quoi is ager vetere*. Johannsen's restoration is unacceptable if the land of the *viasiei vicanei* remained public, see commentary on lines 11–12; Hinrichs' is superfluous, if my interpretation of *pro vetere possessore* is correct, see commentary on line 2. For *eidus Martias primas*, that is, the first Ides of March after the passage of the law, see line 18 and cf. line 70 for the Ides of March following the new tax-regulations. To allow a reasonable time for knowledge of the law to circulate, we must assume that this date was chosen at some distance in the future. Hence it is highly unlikely that our law was passed before 15 March 111 BC. The time-limit in question here is, therefore, 15 March 110 BC (see p. 282 below).

The last two chapters, unlike XXVIII and XXIX (lines 33–6), do not proceed on the assumption that there is a dispute about the land in question, though this may have in fact been the case at the time. Their purpose is to provide judicial confirmation of their holdings for those who approach magistrates. This confirmation consists in the magistrate concerned decreeing that the man who has proved his right to ownership of the property may physically take possession. These provisions would have been especially useful to those who had not had direct contact with the land-commission – that is, heirs and purchasers of allotments – and to assignees who, for some reason or another, had left their allotment. The last chapter does not seem to have applied to a man who had not been formally allocated land but was exploiting up to 30 *iugera* for agricultural purposes, as in line 14. *Ab eorum quo emit* implies that all the categories of possessor in lines 16–17 had had the right to sell and that cannot have applied to the occupier of up to 30 *iugera* before the passage of this law.

XIII (line 18) Protection of a possessor from violent ejection

18 (B18, A13) R S S: edd veter (the bottom of the R and the top of the first S are still visible); *sei quis eorum quorum age]r s(upra) s(criptus) est*: Mo, CIL, Jo; *sei quis eorum, quibus utei s.s.est ager in Italia datus adsignatus redditu]s est*: Rud.
IAS: aes, O, Pin, Maz; *Marti]as*: Sig; *eiec[erit, tum pr. consolve quem ex h.l. de eo agro ius deicere oportebit, ante eidus Mart]ias*: Rud; *eiec[erit, quem ex h.l. deicere oportebit, sei is quei ita eiectus est ad eum de ea re in ious adierit ante eidus Mar]tias*: Mo, CIL, Jo. *e[st – restituatur*: Mo, CIL; *e[st, eam possessionem unde vi eiectus fuerit, quaeque tunc ibei habuit, recuperet*: Rud; *e[st, in suam possessionem restituatur*: Jo.

The previous two chapters provided for the confirmation of possession in general, whether there was a dispute over possession or not. This chapter deals with the special case where possession had been disturbed by violence. It orders the restoration of the man who had lost physical control of his land, provided that it belonged to one of the categories previously mentioned in the law and thus he had a title to it, either as the owner of private land or as the possessor of public land, and provided that possession had not been acquired improperly or was a concession by the true possessor. Johannsen (249) took it as a counterpoint to the preceding chapters in a different way. She believed that, whereas XVI and XVII protected ownership of private land, the present chapter protected possession of land not in private ownership. However, there is no reason to confine its scope to cases of possession which fell short of ownership. Violent ejection was a threat to both ownership and possession, which required a special remedy. This chapter is intended as a complement to the other procedures in the law for settling property disputes of all kinds. Nor should we anachronistically ascribe to this period the custom of employing *vis ex conventu*, that is, an understanding between two parties disputing the ownership of land, that one should eject the other by force, in order to set in motion a process arising from the interdicts about possession and dispossession – a more convenient procedure than other forms of private law (Cic. *Caec.* 20ff; Kaser, 1955, I, 336).

It is in fact the earliest text we possess of the *interdictum unde vi*, known to us from *Dig.* 43.16.1ff and Cic. *Tull.* 44: *unde tu aut familia aut procurator tuus illum aut familiam aut procuratorem illius in hoc anno vi deiecisti, cum ille possideret, quod nec vi nec clam nec precario possideret, ⟨eo illum restituas⟩*, cf. Cic. *Caec.* 91 and *Leg.Agr.* 3.11. The basic interdict protecting possession (Festus 260L; *Dig.* 43.17.1) preceded it, since this (including the *vi, clam, precario* formula) is parodied in Terence, *Eunuchus*, 319–20, and, therefore, must have been invented at least before 161 BC. The formulation of *unde vi* here is primitive (there is no mention of *procurator* or *familia*) and, although this interdict may have been devised by a praetor shortly before 111 BC, it is tempting to see the present law as the origin of it. The limitation, *in hoc anno*, incorporated in the later version of the interdict (which was not normally inserted in the subsequent interdict *de vi armata* – Cic. *Fam.* 15.16.3; *Caec.* 23; 89–91) may derive from the terminus of the Ides of March inserted in this law.

On the interdicts see Kaser, 1955, I, 335ff; Serrao, 1954, 74ff; Lintott, 1968, 126ff; Labruna, 1971; Frier, 1985.

XIV (lines 18–19) No tax to be paid in future on land made private under this law

19 (B19, A14) ITO: aes, Sig, Pin; PTO: O; TO: Rud, Mo, CIL. *[Quei ager locus publicus populi Romanei quodve aedificium ex lege plebeive sci]to*: Rud; *[Quei ager locus aedificium publicus populei Romanei in terra Italia P.Muucio L.Calpurnio cos. fuit, quod eius ex lege plebeive sci]to*: Mo, CIL, Jo.

POST H: aes, Sig, Pin; POST H L: O, Mo, CIL; *post h.[l. primum constiterint, nei quis magistratus prove magistratu facito quo quis populo aut p]ublicano*: Rud, *post h.l. [rogatam primum*: Mo, CIL, Jo; *post h.l. [rogatam primum constiterint, ne quis mag. neive pro mag. imperiove sententiam deicito neve inferto, quo quis minus aliterve utei ex lege plebeive scito debet debebit, populo aut p]ublicano*: Saumagne, 1927, 62. PEQVNIA: aes. VECPIGALVE: aes. NEIVE QVIS: aes, edd veter; NEIVE QVIS D (or P): Mo apparatus; *neive quis [de ea re ad senatum referto neive in senatu sententiam deicito neive ferto*: Rud; *neive quis [facito*: Mo, CIL; *neive quis [mag. prove mag. facito quo is ager publice locetur, quove publicanus eum agrum publicum fruendum redemptum conductumve habeat*: Jo.

Mommsen restored the text of this chapter on the understanding that it abolished tax on the former public land made private by this and other laws. Saumagne's proposed restoration was part of an argument that this law did not in fact abolish taxes on the land assigned by the commission and was therefore not Appian's third post-Gracchan law. His formal arguments against Mommsen's restoration in line 20 are either invalid or can be countered by new restorations which preserve the sense that taxes are to be abolished, cf. Johannsen (252ff) and see the commentary on line 20. As Johannsen saw (251–2), the appearance of a *terminus post quem* in these lines indicates that a change was to be made regarding taxation. This would not have been needed, if the situation was to remain the same as it was before this law, as Saumagne's restoration implies. Again, if there was to be a change in taxation other than its abolition, this would have had to be specified somewhere else in the text on Saumagne's restoration, and of this there is no trace, neither in lines 7–10 nor in particular in lines 13–14, where it is quite impossible to find room for a restoration of this kind. The remaining possibility is that tax was abolished. The land of new assignees had been liable to tax since 122 BC at least, when Livius Drusus proposed this tax's abolition (Plut. *C.Gr.* 9.2). It is not, however, known whether his proposal was enacted. The land of prior possessors had been subject to tax since the second post-Gracchan law (App. *BCiv.* 1.27.122). The land made private by this law certainly included the allotments to new assignees and may have included other categories of land mentioned in lines 1–10 (see commentary on line 10 and lines 15–16).

XV (lines 19–20) No tax to be paid in future ?on land assigned to the viasiei vicanei

20 (B20, A15) QVOVE QVID: aes, edd veter (exc. O[1]: QVODVE QVID) – there are traces before QVOVE on the bronze consistent with NT; *[neive quis iudex sententiam deicito quo quis ob eam rem populo Romano aut publicano quid debeat] quove*: Rud; *neve quis [de ea re ad senatum referto, quo minus aliterve utei ex lege plebeive scito debetur ob eos agros locos aedificia quis quid det dareve debeat] quove*: Saumagne. QVAM . . .IGALIA: aes; VECTIGALIA: edd veter.

ṚEIS: aes (only the lower right quarter of the R survives and all the letters are hard to read on the broken bronze); REIS: O; IS: Pin; Sig omits; *ag[ros pecuniae vectigalis scripturaeve nomine pro eo pecore quod in eis ag]reis*: Rud; *ag[ros locos aedificia populo aut publicano dare debeat, neive scripturam pecoris, quod in eis ag]reis*: Mo, CIL; *ag[ros locos aedificia, facito quo minus aliterve atque utei ex lege plebeive scito debetur debebitur, pecuniam vectigal scripturamve pecoris, quod in eis ag]reis*: Saumagne; *ag[ros locos aedificia dato dareve debeto, neive facito, quo quis quid pro scriptura pecoris, quod in eis ag]reis*: Jo, sim. Zancan, 62.

Taken as a single chapter, lines 18–20 are excessively repetitive, even by the standards of this law. I have therefore assumed a second chapter making a similar provision about a different category of land. If we accept that the land of the *viasiei vicanei* was still public (see commentary on lines 11–13 above), this was not embraced by *quod ex lege plebeive sc]ito exve h.l. privatum factum erit*. If the *viasiei vicanei* were bound to perform corvées in return for their properties, it is reasonable to conjecture that they were freed from paying taxes on their land and animals. My restoration of *nei quis – vectigalis sient* seeks to provide a cause, on account of which (*ob eam rem*) money might be demanded. As Saumagne pointed out, a direct prohibition is not expressed in this law by *nei* with the subjunctive but by *nei* with the imperative. We therefore need in the B–A lacuna first a negated imperative referring to the potential taxpayer, followed by a *neive ... facito quo* construction on which the following subjunctive, *debeat*, can depend.

XVI (lines 20–3) Ratification of the possession of certain land given in exchange to prior possessors of public land

20 (A15) POPV: aes, O, Sig, Pin; POPVL: Maz; POPVI: Mo apparatus.

21 (B21, A16) AD XE: aes; E AD XE: Sig; C AD XE: O, Pin; *[quem agrum in eo agro locumve de eo agro L.Caecilius L.Domitius censores] a.d.XI*: Rud; *[quem agrum L.Caecilius – cens] a.d.XI*: Mo, CIL, sim. Jo.

LOC. . .ROMANVS: aes; LOCO CEIVIS ROMANVS: edd veter.

M PVBLICVM: aes (A); VM PVBLICVM: edd veter, Mo; OM PVBLICVM: Rud; *togatorum [milites in terra Italia inperare solent ... agrum loc]um*: Rud, Mo (*lo]cum*: CIL); *solent, agrum locum possesionem habuit posseditve, quem agrum lo]cum*: Hin, Jo. For *ex formula – solent*, cf. line 50.

POSSESO: aes; edd veter; POSSESOṚ: Mo; *posseso[re dedit – conlocaretur*: Rud, Mo, CIL (cf. line 22).

We should take seriously the C seen by the majority of humanist copiers at the left-hand edge of B. The restoration, *ex s.c.*, is then inevitable. *Locatio* did not have to be performed by censors (cf. line 89; Cic. *Verr.* 3.18) and the reference to a *s.c.* is perhaps an indication that the land was let by a consul or consuls (Cic. loc. cit.). This phrase must form part of an exception clause, since land rented out by contract could not have formed part of the public land given to *veteres possessores* in exchange for their former holdings. What is the difference between the public land dealt with here and the holdings given in exchange to the *pro vetere possessore*, dealt with earlier (cf. lines 2, 3, 16)? The chapter concerns land, part of which was contracted out in conjunction with that beyond Curio. This land is probably, therefore, itself a restricted geographical area, for which special arrangements were made, no doubt because part of the area was destined for urban foundations. Curio was presumably a river or mountain: Huschke thought that it was in Aetolia, but it is hard to see how this would be associated with the leasing of Italian land; Hinrichs (275) preferred southern Italy in the neighbourhood of either of the Gracchan colony sites. There is a river now called Curio to the north-east of Dertona (see the map in Fraccaro, 1957) and this may conceivably be relevant. For Italian *socii* as well as Latins being regarded as *togati*, cf. Sall. *Jug.* 21.2 with 26.1; for the *formula* see Livy 22.57.10; 27.10.3.

22 (B22, A17) OPPIDVM: aes, Mo; D OPPIDVM: Sig, O; QVOD OPPIDVM: Pin (QVO not indicated as restoration, but it must have been); *[quo in agro IIIvir coloniae deducendae creatus i]d oppidum*: Rud; *[quo in agro IIIvir i]d*: Mo, CIL, Jo. AGRVM LOCVMVE: edd veter. AGRO LOCVMVE (later): aes. *Roman[ei in terra Italia – fuit]*: Mo, CIL (*Romanei[* – : Rud); *Roman[ei – fuit, IIIvir a.d.a. dedit adsignavit reddidit*: Hin, Jo.

RVM: aes; GRVM: edd veter; *extra eum a]grum*: Sig, Kl, cett edd.

23 (B23) *[IIIvir ei ceivi Romano sociumve nominisve Latini agrum locum aedificium reddidit adsignavit]*: Rud; *[IIIvir dedit reddidit adsignavit, eius, quoi is ager locus datus redditus adsignatus erit]*: Mo (sim. CIL).

OBVENERITVE ... MERITVE: aes; OBVENERITVE EMIT EMERITVE: edd veter; *[queive ab eo emit e]meritve*: Mo, CIL, Jo (Mo realised that *queive ab eo* must have been omitted by the engraver). S AGER: Sig.

ESTO QVE: aes (with no rubric space after ESTO), Pin, O; *esto quam [sei*: Sig.

It is not surprising that here land should be declared private, which had been given to *veteres possessores* or their equivalent in exchange for their holdings, when these were taken over for colonial or other urban territory, since holdings of *veteres possessores* within the legal limit had already been declared private, lines 1–2, cf. 16–17. Whether this chapter merely confirmed a provision of an earlier law or was perhaps the rectification of a previous anomaly, we cannot tell. It should not necessarily be subsumed under Appian's second law, as Johannsen argued. What is remarkable is the appearance of Latin and other allies, since they were not mentioned in lines 16–17 and logically should not have appeared in lines 1–2 (see the review of chapters I–VI above). If the private ownership of *ager Romanus* was only permitted to Roman citizens or those having the right of *commercium* (for this sense of *commercium* see Cic. *Verr.* 3.93), then the grant of private status here could only apply, if the possessor was a Roman or (on the usual view) a Latin. An ally would normally be excluded unless he had been specially privileged. This would have ensured that the land was subsequently only sold or bequeathed to another man of similar juridical status and according to Roman procedures. The word *oppidum* seems to cover any non-colonial settlement created in Roman territory, conceivably a *municipium* created *de novo* or a *forum/conciliabulum*, cf. Brunt, 1971, 583; 1988, 137.

XVII (lines 23–4) Granting of possession by a magistrate to those entitled to it under the provisions of the previous chapter

23 (A18) Q COLONIAM: aes; O COLONIAM: Sig, Pin, O; COLONIAM: Maz; *que[m agrum locum aedificium IIIvir de eo agro loco aedificio pro eo agro loco qu]o*: Rud; *Que[i ager publicus populi Romanei fuit, quem IIIvir de eo agro loco pro – qu]o*: Mo, CIL, Jo.

quei[pr. consolve de eo agro loco aedificio ex h.l. ious deicet, quo de ea re in ious aditum erit]: Rud (Mo, CIL, Jo omit *agro aedificio* but add *ante eidus Martias primas*, cf. lines 18–19).

The practice of the law is to separate chapters about property-rights and statements about procedures for enforcing them. It seems also natural stylistically to begin a new chapter in the middle of this line. It is not, however, certain that we should assume that a paragraph-space was omitted by the engraver after *esto* on the B fragment (see above). It is at least as probable that *que[i]?* introduces a brief qualifying-clause and the new chapter begins later in the line.

24 (B24) REDEMVE: aes; EREDEMVE: edd veter; HEREDEMVE: Bluhme ap. Mo; *is de ea re ious deicito decernitoque secundum eum h]eredemve*: Rud, Mo, CIL, Jo; DEDDIT: aes, O, Pin; DEDIT: Sig, Rud, Mo, CIL, Jo (without indication of correction); R . . . ADSIGNAVIT: aes; REDDIDIT ADSIGNAVIT: edd veter. ADITVN: aes; ERIT: aes, Sig; ER: O, Pin.

For jurisdiction over (probably) newly created private land being reserved for praetors and consuls, cf. lines 33–4. It is significant that land-commissioners (*IIIviri*) and *praefecti iure dicundo* are excluded. For a similar restriction see App. *BCiv*. 1.19.80 on the *s.c.* of 129 BC, which confined jurisdiction over land involving allies to the consul, C.Sempronius Tuditanus.

XVIII (lines 24–5) Free access to be maintained to pasture land in the territory remaining public

24 (A19) *[ager locus quei sup]ra*: Sig, Pin; *locus omnis quei sup]ra*: Rud. SCREIPTVS: aes, Maz; SCRIPTVS: O, Sig, Pin. II.L: aes. *extra eum ag[rum locum quei ager locus ex lege plebeive scito, quod divideretur*: Rud, Zancan, 77; *ag[rum locum, quei publico usui destinatus vel publice locatus est*: Mo, CIL; *ag[rum, quei ager ex lege pl.ve sc. ita utei s.s.e. exceptum – divideretur, extraque eum agrum quei publice locatus venditusve est*: Jo (sim. Hin).

25 (B25, A20) NEIVE: aes (no preceding interpunct visible); *is ager privatus nei esto] neive is ager*: Rud; *in eo agro quei volet pascito . . .] neive*: Mo, CIL; *neive is ager privatus] neive*: Hin; *privatus nei esto] neive*: Jo.

The Q of OQUPATVM appears like an O but a horizontal stroke seems to have been begun at its base.

QVO MI. . . ELIT: aes; QVO MINVS QVEI VELIT: edd veter (this is the last line on this face in which they record an unbroken text for B). IVGRA SINGVLA L: aes (the last letter, not recorded by edd veter, is not an anchor-shaped L as Mo's apparatus suggests, but is clearly neither an I nor any other letter); *L [HS nummos*: Mo, CIL, Jo.

DEBETO: aes, Maz; E DEBETO: Pin, O; *nihil dar]e debeto*: Sig; *dar]e*: Mo, CIL. REDEMPTVW COWDVCTVWVE: aes (for this odd error, cf. line 88).

This chapter concerns the use as pasture of land remaining public property of the Roman people, i.e. land neither retained by or granted to *veteres possessores*, nor newly allocated by land-commissioners, nor converted to private property by cultivation as provided in line 14. The legislator must also have excepted in this chapter the public land already exempted from division – whether this was the *ager Campanus*, as Mommsen thought, or land granted to allied communities and individuals and to *coloniae* and *municipia*, see the note on lines 2–3, including land reserved for public use, e.g. for a *forum* or *conciliabulum* – and any land which had been leased out by contract. The necessary existence of these exceptions has been ignored by Granet (1990, 142ff). The variety of restorations in lines 24–5 reflect differing views about what C.Gracchus' law might or might not have exempted. Since that law was relevant, I cannot imagine that the legislator would have neglected to mention it specifically. Hence the present restoration.

A more difficult problem is created by the provision in line 25. It looks natural to interpret NEIVE at the edge of the fragment as the negative particle. Yet there is a seeming contradiction in providing that land should *not* be *ager compascuus* and then stating that no obstruction should be afforded to any one who may want to *compascere*. Huschke and Mommsen's solution was to appeal to a definition of *ager compascuus* found in the Gromatici and the Digest (cf. commentary on line 15 above). Frontinus (6 Thul = 15 Lach) writes of *pascua/ compascua*, whose ownership, like that of *silvae* belonged *ad fundos, sed in commune*, similarly Hyginus, when discussing colonial assignments (164–5 Thul = 201–2 Lach, cf. Sic.Flacc. 121 Thul). The second-century AD jurist Scaevola (*Dig*. 8.5.20.1) discusses owners jointly purchasing a common pasture area. This form of *ager compascuus* was limited to a definite number of property-holders and in consequence not open to *quei velet*.

However, although this concept of *ager compascuus* had developed by the Principate, in lines 14–15 of this law it is not certain that this sense is to be preferred to a more general one of 'pasture land open to all'. The land in question there seems to be public land, not private, as envisaged by the writers from the Principate. It does not seem to have been allocated by the commission to a restricted number of assignees of agricultural allotments, and, if we were to admit this as a possibility, it would be still odd that there is no statement in this law about its ownership, now that the allotments of agricultural land have been declared private. We would at least have expected a clause to the effect that its status remained unchanged. Moreover, there is contemporary evidence from the *Sententia Minuciorum* of 117 BC (*ILLRP*, 517 = *FIRA* III, 163, lines 32ff): '*Quei ager compascuos erit, in eo agro quo minus pecus [p]ascere Genuates Veituriosque liceat ita utei in cetero Genuati compascuo, ni quis prohibeto nive quis vim facito neive prohibeto, quo minus ex eo agro ligna materiamque sumant utanturque.*' (It is interesting that the same land is both *compascuus* and *silvae*, i.e. this is dry pasture, as opposed to the wet pasture in lines 37ff). This pasture land belonged generally to the Langenses and, according to the decree, was to be generally available to the other peoples, the Genuates and Veiturii, like the other *ager compascuus* in the *ager Genuatis*. The provision against enclosure in the territory of Genua resembles the clause, *neive quis in eo agro agrum oqupatum habeto*, etc., here. In the same sense Cicero (*Top.* 12) takes as an example of a simple literal argument, '*si compascuus ager est, ius est compascere*' – implying that by definition *ager compascuus* was open to any who wished *compascere*. If the legislator of the *lex agraria* was trying to say in this chapter, as Huschke and Mommsen believed, that the land should not be the *compascuus* of a restricted number of farmers, but was open to everyone, he was using a terminology not yet established and in a way which would have puzzled his contemporaries. It would have been better not to use the term *compascuus* at all.

For these cumulative reasons we should in my view admit the possibility that initial NEIVE after the lacuna is not the negative but the end of a word like LATINEIVE or PEREGREINEIVE, and that the sentence ran for example: '*pequdibus ceivis Romanei Lati]neive is ager compascuus esto, neive quis* –'.

For *defendere* meaning 'to bar to outsiders', 'fence off', cf. line 32, also *ILLRP*, 517, line 42, *sei ... malent in eo agro alia prata inmittere, defendere, sicare*, and Hyginus 91–2 Thul = 128 Lach, *ut ... superior possessor in planum usque descendat et sibi defendat omnem locum devexum* (the meaning of this passage is clear from Sic.Flacc. 107 Thul).

The fine for monopolising a piece of land was appropriately calculated *per iugerum*, not by the number of cattle on the land. Fifty sesterces *per iugerum* does not at first sight seem very much. It should have constituted a fair proportion of the price of this sort of land, if it were to have acted as a deterrent. The end of the chapter may refer either to the liability of such an offender to pay his fine to the contractor who had bought the right to collect *scriptura* on these public pastures or simply to the liability of any pasturer to pay *scriptura* for his beasts. It has been stressed by Johannsen in her commentary on this line (cf. Burdese, 95–6; Zancan, 105ff) that there is no evidence for the continuation of outright limits on the number of cattle which could be grazed on *ager publicus*, such as had been taken over by Tiberius Gracchus from earlier legislation (App. *BCiv.* 1.8.37; Cato, *ORF*, frag. 167). The number referred to in line 26 must be the number which can be grazed free (cf. lines 14–15). Obviously this was a valuable concession to those who raised cattle on a large scale, but whether the law was generally intended to favour such men, as Johannsen and recently Granet (1990, 139ff) have believed, is another matter.

XIX (lines 25–6) The right to graze certain animals, which is to be tax-free up to the limit fixed earlier in the law

25 (A20) BOVES EQV: aes, Pin; EQVI: Sig, O; *boves equ[os mulos asinos pecudesve minores*: Rud; *boves equ[os mulos asinos oves capros sues*: Mo; *boves – asinos*: CIL, Jo.

26 (B26) I NVMERVS: aes; NVMERVS: edd veter; OI NVMERVS: Rud; EI NVMERVS: Mo; *[– pascere inpellere usque ad eum numerum qu]oi*: Rud; *pascere ad eum numerum que]i*: Mo, CIL, Jo.

NEIVE SC ... BETO: aes; NEVE SCRI ... RE DEBETO: O; SCR ... E DEBETO: Pin; *scri[pturam dar]e debeto*: Sig. The paragraph space after DEBETO is, unusually, marked with three interpuncts.

The previous chapter granted the right to graze. The function of this one is to grant to certain pasturers the same immunity from tax on small numbers of beasts as has been mentioned in lines 14–15. This would have had a particular point, if Mommsen was right in treating the public pasture here as different from *ager compascuus*. However, this is not the only possible explanation of the chapter. The itemising of the types of beast may be significant: some may have been excluded from the list. Another possibility is that the chapter stressed that not only Roman but non-Romans could graze their beasts on this land.

XX (line 26) Grazing of beasts, while journeying on the drove-roads or public roads, to be free from tax

26 (B26, A21) *indu[xerit impulerit pastasve habebit*: Rud; *indu[xerit ibeique paverit*: Mo, CIL, Jo. *pro eo pecore quod in calli]bus*: Rud; *quod eius in calli]bus*: Mo, CIL, Jo.

VIEIḶỌE PVBLICEIS: aes; VEIIIQE: O[1]; VIEILDE: O[2], Rud; VIEILAE: Pin; VIEISD (the last letter printed in reverse): Sig; VIEILEGE: Maz; *vieisve publiceis*: Mo, CIL, Jo. ∧EIVE: aes. PVBLICANO D: aes; PVBLICANO P: Pin, O; *publicano pe[quniam scripturam vectigalve det*: Sig (sim. Rud); *publicano d[are debeto*: Mo, CIL, Jo.

For the *calles* see Cic. *Clu.* 161; Varro, *RR* 2.2.9; Suet. *Jul.* 19.2; Tac. *Ann.* 4.27 (the *provincia*); *CIL* IX, 2438 = *FIRA* I, 71, pp. 327ff; IX, 2826; *Eph.Ep.* 8, no. 139. Cf. Laffi (1965); Corbier (1983); Granet (1990). For transhumance in Italy during the Republican period see Varro, *RR* 2.1.16 and 5.11; 3.17.9 with Gabba, Pasquinucci (1979). The *calles* are part of the *ager publicus populi Romanei* which cannot be made private, since they are reserved for public purposes, but which, unlike *pascua publica*, are not subject to a charge, when used. The relative importance of transhumance in the agrarian economy of Italy at this time is hard to establish, but it was sufficiently significant to be taken into account by the legislator here. *Viae publicae* does not seem to be a synonym for *calles* here, as Granet (1990, 144) believes, but does refer to main thoroughfares (cf. line 89), which might be used for cattle-movements, where necessary.

XXI (lines 26–7) Former public land given in exchange for private land to be fully private

27 (B27) MMVTAVIT: aes, edd veter; OMMVTAVIT: Mo, CIL; *[quem quis agrum locum ita utei in h.l. scriptum est ex publico in privatum co]mmutavit*: Rud; *[quei ager – fuit, de eo agro loco quem agrum locum populus ex publico in privatum c]ommutavit*: Mo, CIL, Jo.

COMMVTAV . . . MNEIS: aes, edd veter; *commutav[it, is ager o]mneis*: Sig, Rud; *is ager do]mneis*: Mo, CIL, Jo (Mo pointed out that the second syllable of the nominative singular *omnis* was short; for the omission of the short *i* in *domineis* he compared *iugra and tableis*).

utei quei optuma lege privatus est: Rud, cf. Cic. *Leg.Agr.* 3.7, *ea omnia eo iure sunt ut quae optimo iure privata sunt.* If we retain *quoi*, this clause lacks an intelligible subject.

This chapter does not deal with the exchange of public land for that held by *veteres possessores*, which was itself originally public (this was probably dealt with in lines 3–4), but rather with exchange of public land for that formerly fully private. For exchanges carried out by a land-commissioner see Sic.Flacc. 119 Thul = 155 Lach: '*Praeterea scriptum est et REDDITUM ET COMMUTATUM PRO SUO, quod ideo fit, quoniam particulas quasdam agrorum in diversis locis habentes duo, quibus agri reddebantur, ut continuam possessionem haberent, modum pro mod⟨o⟩[um] secundum bonitatem taxabat*, also Hyg. 165 Thul = 202 Lach. Such exchanges might have taken place, however, not only for the convenience of the owners, but also to facilitate land-distribution or to remedy errors, cf. lines 65ff. Here the position of the chapter may be connected with the fact that exchanges had taken place *inter alia* in order to create roads and *calles*. (An interesting example of the relocation of a road, which actually occurred four years before this law, is provided by the newly discovered milestone of M.Aemilius Scaurus near Cosa, Fentress (1984)). How much power Roman magistrates had in this respect, is unclear. Perhaps they could only operate with consent. In principle these exchanges could have occurred at any time in the not too distant past, but the current concern of this law must have been with measures taken in the wake of Ti.Gracchus' legislation, in order to tidy up the agrarian map of Italy. Hence I have restored *IIIvir* as the subject of *commutavit* (*contra* Johannsen).

The chapter is asserting that land so exchanged, even though once public, shall be unquestionably private. This also seems to have been the point of the clause from Rullus' bill reported by Cicero (above). Cicero makes fun of Rullus' promises by suggesting that under his bill the holdings assigned by Sulla will be more secure than ancestral family property – which, other things being equal, they could not have been. Cicero also suggests that Rullus' bill intended that they should be free from any servitudes or mortgages, which may be a closer reflection of what Rullus meant by the phrase. Johannsen, following Kaser (1955), I, 341, has argued that the phrase meant that such land was subject to no public encumbrance such as a servitude to a local community, as in Cic. *Leg.Agr.* 3.9. There is an interesting parallel in the declaration, *utei optimus maximusque esset*, apparently used regularly in private sales from this period (which was the lifetime of the jurist Q.Mucius Scaevola) down to the heyday of the classical Roman jurists in the second to third centuries AD (*Dig.* 18.1.9; 21.2.75; 50.16.126; *FIRA* III, 90, lines 6–7; 92, lines 2–3). On a Roman writing tablet from Somerset of the mid-third century AD, published by E.G. Turner (*JRS*, 1956, 115ff, line 1) we even find *ita uti optumo maximoque iure esse[t. Ut quei optima lege (optimo iure) privatus est* should therefore not be taken to refer to a special category of private land recognised by the law (whatever Cicero suggests in order to ridicule Rullus), but to indicate that the private status was not limited by certain conditions. The land exchanged and made private was thus exempted from servitude as a public right of way and freed from the sort of requirements laid down elsewhere in the law, such as use for agriculture (line 14) or observance of a maximum limit (line 2). Compare the declaration in the *S.C. de Aphrodisiensibus* (J.M. Reynolds, *Aphrodisias and Rome*, no. 8, lines 53–4) – *τὴν ἐλευθερίαν ἔχειν διακρατεῖν τε, καθάπερ καί τις πολιτ⟨ή⟩α τῷ καλ(λ)ίστῳ δικαίῳ καλ(λ)ίστῳ τε νόμῳ ἐστιν* – where the point is that the city's freedom was not being granted subject to any limitations. The *S.C. de Aphrodisiensibus* in fact details all the specific positive privileges awarded to Aphrodisias as part of her freedom: they were not automatically deducible from the *ut quei civitas optimo iure et optima lege est* phrase.

XXII (line 27) Former private land given to the people in exchange for public land to have the same status as public land

27 (B27, A22) IBLICO: aes; VBLICO: edd veter; *ex priva[to in publicum commutatus est, quo pro agro tantus modus agri publici ex p]ublico*: Mo, CIL, Jo. IM PRIVATVM: aes. *L.C[alpurnio – fuisset]*: Mo, CIL, Jo.

Mommsen realised that this chapter must be the exact converse of the preceding one.

XXIII (lines 27–8) Maintenance of contracts for ager patritus *at the same price*

28 (B28) ITIO CENS: aes, Mo, CIL; CENS: edd veter; ORE CENS: Bluhme ap. Mo; *[quomque quei pro patrito praedi]o recens redemptum*: Rud, following Bluhme; *[quei ager pro agro patrito ex publico in privatum commutatus est, ... pr. consolve, quei post hac factus erit, quanti agri patriti publicani publicum*

L.Caecilio Cn.Dom]itio cens: Mo, CIL; *[quei ager patritus in terra Italia est, quanti pro eo agro patrito publicani – Dom]itio cens*: Hin; *[... pr.consolve, quanti publicani pro patrito – Dom]itio cens*: Jo.

HABE.T: aes, edd veter. FACIV...VOLENT: aes; FACIVN...VOLENT: Pin, O[1]; FACI: O[2]; *faciunto [ut]ei [quei] volent*: Sig; *faciu[nto utei quei praedium supsignare] volent*: Rud; *faci[unto utei, quom p.p. supsignare] volent*: Hu; *faci[unto id publicum, sei] volent*: Mo, CIL; *faciu[nto quo publicani, sei] volent*: Hin, Jo.

Mommsen's comment, '*locum difficilem et a prioribus coniecturis varie temptatum*', is as apt as ever. If we restore, as seems inevitable, a reference to the censors of 115 at the beginning of the B fragment, the remaining problems are: (i) What exactly is *ager patritus*? (ii) Who are the subject of *faciunto*? (iii) Who are the subject of *redemptum habent* and *supsignent*? (iv) For what is *p.p.* an abbreviation? (v) What, if any, is the relationship of this chapter to the preceding one?

The traditional view since Rudorff is that *ager patritus* is ancestral land in private ownership. However, although we have references to land which is *paternus* or *paternus et avitus* (Cic. *Verr*. 3.97; *Leg.Agr*. 3.7), an inscription from Ferentinum refers to land being handed over *in avitum rei publicae* (*ILS* 6271 = Bruns, no. 151, line 10) and *patritus* is clearly a technical term for a specific kind of land inherited from ancestors, whose meaning goes beyond the usual sense of *paternus* or *avitus*. The important parallel, noted by Kniep (1896, 27), is in a receipt from the Iucundus archive from Pompeii of 53 AD (*CIL* IV, Supp., pp. 382–3, Tab. 138, lines 6–9 = *FIRA* III, 131a = Bruns, p. 360): '*Secundus [c]o[lonoru]m nomine coloniae Ven[e]riae Corneliae servo[s]: accepi [a] Terentio Prim[o] HS DCCLXXVI reliquos ob avitum [et] patritum fundi Audiani nomine Stali Inventi.*' Rent is here received by the *colonia* through a contractor Terentius Primus for a farm whose tenure is nonetheless described as *avitus et patritus* (the later summary on the tablet simply has *ob avitum fundi* – line 19), presumably because it is rented out on a long term basis, while remaining the property of the *res publica* of Pompeii. (See J. Andreau, *Les Affaires de M.Iucundus* (Rome, 1974), 56–7, 61). The land which was given over into the *avitum* of Ferentinum was to be similarly let out in due course. The relevance of an inscription from a sepulchral monument at Stabiae (*Not. Sc.* 1897, 64–5) remains obscure; this begins: *L.Urinae(us) L.f. Vare(nus?) ... AVITV PATRF.*

Hinrichs (302ff) has compared the contracts for renting land to people in Egypt εἰς τὸ πατρικόν or τὰ πατρικά (*P.Teb*. I, no. 5, 10ff – 118 BC) and those from the territory of Mylasa and Olymos in Caria (Blümel – *Inschr. v. Mylasa* I, 201.5; 206.2, 19–20; 207.16; 212.7; 216.7–8; II, 801.15–16; 802.6–7; 818.5; 819.6; 822.6–7; 831.2 – (Olymos), dateable on prosopographical grounds to the later second century BC). There is also now evidence from the same area relating to the land given to the temple of Zeus Osogoa at Labraunda *c*. 220 BC (Crampa, 1969, no. 8, lines 8–9, 23–4, cf. *Bull. Ep*. 1971, no. 549), where Olympichos suggests to the people of Mylasa that the land should be rented εἰς τὰ πατρικὰ τάκτου φόρου, that is, for a tribute of money fixed in advance and presumably valid over a long period. The invention of this formula for a type of lease in the Hellenistic world must at least be as old as the mid-third century BC. (For εἰς τὸ πατρικόν as a hereditary lease, cf. Y.H. Landau, *IEJ* 16 (1966), 54–70, at 58–9, line 23, also *SEG* XXXV.1476, line 32.) It was used at Mylasa for long-term leases by temples or communities intended to provide a steady income. We may reasonably speculate that it may have also been used in Italy to finance temples or shrines.

If we conclude that *ager patritus* here is land rented out by the Roman censors on a renewable contract, such that the land can pass from one generation to the next, *pro patrito* should refer to land given in place of this when the original *ager patritus* became unavailable – probably, as Mommsen implied by his restoration, when it had been taken over by the land-commission. The chapter then will be providing that at the next censorship a contract should be renewed in relation to this land, as if it had been in the possession of the family for a long time.

Rudorff, Huschke and Mommsen all believed that the contractors were *publicani* using this land as security for their contracts in the light of the term *supsignare*. For *praedia supsignare*, the registration under seal of property at the treasury in Rome or with local officials, see lines 73–4, 84; Cic. *Flacc.* 80; *Schol.Bob.* 106St and *ILLRP*, 518, I.5ff; III.13ff; *lex Malac.Irnit.*, cap. 63–4 respectively. *Praedia* at Rome would normally have been property owned according to the *ius civile* and registered in the census (Cic. *Flacc.* and *Schol.Bob.*, cit.). Therefore, if *patritus* was rented, it is unlikely to have been used as security. Nor is it easy on the traditional view to translate *pro patrito redemptum habeant*. Hinrichs, followed by Johannsen, therefore concluded that the contractors were *publicani* contracting for the rents of the land in question. The chapter then would become a guarantee to them that they would not have to pay more for their contract to collect rents than they currently did. On this view it is not obvious why the *contractors* had to register the land: the treasury should have had a record before the contract was let. More generally, the whole provision becomes puzzling. Why should the *publicani* have been guaranteed a tax-contract at the same price? (This is not equivalent to fixing the rents of the *ager patritus* paid by its occupiers, and it is doubtful whether a clause to that effect could be inserted in the lacuna in lines 27–8, since an introductory definition must first be supplied.)

Accordingly, I prefer to believe that the subject of *redemptum habeant* is not the *publicani* but the possessors themselves, who rented *ager patritus*. They had been given new land, *pro patrito*, in exchange for their traditional holdings and would make a new contract for this which would be registered at the treasury at the next censorship. The subject of *faciunto* on Mommsen's view was the praetor or consul, as magistrates involved in executing the law. Yet it would be odd that these magistrates should be urged to do something as part of the operations of the censors – in effect to tell the censors what to do. I suspect that there is a loose piece of drafting and that *ei* refers to the censors who have already appeared in an ablative absolute as an indication of time (*censoribus ... erunt*). As for *p.p.*, even Mommsen, who held that land was being registered as security, thought it more likely to stand for *pro patrito* than *pro praede* (the only parallel is P.P.L.V. = *pro praede litis vindiciarum* in Val.Prob. 5.22). In the Ba–b gap (*c.* 12 letters after *faciunto*, including *quei* or *sei*) one might restore *mancipes* as the contractors for the *ager patritus*; *colonei* in the sense of farmers/tenants is also possible. There is not enough room for *conductores*. For the renting of farms by wealthy or moderately wealthy tenants in the Republic, cf. Cic. *Verr.* 3.53; *pro Caec.* 10ff; *Dig.* 19.2.15.2; 30.4; de Neeve (1984, esp. 45ff, 82ff).

XXIV (line 28) The maintenance of public rights of way

28 (B28, A23) IIVIRVM: aes, Rud, Mo, CIL; *IIvir⟨i⟩*: Jo, but cf. *lex rep.* 13 (*quei...IIIvi]rum a.d.a. siet*) and *ILLRP*, 536 for the genitive plural being used in effect for the nominative singular or plural; *IIvirum qu[ei ex hac lege facti creative erunt, ei...*: Rud. *quae viae publicae p]er*: Rud, cett edd. EVERINT: aes. SIE: aes; SIEN: edd veter, Mo, CIL.

The chapter must concern roads or other public rights of way. A similar provision about roads in Africa may have stood in the lacuna at the beginning of line 90. Much more elaborate regulations about the maintenance of free movement on roads within the city of Rome are to be found in *Tab.Heracl.* 56–72. The *IIviri* created by this law are those concerned with land in Africa. So Rudorff's supplement is implausible. Mommsen seems to have been right in identifying the *IIviri* here with those mentioned in *Tab.Heracl.* 50–1 (*IIvir(ei) vieis extra propiusve urbem Rom(am) passus ⟨M⟩ purgandeis*), who, as he showed by comparing *ibid.* 20, were concerned with clearing roads outside the city *and* the area up to the first milestone. See also Dio 54.26.7.

Roads were intimately connected with Roman land-division. The axis of a centuriation was usually a main road and the *limites* between *centuria*-squares were the capillaries to that road. It was important for those who were living on allotments to have communication with towns or *fora*, in order to exchange produce for money or goods and to have access to justice.

XXV (line 29) Those non-Romans, who had in 112 BC *the same rights as Romans to possess land dealt with by this law should be permitted to enjoy the same freedoms on this land as Romans*

29 (B29, A24) A VTEI S.S.: aes, O[2]; VTEI S.S.: Sig, Pin, O[1], Mo; *[quod quoieique – it]a*: Rud, cett edd. QV...LIA: aes; QVEI IN ITALIA: edd veter. POPVLI R...ROMANO: aes, O; POPVLI RO...ROMANO: Sig, Pin; *R[omani fuerunt, ceivei] Romano*: Rud, Mo, CIL, Jo (but there is not room for *ceivei*, when allowance is made for the warp of the bronze; perhaps *c.] Romano*).

cos [agrum publicum populi Romanei possidere: Rud; *cos [in eis agreis id facere*: Mo, CIL; *cos [in eis agreis possessio erat, quibusve in eis agreis id facere*: Jo. EIVE: aes, edd veter; *ex lege pleb]eive*: Sig, cett edd. EOEDERE, ERAVDE, EACERE: aes.

This chapter concerns rights on land public in 133 BC. Those rights available to Roman citizens are extended to Latins and *peregrini* (it is worth noting that Latins are here distinguished from *peregrini, contra* Gaius 1.79; Richardson, 1981, 6–7), but only to those Latins and *peregrini*, to whom the relative clause, *quibus M.Livio L.Calpurnio cos* . . ., applies. This last clause provides a *terminus ante quem* for the possession of certain rights on this land by virtue of law, plebiscite or treaty – presumably rights to enjoy possession or use of that land in some way. However, the present chapter seems not to be restating these rights but elaborating on them, permitting certain unspecified actions (*facere*) to non-Romans, already allowed to Romans by this law. I do not think that there can be any question here of permission to non-Romans to make the land private. This topic was discussed earlier – in lines 1–10, 13–14 and again, in connection with certain lands received in exchange, in lines 21–4 – with different formulae and in a different manner. Could the land in question here have been changed from public into private property already, in so far as the Latins possessed *commercium* and the *peregrini* may have been specially granted it (Johannsen, 272)? This seems to me unlikely, since the Latins and *peregrini* are not classed as *veteres possessores*. Moreover, in that case it would have been more appropriate to put the following chapter relating to law-suits involving Latins and *peregrini* after chapters XI–XIII (lines 15–18). It is more probable that this chapter relates to public land occupied by non-Romans, which was exempted from the commission's operations because it was legally held by them (according to law, plebiscite or treaty). It may be significant (cf. Hinrichs, 281) that the clause making an exception for land exempted from distribution by C.Gracchus does not appear here. This would be natural if the chapter referred precisely to land which Gracchus had kept for the allies. What then are the Latins and *peregrini* being permitted to do? *Ita utei s.s.est* should refer to the preceding chapters concerned with specific activities rather than rights to property – XIX, XX, XXIV about pasturage and the use of roads and paths (Johannsen, 271–2), conceivably also XXIII about the right to rent *ager patritus*.

XXVI (lines 29–30) Law-suits seeking to enforce the provisions of this law should be handled by Roman magistrates in exactly the same way (?), if a non-Roman is involved, as if the suit were between two Romans

29 (A24) QV: aes; QVEI: Sig; QVE: O, Pin; *que[i in terra Italia sunt, quei eorum P.Mucio L.Calpurnio cos. publicei populi Romanei fuerunt, facere licuit*: Rud; *que[i s.s.sunt, Latinum peregrinumque facere vel non facere oportebit*: Mo, CIL, Jo.

30 (B30, A25) M QVIS: aes; *[quod eius quis facere prohibuerit quodve] quis*: Rud; *sei eorum] quis*: Mo, CIL, Jo. QV...ACERE: aes; *qu[od eum ex h.l. f]acere*: edd veter.

EORVM (vac. 2) E...ROVE: aes; EORVM EX H.L....PROVE: O, Pin; *eorum ex h.l. omiserit [mag.] prove*: Sig; *eorum [quae in h.l. scripta sunt, mag.] prove*: Rud; *eorum [h.l. prohibitus erit, fecerit, mag.] prove*: Mo, CIL, Jo. QVOD EA RE: aes.

The bronze at the right-hand edge of Bb is warped inwards. There appear to be perhaps two letter-spaces uninscribed and then E before the lacuna, which covers about 15 letter-spaces. Rudorff's and Mommsen's restorations are therefore excluded by lack of space. Sigonio's *omiserit* is not confirmed by other early copyists and repeats the meaning of the previous clause. So I have regarded it as a restoration printed as if it was surviving text. The simple restoration of *fecerit* seems to give adequate sense. The initial supplement, *de ea re quod eorum] quis*, is intended to produce parallelism between the clauses.

iudi[cem recuperatoresve dato: Sig; *iudi[cem recuperatoresve ei et in eum non dederit quum ei] et in eum*: Rud; *iudi[cem recuperatoresve dato atque cos pr.ve ei*: Hu; *iudi[cem recuperatoresve facito ei, quei ex h.l. petet, et in eum ita det, utei ei] et in eum*: Mo, CIL, Jo – somewhat awkward, since the subject of *facito* and *det* are the same. *iudiciu[m petisset, quod civem Romanum contra h.l. fecisse diceret*: Mo, CIL, Jo. My own text allows for the possibility that the non-Roman might be on either side of the case.

Rudorff restored this chapter as a sanction against a magistrate or promagistrate who failed to enforce the law; Huschke as a provision for magistrates and promagistrates acting in place of consuls or praetors, when either Romans or non-Romans were concerned. Mommsen, however, believed that the chapter required that the same legal procedure should be used for non-Romans as for Romans – a natural development from the statement about the rights of non-Romans in the preceding chapter. This still seems the most convincing explanation of a chapter about litigation appearing shortly before the main regulations in lines 33ff. If Mommsen's interpretation is correct, then we have here an instance of how Rome's Italian allies were being drawn into her judicial system. Of course, one would normally expect disputes arising over Roman territory to fall within Roman jurisdiction. Again, the allies may have considered themselves privileged, rather than disadvantaged, in being treated on the same level as Roman citizens. Nevertheless, there is no suggestion that, because they are allies, Italians deserve special treatment, such as was apparently put about in the aftermath of Ti.Gracchus' land-bill (App. *BCiv.* 1.19.78ff; Cic. *Rep.* 1.31).

XXVII (lines 31–2) Confirmation of the existing right to enjoy the use of land possessed by those renting from colonies and municipia *and those in the* trientabula

31 (B31, A26) NICIPIEIS: aes, omitted by edd veter, read as FCIRIBIT by Bluhme and taken to be an error for FVERIT by Rud and Hu (who restored respectively clauses referring generally to distributions to citizens and allies and to distributions within the city of Rome); *sei(ve) quei (ager) colonieis seive moi]nicipieis*: Mo, CIL, Jo. COL ... NOMINISVE: aes; COLO: edd veter; SOCIISVE NOMINISVE: Sig, but *sociisve* is not confirmed in the other early copies and should be regarded as restoration; *colo[nieisve civium Romanorum]*: Rud; *colo[nieisve sunt civium Rom(anorum)*: Mo, CIL, Jo. *Sunt* is needed to complete the relative clause. By my calculations there is then room for no more than the initial letter of *Romanorum.*

datus [est, seive quei in trientabuleis est, quei (colonei moinicipesve prove moinicipieis)..fruentur, queiv]e: Mo, CIL, Jo. *Prove moinicipieis* was inserted in the lacuna, although also present in the succeding text on the A fragment, because on the second occasion it means *pro pro moinicipieis*, 'people on behalf of the equivalent of a *municipium*'. I have taken the restoration, *colonei moinicipesve* to cover the actual inhabitants of any *colonia, municipium* or its equivalent.

Quei⟨ve⟩ in trientabule[is: Mo, CIL, Jo. Rud understood *ager* with *quei* and assumed a new clause in parataxis, *quei in trientabule[is pro tertia parte eius pecuniae, quae M.Valerio M.Claudio cos. populo credita fuit, datus est.*

32 (B32, A27) *[quibusve ab eis heredibusve eorum is ager locus testamento hereditate deditioneve ob]venit*: Rud; *[quod eius agri eis in trientabuleis testamento hereditate deditione ob]venit*: Mo; *[quod eius agri colonei moinicipesve prove moinicipieis habebunt queive a colonia moinicipiove prove moinicipieis habebunt quodve eius agri – ob]venit*: CIL, Jo.

ANTE...DVCTVM: aes; ANTE H...DVCTVM: O; *ante h.[l. rog. redemptum con]ductum*: Pin, Sig; *ante – rog. eum agrum redemptum con]ductum*: Rud; *ante – rog. eum agrum locum con]ductum*: Mo, CIL, Jo. A noun is needed for *conductum* to agree with. In that case there is not room for *redemptum* nor for all of *eum agrum locum.*

\ VE: aes (A27), Mo apparatus; MVE: O², Pin; VE: Maz; E: O¹; *dar]e*: Sig; *[quem agrum locum ex h.l. venire dare reddi]ve*: Rud (sim. Mo, CIL, Jo). The evidence for MVE should not be disregarded: we should therefore conclude that two nouns or adjectives/participles in the accusative stood in the lacuna before *oportet.*

HABERE: aes, edd veter; HABERE Ọ [*eti frui*, etc.: Mo, CIL, Jo, but the trace Mommsen saw is consistent with the initial letters of other infinitives or *c[onductum*, nor does *oeti* appear earlier in the line; *habere [frui possidere defendere post h.l.rog. liceto]*: Rud.

This chapter clearly deals with land which was still public, whether it had been assigned to communities in Italy for exploitation (*poplice deve senatus sententia ager fruendus datus*) or was in the *trientabula*. The latter was land within the fiftieth milestone from Rome, handed over to creditors of the *populus Romanus* after the second Punic War in place of a third of the debt owed them, because there was no cash available to repay them (Livy 29.16.3; 31.13.2ff; 33.42.3). The land was taxed at I *as per iugerum*, in order to make clear it was public (*testandi causa publicum agrum esse*), and could be restored to the *populus* in exchange for its cash value, whenever the occupier wished, once the treasury was solvent. If restored correctly on the analogy of line 23, the references to inheritance and cession in line 32 (*testamento hereditate deditioneve ob]venit*) can only apply to this land *in trientabuleis*. For it must have been legitimate to hand this on as if it were private land: otherwise its legal existence would have been extinguished long before 111 BC. (By contrast with line 23, there is no mention of sale, and this is appropriate, since this land was not private and its value could only be realised by transfer back to the *populus Romanus*.)

The land given to communities seems to have been either enjoyed directly by the community as a whole (such is implied by the contrast, *queiv]e pro colonia moinicipiove*, which necessitates a restoration such as *colonei moinicipesve* in line 31), or to have been leased (*con]ductum habere*) to others, who need not have been members of the community, in order to yield an income for it. What precisely *quae pro moinicipieis colo[nieisve sunt* were, is a problem that baffled Mommsen. It was probably a formula intended to cover a whole range of territorial organisations in which Romans or Latins might live (cf. Brunt, 1988, 136–7, criticising the view of Sherwin-White, 1973, 213–4, on *municipia*). One may conjecture that *pro colonieis* were men with viritane allotments on the *ager Romanus* with some local organisation based on the *forum* or *conciliabulum*, while *pro moinicipieis* were men with Roman citizenship, perhaps those formerly *cives sine suffragio*, living in their own traditional communities, not in new Roman foundations. Obvious candidates for inclusion in this latter category are the Campanian towns who had lost their political, but not their social and economic existence in 211 BC. Originally the Campanians were left as *peregrini* but recovered their citizen status in 188 (Livy 26.16.7–9; 31.29.11; 38.36.5–6; Vell. 2.44.4; cf. Festus 262L for the *praefecti Capuam Cumas Casilinum Volturnum Liternum Puteolos Acerras Suessulam Atellam Calatiam*). Volturnum, Liternum and Puteoli became colonies, but the rest could have been regarded as *pro municipiis* in this period. See, in general, Frederiksen, 1984, 244–54, 264–80.

The law now ceases its review of the various types of land in Italy. Accordingly, it may be helpful to catalogue those discussed or mentioned in passing since the summary of chapters I–VI (pp. 212–3 above).

1. Categories of land which were no longer public land of the Roman people:

(a) Holdings of up to 30 *iugera* of unassigned public land used for agriculture (ch. IX, lines 13–14).
(b) Land given to a prior possessor in exchange for land used to found a colony (ch. XVI, lines 22–3).
(c) The actual land given to colonies themselves (ch. XVI, lines 21–2).
(d) Land given in exchange for private land, for example in the course of changing the line of a public road (ch. XXI, lines 26–7).

2. Categories of land, which still remained public land of the Roman people:

(a) Land assigned to villagers by the roads, i.e. *viasiei vicanei* (chs. VII–VIII, lines 11–13).
(b) Open pasture land – in my view identical with *ager compascuus* in this period (chs. XVIII–XIX, lines 24–6, cf. X, lines 14–15).
(c) Drove-roads, i.e. *calles* (ch. XX, line 26), and public roads (ch. XXIV, line 28).
(d) *Ager patritus* – a type of public (? or sacred) land rented out on long-term contracts (ch. XXIII, lines 27–8).
(e) Public land occupied by non-Romans on a long-term basis according to law or treaty (ch. XXV, line 29).
(f) Roman public land given to *coloniae* or *municipia* or their equivalents by virtue of an apparently revocable grant, either for the use of their inhabitants collectively or individually or to provide the community with income through rent to outsiders (ch. XXVII, lines 31–2, cf. Hardy, 1910, 269, 274).
(g) Land in the *trientabula*, leased at a nominal rent to the successors in law of creditors of the Roman people during the Second Punic War, in consideration of the capital sum owed to them and as yet unpaid (ch. XXVII, lines 31–2).

One category of public land, which does not appear in the surviving text, but should have been mentioned in exception clauses (cf. ch. XVIII, lines 24–5) is land, such as the *ager Campanus*, rented out for agriculture by the censors or consuls.

There is finally the land devoted to public buildings and public space, which, Mommsen believed, was also mentioned in the lacuna in lines 24–5. This was certainly an important type of public land, but I am not certain that the legislator would have thought it necessary to mention it as a separate category. Roman public land assigned to *fora* and *conciliabula* in the countryside would probably have been comprised in ch. XXVII, lines 31–2. The actual territories of *coloniae* and *municipia* were not public land of the Roman people, while the territory of the city of Rome itself probably did not come into question (cf. commentary on line 1).

XXVIII (lines 33–4) Regulations for jurisdiction about land made private under the law

33 (B33, A28) QVEI AGER LOCVS PVBLICVS P: aes; QVEI – POP: edd veter; RA: aes; RRA: O, Pin; *pop[ulei Romanei in t]erra*: Sig. L. .E: aes; LEGE: edd veter; *lege [plebeive sc. IIIvir sortito ceivi Romano dedit adsignavit sei qu]id*: Rud; *lege [plebeive scito exve hac lege privatum factum est, ante eidus Martias sei*: Mo, CIL, Jo.
QVEI QVOMQVE: edd veter; *iuris[dictio – esto*: Sig (cf. line 35 and for a parallel to this formula *lex prov.praet.* Cnidos IV.35–6).

34 (B34, A29) ERNITO: aes; NITO: edd veter; *[neive mag. prove mag. – dec]ernito*: Mo (sim. Rud, CIL). IVDICIVM N. . . ECVPERATORES: aes; NEIVE . . .RECVPERATORES: edd veter; *neive [iudicem neive] recuperatores*: Sig. RE.C: aes (B34), Pin; RE: Sig (the I of REI has been lost in a scar on the bronze). EI CAVSA: aes (A29); I CAVSA: edd veter. *re[i] c[ausa promissum erit, quo minus cos. pr.ve non tenere eius r]ei* *causa*: Rud; *rei c[ausa cos pr.ve promitti iusserit, quei ab eo ea re mag. appellati erunt, quominus eius] rei*: Mo; *c[ausa promissum erit – mag. appellati, quominus eius] rei*: CIL, Jo.

QV. . .RECVPERATOR: aes(Aa); QVOD IVDICIVM IUDEX RECVPERATOR; Sig, Pin, O; QVOD – RECVPERATO: Maz.

Quod – recuperator[esve eius rei causa datume erit, quominus ei tr.pl. ex h.l. intercedat eius h.l.n.r.: Rud; *quod – recuperator[es – datei erunt, cos. pr.ve, quei ab eo de ea re mag. appellati erunt, quominus eius rei causa decernant, e.h.l.n.r.*: Mo; *quod – datei erunt, sei magistratus appellati erunt, quoi eorum e re publica non esse videbitur, quominus id inpediat vel intercedat, e.h.l.n.r.*: CIL, Jo. The supplement from *non esse videbitur* onwards is provided by line 36.

There is a reference to *intercessio* in the parallel chapter (line 36) and *appellatio* may be plausibly restored as the assumed occasion of *intercessio* both there and in the corresponding part of this chapter. In relation to the *vadimonium* I have suggested a clause concerning the refusal to provide this surety for appearance at Rome before the consul or praetor, whereby the magistrate there may decide about the case of such a man in his absence. The clause is adapted from *lex Rubr.Gall.* XXI.21ff – *quo minus in eum, quei ita vadimonium Romam ex decreto eius. quei ibei i(ure) d(eicundo) p(raerit), non promeisserit aut vindicem locupletem ita non dederit, ob e(am) r(em) iudicium recup(erationem) is – ex h.l.det – ex h.l.n.r.*

In this chapter and that following (lines 35–6) there are apparently two parallel provisions about jurisdiction, which, after the introductory description of the land concerned, cover at most points (apart from the long lacuna in lines 33–4) an almost identical space on the bronze and can be restored in the same fashion. The only visible discrepancy is that in line 35 the censor is listed as one of the magistrates to whom jurisdiction is given. It is unlikely that either of these dealt with one of the precise categories of land in this law, e.g. those listed in lines 1–7, as Rudorff believed (though he realised that the following chapter dealt with public land). More probably there are two major categories and the best candidates for these are the land declared private by this law and the land remaining public after it. *Quod eius agri loci ex lege [plebeive scito* in line 33 recalls line 19, *quod ex lege plebeive sc]ito exve h.l. privatum factum est eritve*, rather than *quod eius agri locei post h.l.rog. publicum populei Romanei erit* (line 24). Hence our present chapter should be dealing with private land, the following one with public. This will also explain why the censor is involved with jurisdiction in the second chapter – because of his concern for the contracting of public land, as Mommsen pointed out (see also Baumann, 1979, 398–9). This has also a more general implication: the law is no longer dealing with the settlement of immediate problems of possession and ownership, as in lines 15–18; otherwise the censor is irrelevant. Mommsen inserted *ante eidus Martias preimas* before *sei qu]is de eo agro ambigetur* in lined 33, but this obviously cannot be repeated in the following clause, where the censor appears, and anyhow is hardly consistent with *cos. pr. quei quomque erit*, which suggests a future array of magistrates rather than a few magistrates of 111 and the first two to three months of 110. The importance of this and the following chapter lies not only in the removal of future jurisdiction from a *IIIvir a.d.a.* but also from any local magistrates or *praefecti iure dicundo*.

XXIX (lines 35–6) Regulations for jurisdiction about land remaining public after this law

35 (B35, A30) *[Quei ager locus post h.l.rog. publicus populi Romanei in terra Italia erit, sei quid de eo agro loco ambigetur]*: Rud, Mo, CIL. My own restoration seeks to maintain as close a parallel as possible to the preceding chapter.

QVEI QVO: aes; QVEI QVOM: edd veter; *quei quom[que erit, de ea re iu]risdictio*: Sig; *quei quom[que tum erit –* : Mo, CIL, Jo, perhaps rightly. There is space for 3–4 more letters than in Sig's text. E.R.P.F.S.: aes, Sig; E.R.P.F.S.V.: O; E.R.P.F.R.: Pin.

Ọ AGRO: aes (Aa30), Sig, Pin, O; G AGRO: Maz. IDVS for IOVS: Maz.

NEIVE DE ... IVE IVD: aes (Aa); NEIVE DECERNITO NEIVE IVDICIVM: edd veter (from Aa + Ab). But there is room for more in the lacuna in the bronze than CERNITO NE. Hence Mommsen assumed that the humanist copiers had failed to record EO AGRO DE before CERNITO, because this had been destroyed by damage to the bronze. The line drawn in the Pinelli copy, *Vat. lat.* 6531, fo. 181r. dividing Aa from Ab suggests that there was a lacuna at the time. However, in that case it is not clear where Mazzochi's copyist found the full word IVDICIVM, since there would not have been room for it at the right hand edge of the bronze and this copyist did not make supplements. I have restored the text here on the assumption that DECERNITO NEIVE IVDICIVM could be read at the top of Ab by Mazzochi's copyist, followed by Sigonio and Orsini, but that the poorly preserved letters at the bottom right corner of Aa were ignored by them. Then Pinelli, comparing the fragment Aa with Mazzochi's copy of A, assumed that IVE IVD belonged to NEIVE IVDICIVM, when it was in fact part of the following NEIVE IVDICEM.

36 (B36, A31) ṆON ESSE: aes; ESSE: edd veter. *[quod vadimonium eo, quo ex h.l. vadimonium promittere oportet, promissum non esse videbitur, quodve iudicium ita, utei in hac lege scriptum est, datum n]on*: Rud; *[quod – quodve iudicium ab eo, a quo ex h.l. dari oportet, datum no]n*: Hu. The restorations in lines 35–6 here repeat what was suggested in the previous chapter. QVO: aes; QVOI: edd veter; *quo [minus ei trib.pl. ex h.]l. intercedat*: Rud; *[minus id inpediat ve]l*: Mo; *[minus inpediat ve]l*: CIL, Jo.

XXX (lines 36–9) Special regulation about tax-collection, permitting tax-collectors to sue before recuperatores

36 (B36, A31) At most a single letter-space is left after R(*ogatur*) on Bb, but there can be little doubt that a new chapter begins here, given the appearance of a new topic which extends over the next three lines.

M FACITO: aes (Aa31); EM FACITO: edd veter; AGRO – V: edd veter (Ab).

debebitur [de ea re neiquis mag.ious deicito neive iudicium dato neive quis sponsion]em facito – v[ectigal decumas ei publicano det dareve debeat atque utei ex h.l. scripturam vectigal decumas dare oportet: Rud; *debebitur[nei quis mag(istratus) . . . quid ob eam r]em – v[ectigalve det atque utei ex h.l. dare debet debebitve*: Mo, CIL, Jo.

37 (B37, A32) DARIVE OPORTERE DE . . . S PR: aes, edd veter; *de[cretum erit, cos prove co]s*: Sig; *[Sei quid publicanus eius rei causa sibi deberi] darive – de[icat, de ea re cos prove co]s*: Mo, CIL, Jo (but their Bb–a supplement is a little too long for the lacuna). I have suggested *eis* instead of *de ea re* with the additional purpose of providing a subject to be understood with *adierint*, i.e. the two parties to the dispute, and inserted accordingly *a quo eorum* earlier. It is also possible, however, that we should read *de[icat, cos prove cos cen]s pr*, since such contracts are part of the censors' province.

VIBVS L: aes (A32), edd veter; *ci]vibus*: Sig; *qu[ibus de ea re in ious aditum erit . . . recuperatores ex ci]vibus*: Mo, CIL, Jo (for *recuperatores*, cf. line 38); *du[mtaxat – facito*: Mo, CIL, Jo.

The V in VIBVS may be part of a broken N. The jurors concerned must indeed be Roman citizens (if for no other reason, because of the reference to the *prima classis*), but it is not clear why the legislator should have wished so to describe them. It may be that the text read in fact something like *ex iudicum nomi]nibus* or *ex homi]nibus*. With any of these restorations the text is still ambiguous. The reference to a specific number of possible jurors shows that the magistrate concerned was not required to select *recuperatores* from all the members of the first class at Rome but from an album of some kind. The implication of the subjunctive in *quei primae classis sient* remains a problem. Either (i) there was an album of precisely fifty men drawn from the first class, or (ii) there were fifty men from the first class who formed part of a larger album, which included men of other statuses (senators, *equites* or members of the second class), or (iii) the whole panel comprised fifty men of whom some, not less than eleven, were members of the first class. On this last view the word order is awkward, since the relative clause refers to the eleven. However, *quei – sient* seems to have a limiting sense, 'such that they are members of the first class', which is an argument in favour of solutions (ii) or (iii). It should be noted that the use of non-senatorial jurors in such cases is important in the light of the controversy over whether C.Gracchus' jury-reforms extended beyond the *quaestio de repetundis* and in particular to civil cases. On this topic see Brunt, 1988, 194ff, esp. 227–36.

Mommsen's supplement *quaternos* implies an eventual jury of three; *ternos*, producing a jury of five, is equally plausible (cf. V. Arangio-Ruiz, *RFIC* (1928), 357, n1), so is *binos*, producing a jury of seven (cf. Huschke, 598) – this is the number prescribed in the Flavian municipal law (see below). We have other epigraphic evidence for *recuperatores* being selected by *sortitio* followed by *reiectio*: *lex Genet.Urs.*, cap. 95, line 27; *Falerio frag.* (*CIL* I², 2677) A, lines 18 and 22, where we find a *recuperator* drawn from three *decuriae* and a reference to allotment; *S.C. Calvisianum* (*FIRA* I, p. 410ff), lines 106–23 – here the nine senators allotted are reduced to five by alternate rejection; probably also *lex prov.praet.* Cnidos V.15–24, where a jury of fifteen are to be formed after allotment and perhaps rejection from a preliminary panel of forty-five. In the Flavian municipal law (*lex Irnitana*, tab. IXC, cap. ⟨LXXXVIII⟩, cf. ⟨LXXXVII⟩) seven *recuperatores* are to be chosen either by rejection of *decuriae* and then rejection within the surviving *decuria* or else by allotment. For time-limits being set in such cases for the delivery of the verdict as here (*in diebus X proxsumeis*), see *lex Genet.Urs.* 95, 2–3; *lex prov.praet.* Cnidos V.25; *S.C. Calvisianum*, 134.

38 (B38, A33) *[quodque eius is, unde petetur, condemnatus est, cos prve facito utei primo quoque die ab eo deve bonis eius exsigatur*: Rud; *[quei eorum XI hominum tres pluresque supererunt, eos primo quoque die de ea re iudicare iubeto]*: Mo, CIL, Jo. VAE RES SOLVTA N: aes (Bb); QVAE RES – NO: Pin, O; QVAE – N: Sig. O NON SIET: aes, O, Pin; NON SIET: Sig; *soluta no[n siet inve iudici]o non siet*: Rud, cett edd.

quod eius praevaricationus [causa solutum non siet inve iudicio non siet iudicatu]mve: Rud; *praevaricationus [causa . . .vel per dolum malum petitorum patronoru]mve*: Mo, CIL, Jo.

RECVPERATORV: Maz; RECVPERATORVM: Sig, Pin, O; *recuperatorum [quos cos pr prove pr, ita utei supra screiptum est, recuperatores dederit*: Rud (sim. Hu).

It is not clear how *praevaricatio* (collusive accusation) can relate to the phrases restored by Rudorff: if anything, it should concern payment or judgement but of an inadequate and fraudulent kind. However, it is only fair to add that *praevaricatio* would have been highly improbable in a lawsuit conducted by a *publicanus* for tax-money owed to him (unless one can imagine one of a group of *socii*, who was a friend of the defaulter, suing him collusively in order to prevent one of his partners doing so more effectively). For the clause, *quod praevaricationus causa factum non siet*, cf. *lex rep.* 5, 55, 56; *lex prov.praet.* Cnidos V.34–5, '*ὥστε προκρίματος ἀδίκου* [*μηδὲν* (?) *γεγ*]*ονέναι*'.

39 (B39, A34) AVDẸ. . .ENTIA; aes; TENTIA: edd veter; \ ID SENTENTIA: Mo; *sententia [pronuntiato quod eius] rei*: Mo, CIL, Jo. COMMPERRIT: aes.

RIT: aes; *[quod ita iudicatum e]rit*: Mo, CIL, Jo.

SEDVLOM ∧ I: aes; SEDVLOMN: Sig, Pin, O; SEDVLOM: Maz; *se dulo (dolo) m⟨alo⟩*: Mo, CIL, Jo. DARE OPORTEAT: Sig, Pin, O; OPORTAT: Maz; *oport[ere solvat*: Mo, CIL, Jo (but we should trust the ancient copyists nor should we necessarily suppose an engraver's error: *oporteat* may be construed as jussive subjunctive dependent on *iudicatus erit*).

If I correctly read AVD at the beginning of the line, then *sed fr]aude* is the only plausible restoration. It presumably means 'without prejudice (to himself)', like *sed fraude sua*. It may be explained on the assumption that the magistrate is being required to take an unusual and perhaps controversial initiative. In this case it is to announce a verdict based on the investigations of the *recuperatores*, which is nevertheless represented as his own view of the truth (cf. perhaps *lex prov.praet.* Cnidos V, 27–8: '*καὶ καθὼς ἐκείνωι τὸ πλέον μέρος γενόμ*[*ενον περὶ*] *τοῦ πράγματος γνώμην ἀπεφήναντο*'). It is hard to tell whether this is the same as the majority decision of the *recuperatores* or results from some failure by that jury to produce a majority decision. The end of the chapter seems to instruct the magistrate concerned to see to the enforcement of the decision of the *recuperatores*, cf. *lex lat.Bant.* 10–12; *lex rep.* 8; *lex prov.praet.* Cnidos v.45ff. Kelly (1976, 51ff) held that it was a characteristic of trials before *recuperatores*, as opposed to trials before *unus iudex*, that the judicial authorities were empowered to enforce the judgement. However, he mistakenly ascribed this activity to the *recuperatores* themselves, whereas it appears to belong to the magistrate with jurisdiction in the case.

XXXI (lines 40–1) ? Immunity for those who refuse to swear oaths to previous legislation

40 (B40, A35) AẸ: aes; *q]uae*: Rud; *q]uae ag[rum*: Mo, CIL, Jo. FRVIE: aes, Pin; FRVIVE: Sig, O. FRVETVR (Ab): Sig, O, Pin; FAVETVR: Maz. *[Quas in leges plebeive scita de ea re, quod, quei agrum publicum populi Romani ita habebit possidebit fruetur, utei ex h.l. licebit, eum earum q]uae ag[rum, quem ita habebit – de ea r[e, quod earum quae ei, quei agrum publicum populi Romani aliter habebit] – quem [ita habebit, habere possidere fruive permittat, is quei earum legum plebeive scitorum, quo iurare iubetur iubebitur non iouraverit, ei poena multa remissa esto*: Mo, CIL; – *permittat, is quei in eas leges plve sc. iurare iubetur*: Jo.

41 (B41) *liceto neive q[uid ei ea res fraudi esto*: Mo, CIL, Jo. For the present restoration cf. the penalties in *lex lat.Bant.* 19–20: '*Qu]ei ex h.l. non iouraverit. is magistratum inperiumve nei petito neive gerito neive habeto, neive in senatu [sententiam deicito deicereve eum] ni quis sinito, neive eum censor in senatum legito*'; also *frag.Tar.* 21 and, for a more elaborate provision of penalties, *lex prov.praet.* Delphi C.15ff.

Rudorff realised that this chapter must be closely associated in sense with the following one concerning oaths to laws – cf. *quasve in leges pl.ve sc. de ea r[e* (40) and *inque eas leges pl.ve sc. de ea re* (42). The clause in the first half of line 41 appears to be abolishing a possible penalty on a man of the office-holding class. We know from *lex lat.Bant.*, *frag.Tar.* and *lex prov.praet.* that penalties were imposed on those who failed to take oaths. The present chapter, therefore is likely to have indemnified those who failed to take oaths to other laws which were in conflict with this one. *Possidebit fruetur, quam ex h.l. licebit* (40) suggests that one justification for failure to swear was that the provisions of the laws in question allowed possession of public land under terms contrary to the provisions of the present law. Mommsen's restoration, although undoubtedly speculative, was a brilliant reconstruction on these lines. I have reformed this, utilising the full width of the B–A lacuna, and brought the refusal to take the oath to the beginning of each clause, in order to increase intelligibility. On similar grounds I have substituted *ex h.l.* and *contra h.l.* for *ita* in Mommsen's text.

The effect of the indemnification of those who transgress other laws in order to observe the present one is to confirm the abrogation of or derogation from these laws in the matter in question. Collisions are to be decided in favour of the agrarian law of 111 BC. Thus this and the following chapter are in effect similar to the *sanctio* of the *lex de imperio Vespasiani* (*FIRA* I, 15, p. 154, lines 34ff). For another immunity clause indemnifying those who obey the current law from the consequencesof earlier laws see *frag.Tudert.* (*CIL* XI, 4632. Bruns, pp. 137–8), lines 7–8. The reference to *leges pl.ve scita* here shows that the oaths whose omission our present law is indemnifying are those incorporated into statutes, such as those in *lex lat.Bant.*, *frag.Tar.* and *lex prov.praet.* (see also App. *BCiv.* 1.29.131; 2.12.42; Cic. *Clu.* 91; *Att.* 2.18.2; Plut. *Cato mi.* 32.5; Dio 38.7.1–2) – not the general oath taken by magistrates on entry into office. Indeed our text shows that the incorporation of such oaths into statutes antedates 111 BC and was not an invention of Saturninus and Glaucia (cf. Lintott, 1968, 139–40, and 1978; Tibiletti, 1953, 61ff). Note that the present subjunctive *vetet* in line 40 does not allow us to infer a reference to future legislation contrary to the present law (cf. Huschke, 599), nor could the legislator have indemnified those obeying his law against the consequences of infringing subsequent laws which might override it.

XXXII (lines 41–2) Magistrates in their actions and legal decisions are to disregard the enactments in, and oaths to, previous laws which conflict with their duty to this law

41 (A36) We are now completely dependent on humanist copies of this fragment. Mommsen claimed to have seen a trace of the V of QVAE, but he may have been confused by a fissure in the bronze.

MAS: edd veter. *[de aliqua re – decernito*: Mo, CIL, Jo; *[petere capere habereque licet, petere – vetet, eum nei minus petere-liceto*: Rud.

42 (B42, A37) *[quaeque eis legibus plebive sc. facere quis prohibetur, quod quem eorum haec lex facere iubebit, ea omnia ei sine f]raude*: Mo, CIL, Jo; *[quodque consulem praetorem censorem prove pr. ex h.l. facere decernere oportet oportebitve id ei sine f]raude*: Rud. *quod ex [h.l. non decreverit*: Mo, CIL, Jo; *quod ex [h.l. consulem praetorem censorem prove praetore facere]*: Rud.

neive [ei ea res fraudi multae poenaeve esto: Mo, CIL, Jo; *neive [quid ob eam rem quod ex h.l. quid fecerit decreverit dare damnas esto*: Rud.

Any restoration here, as in the previous chapter, must be highly conjectural, but the general sense is clear. This chapter is also concerned with oaths to prior laws but in relation to the actions required by this law from magistrates. They are urged to carry out their duties under this law without fear of reprisal. *Si quae lex plebeive sc.est* shows that the chapter is dealing with possible collisions with existing, not future, measures.

Lines 43–48

Provisions such as those in the two foregoing chapters concerning the enforcement of the law and its relationship to other legislation come most naturally at the end of a legal text (apart from the *lex de imperio Vespasiani* cited above, there is the clause which avoids any collision with sacred law, to be found at the end of *fragmentum Tarentinum* and *lex de Delo*: *sei quid sacrosanctum est*, etc.). It is reasonable to deduce, therefore, as Rudorff originally did (84ff, cf. Huschke, 599), that this is the end of a major section of the law. What follows is, for a number of lines, too fragmentary for even a tentative reconstruction into chapters. There is a reference to the province of Africa in line 48. The language of lines 44–8, in which we find land-purchase, *mancipes* and *praedes* mentioned, resembles that in the later (African) part of the law, e.g. lines 62–5, 73–4.

Mommsen was prepared to accept lines 45–8, but not lines 43–4, as part of the African section; Johannsen made a small modification, beginning the new section in the middle of line 44. Their problem was that the appearance in line 43 of a law passed by M.Baebius as tribune and *IIIvir coloniae deducendae* could hardly be accommodated in an African context, as Rudorff and Huschke (602) thought. This law is not mentioned later in the African section, where we have references to the rescinded Gracchan *lex Rubria* as a reference point for the status of the colonists in the territory of Carthage. Baebius' law can hardly be a Gracchan law about Carthage, earlier than the *lex Rubria*, which was left in force when the latter was abrogated, since the object of Gracchus' opponents was to eliminate the colony of Iunonia. Nor can it, on the other hand, be a later law reinstating part of Gracchus' programme in Africa, since then it would have been necessary to mention it in the subsequent African section of this law. The *lex Baebia*, therefore, did not concern Africa.

Mommsen (ad loc.) believed that the Baebius mentioned here was the founder of the colony of Sipontum in 194 BC (Livy 34.45). Johannsen (295) found the idea of a special chapter here about Sipontine territory, eighty years after the foundation of the colony implausible and preferred to see a reference to a Baebius of the Gracchan period, whose tribunate and colonial activities are otherwise unknown. She noted that a M.Baebius Q.f.Tamphilus was *monetalis* about this time (dated to 137 BC, Crawford *RRC*, no. 236). Carcopino (1928, 269ff) held that he was in fact the author of the first post-Gracchan agrarian law in Appian, which, in Carcopino's view, applied both to Italy and Africa and so restricted the scope of the land-commission that it led to a *de facto* cessation of land-distribution. But there are obvious difficulties about this view in relation to Africa (see above) and as a conjecture about developments in Italy it finds no support in other sources (Johannsen, 291ff). We may agree that the *lex Baebia* is more plausibly to be identified with a recent law than one of 194 BC. However, it would be very odd if this law had been mentioned immediately after the chapters ensuring the enforcement of the Italian provisions, when in fact it related to Italy. Moreover, a recent colonial law about Italy, for which the present law was making exception, would have been mentioned by name in the Italian section like C.Gracchus' *lex Sempronia.* We are left with the possibility that the *lex Baebia* concerned a colonial foundation outside Italy, but not in Africa. For example, it is not clear from our texts (Cic. *Brut.* 161; *Clu.* 140) that the colony of Narbo Martius was actually founded in 118 BC by a *lex Licinia*, rather than a *lex Baebia.* Only two founding magistrates seem to be mentioned on the relevant coins (Crawford, *RRC*, no. 282): Baebius may have been a third, who died or was unable to participate on the spot in the foundation. Alternatively we may suppose that our Baebius was the legislator behind the colony founded in the Balearic islands (Strabo 3.5.1) by Q.Metellus Balearicus (*cos* 122) or that at Dertona in Cisalpina (Vell.Pat. 1.15.5; Fraccaro, *Opuscula*, III.1.123–50).

This in turn raises the question of the attribution of lines 44/5–48 to the African section, since the two lines 43–4 are unlikely to have been sufficient to deal with the agrarian situation in a newly settled part of the empire. An independent argument against the traditional ascription of lines 45–8 is provided by line 45 – '*e]um agrum locum, quem ex h.l. colonei, eive quei in colonei numero [scriptei sunt*'. Settlers are recognised here as *colonei* without qualification, which contrasts with the cautious references later to those given land under the Gracchan law about Africa – '*neive unius hominis nomine, quoi ex lege Rubria, quae fuit, colono, eive, quei in colonei numero scriptus est, agrum dare oportebit licuitve*' (lines 59–60, cf. 55 and 61). It is difficult to begin a new section in the lacuna immediately after *quem ex h.l. colonei – sunt* in line 45 and the surviving text of line 46 seems to be a continuation of the provision for sale of land in line 45. However, there seems to be no objection to believing that the African section began either in the lacuna between the preserved texts of lines 46 and 47 or in line 48 where the word *Africa* is first mentioned. More generally, there is nothing implausible in provincial territory being sold as well as distributed to colonists in this location unknown to us, when it was being sold in this way in Africa and Greece.

43 (B43, A38) VS: aes, edd veter; TVS: Mo, CIL, Jo (Mo saw the crossbar of a T at the edge of the fragment); perhaps *colono eive quei in colonei numero scrip]tus est* (cf. lines 45, 55, 59, 60). The G of AGRO is blurred by damage to the bronze. COLONIAE: Sig, Pin, O; COLONIE: Maz.

44 (B44, A39) M ADSIGNATVM: aes, Mo (the first M can only just be discerned at the top left-hand corner of Bc and was not read by Orsini or Vettori). QVEI L (apparently followed by interpunct), hence *quei l(ege) ? Baebia.*

Even if there was no sign of an interpunct after L, the only likely restorations are *l[ege]* or *l[ocus]*. If *lege* is correct, *quei* will refer back to an antecedent *ei*, the indirect object of *datum adsignatum esse*, i.e. a man whose tenure of land is confirmed by the present law. *Ioudicaverit* indicates a future act of review by a magistrate or land-commissioner. This will probably have been provided for in the lacuna between lines 43 and 44 (cf. *utei in h.l. scriptum est*). For *cen[turia supsicivove*, cf. line 66.

45 (B45, A40) VM AGRVM: aes, edd veter; EVM: Mo; *extraque] eum*: Mo, CIL, Jo.

It is tempting to read *extra* or *extraque eum agrum locum*, since the relation of *eum – scriptei sunt* to the second half of the line seems to be that of an exception clause: land bought is outside the territory assigned to colonists. For *colonei – scriptei sunt*, cf. lines 55, 59, 60. On the contrast between this line and those in the African section see the introductory discussion to this section.

There remains the problem of the contrast between *colonei* and those *in colonei numero*. Both are accepted as having rights under the present law (*ex h.l.*, which must refer to the whole clause not just the word *colonei*). Mommsen, comparing *dediticiorum numero* (Gai. *Inst.* 1.15) and *maritorum numero* (*lex mun.Malac.*, cap. 56 = *FIRA* I, p. 212), argued that those *in colonei numero* were treated as colonists, although they were not properly enrolled as such. On the assumption that this line concerned Africa, he referred to the allegations (App. *BCiv.* 1.24.104) that C.Gracchus and Fulvius Flaccus enrolled more colonists at Iunonia than they were permitted to under the *lex Rubria*. However, it is clear that even the man *quei in colonei numero scriptus est* was regarded as having rights in law at the time and not merely as a *de facto* recipient of land, cf. line 60: '*quoi] colono[eive quei in colonei nu]mero scriptus est, agrum dare oportebit licuitve*'. An alternative explanation of the phrase *in colonei numero scriptus* may be found. It may refer to a man, not on the original list, who was incorporated in the colony on the spot by the commission, perhaps in place of an original colonist, who failed to appear.

46 (B46, A41) MANCV: aes; MANCVP: O; *mancup[is*: Sig, Pin; *mancup[um*: Mo, CIL (Jo adds *praevidum*).

In line 100 the reading is probably *nomina mancupum*, but the singular *mancupis* corresponds better with *manceps* earlier in this line. *Praevidum* presumably followed. For the provision of personal guarantors for financial liability after purchase and the registration of property as security with the treasury cf. lines 73–4, 83–4, 100. For the recording of debts to the treasury by the quaestor at the *aerarium*, cf. line 70.

47 (B47, A42) MAG: aes, edd veter; Mo printed DE MAG on the basis of an E in Ritschl's illustration, but confessed that he had no evidence for the E from autopsy or earlier editors.

PEQVNIA: aes, edd veter; PEQVNIAM: Mo, CIL, Jo. NE: aes; NEI: Sig, Pin, O; *nei[ve praedia populo (nei) dato*: Mo, CIL, Jo. *neive –] – est[o*: Mo (adapting Rud), CIL, Jo.

Can *pequnia*, the reading of the bronze, be defended? In a similar situation in lines 73 and 83–4 we find only *pro eo agro loco*. Assuming that the clause relates to land bought already (*emit*) in such a way that there can be no question of anyone demanding security for the price owing to the *populus*, this must have been either because the price had already been paid or such purchases had to be made with cash. If we retain the reading of the bronze, the clause excludes the giving of security for certain types of purchase: cash must be produced, cf. line 74. Yet the notion of giving security for money owed as well as property bought is unusual and somewhat confusing: surely it would have been given for either one or the other? If *pequniam* is read, the clause may be wholly negative (Huschke, 606, wished to insert *neive* before *pequniam*) or may be positive in relation to *pequniam*: on the second interpretation once again the clause will be an injunction to pay ready cash. The view of Hinrichs (285) that this chapter refers to purchases declared void seems inconsistent with the use of the perfect tense *emit* (cf. *emptum est* in line 45) and the absence of any immediate qualifying clause. In the second half of the line we have a clause which cancels any obligation on a guarantor, who has been improperly given by the purchaser in this situation.

48 (B48, A43) QVODQVE. . .EDIVM: aes; *pra]edium*: O, Sig, Pin; *pr]aedium*: Mo (seeing the trace of an A), CIL, Jo. VEI AGER: Maz; QVEI AGER: O, Sig, Pin. *Publice [venieit venieritve*: Rud, Jo.

In the first half of this line, as in the second half of line 47, it is assumed that a purchaser may have given a personal guarantor or a security in property, but it is not clear whether this is the same situation as in the previous line, where such security was not required or permitted, or a different one, where the provision of security for purchase of public land was permitted as usual.

In the second half of the line there is the first mention of Africa. Clearly this term is not purely geographical: the focus is on the area where the Romans have power. We may identify it with the province, as Johannsen does (301), with the proviso that it may apply to land assigned to free peoples, since the phrase, *ager locus in Africa*, appears later in the context of land assigned to them but subsequently improperly sold (lines 74–7). It should be noted that in the introductory formula *quei ager locus in Africa est*, the land is not specifically qualified as 'public', as the land of the Roman people in Italy was. This is presumably because it was believed that the people were the original owners of all the territory over which they acquired sovereignty through the defeat of Carthage.

Lines 49–58 Provisions regarding the sale of public land in Africa: ratification of its status, requirements for its registration, adjudication by the duumvir

49 (B49, A44) *heredeive] eius*: Mo (not followed by CIL, Jo). To the left of EIVS there is a scar on the bronze about 2 letter-spaces wide; to the left of this, as Mo saw, there is a trace of a vertical stroke. ITALIA: Maz, ITALIAM: Sig, Pin, O (*extra* with the ablative seems to be an unparalleled construction).

Mommsen rightly identified traces of a V after *vectigalisque*, probably the beginning of VTEI, perhaps *utei in h.l. infra scriptum est*, cf. line 66. On this category of land see below.

50 (B50, A45) GATORVM: aes; OGATORVM: O, Vett. EIS P: aes, edd veter; EIS PO: Rud, Mo, CIL (at best the apex of the O at the edge of the fragment can have been read); hence *po[plice deve senatus sententia datum est*: Rud; *po[puleis*: Mo, CIL, Jo.

For the *formula togatorum*, cf. line 21. Rome's Latin and Italian allies must come into question here as potential purchasers of African land. Hinrichs (285) and Johannsen (300–1) assumed that its effect was to deny them this right in view of line 76 (*quantum agri – ceivis Romanei factum erit*), but the assignments mentioned there at the expense of the *populei leiberei* and the *stipendiariei* may have been only the colonial allotments of the *lex Rubria*. The implications of *ceivi Romano* in line 58, a chapter dealing with compensatory grants in relation to the sale of land, are also unclear. Overall, it seems unsafe to conclude that Latins and Italians were completely excluded from acquisition of land by sale. Cf. lines 76 and 83 with commentary.

51 (B51, A46, E1) E REI: aes, O, Vett; *eiusv]e rei*: Mo, CIL, Jo. *in[mittito*: Mo, CIL, Jo.

LO. . .MAÇ: Peir; ALO QVEI AC: D, Br; ALOQVEI AC: Scal, Bo. *se dolo m]alo (space between chapters) Quei ag[er locus in Africa est*: Mo, CIL, Jo.

For the mutual relationship of the A and E fragments see the introduction to the text of *lex rep.* and the commentary on *lex rep.* 45ff. The apparent join is seductive, but the location of the fragments makes it difficult. *Se dolo m]alo* remains the most likely expansion of ALO. I take *quei ager, etc.* to be a relative construction anticipating a later *is ager*.

52 (B52, A47, E2) IDEAT: aes, edd veter, Rud; SIDEAT: Mo, CIL, Jo. *publi[cus populei Romanei*: Sig; *publi[ce venisset*: Rud.

We do not have any other references to *ager publicus populi Romani* in the provincial section of this law. As with *publice* in lines 48, 58, 65, 67, 75, it is likely that the word refers to a public sale.

IIvir quei ex h.l.] factus: Rud, sim. Mo, CIL, Jo (in their re-arranged line), cf. lines 57, 58, 61, 67, 69. CREATVSVE ERIT EIICI: Maz; CREATVSVE EIICI: O[1], Pin; CREATVSVE ERIT: Sig, O[2]; EIICITO: Rud; *edici[to*: Hu, Mo, CIL, Jo.

I IN BIDW: Peir; IN BIDVO: cett edd veter. After QVO in Peir there is the trace of an inclined vertical stroke, such as the first stroke of M.

The I before IN BIDVO, if correctly recorded, is likely to be the end of a nominative plural, referring to those required by the duumvir's edict to take action. As Mommsen argued, the duumvirs created by the present law were not like ordinary commissioners for a colony or land-distribution in that they were expected to operate both in Africa and Greece (they are not mentioned nor relevant in the Italian section of the law). However, it does not follow that one was assigned to Africa, the other to Greece (cf. Johannsen, 304–5). Provision for their election is not to be found in the surviving text of the law. Their first task laid down in this section of the law seems to have been to create a register of previous land-allotments and unfulfilled claims to land, see lines 53, 56, 57, 59–61, where we find mentioned declarations of land (including land acquired from the original recipient as well as land assigned or publicly sold) and adjudication by the duumvir.

53 (B53, A48, E3) *Diebus] XXV*: O[1]; *in diebus*: Rud, Mo, CIL, Jo. P̣ṚỴ: aes, sim. Mo apparatus – ? *pr(aetor) u[tei...*

ROFITEBITVR: Maz, Sig, Pin; PROFITEBITVR: O. *cognitor[es*: Mo, CIL, Jo.

IDQVE QVOM (followed by two downstrokes from the edge of the fragment, which may simply represent grooves there): Peir; IDQVE QVOM: O, Vett; IDQVE QVON: B (exc. Bo[2] which has QVOM L).

If the suggested restoration on the B fragment is correct, the duumvir was to receive the co-operation of the praetor in Rome in compiling his register of property in Africa, cf. lines 73–4 for the praetor's registration of security given for purchases. *Cognitor[em* is probably not the object of *profitebitur*, both because of the position of the noun after the verb and because the object of *professio* was surely the land in Africa, which the duumvir was registering, cf. lines 56–7, 90. The *cognitor* here is perhaps the legal representative of a man whose land is in dispute (as in Cic. *div.Caec.* 11; *Verr.* 2.2.106–7; 2.3.78; Festus 49L; Gai. *Inst.* 4.83) rather than a witness or reference (Cic. *Verr.* 2.1.13, 5.167), cf. Johannsen, 306, n400. The L recorded after QVOM in Boissard's printed version of the E fragment may be an artistic embellishment by the illustrator de Bry, like the letters added at the bottom of the corresponding *repetundae* face.

54 (B54, A49, E4) *homin[is eius agri privati venditio fuit*: Rud; *homin[is privati eius agri loci venditio fuerit*: Mo, sim. CIL; *homin[is – fuerit, tum quom eum locum emerit*: Jo (for the formula, cf. line 63). IQVE IPSE N: Maz; IQVE IPSE: Sig, O (Pin did not record this line); *ne]que ipse n[eque*: Mo, CIL, *ne]que ipse n[eque heres eius abalienaverit*: Jo (but it is hard to see how the vertical stroke before Q recorded by the ancient copyists could be part of an E); perhaps *quo]ique ipse n[on.* CALPVRNI COS: Peir, O, Vett; C. CALPVRNI COS: B.

QVOD EIVS POS. . .A (followed by a vertical groove or downstroke): Peir; QVOS EIVS POSTEA: O, Vett; QVOD – POST: Bo; QVOD – POSI: Scal, Br, D.

To judge from the Peiresc copy, there was little space at the left-hand edge of the E fragment for a further letter. So it is unlikely that there was a well-preserved C, which could be read in the sixteenth century. The last C.Calpurnius to be consul held office in 180 BC and, as Mommsen commented, it is hard to see his relevance here. It is possible that there was a casually engraved L, which was misread as an angular C. In any case it is likely that the text refers to the consuls of 112 BC in view of the similarity to the provisions of line 63 (see the commentary on that line for the restoration proposed here). This chapter is dealing with declarations by men who have bought land in Africa and who can only properly claim to have purchased it if the seller had the right to sell and (probably) if the purchase had taken place before 112 BC, always providing that the purchaser had not subsequently alienated it (cf. lines 63–4 and note the contrast with *mag. Romano emit* in line 47). Whereas some of the sales by magistrates on behalf of the *populus Romanus* were still incomplete, cf. lines 45ff and 72–3, we seem to be dealing here with sales by private citizens which go back some years before the date of this law. What kind of land was a private citizen allowed to sell? Perhaps only land that had been originally bought from the Roman people, not that received by someone, *qua* colonist of Junonia.

55 (B55, A50, E5) RAEFECTVS: aes; PRAEFECTVS: O, Vett. IN PROVINCIAM E: aes, O, Vett; *in provinciam er[it*: Mo, CIL, Jo (I was unable to see either a final R on the bronze or space for one: the reading is perhaps *e[xierit*).

AG: Maz alone; *ag[er – nu]mero*: scripsi; *quei] ag[er locus in Africa – nu]mero*: Rud; *colono – nu]mero*: Mo, CIL, Jo. SCRIPTOS (the last S being outlined in dots): Peir; SCRIPTVS: cett edd veter.

Whereas Rudorff (108) and Huschke (607) explained the appearance of *praefectus milesve* here by suggesting that special provision was made for them as property-holders if they were absent *rei publicae causa*, Mommsen compared *Dig.* 49.16.9, *milites prohibentur praedia comparare in his provinciis in quibus militant* (cf. 18.1.62 pr.), and understood a ban on purchases of provincial land by soldiers, officers and perhaps magistrates in provinces in which they were serving. Hinrichs' objection (286) that *provincia* did not yet have a territorial significance was rightly criticised by Johannsen (307). Even if Latin counter-examples (Livy 41.28.8; Gell. 15.12.2–3 = *ORF*, no. 48, frag. 26–8 – C.Gracchus' speech on his return from Sardinia) are considered inconclusive, the Greek equivalent ἐπαρχεία is used for a territorial province in Sherk, *RGDE* 44, lines 2–3 (cf. *Syll.*³, 682, 42ff), in two decrees from Claros (L. and J. Robert, *Claros I, Les decrets hellénistiques*, Paris, 1989, p. 13, II.50–4; p. 64, I.39; II.4) and above all in *lex prov.praet.*, Cnidos II.20, III.6 and 22ff; IV.8ff. On the related question of the legality of senators holding private property in the provinces see Rawson, 1976, 91. This line seems to contain the first allusion to the allocations of land under C.Gracchus' *lex Rubria.* The validity of claims to this land were also to be examined by the duumvir (cf. *neive . . .adsignatum esse. . .iudicato* in line 57 and see the commentary on line 59).

56 (B56, E6) EI CVRATOR – ITEM VT: aes, O, Vett; TEI – VTE: Mo, CIL, Jo. O EDICITO: Peir, D, Bo; O EDICTO: O, Vett, Scal, Br; *in. . .proxsum]o edicito*: Rud; *ex e]o edicto*: Mo, CIL, Jo. EMTORE: Br, Bo, Scal; EMPTORE: O, Vett, D, Peir (in the last the P is partly indicated by dots). CVRATOI: Peir (but the last stroke may indicate a fault at the edge of the fragment).

As Mommsen pointed out, Orsini in *Vat. lat.* 6040 wrote *edicito* and then crossed out the second I. Disagreement between copyists cut across the B group with Scaliger and Brisson in one camp, Dupuy and Boissard in the other. It seems most probable that the Peiresc and Dupuy copies were right in recording the second I, but some copyists with a tendency to edit chose to regard this as an error.

This line deals with declarations of land which has been seized by creditors and either is waiting to be sold for their benefit or has already been sold. The *curator* here, as Mommsen argued, must be closely associated with the *emptor* and *magister bonorum*: he will be the trustee appointed by creditors of an insolvent debtor, after they have successfully applied for *missio in possessionem* (*Dig.* 27.10.5 and 9; 42.7.2) – attested by juristic sources under the Principate, the earliest of which is Cassius (*Dig.* 42.7.2.3–5). Cf. Buckland, 1975, 642ff; Kaser, 1966, 306ff. *Missio in possessionem* was the formal permission by the praetor to take possession of property, which in the case of a debtor was followed by its disposal by sale in order to satisfy the creditors. Whereas the *magister*'s job was to sell the proceeds of the seizure (*venditio bonorum*) to the man who offered the highest return on their loans to the creditors (i.e. the *emptor bonorum*), the *curator* was either a temporary administrator before the auction or a man whose function was to dispose of the property of upper-class debtors privately, when there was sufficient to satisfy creditors, without inflicting the *infamia* of an auction. Assuming that *emerit* has been correctly restored here, this text shows that the second function of the *curator* was probably as old as *venditio bonorum* itself. This procedure was introduced by a praetor P.Rutilius (Gai. *Inst.* 4.35) as an alternative to the seizure of the debtor's person by creditors. If that praetor was P.Rutilus Rufus (*cos.* 105, *pr.* 118 or shortly before), the fact that the present legislator chose to take the procedure specifically into account is perhaps an indication of its popularity and rapid growth. However, the procedure may have been devised by P.Rutilius Calvus, *pr.* 166 (Livy 45.44.2), if he became *praetor urbanus* or *peregrinus*, or another P.Rutilius of the second century, unknown to us. On Roman debt procedure from the late Republic onwards see, in general, Solazzi, 1937, 5ff.

XLIII (line 57)*

57 (B57, E7) T QVOD: aes, edd veter; IT QVOD: Mo, CIL, Jo; *[sei quem quid edicto IIvirei ex h.l. profiteri oportuer]it*: Mo, CIL, Jo, sim. Hu. EX H.L.I: aes; EX H.L.: O; EX H.L.N: Vett, Rud, Mo; *n[on erit*: Rud, Mo, CIL, Jo. *ei – lo]cum*: Mo, CIL, Jo. EMPTVM: Peir, O, Vett, D, Br; EMTVM: Scal. A lacuna caused by a leap from *neive* here to *neive* in line 59 begins here in Bo.

FVISE: O, Vett; ...SE: Peir; FUISSE: Scal, D, Br. IVD.CATO (vac) Q: Peir; IVDICATO Q: O, Vett, D, Br; IVDICATOQ: Scal.

If the restoration *professus ex h.l. n[on erit* is correct, as seems likely, failure by a possessor to make a declaration entails that the duumvir cannot judicially confirm the sale or assignation of that land. This, however, does not necessarily mean that the land is forfeit, but its ownership could only have been confirmed after further judicial investigation.

XLIV (lines 57–8)*

To judge from the Peiresc copy, a new chapter began with the last four letters of line 57.

58 (B58, F1, E8) O EI CEIVI: aes; PO – : O[1]; LO – : O[2]; RO – : Vett, Mo apparatus; DO – : Mo, CIL, Jo; *pro eo agro lo]co*: Rud. MOD: aes, O, Vett; MODV Mo, CIL, Jo. The text of this line of the B fragment is omitted in Bruns[7].

ẎEI EIẎ: aes (F1) – initially consistent with *nei*, whether a negative or the end of *ceivis Roma]nei*; VEI L /: Garrucci. VENIEIT: O, Vett; VENIET: Peir, B. Any future event is more likely to have been described with a future perfect verb, cf. lines 73, 75. For *venieit* cf. line 67. Yet there may well have been an engraver's error corrected by O and Vett or their source.

Here we find the first mention in this section of the allocation of land from that remaining undistributed in an exchange or as a recompense to a man deprived of his due, cf. lines 3–4, 21–2, 26–7 of the Italian section and 65ff. Why exchange should be briefly mentioned here is not clear. The chapter is not in the form of an instruction to the duumvir as those in lines 65ff are. It may be a preliminary statement that the receipt of land in compensation is possible, when an injustice has occurred, from the point of view of the prospective recipient, which is followed by a series of directives to the duumvir.

XLV (lines 58–61) The duumvir appointed by this law is to review the assignations to colonists in Africa*

58 (E8) *IIvir qu[ei ex h.l. factus creatusve erit*: Rud, Mo, CIL, Jo, cf. lines 67, 77, 78, 96.

59 (B59, F2, E9) INITIO: aes; ITAQVE I: aes; ITAQVE: O, Vett; ITAQVE H: Mo, CIL. HOMINI: aes (F2). *itaque h[unc agrum locum quoi colono eive, quei in colonei numero scriptus est, ita datus adsignatus est, ei] homini [facito decernitoque utei d]et*: Jo.

COLO. . .EIVE QVEI II: Peir; COLONO EIVE QVEI: O, Vett; COLONO EIVS QVEI: B.

The duumvir is here instructed to begin his work of judication and assignation by reviewing the colonial allotments made under C.Gracchus' law about Iunonia. This law is ascribed to a Rubrius by Plut. *C.Gr.* 10.2; its repeal through the law of Minucius is shown by the perfect tense of *fuit*, cf. App. *BCiv.* 1.24.102ff; Plut. *C.Gr.* 13.3; Flor. 2.3.4; Oros. 5.12.1; *Vir.Ill.* 65.5. The original object of the *lex Rubria* was to refound Carthage as a town of Romans. Appian says that 6,000 colonists were picked, alleging that this was more than the law allowed (*BCiv.* 1.24.104; *Pun.* 136.644). These were to be Roman citizens (Eutrop. 4.21; Oros. 5.12.1; cf. Vell.Pat. 2.7.7).

60 (B60, F3, E10) *data adsign]ata fuise*: Mo, CIL, Jo. HOMINVS: aes; HOMINIS; O, Vett. COLONO: aes (F3); *[colono, eive quei in colonei] numero* had already been restored by Rudorff and subsequent editors, before Mattingly (1969, 135) inserted the F fragment into the agrarian text. The latter produced a compressed line, eliminating almost all the B–F lacuna.

OPORTEBIT LICVITVE: edd veter; *oportuit licuitve*: em. Hu (p. 609), Mo, CIL, Jo; perhaps *oportebit* ⟨*oportuit*⟩ *licuitve. in [singulos homines data adsignata esse fuiseve iudicato*: CIL, Jo; *in [singulos equites*: Mattingly, loc. cit.

Mattingly followed a suggestion of Mommsen's in his introduction to the African section (*CIL* I, p. 97). For differentiation between cavalry and infantry in land-allotment, cf. Livy 35.9.7 and 40.6; 37.57.8. One hundred *iugera* was apparently the maximum allotment under the later *lex Appuleia* about Africa (*Vir.Ill.* 73.1). *Amplius* must be related to a preceding negative, i.e. *[neive ... quoi ex lege Rubria, quae fuit,] colono [eive, quei in colonei nu]mero – licuitve, amplius iug. CC*. We must also assume that the subject of *data adsign]ata fuise* was a certain quantity of *iugera*. Thus there seem to be in lines 59–61 (before *neive maiorem numerum – iudicato*) two closely related provisions with parallel phraseology, each beginning *neive unius homini(u)s nomine*, with the break coming before *neive unius hominus [nomine* in line 60. What is the difference between the two provisions? The first may have been solely concerned with the adjudication of previous allotments, whereas the second concerned allotments which should have been made under previous legislation but had been neglected. But this second problem seems to have been handled in the following chapter. Alternatively, the two clauses may reflect different quantities of land assigned, e.g.: *[quantum uni] homini[– lic]et, neive unius hominis nomine, quoi ex lege Rubria, quae fuit, colono, eive quei in [colonei numero scriptus est – licuitve, quei . . .inter pedites stipendia meritus est, amplius iug. C in agro, quei in Africa est, data adsign]ata fuise iudicato, neive unius hominus [nomine, quei . . . inter equites stipendia meritus est, quoi ex lege Rubria, quae fuit,] colono [eive, quei in colonei nu]mero – licuitve, amplius iug. CC in [agro, quei in Africa est . . .adsignata fuise iudicato.*

61 (B61, F4, E11) SEVE IVDICATO: aes, edd veter; ISEVE: Mo, CIL, Jo. The Q of QVAM is no longer visible. *[neive maiorem numerum – fu]iseve*: Rud, Mo, CIL, Jo.

O QVAE E: aes (F4); *[ex lege Rubri]*⟨*a*⟩{*o*} *quae* {*e*}⟨*f*⟩*[uit*: Mattingly, 1969, 135 (E is a common error for F, but corruption of A into O is more difficult to imagine). The paragraph space on E is shown by Peir, D, Scal.

For the allegation that C.Gracchus and M.Fulvius Flaccus enrolled more men in Iunonia than the *lex Rubria* permitted see App. *BCiv.* 1.24.106, but the issue now may have been claims by men to be colonists above the number actually enrolled by the Gracchan commissioners. See also the discussion of *quei in colonei numero scriptus est* above (line 45).

XLVI (lines 61–2) Adjudication of land by the duumvir ? to colonists*

62 (B62, D1, F5, E12) RE ROM AGRI: Bluhme ap. Mo (Mo himself could not see this), CIL, Jo.; AGRI RE ROM: Rud. Only the apices of a few letters are now visible; I could find no trace of either RE or AGRI.

ATVS A: aes (D1); ATVS AB: Rud; ATVS ADS: Mo; hence *d]atus ads[ignatus*: Mo, CIL, Jo. EIVS NON: aes (F5), hence *quod] eius non [venieit, quod eiu]s agri*: Mattingly, loc. cit., Jo. ADIVDICARI: Peir, O, Vett; ADIOUDICARI: B. ADSIGNATO ESSE IVDICATO: edd veter, Rud; *adsignatum*: em. Mo, CIL, Jo.

I have hesitantly retained *adsignato*, the unanimous reading of the copyists and surely that of the bronze. We should perhaps allow for the specification of two actions to be taken by the duumvir – confirmation of a colonists's holding, *esse iudicato* (cf. *data adsign]ata fuise iudicato* in line 60), and assignation to a man who had not yet received his proper allotment. An alternative emendation is *adsignato* ⟨*adsignatum*⟩ *esse iudicato*. As Johannsen pointed out, the term *adsignare* itself suggests colonial allotments, while the reference to an heir, but not to a buyer, seems to exclude that this was land sold by public authority, which could be resold, as could the land discussed in line 54 and in the chapter following this (lines 63–5). The purpose of this chapter seems to have been to complete the instructions in the foregoing chapter. There the duumvir was told to judge who should hold what land in the former territory of Iunonia, here he is told to put his judgement into effect. The following chapter about land sold includes an instruction to execute a similar judgement, *dato re]ddito*.

XLVII (lines 63–5) The duumvir is to review and confirm the holdings of those who have properly bought land in Africa*

63 (D2, F6, E13) OQVE EIVS AGRI LOC: aes (D2) – only the bases of the last three letters remain visible and there follow some indistinct traces; OQVE EIVS AGRI LOCEI ANTE: O[1], Vett, Pin; OQVE – ANTE ME: O[2]; OQVE – ANTE MEI: Bluhme ap. Mo, Rud; OQVE – ANTE IAṆ.I: Mo apparatus; hence *quandoque eius agri locei ante kal I*: Mo, CIL, Jo. RNIO CO: aes (F6); hence *ante kal I[an P.Cornelio L.Calpu]rnio co[s*: Mattingly, 1969, but there is in fact only room for the names of the consuls of 112 BC, not for the names of those of 111. Some question must also remain over the month: *Iun* or any month whose first letter begins with a vertical stroke is possible.

[quoieique emptum est]: Mo, CIL, Jo. HOMINIS: Peir, O, Vett, Bo; HOMINVS: D; HOMINIBVS: Scal; HOMINES: Br. QVEI: O, Vett, Scal, Bo; QVE: Peir; QVI: D, Br.

If the restoration here of the consuls of 112 BC is correct, then this terminal date suggests a reluctance to accept as valid sales made after the Jugurthine crisis portended war. Sales by private citizens are presumably contrasted with those by magistrates (line 47). A private citizen would have had the right to sell land he had bought, but probably not land he had acquired as a colonist under the *lex Rubria*, cf. App. *BCiv*. 1.27.121 on the Gracchan allotments in Italy; *BCiv*. 3.2.5 on Caesar's legislation; Cic. *Leg.Agr*. 2.78 on Sulla's; and on the general principle see Keppie, 1983, 95. It should be noticed that there is no mention of a buyer of land either at the end of the preceding chapter (line 62 – *id ei heredeive eius*) or in line 67, dealing with colonists in Africa, or in the surviving text of line

68, also dealing with colonists (on the dubiousness of Mommsen's restoration there see the commentary on the line).

64 (D3, F7, E14) T PLANVM – ESSE Q: aes (only the left semi-circle of Q survives), O, Vett, Pin; IT PLANVM: Mo, CIL, Jo (though Mo's apparatus suggests ET). EIVS NE: aes (F7); hence *q[uod] eius ne[que ipse postea*: Mattingly, Jo (a little too short for the lacuna, hence my *ne[que is ipse postea*).

HAERES: D. QVO for QVOI: D. At LOCEI Bo jumps forward to LOCEI in line 65.

Mommsen noted that *planum facere* = 'to prove' is found in Cic. *Verr.* 1.40; 5.165; Lucr. 2.934. The subject of the verb *abalienaverit* seems to have been the owner of a piece of land, resold after it had been originally purchased from the treasury, who had already proved or would in the future prove that it had been bought in such a resale. *Heres eius* must be the heir of the new owner, who had proved his purchase, but *quoi is heres erit* is confusing, since there is an apparent ambiguity about the identity of *is*. *Is* here cannot refer to the *heres* in *heres eius*, since then the whole clause will refer back to the owner who had proved it to be his – the first subject of *alienaverit*. *Is* must therefore refer to the same man as the *eius* in *heres eius*, i.e. the man who *planum fecerit*, who in this situation is assumed to have received it as an inheritance from the purchaser in the first private resale. The implication of this chapter is that sales of land in Africa to private citizens had been going on for some time before 111 BC, thus leading to inheritance and resale, as well as seizure by creditors (cf. line 54 and commentary there). Sales must have begun at least about the time of the *lex Rubria*, if not earlier – perhaps from the creation of the province, cf. Broughton, 1929, 18; Romanelli, 1959, 55; Chevallier, 1958, 69.

65 (D4, E15) ḌITO: aes; DDITO: edd veter; *[quoieique is ager emptus erit, de eo agro loco re]ddito*: Rud; *dato red]dito*: Mo, CIL, Jo. VENIE: aes; VENIEI: Mo; VENIER: edd veter.

XLVIII (lines 65–5) The duumvir is to compensate a legitimate private purchaser, whose land has been publicly sold in error, with an equivalent amount of public land as yet unsold*

65 (E15) EMPTVS: O, Vett, D, Br; EMTVS: Scal. VENIEIT: Peir, Br; VENIET: O, Vett, Scal, D. AGER LO: Peir, B; AGER LOCVSVE: O, Vett (these copies here seem to reproduce a supplement).

Venieit, a reference to past sales by the Roman people, seems more appropriate than the future, *veniet*, since the duumvir, with the aid of the land-register he was about to make, should have been able to prevent the public sale of land no longer in public hands.

66 (D5, E16) *lo[cus in Africa est, quei publice non venieit, ei quei ita emptum habuerit*: Mo, CIL, Jo. The present restoration is on the model of line 67.

CTVS: aes; ACTVS: edd veter; *[quei – f]actus*: Mo, CIL, Jo, sim. Rud. VECTIGALISQVE III: aes, edd veter (Mo saw the last stroke as oblique).

ita [utei in h.l.] scriptum: Rud; *ita [utei supra]*: Mo, CIL, Jo. The paragraph space after *esto* appears in Peir and O, not in Vett or the MSS of the B group; in O[1] it is a correction, perhaps the result of editing, but Peir suggests that this is the true reading of the bronze.

I have suggested *infra* rather than *supra* in the D–E lacuna, because, although *ager privatus vectigalisque* has been mentioned earlier (line 49), the way in which *vectigal* was to be exacted is on my view specified below (line 70 with commentary).

Buying for one sesterce was not a fictitious sale, but a genuine conveyance of property, as when property was transferred as real security, *fidei fiduciae causa*, for which only a token price was paid (cf. *FIRA* III, pp. 291–7; *Tab.Pomp.* 19, 21, 22 = *AE* 1973, 139, 141, 142). This is the first time that we find this as a form of conveyance in this law. There is no evidence that it was used in the Italian section, though it might have been appropriate when the land assigned was made private. Here it seems to be used to distinguish land, which was to be private property, from assignations to men treated as colonists.

For *ager p.v.que* being truly private see Weber, 1891, 156ff; de Martino, 1956, I.557ff; Kaser, 1942, 9–10; Burdese, 1952, 102; Levi, 1929, 235. Mommsen interpreted the *vectigal* here as a token rent, but from what follows it seems to have been a considerable sum, see the commentary on line 70 (cf. de Martino, Weber and Kaser cited above). The *populus Romanus* was prepared to sell land as private property in the provinces and thus to cease being landlord of these holdings: it was not prepared to give up its right to tax them. This last principle was probably maintained even in the agrarian bill of 63 BC, in which Servilius Rullus proposed to sell large quantities of Roman public land outside Italy (Cic. *Leg.Agr.* 2.38ff), though one would not guess this from Cicero's own presentation of these proposals.

XLIX (lines 66–7) The duumvir is to compensate a colonist, who has been deprived of his formal allotment, with an equivalent amount of land as yet unsold*

66 (E16) EIVS for EIVE: O[1]. SVPSICIVOV: Peir, Scal, D, Br, O[1]; SVMPSICIVOV: Bo; SVPCISIVON: O[1] correction, O[2]; Vett.

Orsini should have known the word *supsicivum* from Varro's *Res Rusticae*: perhaps his and Vettori's source had *supcisivon* and he returned to that reading, because he could not be sure that it was an error.

67 (D6, E17) O LOCO: aes; RO LOCO: edd veter, Rud; GRO LOCO: Mo, CIL, Jo; *supsicivov[e de eo agro, quei ager in Africa est, datus adsignatus est, quae centuria quodve supsicivom Romae publice venieit venieritve ... si quid eius agri IIvir, quei ex h.l. factus creatusve erit, ei heredeive eius minus adiudicaverit, tum* *tantundem modum agri locei pro eo agro loco de eo a]gro*: Mo (developing a suggestion of Rud), CIL, Jo.

EI HE: aes, Pin, Vett, O[2]; EI HER: O[1]; *ei he[redeive ei]us*: Rud, Mo, CIL, Jo. VS IIVIR: O, Vett, Scal, D, Bo; S IIVIR: Peir; VS HVIR: Br.

The duumvir is to deliver land, taken from the territory as yet unsold, to a colonist or his heir, presumably because the latter had lost his original allotment through no fault of his own. It is plausible to compare this and the following chapter with XLVIII* (lines 65–6), where compensation is given with an equivalent amount of land (*tantundem modum*). The reference to an *heres* suggests that the colonist may have been unjustly deprived of his land some time before. Mommsen's supplement (following line 69) does not actually place the responsibility for the loss on the duumvir himself, but rather expresses a condition in which the IIvir found himself unable to award to the colonist his original patch of land. The reference to *centuria* and *supsicivum* emphasises that the allotments were made by the *IIIvir coloniae deducendae causa* on the grid-plan (*forma*) of the colony of Iunonia.

For the results of work based on air-photography of the centuriation of the province of Africa, see A. Piganiol, *Atlas des centuriations de Tunisie* (1954); Caillemer–Chevallier, 1954; Chevallier, 1958. A major grid of *centuria* squares covers most of what is now northern Tunisia, with an axis running roughly NW–SE from a point NW of Bizerta to the neighbourhood of Sidi-bou-Ali (north of Hadrumetum = Sousse). This is oriented differently to what must be the Caesarian and imperial grids to the south. The *centuriae* are each of 200 *iugera*, the standard size (Dilke, 1971, 85ff) and apparently the maximum allotment under the *lex Rubria* (line 60). This must be the centuriation to which our law refers here and in line 89. It must have been begun at least at the time of the founding of Iunonia, but there is a case for believing that the first steps go back to 146 BC (so Johannsen, 353ff, following Caillemer–Chevallier and Chevallier, opp. citt.). A *supsicivum* was either an unassigned area between *centuriae*, usually because it was uncultivable, or an area less than a *centuria* square between the grid and the outer boundary of the territory (Front. 2–3 Thul; Hyg. 96–7 Thul).

L (lines 67–8) The duumvir is to compensate a colonist, who has been deprived of land (? which he was not formally allotted), with an equivalent amount of land as yet unsold*

67 (E17) Paragraph space noted only by Peir, Scal, O[1], Br.

68 (D7, E18) ṢEVE: aes; EVE: O[2], Vett, Pin; ESSE: O[1]; *[ager in ea centuria supsicivove de eo agro, quei in Africa est, datus adsignatus est, quae centuria quodve supsicivom Romae publice venieit venieritve, si quid eius agri IIvir, quei ex h.l. factus creatusve erit, ei quei ab eo colono heredeve eius emit habuitve, minus adiudicaverit, tum tantundem modum agri ei, quem ita emisse habui]seve*: Mo, CIL, Jo. AGRO I: aes, Mo apparatus; AGRO: edd veter; *agro [IIvir reddi]to*: Mo,

CIL, Jo. O QVOI EIQVE: Peir; TO QVOIEIQVE: B, O[2], Vett; EO (corrected to *reddito*) QVOI EIQVE: O[1].

Mommsen's assumption that this chapter, like LI*, concerned a man who had bought land, does not seem justified. (His restoration also assumes a complex and puzzling situation, where the land in question was first assigned to a colonist, then publicly sold at Rome and finally privately bought from the colonist or his heir.) The chapter is closer in form to the foregoing chapter concerning colonial allotments (XLIX*) than the following (LI*) concerning land sold. It begins in the same way as XLIX*, not LI* – *quoi colono eive quei in colonei numero*, as opposed to *quoi agrum de eo agro.* Again, although its end, *adsignatum fuisse iudicato*, may be reproduced in chapter LI*, as Mommsen thought, an alternative restoration there is more attractive (see below). Moreover, it is unlikely that colonial allotments could have been freely sold, see commentary on line 63 above and note the absence of any reference to a buyer in line 67. My own conjecture is that the chapter deals with a colonist never formally assigned land, who helped himself amid the confusion caused by the repeal of the *lex Rubria* (hence *habuisse possedi]seve comperietur*) and later found that this plot had been sold at Rome. Such a man was also to be given a quasi-colonial allotment out of unsold territory.

LI (lines 68–70) The duumvir is to compensate a man, who has purchased in good faith land which has been adjudged to belong to a colonist, with an equivalent amount of land*

68 (E18) COLONO E: Peir, B; COLONO C: O, Vett (C very faint in O[1]); *colono e[ive]*: Mo, CIL, Jo.

69 (D8, E19) Ş ADIVDICAVERIT: aes; S ADIVDICAVERIT: O, Pin, Mo; IVDICAVERIT: Rud; *[quei in colonei numero scriptus est fuitve, datus adsignatus est, magistratus Romae publice vendiderit . . . sei quis eius agri IIvir, quei ex h.l. factus creatusve erit, ei, quoi ita emptus esse comperietur, emptorive eius procuratoreve eius heredive quoius eorum minu]s adiudicaverit*: Mo, CIL, Jo; *[si IIvir eum agrum locum, quem ei emptum esse comperietur, colono eive quei in colonei numero scriptus est] adiudicaverit*: Rud.

COMPERIE: aes, edd veter; COMPERIET: Mo; *comperie[tur heredive ei]us*: Rud; *comperiet[ur emptorive ei]us*: Mo, CIL, Jo. PROCVRATORVE: O. HVIR: Br, O[1]. REDDIDERI: Peir.

Mommsen's supplement of *minu]s* as a negative at the left-hand edge of fragment Da is attractive but far from certain. For *emptorive ei]us* he compared line 23, but *emptorve eius* is not equivalent to *quive ab eo emit* and does not naturally convey the sense of 'the buyer from the buyer'. It seems more probable that we should supply another person who can represent the buyer in law, like the *procurator*. Hence the suggestion, *sociove*, a partner in the purchase. A non-emancipated son would probably have been covered by *heredive quoius eorum*.

70 *[ei adsignatum fuisse iudicato...]*: Mo, CIL; *[ei is ager HS n.I emptus esto, isque ager locus privatus vectigalisque ita utei in h.l. scriptum est, esto*: Rud, sim. Jo.

Mommsen' supplement reproduced the end of chapter L* in line 68, but, as Johannsen remarked (362–3), there the duumvir is in fact making a new colonial allotment to replace one which had become void. Here a closer parallel is line 66, since the buyer, who had been sold land, which should have been a colonial allotment, and had been therefore deprived of it, should have received an equivalent amount on the same terms as his original purchase. On this account Rudorff's restoration seems more appropriate.

LII (lines 70–2) Regulations for the collection and payment of tax, presumably on* ager privatus vectigalisque

70 (D9, E20) *[Quei agri quae loca quaeque aedificia ...quei eorum publice venierit, quantum ei, quei eos agros emit, pe]quniae*: Rud; *[Quantae quis pequniae ab populo mercassitur, quam pequniam, quei agrum locum publicum in Africa emerunt emerintve, pro eo agro loco populo dare debent debebuntve ... quod eius p]equniae*: Mo, CIL, Jo.

ERITV: aes; ERIT: edd veter; *erit[ve tantam pequ]niam*: Rud, sim. Mo, CIL, Jo. CONSTITENT QVE – CONSISTENT: Scal, Br; CONSTITENT QVAE – CONSISTENT: Bo[1]; CONSTITENT QVAE – CONSTITENT: Bo[2]; CONSISTENT QVAE – CONSISTENT: O, Vett. The engraver may well have erred over the first *consistent*.

Since Rudorff, scholars have assumed that the money, entered on public records as due to the people and payable from the Ides of March following the first tax-settlement after the passage of this law, is the price of land bought in Africa. On this view a *publicanus* (*quei eo nomine ab populo mercassitur*) is purchasing the right to collect a debt to the Roman people. I do not know of any example of the use of a *publicanus* for the collection of public debts, though there seems no objection to this on principle. However, in the present context it is a highly unlikely supposition, when the purchasers of land in Africa were liable to provide *praedes* and *praedia*, from which cash could be derived (line 73 and cf. lines 46–8, 100–1). Moreover, on any occasion, presumably a very recent one, when a property was sold but neither *praedes* or *praedia* were furnished, the property was to be resold for cash (line 74).

It is therefore far more probable that this chapter ordered the payment of the *vectigal* on land bought under the provisions of this and earlier laws (cf. lines 49 and 66) – especially when the next round of tax-arrangements is used as a starting-date for liability to pay to the people the money due. The *vectigal* must therefore be a considerable sum, not a token rent, as Mommsen believed, cf. commentary on line 66. Against Mommsen, Weber (1891, 156ff) thought the rent/tax to have been substantial, similarly de Martino (1956, 1.557ff). Kaser (1942, 1ff, at 9ff) held that the Roman people took a percentage, whenever the property changed hands, but such occasional exactions are not suitable for letting out to contractors.) This tax was no doubt understood in general terms by the buyer of land. It was to be formally fixed with the other taxes (by censors or consuls) and would have become due after what was in effect the start of the new tax-year. This commenced on the Ides of March (15th) under the Republic, cf. *Dig.* 39.4.15 (Alfenus Varus), Macr. *Sat.* 1.12.7.

For general evidence about the letting of tax-contracts see by contrast the new dossier about the Asiatic *portoria* found at Ephesus (Engelmann, Knibbe, 1989), especially lines 99–103, 105–12; 123–8; 137–47 – regulations from the early Principate, in which payments are due annually from the tax-contractors on the Ides of October (15th) and the contracts themselves run from the Ides of January (13th).

71 (D10, E21) *[neive is quaestor, qui aerarium provinciam optinebit . . . eam pequniam, quae . . . populo, eive quei eo nomine ab populo mercassitur, debebitur, propiore die exigito atque]*: Rud; *[Quei eo nomine ab populo mercassitur, ex eid. Mart. eisdem, quem pequniam, qui agrum locum publicum in Africa emit emeritve, pro eo agro loco populo dare debet debebit, ab eo exsigito . . .neive quis eam pequniam propiore die exsigito atque]*: Mo, sim. CIL. Jo (but see commentary on line 70). PROPIOREM DIE EX ACTVM: aes (with interpunct separating the last two words). VE IN H.L.S.E. IS: Peir, Vett, D; IE – IS: Scal, Bo, Br; NE – IS: O²; VE – EIS: O¹; *er[it atque uteiq]⟨u⟩e*: Rud, Mo, CIL, Jo (not realising that v had MS authority). PECVNIAM: Bo². NOMINE: O, Vett, Bo; NOM NE: Scal, D, Br (perhaps the actual reading of the bronze). IS QVEI for EI QVEI: Bo².

For the Latin legal language appropriate to the buying of tax-contracts, cf. *lex Flav.mun.*, cap. LXIII V (*lex Irnit.* VIIB–C, *lex Maluc.*, col. 4).

72 *[minus solvito . . .*: Mo, CIL, Jo.

Mommsen seems to have meant by this that there was no relief or reduction for early payment. But it seems better to restore a complementary provision. The tax-collector should not exact early and, if he does, the taxpayer should not pay.

LIII (line 72) No magistrate is to contravene and no senator is to propose the contravention of the tax provisions in this law*

72 (D11, E22) NVM FIAT: aes, Mo; VM edd veter; *[. . .neive eam pecuniam ante dato, quam eos locos eaque aedificium emptos esse plan]um fiat*: Rud; *. . .pla]num fiat*: Mo, CIL, Jo. DECERNITO Q̣: aes, Pin; – O: Vett, O; *decernito q[uo ea pequnia]*: Rud, Mo, CIL, Jo.

VAE: Peir; QVAE: cett. edd veter. AEDIFICEIS: Ha. QVEI S.S.S.: Peir, Scal, D, Ham; QVEIS S.S.: Bo; QVOI S.S.S.: Br; QVAI S.S.S.: O; QVAE S.S.S.: Vett. DEBERETVR, EX. SIGRATVR, IN II.L.EST: Ha.

For similar clauses forbidding contravention of this law by magistrates and senators, cf.lines 9–10, 20, 87–9 and see the commentary on *lex rep.* 70.

LIV (line 73) Security and guarantors are to be provided to the treasury at the discretion of the praetor by any buyer of public land, who has not paid the price*

73 (D12, E23) ENIERIT: aes; VENIERIT: edd veter, Rud, Mo; *[Quei agrum locum publicum in Africa emit emeritve . . . sei ea pequnia, quam eo nomine populo dare debet debebitve, in diebus .. proxsumeis, quis is ager locus Romae publice venieit] venierit*: Mo, CIL, Jo; *[Quiquomque pro eo agro loco aedificio, quei in Africa est, quei ager locus Romae publice venieit venieritve, populo eive, quei eo nomine ab populo mercassitur, pequniam dare debebit, quae pequnia in diebus .. proxsumeis, quibus is ager, quei in Africa est, Romae publice venieit]*: Rud.

EA: aes, edd veter; QVAE: Peir (showing only the tail of Q), O, Vett, Scal, Bo, Ham; IVAE: D; VAE: Br; *ea [praedia] quae*: Rud, Mo; *ea[rum summarum nomine] quae*: CIL, Jo.

INTER: O, Vett, Bo; INTE: Scal, D, Br, Ham (almost certainly the actual reading of the bronze). IOVS: O, Vett, Scal, D, Ham; IVS: Br, Bo[1]; IDVS: Bo[2]. The paragraph space is shown by O, Scal, D, Br.

It is almost inevitable that a time-limit was imposed for the payment of the money due to the Roman people: hence the restorations of Rudorff and Mommsen at the beginning of the line. However, so much of the sense in the long lacuna is beyond reconstruction that it is hard to suggest plausibly how this limit was formulated. My own supplement aims to provide the essential minimum for the sense. *Praedia* by itself is too short for the D–E lacuna, as Mommsen realised, but his second attempt was too long. If *satis* is adequate as the object of *supsignato*, it seems appropriate to define more closely the period of 120 days prescribed for the furnishing of guarantors (cf. the starting-points provided in lines 52, 53, 70, 76, 77, 96). On the procedure and formulation see also *lex Flav.mun.* LXIV, esp. *Malac.*, col. 4, 37–8 = *Irnit.* VIIB, 29–30. Although the actual registration of securities and guarantors had to be made with the quaestor at the treasury (cf. line 46, *lex rep.* 57), the determination of the value of *praedes* and *praedia* required rested with the *praetor urbanus*.

LV (lines 73–4) The praetor is to sell for cash any property, whose purchase is incomplete and for which no security has been provided*

73 (E23) IOVS DEI: O, Vett; DE: Scal, D, Br; DI: Bo[1]; DIC: Bo[2].

74 (D13, E24) RAEDIVM: aes; PRAEDIVM: edd veter, Rud, Mo; *[si in diebus CXX proxsumeis, quibus is ager locus, quei in Africa est, Romae publice venieit venieritve, neque praes pro ea pequnia, quae ob eum agrum locum populo debetur debebiturve, populo eive, quei eo nomine ab populo mercassitur, datus erit,* *neque] praedium*: Rud; *nisei] praedium*: Mo, CIL, Jo. OBLIGAIVM: aes. E AGRVM: Peir, O[1], B; T AGRVM: O[2], Vett.; *in publicu[mve supsignatum eri]t*: Rud; *in publicu[mve praes datus eri]t*: Mo, CIL, Jo (but the authority for T is weak).

ARB.PR: O, Vett, Scal, Br (D omits ARB); ARB.PRP: Bo. SUBSIGNATVM, PRESENTI: D, Br. The paragraph space is indicated in Peir, O, D, Br.

Clearly what is missing in the first part of the line is a statement of the condition, whereby a purchaser had neither paid for property nor provided guarantors or security as detailed in the previous chapter. E is the better supported reading for the letter at the left-hand edge of the E fragment: we should perhaps supplement: *in publicu[mve praes datus erit u(tei) s(upra) s[criptus)] e(st)*. The regulations determining who could act as a *praes* and what could be registered as *praedia* were probably stated earlier in the law. For the word *obligatum* with *praedium*, cf. *lex Flav.mun.*, LXIII–LXIV (*Malac.*, col. 4, *Irnit.* VIIB); for *in publicum* in this connection, Varro, *L.L.*6.74; Cato, *ORF*, frag., 106 = Festus 312L (with Orsini's emendation); for *pequnia praesenti*, the *formula Baetica* (*FIRA* III, 295ff = Bruns[7], 335, line 14).

LVI (lines 74–7) The duumvir is to make an equivalent reparation for any land taken to satisfy a Roman citizen at the expense of the free peoples and those who deserted to the Romans*

74 (E24) QVE: Peir, B; QVAE: O, Vett; *quae [pequnia . . .*: Rud. I have given preference to the consensus of Peiresc and the B group, since the alternative reading may be based on a tacit emendation. Rudorff's restoration of a clause relating to money in this and the following line is not very plausible and it is unsafe to use the reading *quae* as an argument for restoring *pequnia*.

75 (D14, E25) AGER Ḷ. . .IN AFRICA: aes; A AGER LOCVS IN AFRICA: O; A AGER LOCVS (on line above), LOCO IN AFRICA: Vett; A AGER LOCVS PTIVI: Pigh (only knowing the bases of the last letters on frag. Dbc); *[Que]i ager locus in Africa*: Mo, CIL, Jo, sim. Rud. VENIEI: aes.

AGR: aes; AGRI: O, Pin, Vett, Mo. EIS LIBEREIS: edd veter (exc. D: IS); *agri [locei eorum erit qui popul]eis*: Rud; *agri [locei, quei popul]eis*: Mo, CIL, Jo (*populeis* in fact was first restored by Scaliger, quoting this line in his edition of Festus, *s.v. Punicus*).

EORVM AMEICITIAM: O[2], Vett; S.ORVM AMEICITIAM: Scal, Br; S.ORVM (omitting AMEICITIAM): D; SVORVM AMEICITIAM: Bo; EORVM IN AMEICITIAM: Scal(Festus). POPVLEI ROMANEI: Scal; POPVLO ROMANES: D. POINICIO: O, Vett; POINICO: Peir; POLNICIO: B; POENICIO: Scal (Festus). QVEIVE: Peir, B; QVEIVE A: O, Vett.

In this line we reach the top of fragment Dbc, whose recording by Orsini, Vettori and Pighius enables us to reconstruct the text of a very worn piece of bronze. Pighius had no knowledge of Da: his PTIVI is the result of trying to read the lowest parts of the letters IN AFRICA. However, we cannot ignore the A seen before AGER LOCVS by Orsini and Pighius – perhaps the last letter of an adverb like *postea* or *propterea* or even a phrase *ex lege –a*. In any case *ager locus* does not mark the start of a new chapter.

For the *populei leiberei*, cf. line 79. The land in question here is not said to be within their boundaries, as it is in that line, and it is associated with land given to *perfugae* (line 76): hence it may not have been the home territory of these free cities, but land given to their members as a reward for taking the Roman side in the Third Punic War, cf. App. *Lib.* 135.640 – 'And they gave land from the conquered territory to each of the cities that had helped them in the war, and first of all to the Uticans the land stretching to Carthage itself and to Hippo in the other direction.'

76 (D15, E26, C1) *queive a[g]er locus in Africa est, quei Romae publice veniet venieritve, quod eius agri locei eis hominibus publice deve senati sententia datus adsignatus est, qui bello Poenicio proxsumo ad imperatorem populi Romani perfugerunt*: Rud (but the engravers of these laws on our evidence do not split words between lines); *queive a[d] imperatorem populi Romanei bello Poenicio proxsumo ex hostibus perfugerunt, quibus propterea ager datus adsignatus est de s(enati) s(ententia), eorum quisque habuerunt*: Mo, CIL, Jo.

IBVS IIVIR . . . REATVSVE: aes; DVS II VIR EX H.L. LAVTVS CREATVSVE: Pigh; REATVSVE: O, Vett; *[pro eo agro loco – qu]ibus II vir ex h.[l. fact]us creatusve erit*: Rud, Mo, CIL, Jo. QV. .TVM: aes; QVANTVM: O, Vett; QVAM: Pigh.

AGR: aes, Pin; AGRO: O, Vett. OCVS: edd veter (exc. Bo – LOCVS); *agr[o loco, quei ager l]ocus*: Rud, Mo, CIL, Jo.

D omits LOCO before AGER LOC. LOC: Peir, B; LOCVS: O, Vett. The central angle of the M of RO]MANO is just visible in C1; *loc[us ceivei Ro]mano*: Rud, Mo, CIL, Jo.

77 *[commutatus redditusve non erit, tantundem modum agri locei quoieique populo leibero perfugeisve det adsignetve]*: Mo, CIL, Jo, sim. Rud. Hu added: *idque in formas publicas facito utei referatur i.u.e.r.e.v.*

For *redditus commutatus*, cf. line 80. For deserters from the Punic side see App. *Lib.* 107–8, esp. 108, 513–14; Livy *Per.* 50. If any land assigned originally to African allies and friends of Rome had later been assigned to a Roman citizen, but land was made available for him in exchange, then the original assignment remained valid and no new provision needed to be made.

The chapter assumes that the assignments in question were only made to Roman citizens. This has been used as an argument that non-Romans were ineligible not only to receive land as colonial allotments but also to purchase land in Africa (see commentary on line 50). However, the land granted to members of the free cities and deserters is likely to have been that closely connected with the city of Carthage itself and this would have probably have fallen within the ambit of the colony of Iunonia. We know in particular that the land between Carthage and Hippo Diarrhytus was given to the Uticenses (App. *Lib.* 135.640). It remains possible that land was sold to non-Romans in parts of Africa beyond the territory of the planned colony. See also line 83 and commentary. Heurgon (1969) published four *termini* with identical Etruscan texts from the region between Thuburbo Maius and Ziqua (Zaghouan), but these may derive from Etruscan emigration in the eighties BC.

LVII (lines 77–8) The duumvir is to ensure that the tribute-paying peoples in Africa possess the land assigned them*

77 (D16, E27, C2) QVAN: aes, Pin, Vett; QVAM: O; *quan[do X virei, quei ex] lege*: Mo, CIL, Jo; *qu⟨e⟩m X[virei, quei ex]*: Rud. CREATIVE: Br. ADSIGNAVERV: Peir, B; ADSIGNAVERVNT: O, Vett; *adsignaveru[ntv]e*: Mo, CIL, Jo (Mo claimed to have seen the lowest horizontal bar of an E before QVOS on C2).

Quantum seems a more apposite supplement in the D-E lacuna than *quando* in the sense of 'inasmuch as'. For the time-limit on the magistrate's activities, cf. lines 52, 53, 78. The legislator seeks to schedule the activities of the duumvir in a manner which recalls the decrees of classical Athenian democracy. For the ten-man commission appointed by the *lex Livia*, cf. App. *Lib.* 135.639, where the commission is said to have been chosen by the senate in 146 BC. *Decem legati*, sent to organise a province or other conquered territory, were normally appointed *ex senatus consulto* (cf. e.g. de Martino, 1958, II.283ff). It does not follow from this chapter that all land, apart from that given to free cities and *perfugae*, was assigned to the *stipendiarii* in 146 BC, as Hinrichs thought (297).

78 (D17, E28) ROMANEI: aes, O, Vett; I ROMANEI: Pigh; *[populo Romano dare oportet, sei quid eius agrei locei ex h.l. ceivis Romanei esse oportet oportebitve, utei de eo agro, quei publicus populei Romanei in Africa est, quei publice non venierit, tantundem modum agrei locei quantum agrei locei ex h.l. ceivis] Romanei*: Hu (613), modifying Rud; *[pro eo agro populo Romano pendere oportebit, sei quid eius agri ex hac lege ceivis Romani esse oportet oportebitve ... de agro, quei publicus populi Romanei in Africa est, tantundem, quantum de agro stipendiario ex hace lege ceivis] Romanei*: Mo, CIL, sim. Jo.

STIPENDIARIEI: aes. VTE: aes; VTEI: O, Pin, Vett.

Q.E.E.V.: B; Q.E.P.V; Peir; R.E.E.V.: O, Vett (in the latter the second E is an addition); *utei [referatur ita utei ei e.] r.e.v.*: Rud; *ute[i referatur i(ta) u(tei) e r(e) p(ublica) f(ide)]q(ue) e(sse) v(idebitur)*: Mo, CIL, Jo (to which we should add the E=*e(ius)* seen by the majority of ancient copyists). The paragraph space is indicated in all copies.

The restorations of earlier editors in the initial lacuna are put into question by the I recorded by Pighius at the beginning of D17, which suggests *popul]i Romanei* rather than *ceivi]s Romanei*. In fact there may well be no mention of individual Roman citizens at all nor of any exchanges of land as such. *Is* before *stipendiarieis* must be dative plural agreeing with that noun, as Mommsen saw. The subject of *det adsignetve* and *facito* can only be the duumvir who is the grammatical subject of the chapter as a whole. If the *stipendiariei* had less land than what was due to them according to the *lex Livia*, then the duumvir was to see that they received it. The *stipendiariei* are probably paying tax in proportion to the land, the *certum stipendium*, which, according to Cicero, the majority of Punic peoples paid (*Verr.* 3.12). Appian (*Lib.* 135.641) mentions a tax both on land and on persons (i.e. a poll tax). The latter was perhaps an alternative to land tax, used with nomads or artisans and craftsmen. The standard formula, *utei e re publica fideque (sua/eius) esse videbitur*, is well established by this time, cf. line 35; *S.C. de philosophis* (Bruns[7], 26); *S.C de Thisbensibus* (Bruns, 37 = *RGDE* 2, lines 39–40, 40–5); also *RGDE* 6, line 9; *RGDE* 7, 50–1; *RGDE* 8, 71–2; *RGDE* 10, A11, B14; *RGDE* 12, 19. Our text seems to have *fideque eius*, not *fideque sua* which is normally used to emphasise that it is the magistrate's own good faith which is in question (cf. the Greek translation, ἴδια πίστις).

LVIII (lines 78–82) The duumvir is (?) to make a record of land remaining public after the various allocations and sales*

78 (E28, C3) CCL (the L being anchor-shaped, like the L in CL in line 77): Peir, B, Ha; CCCL: O, Vett.

79 (D18, E29, C4) *[utei ... com]mutatus*: Mo, CIL, Jo, sim. Rud. LEIBERLRVM: aes. VTICENSIVM Ḥ: aes (the left-hand vertical and a fraction of the cross-bar of H survive); VTICENSIVM: edd veter. TAMPSITANORVM: Ha; AMPSITANORVM: cett edd veter; *H[adrumetinorum T]ampsitanorum*: Rud, Mo, CIL, Jo. AQVIILITANORVM: Peir; AQVILLITANORVM: O, Ha; AQVILITANORVM: B, Vett. TEVDALENSIVM: O, Vett, Ha; TEVBALENSIVM: B. The E fragment ends with the first P of *populei*, which Bo converted into P.R.

The reference to exchange, *com]mutatus redditusve*, shows that in the lost part of the line there must have stood one of the categories of land, in respect of which exchanges could occur. The land sold and declared *ager privatus vectigalisque* is mentioned later in the chapter (line 80). It is, therefore, almost inevitable that a reference to colonial allotments should be restored.

The law then excepts the land of what must be a complete list of the communes, previously allied to Carthage, which after her defeat were rewarded with the status of free people by Rome because of their timely desertion to the Roman cause. That of Utica was critically important for the Romans (Pol. 36.3.1; App. *Lib.* 75.347–8). The Tampsitani seem to be the people of Thapsus, the Aquillitani the people of Acholla; the people beginning with H are surely the Hadrumetini (see the list of defectors in App. *Lib.* 94.446). Usalis (cf. Pliny *HN* 5.4.29 – Uzalis) was identified with Strabo's Zella (17.3.12,831) by Mommsen and Gsell (1914–30, VII.39) – said to be a free city in the neighbourhood of Thapsus and Acholla, i.e. near the coast south of Hadrumetum. Teudalis is located by Pliny (5.3.23) near Hippo Diarrhytus (Bizerta).

80 (D19, E30, C5) EXPRA: aes, Pigh; EXTRA: O, Vett; S EXTRA: Rud, Mo, CIL, Jo (it is unclear what was taken to be the trace of an s); *[venerunt, fuit – adsignatus est de senati] s(ententia)*: CIL, Jo, sim. Mo; *[venerunt, fuit, extra eum agrum* *locum, quei ager locus eis hominibus publice deve senati sententia in Africa datus adsignatusve est, quei ad imperatorem populi Romani bello Poinicio proxsumo perfugerunt, utei s(upra)] s(criptum)*: Rud.

QVA EVM AGRUM LOCVM: O[1]; QVAE: O[2], Vett; -QVE: Scal; IQVE: Bo; \ QVE: D, Br; *commutatusve [non erit, extra] quae*: Rud; *[non erit, extra]que*: Mo, CIL, Jo. IIVIR EX H.L.: O, Scal; II VIREI EX H.L.: Br; II VIREI QVEI EX H.L.: Bo.

D conflates this line of the E fragment with the following one. SIIPENDIARIEIS: Scal; ADSIGNAVERIT: O; ADSIGNAVERITVE: Peir, Vett, Scal, Bo, Br.

QVOD EIVS EX H.L.: O, Vett, Scal; QVOD EIVS: Peir; QVOD EX H.L.: Br, Bo. IN EO: O, Vett, Scal, Br, Bo; RMAM: aes (C5); *in formam*: Rud, Mo, CIL, Jo.

The restoration of a conjectural formula describing the *perfugae* was first made in line 76. The reference to the *forma* at the end of the line picks up the provision in lines 77–8 that the duumvir should record on *formae publicae* the amount of land he had assigned to the *stipendiariei* as their due under the *lex Livia*. For such maps, compare the commentary to line 7 and especially Piganiol (1962) on the *formae* at Arausio (Orange). It may be noted that the latter even recorded rents due to the community from the *centuriae* (*ibid.* 58–62) – very small, it must be admitted, and probably well below the scale of the taxes of the *stipendiarii* here.

81 (D20, E31, C6) ẸREIS: aes; EREIS: O, Vett; GREIS: Pigh; *[erit – leib]ereis*: Mo, CIL, Jo; *[erit, extraque eum agrum locum, quem agrum locum P.Cornelius P.f. procos de eis agreis, quei in Africa sunt, quod eorum poplicum p.R. factum est, de X legatorum sententiis leib]ereis*: Rud. IVSII: aes.

OPPODVM CẠṚT (4 letter-spaces) FVIT QV: aes; OPPIDVM: O[1]; OPPODVM: Pin; OPPODVM CHA: O[2]; OPPIDVM ...FVIT Q: Vett; VPLI ..MLHAB: Pigh; OPPIDV MLHAG: Rud.

E EVM AGRVM: Peir, Scal, Bo, Br; EVM AGRVM: O[2], Vett; QVE (erased) EVM AGRVM: O[1]; *Char[tago] fuit qu[ondam extraqu]e eum agrum*: Mo, CIL, Jo (but the surviving lower halves of A and R are easily confused with H and A and there is no reason to assume an abnormal spelling of CARTHAGO).

EX H.L.LIVIA: Peir, B and (with H. erased) O[1]; EX LEGE LIVIA: O[2]; EX N.L. LIVIA: Vett. FACTI: Br. VTICENSIBVS: O, Vett; VTEI CENSIBVS: Scal, Bo; VTI CENSIBVS: D, Br. RELIQVEI: Peir, O, Vett; RELIQVE: B; RVNT: aes (C6). CE ERVM: aes.

The singular donor of land to Massinissa's family must be Scipio Aemilianus, the victorious commander. However, there is no reason to believe that he can only have done so on the advice of the senatorial commission, especially as the *X viri* created under the *lex Livia* are mentioned later in the line, apparently acting in their own right (this presumably was after Scipio had returned home to his triumph). Scipio's action is described by Pliny (*HN* 5.25) as the creation or recreation of a trench separating Roman territory from that of the kings – a successor to the Punic trenches (cf. Eumachos of Neapolis, *FGH* 178, F2; App. *Lib.* 54.235–6) and later the boundary between Africa Vetus and Nova. Massinissa had claimed in the period preceding the Third Punic War the so-called Great Plains (in the Bagradas valley) and 'the territory of fifty cities which they call Tusca' (App. *Lib*. 68.309). Gsell (1914–30, III, 320) thought that the latter was the area of Thugga. But a recently discovered Numidian boundary stone, dated to the twentieth year of king Mikipsa, shows that the *pagus Thuscae* was in the region of Mactar (Picard, 1966). An imperial inscription reveals that the later *pagus Thuscae et Gunzuzi* had sixty-four *civitates* (*CRAI*, 1963, 124ff). So it seems that in part at least Scipio's action was to give the Numidian royal house what it had previously sought. The language of this law seems to imply that the grant had been formally *precario* and thus liable to retraction at any time, as was maintained by Mommsen (*Ges. Schr*. I. 131–2; cf. Weber, 1891, 186–7; Kaser, 1942, 56). It may be argued that in fact the Romans would not have taken such land back. However, lands which Hiempsal II later occupied in the coastal region, whose possession he subsequently sought to confirm by a clause in a senatorial treaty, had to be specifically excluded from sale in Rullus' agrarian bill and hence must still have been considered the property of the Roman people in 64 BC (Cic. *Leg.Agr*. 2.58).

For the *consecratio* of Carthage, cf. Cic. *Leg.Agr*. 1.5; 2.51; App. *Lib*. 135.639; *BCiv*. 1.24.103. An imperial inscription claims to be a republication of a stone carrying Scipio's dedication of the site to the Lord Baal (*CRAI*, 1966, 61ff). It appears from the reference to wolves seizing the *termini* of Gracchus' land-commission that they had begun surveying the territory of the city, but either no agricultural allotments were made in the area or any recipient of such an allotment was given another outside the site of Carthage in exchange (this situation may have been catered for in lines 66–7 of this law). The centuriation of the Augustan *colonia Iulia Carthago* is oriented differently to the rural centuriation created in the Republic (see the works cited in the commentary to line 67).

The land newly granted to Utica or maintained for that city by the Livian commission is specified here in contrast to the original territories of recognised free cities (line 79) and land assigned to individual deserters to the Roman cause (line 76, probably to be restored in line 80). Appian (*Lib*. 135.640) states that the Romans increased the territory of other free cities and there seems to be a reference to this land in line 75. Possibly there was a general reference to additional land given to the free cities in the lacuna at the beginning of line 80, whereas Utica's privileged status was repeated because it possessed territory previously Punic close to the site of Carthage itself. However, it has been suggested on the basis of this line that Appian was wrong to assert that other cities than Utica profited from an increase of territory (Johannsen, 377–8).

82 *[omnem agrum metiundum terminosque statui curet, eique operei diem deicat, ubi confectum siet*: Rud (cf. lines 97–8); *[agrum omnem, quei in Africa est, quei de eo vectigal decumas scripturamve pro pecore populo aut publicano debebunt, quei ager eis ex h.l. datus redditus commutatus erit, habeant possideant fruanturve et pro eo agro loco vectigal decumas scripturamve, quod post h.l. fruetur, populo aut publicano dent*: CIL; *[agrum – est, iei habeant possideant fruanturve, quei de eo agro vectigal decumas scripturamve pro pecore populo aut publicano dare debent* *debebuntve]*: Mo; *[agrum – est, quibus ager ex h.l. datus redditus commutatus erit, ei habeant possideant fruantur et pro eo agro vectigal decumas scripturam populo aut publicano dent*: Jo.

The interpretation of the chapter hinges on what is considered the most probable restoration of this line. The legislator seems to have carefully listed as exceptions the various categories of land already mentioned by the law and then given an instruction about what remained. This land is not land made private by the law, nor land assigned to colonists, nor land assigned to free peoples, tribute-paying subjects or the royal house of Numidia. It is therefore likely to have the same status as the land left public in the Italian section of the text. Such land would normally have been rented out for agriculture or grazing, and appropriately the law goes on in the following chapters to deal with the collection of rents and taxes. Hinrichs' view (294ff) that there was no *ager a censoribus locatus* in Africa, only *ager privatus vectigalisque*, runs counter both to the probable sense of this chapter and to the references to *vectigal* and *scriptura* in parallel in lines 83–9 (cf. Johannsen, 379ff).

It is therefore likely that the law stated that this remaining public land was subject to rent or tax. However, the chapter is framed as an instruction to the duumvir to accomplish something in 250 days (line 78) and we need to suppose a task defined in scope to match the limited period available. Hence the restorations of Mommsen and Johannsen seem too vague and all-embracing. How could the duumvir, in addition to his other tasks, have ensured within the next 250 days that the people concerned paid their taxes, especially as the next tax-period applicable to those paying *vectigal* on *ager privatus vectigalisque* was some time in the future and those taxes were not due before the Ides of March, 110 BC at the earliest (line 70)? Rudorff's suggestion was more realistic – the demarcation of the remaining public land. However, the surveyors' fieldwork would have been largely over by now, and what was required was a proper record of the land which had not been distributed in the course of the duumvir's operations and a report of this to the relevant authority in Rome. Hence the supplement proposed in the text.

LIX (line 82) Freedom from taxation under the* lex Sempronia *is to be maintained*

82 (D21, E32, C7) PECORE (preceded by an undecipherable trace): aes; O PECORE: Pigh; PECORE: O, Vett; *[Queicumque – pr]o pecore*: Mo, CIL, Jo; *[Queicumque de eo agro, quem agrum locum possident fruunturque vectigal – p]ro pecore*: Rud.

ERI. . .Y: aes; ERIT: Pigh; ER: O, Vett; *eri[t, quei eor]u[m eum agrum habebit] possidebit*: Mo, CIL, Jo; *eri[t quod quis ei]u[s agri]*: Rud. (Neither quite matches the spaces available.) WEIVE: Peir, D, Bo; WVE: Scal; MEIVE: Br; NEIVE: O, Vett (cf. lines 25 and 88 for similar engraver's errors). NEI SCRIPTVRAM: edd veter (exc. Br: NE).

Two questions immediately arise: what sort of land is being discussed here? what is the *lex Sempronia*? Although the reference to *scriptura* at first sight suggests that the subject is unassigned public pasture-land, *ex h.l. datus redditus commutatus erit* must refer to one or more of the operations of the duumvir described in lines 58–77 – with regard to land purchased, land of colonists, etc. It is therefore improbable that the chapter deals with possessors of land leased by the censors as Mommsen thought (*Ges. Schr.* I.153ff), who in any case were most unlikely to have been allowed to escape tax or judged exempt from it. Rather, some category or categories of land-holder are excused *vectigal decumas scripturamve* either on their own land or on nearby *subseciva* or *pascua*. They were evidently not purchasers of land, whose property was *privatus vectigalisque*, nor *stipendiariei*. This leaves the colonists of the *lex Rubria*, the peoples of the free cities and the *perfugae*. Of these the most likely group to be affected by the provisions of a *lex Sempronia* are the colonists or quasi-colonists.

In Mommsen's view the *lex Sempronia* here is the law of C.Gracchus, otherwise known to us as establishing *locatio censoria* for the taxes of Asia (Cic. *Verr.* 3.13): that law would have dealt with more than one province just as the present law did. Similarly, Hardy (1910) argued from this text that C.Gracchus passed a general law dealing with taxation in the provinces (or at least in certain provinces including Asia and Africa). If this solution seems improbable, since the Asiatic taxation was an immensely complex matter in its own right (cf. Engelmann and Knibbe, 1989), and C.Gracchus' law may have had to begin by settling the political organisation of the new province, then the best hypothesis for the present *lex Sempronia* is a complementary plebiscite of C.Gracchus concerned with the taxation of Africa (perhaps also with the sale of land), whose subject-matter was distinct from that of the *lex Rubria*. Hinrichs (289–90, cf. Johannsen, 378) argued that this *lex S.* was a *lex data* relating to the foundation of Iunonia, but it is not termed *quae fuit*, and, although an exception to it has developed, either *de facto* or as the result of interpretation by magistrates (*dare non solitei sunt*), its provisions have been regarded as valid over a period. Nor is there any mention of the repealed *lex Rubria* as an ultimate authority as in earlier chapters relating to colonial allotments.

LX (line 83) Land in Africa is to be leased (? to Latins and* peregrini*) on the same terms as it is to Roman citizens*

83 (D22, E33) *[quem agrum locum populus Romanus ex h.l. locabit, quem agrum locum Latinus peregrinusve ex h.l. possidebit, is de eo agro loco vectigal decumas]*: Mo, CIL, Jo; *[Quei populus leiber, queive socium nominisve Latini, quibus ex formula togatorum milites in Italia imperare solent, agrum publicum in Africa possidebit frueturve, is pro eo agro vectigal decumas]*: Rud.

POPVLVS: aes, edd veter; POPVLV: Mo, CIL, Jo; M AGRVM LOCVM: edd veter; *populu[s Romanus ex h.l. locabit que]m*: Mo, CIL, Jo; *populu[s Romanus aut que]m*: Rud; *populus [Romanus ex h.l. pr. quaestoremve vendere iubebit que]m*: Hin.

The paragraph space at the end of this chapter is not recorded in any humanist copy of E, but follows from the line-length which can be reconstructed from the text of the *repetundae* face.

Rudorff's restoration of the D–E lacuna is too short and Hinrichs' too long. The latter was seeking to avoid any reference to the leasing of land in Africa, but this is precisely what is implied by the references to *vectigal, decumae* and *scriptura* (cf. the commentary to line 82). This chapter prescribes treatment similar to that received by Roman citizens for non-Romans, either as a whole or a particular section among them. For a similar provision, cf. lines 29–30, where we find *Latino peregrinoque*.

LXI (lines 83–4) The praetor is to obtain adequate security for (?) the purchase of the tax-contract relating to land sold in Africa*

83 (E33, C8) PR.QVOIVS ARB.PRO AGRO LOCO: O, Vett, Br, Bo[1]; QVOIVS ARBITRIO AGRO LOCO: Scal; P.R.: Bo[2]; QVOVIS: D. Since we have here a specific category of land defined by a relative clause, I have inserted a demonstrative, *eo*.

84 (D23, E34, C9) *[satis supsignari oportebit . . . praedia empto]ris*: Mo, CIL, Jo; *[ita utei supra scriptum est, populo satis supsignari oportet oportebitve, is facito utei pro eo agro loco, quem publicanus fruendum conduxerit, ita utei s.s.e. praedia dentur. Quibus pro agris praedia data non erunt, pro eis ag]ris*: Rud.

IIIVITO: aes, Pigh; INVITO: O, Vett. IT QVOMINVS: Peir; SIT QVOMINVS: cett edd veter; *supsig[natum] sit*. Rud; *supsig[netur – fax]sit*: Mo, CIL, Jo.

PRAESQVE QVE: O, Scal, D, Br; PRAESQVE QVAE: Vett; PRAES QVAE: Bo; I QVOMQVE: aes (C9).

Mommsen's view of this chapter (*Ges. Schr.* I.140), followed by Johannsen, is that it was a reversion to the matter discussed in chapters LIV–LV* (lines 73–4), the taking of security from purchasers of land in Africa who had not paid the price. He also assumed that the *publicani* were involved in collecting the purchase-money on the basis of his interpretation and restoration of line 70 (for the dubiousness of this interpretation see the commentary on that line). His view of the present chapter does not depend on this extra assumption, but it is not convincing in itself. For it would have been odd that the taking of security from purchasers should have been treated separately and differently in lines 73–4 and 83–4. The alternative view of Rudorff (129) and Hinrichs (289) is that the security concerned here is that given by a tax-contractor for the taxes whose exploitation he has acquired. *Eo quei dabit* is presumably the man who has bought the tax-contract, but the sense of *dabit* is obscure – 'will be giving security', 'will be paying money'? Perhaps the sense of this chapter is that the purchaser must either make a down-payment combined with the furnishing of guarantors and security or else, if he is unwilling to make the down-payment, the praetor must ensure that the amount of security to be taken is trebled. For the taking of security from contractors, compare the Asiatic customs law (Engelmann and Knibbe, 1989), lines 101ff, 109ff, where an upper limit of fivefold security is set, and, for the contractor under the Principate paying in yearly instalments, *ibid.* lines 99ff. The restoration *empto]ris* is possible, but far from certain. If the present view of the chapter is correct, *conducto]ris* is also a possibility, or *cognito]ris*, cf. the *praediorum cognitores* in *lex Flav.mun.* (*Malac.*), chs. 63–5 = *lex Irnit.* VIIB.

LXII (lines 85–6) The terms established by the censors of 115* BC *for the payment of tax on land and grazing are to remain in force for the relevant tax-payers*

85 (D24, E35, C10) *[Quantum vectigal decumas scripturamve pecoris eum, quei agrum locum aedificium in Africa possidebit ... quei ager]*: Mo, CIL; *[Quantum – possidebit, quei ager locus colonei eiusve, quei in colonei numero scriptus est, non fuerit, queive ager]*: Jo; *[Quae vectigalia, quas decumas quasve scripturas pecoris eum, quei quomque agrum locum aedificium in Africa possederit, quei ager locus aedificium Romae publice venierit, quei ager]*: Rud. LEIBERORVM: aes (with a space after the first R, owing to a flaw in the bronze which continues through the next three lines below); LEIBERORVM: edd veter; *leiber{t}orum*: Jo. AEDIEICIO: aes. DICTA: aes, edd veter; *dicta q[uam L.Caecilius Cn.Domitius cen]s*: Mo, CIL (*dicta [quam –* : Rud); *dicta q[uam Cn.Paperius cos. quamve L.Caecilius – cen]s*: Jo (but there is not enough space for this).
AGREI AEDIFICIEI LOCEI: Bo; *agri⟨s⟩ aedificii⟨s⟩ loci⟨s⟩*: Rud.
DEIX: Peir, Scal, Br; DE IX: Bo; DEIXE: D; DEI: O, Vett; ERVNT: aes (C10).

There is no need to emend *agri aedificii loci*, as Rudorff proposed, since it can be construed as a genitive dependent on *legem*. The apparent distinction drawn between the *lex agri aedificii loci* and the *lex vectigalibus publiceis fruendeis locandeis vendundeis* has been stressed by Mommsen (*Ges. Schr.* I.144) and Johannsen (391). However, the *lex* remained a single *lex* (*e.l. dicta quam – legem deixerunt*), which had two aspects – the terms under which the taxpayer had to pay for his land, territory or building, and the terms under which the tax-collector had to contract for and exploit the taxes (cf. Burdese, 1952, 104). The types of land in question here would have been (i) *ager privatus vectigalisque* and (ii) land leased from the censors for grazing and other purposes. A further possibility is the land of the *stipendiariei*. However, although an early imperial dedication to a quaestor by the *mancupes* of the *stipendium* from Africa (*ILS*, 907 = Ehrenberg and Jones, *Documents*, 191) shows the collection of *stipendium* by contractors then, their farming of this tax was probably not through *censoria locatio*, but handled by the quaestor, as the dedication suggests. Here the *censoria locatio* seems to preclude any direct payment of tax to a Roman magistrate. Johannsen was right to supplement in the initial lacuna an exception for the territory of the colonists, but there is room for other exceptions.

86 (D25, E36, C11) *[tantundem post h.l. rogatam, quei agrum locum aedificium in Africa possidet possidebit, publicano vectigal decumas scriptura]mque*: Mo, CIL, Jo; *[idem is, quei eum agrum aedificium locumque, quei ager locus aedificium in Africa est, quei Romae publice venieit, quei ager locus populorum leiberorum perfugarum non fuerit, ex h.l. possidebit, publicano vectigal decumas scriptura]mque*: Rud. A space is left after PECORIS on account of the flaw in the bronze. ALITERVE DARE DEBEO: aes. PEQVSQVE NE: aes; PEQVSQVE: edd veter; *ne[i aliter alieisve legibus]*: Mo, CIL, Jo; *ne[cubei nisei]*: Rud; *ne[i quod aliud]*: Hu (the last two supplements are too short for the lacuna). The paragraph-space is shown by Peir, O, Scal, Br.

This line reveals something of the details of the *lex censoria*. Not only the amount of tax-payment was specified, but the manner and place of payment (*aliubeive aliterve*). It is not clear from the surviving text whether the fixing of the maximum sum payable at the level laid down by the censors of 115 BC was to be permanent or only valid until the next auction of tax-contracts. However, it is unlikely that the yield of this tax was being fixed for all time.

LXIII (lines 86–7) The terms established by the censors of 115 BC for the tax-collectors in Africa are to remain in force*

86 (E36, C11) QVE VECTIGALIA: Scal, Br. PVBLICA: om. Bo[2]; ROMANEI: Bo[2]; Bo[1] merges this text with that of the following line. SVNT QVAE: O, Vett; SVNT QVA; Peir, B (the final E of QVAE is in fact on the C fragment).

87 (D26) *[locaverunt vendideruntve, queiquomque magistratus post hance legem rogatam ea vectigalia locabit vendetve, quominus publicano eam legem dicat quo pl]us*: Mo, CIL, Jo; *[locaverunt vendideruntve, quei quomque ea vectigalia fruenda conducta redemptave habebit, quod ob ea vectigalia fruenda populo dare debebit, ubeive eam pequniam solvere debebit, id ibeive quominus] is*: Rud.
The lacuna after DEBEAT is caused by the flaw in the bronze.

Mommsen's restoration allowed the price of the tax-contract to be changed in future, but in that case we might have expected *quo plus minusve populo dare debeat*. It is more likely that we have a provision parallel to that in line 86 about the taxpayer: just as the latter was protected against a change in terms regarding what he was expected to pay, so the tax-collector was protected against a change in terms which would have put him at a disadvantage. Hence the restoration *min]us* is unlikely. I have preferred *ampli]us*, as in line 86 (cf. line 60), to Mommsen's *pl]us*. The rest of my supplement is on the analogy of line 89. The protection of the terms granted to the *publicani* would only have been valid as long as that contract was valid. It was important, because the price of the contract was paid in arrears, either in instalments or in a lump sum at the end of the contract, perhaps after an initial down-payment (see commentary on line 84). It should be noted that the proceeds of *ager privatus vectigalisque* assigned by the duumvir according to the provisions of this law would not become available to the *publicanus* until after the next tax-contract (lines 70–2 with commentary).

LXIX (lines 87–9) The magistrate who in future sells a tax-contract in Africa shall not alter the rules for the collection of tax or pasture-tax laid down by the censors of 115* BC *without the consent of those who possess the land*

87 (D26, E37, C12))VBLICA: Br; PVBLICA: O, Vett, Scal, Bo²; *iudicio [suo quae] publica*: Rud; *iudicio [curationeve erit, quei quomque quae]*: Mo; *[potestateve – quae]*: CIL, Jo. ROMANEI: Bo². VENDETVE O: Peir; VENDETVE: cett edd veter. The tail of the Q of QVOM is visible on the C fragment.

There does not seem to be enough space to restore *quei quomque* in the supplement in the D–E lacuna. For *mag. prove mag. queive – potestateve erit*, cf. *lex Rubr.Gall.* XX.50: *neive mag. prove mag., neive quis pro quo imperio potestateve erit*; *lex Gen.Urs.*, cap. 94: *neive quis pro eo imper. potestat.ve facito* (see also line 10 and *lex rep.* 70).

88 (D27, E38, C13) EX LEGE (preceded by a trace of a horizontal bar): aes; E EX LEGE: Pigh; EX LEGE: O, Vett; *[nei eis vectigalibus legem deicito, quo invitieis ieis, quei eum agrum possidebunt, publicano quid facere liceat, quod ei non licuit . . facer]e*: Mo, CIL, Jo; *[neive alia lege ea vectigalia fruenda locato neive vendito atqu]e*: Rud (more plausibly regarding the end of the lacuna).

LOCAVERVN (followed by a trace of a horizontal bar): aes, Mo; LOCAVERVNT: edd veter. M DEIXERINT NEIVE QVOI: Scal, Br; DEIXERVNT NEIVE QVOI: Bo; QVOD: O, Vett (omitting previous letters). ∧ VCETVR: Peir; INWCETVR: Scal; IWCETVR: Bo; IMCETVR: Br; . . .CETVR: O², Vett; ⟨*pas*⟩*cetur*: O¹, Rud, Mo, CIL, Jo. For intrusive Ws, cf. lines 25, 82. LEGE DE: edd veter; CITO: aes (C13). O and Vett make no break between E38 and 39.

89 *[aliter pascatur – deixerunt]*: Mo, CIL, Jo; *[pro eo pecore, obve id, quod in eo agro pequs pascetur, scripturae nomine plus exigatur, atque ex lege dicta quam L.Caeci.Cn.Dom.cens legem deixerunt]*: Rud.

The two previous chapters seem to have been preserving unaltered the tax-contracts laid down by the censors of 115 BC from the point of view of both taxpayer and tax-collector. The present chapter apparently instructs future magistrates (i.e. censors or any magistrates carrying out their functions, such as consuls in Rome or pro-magistrates in Africa), who are letting contracts according to a certain code of regulations (*lex*) in Africa, to maintain in force the *lex* established in 115 BC. Rudorff's restoration here would entail that these magistrates were not entitled in the *lex* to change the amount of tax payable. But this is perhaps not the point. The legislator clearly seems to have wished to maintain the principles and modalities of the taxes (which would have included the basic rate of tax), cf. the Asiatic tax-dossier (Engelmann and Knibbe, 1989), which contains an accumulation of *leges dictae* of successive magistrates. However, this would not have excluded variations in individual assessments and hence in the global sum collected. This chapter applies to the taxes on land and pasturage in Africa handled by the censors of 115 BC (see line 88, *quom eorum agrorum – locaverunt, quod in eis agreis pequs*). We should perhaps supplement after *vendetve* (at the beginning of line 88) *quae vectigalia L.Caecili.Cn.Dom.cens,fruenda locaverunt vendiderunt*. Although the reference to the possessors of land, whose consent is required for any change, occurs in the surviving text only in relation to *scriptura*, it could have appeared earlier in relation to the tax on land.

LXV (line 89) The terms established by the consul of 113* BC *for taxes in Africa are to remain in force*

89 (D28) OMINVS: aes, edd veter; *[Quae vectigalia fruenda in Africa Cn.Paperius cos. vendidit locavitve, qu]ominus*: Mo, CIL, Jo; *[Quae vectigalia in Africa sunt, quae Cn.Paperius cos. vendidit locavitve, ea qu]ominus*: Rud. For the restoration here, cf. line 86.

VENDVNDEIS E.H.N.R.: aes, Pigh; – E.H.L.N.R.: O, Vett, Rud; *vendundeis ⟨locandeis deixit⟩ e.h.⟨l.⟩n.r.*: Mo, CIL, Jo.

The contracts let by Cn.Papirius Carbo (*cos.* 113) were presumably for land which had only recently become taxable – probably *ager privatus vectigalisque* which had been purchased by individuals since the censorial auction in 115 (cf. Johannsen, 386). The briefness of this chapter suggests that it only sought to maintain Carbo's regulations until the auction of a new contract.

LXVI (lines 89–90) (?) Existing roads and paths should not be closed or obstructed*

89 (D28, E39, C14) *Quei [ager in Africa est,. . .quae viae in eo] agro*: Rud, Mo, CIL, Jo. CENTVRIA: aes (C14) – the engraver ran out of space at the edge of the tablet.

90 *[itineri publico inserviunto]*: Rud.

The *limites* form the grid of dividing lines between the centuries and also serve as paths around them, cf. e.g. Front. *De limitibus*, 10–15 Thul; Hyg. 156ff Thul; Dilke, 1971, 88ff. The objection can be made to the restoration of *viae*, that, if the Romans had been imposing a new grid of centuriation on Africa, this would have been incompatible with the maintenance of the old Punic roads. Yet it is difficult to conceive an alternative to *viae*. What is being declared public here is closely allied to the *limites* between centuries and existed before 146. The text may have had the form, *Quei [ager in Africa est, quae quomque viae post h.l.r. erunt, quae in eo] agro . . .* The implication of this would be that the Romans had been satisfied with maintaining some Punic roads and had not added more themselves, but that the system of *limites* had been linked to them.

LXVII (lines 90–1) False declarations and information laid about such offences*

90 (D29, E40, C15) RVM (preceded by trace): aes; GRVM: O, Pigh; AGRVM: Vett; *[IIvir, quei ex h.l. factus creatusve erit, sei apud eum, quoi ager in Africa adsignatus est, eum agrum professus erit, ei eum agrum, quem a]grum*: Mo, CIL, Jo; *[Quoi ager in Africa est, quem is a]grum*: Rud. *Adsigna[tus est, professus erit, profiteri non oportuit . . . nei dato]*: Mo, CIL, Jo; *adsigna[tus est – non oportuit, eum agrum ei IIvir nei dato]*: Rud. ADIOVDICATO: Bo. *rem [ita]indicio*: Mo, CIL; *rem [ita esse]*: Rud, Hu; *rem [ita ⟨esse⟩]*: Jo.

The present restorations seek to make those of Mommsen more intelligible. I have preferred the future perfect, *oportuerit*, to *oportuit*, since the *professio* is something that the law is prescribing for the future. There is only space for three letters in the E–C lacuna. Hence Johannsen assumed that *esse* was omitted by the engraver. But a noun clause in this law would have been more elaborate and it is possible, as the text stands, to construe *eam rem* as an accusative of respect.

This law provides that, after the creation of *IIviri*, one of them should demand the declaration by possessors of land held in Africa as a preliminary to the ratification of these holdings (lines 52–7). This certainly applied to land purchased and now private (line 54) and probably to allotments under the *lex Rubria*. The latter are mentioned in line 55, and *neive emptum neive adsignatum esse – iudicato* (line 57) seems designed to cover both types of land. *Professio* in the wrong *numerus* would have covered declaring purchased land to be colonial land – in order to avoid tax – and doing the converse, in order to avoid the restrictions attached to such allotments. For the use of informers, cf. App. *BCiv*. I.18.73 (referring to the situation after the *lex Sempronia* of 133, when the possessors failed to declare their holdings of *ager publicus* in Italy) and Baumann, 1979, 396.

91 *[quei eam rem ita indicaverit, in eo numero agri, quo non oportuit, professus esse iudicatus erit . . . partem . . . magistratus, qui de ea re iudicaverit, dato adsignato.]*: CIL, Jo, sim. Mo; *[in eo numero agri, quo in numero agri profiteri oportuit, professus non esse convictus fuerit, partem .. dato adsignato esse iudicato]*: Rud; *[in eo numero – convictus fuerit, quantum pequniae sit, inde decimam partem dare damnas esto, deque ea re IIviri, quei ex h.l. factus creatusve erit, iurisdictio reciperatorumque datio addictio esto*: Hu.

Mommsen and Rudorff took *is* in *quod is indicio eius* (line 90) to be the culprit. However, the parallel of *quei eam rem indicio fuerit* suggests that he is the informer. Moreover, it is difficult to understand this *is* as the culprit when the *ei* in *ei eius agri* immediately preceding this refers to the informer. Hence the restoration offered in the text. *Eius agri* implies that the reward was to be land in Africa. Huschke suggested that the reward would have been a tenth of the value of the land involved on the basis of Livy 28.46.4–6: '*agri Campani regionem a fossa Graeca ad mare versam vendere quaestores iussi, indicio quoque permisso qui ager civis Campani fuisset, uti is publicus populi Romani esset; indici praemium constitutum, quantae pecuniae ager indicatus esset, pars decima*'.

LXVIII (lines 91–2) Land should be provided in exchange for allotments that were publicly sold*

91 (D30, E41, C16) ACTVM: aes, O, Vett; FACTVM: Pigh; *[Quibuscum trans]actum est*: Rud, Mo, CIL, Jo. *Haberent [possiderent fruerentur, eis . . .quantus]*: Mo, CIL, Jo; *[possiderent fruerenturve, . . .queiquomque]*: Rud. AGRI: Peir, Br, O, Vett; AGREI: Scal, Bo. DE: O, Vett, Scal; D.L.: Bo, Br.

Pighius was the first man known to us to copy fragment Dbc and regularly preserves a little more of the text than can be discoverd from the bronze or other sources. We should therefore assume that FACTVM is correct. This suggests a clause such as *quod eius publicum populi Romani] factum est*, limiting a reference to a certain piece of territory, or *de quibus senatus consultum] factum est*, providing the authority for the *utei* clause.

92 *[agri de eo agro, quei publicus populi Romani in Africa est, quei publice non venieit, magistratus commutato]*: Mo, CIL, Jo; *[agri loci de eo agro quei ager locus publice non venieit venieritve, IIvir reddito: quoi ita reddiderit, ei adsignatum fuisse ioudicato]*: Rud.

Mommsen (*Ges. Schr.* 1.133), followed by Johannsen (395), held that this chapter concerned land in Africa given in exchange to those, who had possessed land rented from the censors, but whose land had been publicly sold. However, '*utei bona, quae habuisent, agrumque, quei eis publice adsignatus esset, haberent*' does not seem appropriate language for land leased on a contract (contrast line 32). Rather, possessors of another kind had been confirmed in their holdings of property and land publicly assigned to them, but some, if not all, of this land had been later sold and a compensatory grant was to be made. Such language would suit the African *stipendiariei* (lines 77–8, 81) or the free peoples (75–6, 79, 81). There seems, however, to be no need for a further chapter about them, in view of the provisions of lines 75–81, or indeed about the former colonists or the purchasers of land in Africa.

Must, then, this chapter refer to Africa? After the end of the preceding chapter on informers, there is nothing which certainly relates to Africa and there are contrary indications. Apart from the problem arising from line 92, *is ager ex s.c. datus ads[i]gnatus est* (line 93) does not fit well with the rest of the African section, where land-distribution has been authorised by the *lex Livia*, the *lex Rubria*, possibly (though not in my view) the *lex Sempronia* (line 82) and the present law. Although the first, and indeed the only specific mention of Greece comes in line 96, where the duumvir is organising the *ager Corinthiorum*, that is no reason for believing that a section on Greece began precisely there. If we take the African section as a parallel, it runs at least from lines 48 to 52 of this text before it reaches the operations by the duumvir to register and allocate land. There was of course land in Greece, other than the *ager Corinthiorum*, which had been taken over by the Roman people in 146 BC after the defeat of the Achaeans and their allies. Cicero states that Mummius brought many cities of Achaea and Boeotia under Roman rule (2 *Verr.* 1.55), while Pausanias (7.16.9–10) speaks generally of the imposition of tribute on Greece and political measures against Achaean, Boeotian and Phocian cities, cf. Accame, 1946, 10ff. We know that later tax-contracts related to land in Euboea (*S.C. de Asclepiade*, Sherk *RGDE* 22, Lat. 11, Greek 23) and land in the neighbourhood of Oropus (*S.C. de Oropiis, RGDE* 23, 19ff), while Sulla was able to give 10,000 *iugera* in Euboea to Mithridates' general, Archelaus (Plut. *Sulla* 23.2). The only Greek land which apparently figured in Rullus' sale-list in 64–63 BC was the Corinthian (Cic. *Leg.Agr.* 1.5; 2.51), but this may be explained by the fact that other Roman public land in Greece had already been disposed of. It may therefore be suggested that the subject of this chapter is Roman allies who were publicly assigned land in Greece in 146 BC or later. We know from Strabo (8.6.23 – 381), for example, that the people of Sicyon were given the majority of the territory of Corinth.

LXIX (lines 92–3) Neither pasture tax nor other tax shall be paid in respect of land or buildings which the quaestor has publicly sold*

92 (D31, E42, C17) E FRVITVRVE: aes (only faint traces of first E); Pigh; FRVITVRVE: O, Vett; *[Quei in Africa agrum – possidetv]e*: Mo, CIL, Jo; *[Quem quis in Africa agrum possessionem quoiusve agri possessionisve superficium posside]t*: Rud. PR.VE PV: aes, O, Vett; PRVE P: Pigh; OB EVM AGRVM: O, Vett; 3 EVM AGRVM: Scal, Br, Bo[1]; 7 EVM: Bo[2]; *pu[blice vendiderit ... o]b eum*: Mo, CIL, sim. Jo; *pu[blice in agro manu capto inve bonis sectionis quoius vendidit], ob*: Hu (comparing Varro *RR* 2.10.4: *tumve cum in bonis sectioneve cuius publice veniit*, referring to purchases of slaves). POSSESIONE: Peir, Scal, Bo, Br; POSSESIONEM: O, Vett; IVM: aes (C17); *possesione[m – superfic]ium*: Mo, CIL, Jo; *possesionem [superficium vectigal decumas stipend]ium*: Rud. SCRIPIVRAM: aes.

93 *[vectigal solvito]*: Mo, CIL, Jo; *[solvito]*: Rud.

The term *superficium* only occurs here in the surviving text of the law. This is, moreover, the first reference to buildings in the provincial section and the first occasion when the term *possesio* is used in this section. In spite of the frequent discussion of the sale of public land earlier in the sub-section which unquestionably deals with Africa, this chapter speaks in different terms about what seems to be a different matter, as Huschke (647) realised, although his argumentation is not entirely sound. Johannsen explained this chapter as exempting from tax the man who had lost his land, because it had been publicly sold to some one else, but such a provision seems otiose nor is there any good reason why it should have appeared at this point. In my view the law here deals with sales of land, which did not become *ager privatus vectigalisque*. Exemption from *scriptura* in respect of a *superficium*, i.e. a building of some kind, seems odd, but may be explained by assuming that the sales involved pasture-land and its associated steadings. Land used primarily for pasture is a feature of Greece as much as, if not more than, of Punic Africa.

LXX (lines 93–4) Confirmation of assignments of lands made in consequence of a* senatus consultum

93 (D32, E43. C18) *h[ominum . . .dum magistratus, quo de]*: Mo, CIL (Jo omits *dum*); *h[ominum sunto, facitoque is pr. prove pr., quo de]*: Rud. EA RE: O, Vett; A RE: Peir, Scal, Br. IN IOVS: O, Vett; IM IOVS: Peir, Scal, Br; A REI MIOVS: Bo[1]; A REMIOIVS: Bo[2]. Ṭ VTEI: aes (C18) – there is a trace of a crossbar at the edge of the fragment.

[ita – de]t utei: Mo, CIL, Jo; *[. .neive aliter atque] utei*: Rud.

Mommsen (*Ges. Schr.* I.135, cf. Johannsen, 395) believed that this chapter still concerned African *ager censorius*, but what survives of the language does not lend support to his conclusion. Weber (1891, 163) thought that land was being granted to *navicularii* who transported grain to Rome, but this seems an anachronism in the Republic. Allocation in accordance with a *senatus consultum* does not occur elsewhere in the provincial section of this law (except perhaps in line 91 above). The obvious occasion for such a decree would be before the despatch of a commission (*decem/quinque legati*) to settle conquered territory. The recipients, like those in chapter LVIII* (lines 91–2), are probably allies of Rome. The magistrate, who is required to perform jurisdiction, would be a proconsul or propraetor.

Division into chapters now becomes again too conjectural to be worth attempting.

94 (D33, E44, C19) OS: aes, edd veter, Mo; *[IIvir, quei ex h.l. factus creatusve erit, is in diebus . . proxsumeis, quibus factus creatusve erit, facito utei horrea certis locis constituantur, quo fructus s]uos*: Rud. *adsignatus[ve est . . . agrum locum ex h.l.]*: Mo, CIL, Jo. DARI REDDI ADSIGNARI: O, Vett; DARI – ADSIGNAR: Scal, Br, Bo; RI REDDI ADSIGNAR: Peir. *ceivis R[omanus*: Mo, CIL, Jo. *adsignatus [relictusve est, quibusve agrum locum ex h.l.] dari reddi adsignari [oportebit. Quei ager locus . . . e]um agrum locum ceivis R[omanus*: Rud.

Rudorff and Mommsen deduced from the word *comportent* that this line referred to the transport of the fruits of the harvest. However, *comportare* is used for the transport of supplies of all kinds, and it could refer to the new settlers bringing in their chattels, when they occupied the land.

95 (D34, E45, C20) VODQVE: aes, O; QVODQVE: Pigh, Mo. L.C: aes, O, Pigh; L.CA: Vett; *L.C[alpurnio – fiet*: Mo, CIL, Jo.

A possible explanation of the mention of harvests in III BC and perhaps later is that the law was prescribing that the man who was in possession of certain land at the time of the harvests in question, was responsible for taxes or rents due on the crops. This would have been important, if land, which had been rented, was about to be distributed or purchased before the next harvest.

96 (D35, C21) IS QVIBVS: aes (apex of the first I just visible), Mo; S QVIBVS: edd veter, Rud; *[Quei–proxsume]is*: Rud, Mo, CIL, Jo. DRIT: aes. M LOCVM: aes, O, Vett; VM LOCVM: Pigh, Mo.; *a[gru]m locum*: Rud.

Corinthiorum [fuit, quod eius agri locei publicum populei Romanei factum est, e]xtra: Rud.

For the confiscation of Corinthian territory in 146, cf. Cic. *Leg.Agr.* 1.5; 2.51; for the cession of the greater part to the Sicyonians, Strabo 8.6.23 (381). No doubt up to this time holders of this territory had paid rents to the Roman people, perhaps collected through a censorial contract, as Mommsen conjectured (*Ges. Schr.* I.145). Whether the Sicyonians paid rent or they were given the land, as apparently the Uticans were given Punic territory in Africa (line 81 and commentary), is not clear.

97 (D36, C22) *[... agrum locum] quem*: Mo, CIL, Jo; *[...extraque eum agrum locum] quem*: Rud. *me[tiun]dum*: Rud, Mo, CIL, Jo. STATVI: aes, but the final downstroke is at the very edge of the bronze, hence probably the vertical of an E. ỌM A: aes (with apparently an interpunct between M and A); *eu]m a[grum*: Mo, CIL, Jo.

It is interesting that a magistrate, probably the duumvir mentioned in the preceding line, is required to carry out centuriation in the *ager Corinthiorum*. For centuriation already existing in Africa, cf. lines 66 and 89. The operations in Greece may be relevant to the subsequent proposal of Saturninus to put a colony or colonies in Achaea (*Vir.Ill.* 73.5).

98 (D37) SQVE LOC: aes, Pigh; SVE LOC: O[1]; SVE LOCV: O[2], Vett; *opu]sque*: Mo, CIL, Jo; *loc[at]o*: Rud, Mo, CIL, Jo. ECTVM: aes, edd veter; *u[bei conf]ectum*: Rud; *u[bei perf]ectum*: Mo, CIL, Jo.

There seems little point in fixing a date for work which has already been completed (*perfectum siet* can hardly mean 'will be'/ 'is to be completed'). Hence the restoration, *infe]ctum*, proposed here, which has the additional advantage of fitting better into the short lacuna.

Mommsen (*Ges. Schr.* I.145) compared *Dig.* 11.6.1 pr., where it is stated that a contract of *locatio conductio* was not thought to exist with a *mensor*, and argued that the passage was not in conflict with the present text, since the *mensor* was not entering into a contract with a private citizen but a community. I assume that the contract was being let by the duumvir on behalf of the Roman people. However, the contractor may not in fact be measuring and assigning land here but carrying out some other public work in Corinthian territory.

99 (D38) RV: aes (the top of the two letters are preserved); CRVM: Pigh; not recorded by O, Vett, nor by Rud, Mo, CIL, Jo. S AGRI: aes; *[...quod eius] agri*: Mo, CIL, Jo; *[Quei ager locus aedificium Corinthiorum fuit, quod eius agri locei aedificiei ex h.l. venire oportebit, quod eius]*: Rud. *Quoieiqu[e emptum] erit*: Rud, Mo, CIL, Jo. PEQVNIAI O: aes; PEQVNIAI Q: Pigh; PEQVNIAE O: O; PEQVNIAE: Vett; *pequniae q[uam ob eos agros loca aedificia populo dare debebit, praedia praevidesque dato*: Rud.

In the light of the word *pequniai* and the following line, this chapter seems to be concerned with the purchase of land. *Emptum*, therefore, is an inevitable restoration in the space available. If Pighius correctly read CRVM, and not GRVM, then the most likely restoration is *sa]crum* and the line may have run, '*quod quomqe, extra quod... sa]crum[est, eiu]s agri loci aedificiei quoieiqu[e emptum] erit*'.

100 (D39) VIDES: aes; *manceps praedia prae]videsque*: Rud, Mo; *manceps prae]videsque*: CIL, Jo. SV: aes, O; SVN: Rud, Mo; *sun[to eaque]*: Rud, Mo, CIL, Jo. MANCVPVI: aes; MANCVP VS: Pigh; MANCVPV: O; MANCVPI: Vett; *mancupu[m praevidum is quaestor, quei aerarium provinciam optinebit, in tabuleis publiceis scripta habeto*: Mo, CIL, Jo, sim. Rud (cf. line 46).

101 (D40) ḌIBVSQVE: aes, O; *here]dibusque*: Rud; *ab ipsis here]dibusque*: Mo, CIL, Jo. PERSEQVTIO E: aes, O; *persequtio e[sto. Quei] ager*: Mo, CIL, Jo; *persequtio h[ac lege esto. Quei]*: Rud. EDIF: aes; EDIFI: Pigh; EDI: O; AED: Vett.

If a purchaser of land should have failed to pay the price but had provided *praedes*, then they were liable. If such security was unavailable, land in Africa was to be resold for cash (cf. lines 73–4). Hence *praevi]dibusque* seems a safer supplement here than *here]dibusque*. It has been assumed since Mommsen (*Ges. Schr.* I.145) that the land up for sale here is Corinthian land. However, as Mommsen noted, according to Cicero (*Leg.Agr.* 1.5; 2.51) this land was still on Rullus' sale-list in 64–3 BC. It was certainly *vectigalis* at that time, but cannot have been *ager privatus vectigalisque*, like other land sold under the present law. We must therefore conclude that either the sale of Corinthian land initiated by the present law remained incomplete – which would be understandable if the legislator had reserved some land for distribution in colonial allotments – or else these last three lines refer to some other land than that of Corinth.

102 (D41) *populo] dare*: Mo. PỴ ... RE IN IOVS ADI: aes; RE IN IOVS ADV: Pigh; RE IN IOVS A: O, Vett; *pr. [prove pr. quo de ea] re in ious adi[tum erit*: Mo, CIL; *– adi[tum erit, ita de ea re iudicium det, utei de ea re in h.l.s.est*: Jo (cf. line 93).

This chapter seems to be prescribing a sanction against infringement of the law (cf. *Tab.Heracl.* 19; *lex lat.Bant.* 9ff). In this case the magistrate to be approached might well be the praetor in Rome. However, the bronze does not read PR. The P is followed by what is most probably a V (or conceivably the intrusive W that corrupts the text in lines 25, 82 and 88). Perhaps, however the P is corrupt and the line should read, '*Qu[em mag. de ea] re...*'.

103 (D42) I VENIERIT N: aes (the T is blurred and there was a letter now almost obliterated before N). The base of Db has unintelligible traces.

104 (D43) POSSES: aes; POSSESI: O, Mo; POSSESSI: Rud; *possesi[ones]*: CIL, Jo.

105 (D44) OI. I: aes; OI: O; PLI: Mo, CIL, Jo. Perhaps *qu]oi i[s*.

Date and identity of the lex agraria

The general historical context of the law is clear from its frequent references to the laws of Tiberius and Caius Gracchus: it must belong to the aftermath of their legislation. More precisely, it refers to the future wine and oil harvest in what can only be the consular year 111 BC (line 95 – *P.Cornelio L.C[alpurnio]*). Note also the reference to the preceding censorship of L.Caecilius and Cn.Domitius in 115–4 (lines 87–8), the consul of 113 (line 89) and the consuls of 112 (line 29, probably also 54 and 63). The reference in line 95 in itself dates the law after the election of the consuls of 111, probably late in the year 112, as was customary before Sulla, and before the next vintage and olive harvest. However, the use of the next Ides of March as a terminal date for law-suits about possession (lines 18–19) suggests that a reasonable interval would elapse before this date (the reference in line 70 is less significant, because this is only to the first kalends of March after the new tax-assessment). The law, therefore, was passed some time between 1 March 111 BC, and the vintage in the August following – about the time that the Romans first sent an army to oppose Jugurtha. Just as the *lex repetundarum* was originally identified by humanist scholars with the *lex Servilia* of Glaucia, so the agrarian law was identified with the *lex Thoria* by Sigonio (*De antiquo iure Italiae*, 220) and other scholars – though Pighius (*Annales urbis Romae*, III, pp. 136–7) expressed some doubt. Cicero makes two references to an agrarian law passed by a Sp.Thorius in this period. One is to a *bon mot* of 'Appius maior' in a debate '*de agris publicis et de lege Thoria*' concerning the cattle of Lucilius, presumably the satirist (*de Or.* 2.284). If the Appius is the later consul of 79, the incident falls in the late second century, at the earliest *c.* 115–110. Alternatively, if he is the *cos. suff.* 130 or we assume an otherwise unknown elder brother of the *cos.* 79, the *lex Thoria* has a wider time-bracket, but may still belong in the aftermath of the Gracchan legislation (see below). The other passage is the well-known crux, *Brutus* 136: *Sp.Thorius satis valuit in populari genere dicendi, is qui agrum publicum vitiosa et inutili lege vectigali* (codd. meliores: *vectigale*) *levavit*.

I have quoted earlier (pp. 47–8) the passage from Appian (*BCiv.* 1.27) listing three post-Gracchan agrarian laws. The second of these, said to have been passed by a Sp.Borius, brought to an end land-distribution, but confirmed holdings of current possessors, while imposing a rent on them; the third of these, according to Appian, abolished the rents. The problem of interpreting the text from Cicero's *Brutus* has been compounded by attempts to identify Appian's Sp.Borius with Cicero's Thorius and to reconcile the accounts given of their laws in the two sources. How should the *Brutus* passage be translated? One solution (proposed by Rudorff, 1839, 77ff and Zancan, 1935, 66, *inter alios*) is to render *lege* as an instrumental ablative, while reading *vectigali* and understanding this as separative. Hence, 'Thorius ... relieved public land from rent by a defective and worthless law' (or, in Zancan's view, 'legal status'). This interpretation might be a description of our epigraphic law, since it did remove rent from the chief categories of land dealt with by the land-commission (cf. lines 19–20 and see below) but hardly one of Appian's second law. Alternatively, with for example Mommsen, *Ges. Schr.* 1.69ff, and Badian, 1964, 235ff, we may take *lege* as separative and *vectigali* as instrumental. Thus, 'Thorius ... relieved the public land from a defective and worthless law by a rent.' Consequently, Thorius and Borius might be identical but it would be unlikely that Thorius was the author of the law on the bronze. It has further been suggested, recently by Burdese, 1952, 97–8 and Douglas, 1956, that *vectigali* agrees with *lege* and the sentence means 'Sp.Thorius ... relieved the public land of a faulty and useless rent-law.' This at first sight attractive interpretation is, however, unacceptable, since the adjective *vectigalis* means 'liable, subject to rent' (see Badian). Similarly, the view that both ablatives are instrumental – 'Thorius ... relieved the public land by a defective and worthless law with a rent' – is unacceptable, apart from any other implausibilities, because *levo* is not used in this sense absolutely.

To return to the first two main alternatives, it is hard to find convincing criteria for a decision between them. Cicero's attitude to the taxation of public land varied with his situation (contrast *Leg.Agr.* 1.10; 2.50; *Att.* 1.19.4 with *Att.* 2.16.1). There is a general problem over sense, stressed by Badian, 1964, 238. If we take *lege* as instrumental, Cicero would be asserting that a defective and worthless law had brought relief. This point may be reinforced by noting Cicero's use of the aorist/perfect *levavit*. If Cicero was sarcastically describing a failed attempt, he would surely have used an imperfect tense. On the other hand, although it is consistent with both grammar and sense to take *vectigali* as instrumental and *lege* as separative, the sense that results is still elliptic and would have baffled anyone who did not already know what the law was about. Since no entirely satisfactory explanation of the preserved text has been found, it has been argued that *vectigale levavit* was the product of corruption and emendations have been proposed – *vectigali vexavit* (Seager, 1967); *vectigali locavit* (Willcock, 1982); *vectigali oneravit* (Lintott, 1975). All these solutions would lead to an identification of Borius with Thorius and to a disassociation of the *lex Thoria* from the law on the bronze.

A further possibility, however, may be mentioned, that *vectigale* is a corruption from *vectigalē* = *vectigalem*: hence, 'Sp.Thorius ... relieved the public land which was burdened by rent through a defective and worthless law (Douglas, 1966). Although this proposal must be rejected as it stands, since *levavit* is not attested as meaning 'relieved', except in conjunction with a separative ablative, and *lege* cannot be both instrumental qualifying *vectigalem* and separative qualifying *levavit*, a further emendation avoids this difficulty: *is qui agrum publicum vitiosa et inutili lege vectigale⟨m⟩ l⟨ib⟩e{v}⟨r⟩avit*. For the use of *libero* absolutely in this sort of context there is the parallel in Cic. *Att.* 1.19.4, *liberabam agrum eum, qui P.Mucio L.Calpurnio consulibus publicus fuisset*, where the verb means 'free from public intervention'. The corruption is not implausible in view of the confusion between *b* and *v* in early mediaeval manuscripts. With these emendations it would be possible to identify the *lex Thoria* with the law on the bronze, which removes a great deal of land from the public to the private sector.

If we assume, in spite of the problems in his account, that Appian is right in stating that there were three laws after C.Gracchus' *lex Sempronia* and that he has grasped their nature in part at least, there can be little doubt that of Appian's three laws the third is most easily equated with the law on the bronze, as scholars from Rudorff and Mommsen to Johannsen have believed. Even if the law of 111 did not remove the rents from all public land, it removed them from land public in 133 which had subsequently been assigned in one way or other by the land-commission (*IIIviri a.d.a.*) and made private by the law (lines 19–20) – the land in which Appian is most interested. This view was rejected by Saumagne (1927), who argued that one should supplement lines 19–20 in such a way that they express an injunction to continue the existing rents, but Saumagne's solution will not hold water, even if he was right to criticise Mommsen's supplement (see commentary on *lex agr.* 19–20). The second law, by contrast, if we believe Appian, actually imposed rents on old possessors of public land (the new assignees had apparently already become liable to rent under C.Gracchus' *lex Sempronia* – Plut. *C.Gr.* 9.4). It is anyhow plain that it is rents on these legitimate holdings that the epigraphic law is trying to abolish. The law of 111 has, moreover, the appearance of a winding-up measure, intended to settle problems and provide stability over a period: it was to some extent disengaging the *populus Romanus* and its magistrates from the management of the land – see in particular the permission granted for the occupation and conversion into private property of up to 30 *iugera* of agricultural land without the intervention of any land-commissioner – lines 13–14. (It is usually assumed that land-commissioners were no longer elected after Appian's second law, but this inference is not quite secure, since, even if no land was actually distributed afresh, problems of determining the boundary between public and private land might still subsist.)

What, then, of the identification of our epigraphic law with that of Sp.Thorius? If the *Brutus* passage means that Thorius freed public land from a faulty and useless law by imposing rent, then, *pace* Badian 1964, 241, I cannot see how the limited tax or rents imposed by the law on the bronze can amount to the saving of public land from a previous pernicious bill – note that even with surviving public land, free grazing is allowed up to a point on *ager compascuus* (lines 14–15) and on the *calles* for those in transit (line 26). It would then follow that we are free to identify Appian's Sp.Borius with Sp.Thorius but the epigraphic law is not his. The same is true if we accept any of the emendations which imply that Thorius was imposing a rent. On the other hand, if Thorius was freeing public land from rent by a defective and worthless law, this is consistent with the epigraphic law about the rent, but is a poor description of a law whose effects seem to have lasted for some time and which provided security for *possessores*, with whom Cicero is normally in sympathy. Finally, if the emendation that I have tentatively proposed here is acceptable – *agrum publicum vitiosa et inutili lege vectigalem liberavit* – then the faulty and worthless law which imposed the tax will be Appian's second law (cf. Burdese, 1952, 86) while the law of Sp.Thorius will be both Appian's third law and the law of 111 in this inscription.

If 111 BC was the end of an era in agrarian history, can this be related to Appian's view that Gracchus' plans were brought to nothing fifteen years after his legislation? In the context this seems to be a reference to the *lex Sempronia* of 133, since it is this law which Appian regarded as excellent and most valuable in principle, if only it could have been put into effect. Thus Appian is suggesting that Ti.Gracchus' plans collapsed about 118 BC – which would perhaps fit the second law which brought distribution to an end. We should not in any case be looking for a law of *c.* 108 BC, fifteen years after the legislation of C.Gracchus. In fact, after the law of 111 there would have been no more need for conservative stabilising measures. A new law would have probably been in the interest of further reform and redistribution.

Appendix 1 K. Johannsen's Identification of the *lex Thoria*

Johannsen (1971, 69ff) rightly saw that the nature of the provisions in the inscribed *lex agraria* do not fit either of the first two post-Gracchan agrarian laws as described by Appian. She also interpreted the *Brutus* passage with Mommsen and Badian as meaning that Thorius freed public land from a defective and worthless law by a rent. However, because she identified 'Appius maior' in Cic. *de Or.* 2.284 with the consul of 79, she thought that the discussion in the senate of the *lex Thoria* in which Appius maior participated must have been after 111: therefore the *lex Thoria* must have been the final post-Gracchan agrarian law of 111. To sustain this view she argued that the *ager publicus* in the Cicero *Brutus* passage did not mean the land assigned by the commission, which in her view had become private at least after Appian's second law, but the land remaining public in 111, indeed a particular section of this – pasture land. Thus, Thorius removed the upper limit on the grazing of animals on public pasture-land imposed by the *lex Sempronia* of Ti.Gracchus, the *vitiosa et inutilis lex*, but merely subjected such grazing to a tax.

A number of points may be made against this view:

(a) This makes Cicero's statement in the *Brutus* even more elliptic and obscure.
(b) It is not certain that the law of 111 itself removed an upper limit on the number of cattle to be grazed on public land. Johannsen can only argue from silence.

(c) If the law of 111 did remove an upper limit on grazing, this was a traditional limit confirmed by Ti.Gracchus, not merely the product of a *vitiosa et inutilis lex*.

(d) It is far from secure that both the new allotments of the *IIIviri* and holdings of former possessors had been removed from the category of *ager publicus* before 111 (see the commentary on lines 1–10).

(e) Given that grazing on public land was traditionally subject to *scriptura*, then it is hard to see how Cicero could have regarded the *vectigal* as the instrument by which Thorius freed the public land.

(f) The problem of *Appius maior* can be solved in a different way. He might well be (Badian, 1964, 239) the *cos. suff.* 130, who could still have been active in the senate about 20 years after his consulship. Alternatively given that *Appius maior* should mean the elder of two brothers with that name (cf. Cic. *Fam.* 8.8.2–3; Asc. 39, 41C), we may postulate a hypothetical elder brother to C.Claudius Pulcher (*cos.* 92) and the Appius who was *cos.* 79, one who died before he could reach the consulship.

For a critique of these views of Johannsen tending to re-establish the view of Badian, see Meister, 1974.

Appendix 2 *Sp.Borius*

Borius is otherwise unknown as a Roman *nomen* and even if no other considerations came into question, it would have seemed likely that there had been a fault in the transmission of Appian's text. The *praenomen* Spurius is also rare and it is thus very attractive to emend Borius to Thorius, though not inescapable – Broughton, *MRR*, I, 542 suggested Aburius. Given, however, that Appian is not absolutely reliable on the post-Gracchan legislation, the interpretation of the text from Cicero's *Brutus* should not hinge on him.

POSTSCRIPT

When this book was already in proof, I was shown by Michael Crawford casts of the base of the B fragment and the apex of the D fragment, which suggest strongly that a join could be made there. What are the implications of this for the text and the reconstruction of the fragments?

In *lex rep.* 53 Mommsen's doubts about the E in '*r]eum*' were justified and the reading will be in fact '*iudicium sententiam*'; in *lex rep.* 54 the text must read after the *vacat 'De reo ap[solvendo'.* The compressed lines proposed by Mattingly (1969, 134) for *lex rep.* 51 and 53, or something similar, will come into play, equally those proposed by him for *lex agr.* 60–4.

The implications of the attachment of B to D for the organisation of the fragments will be more important. It appears at first sight that either Mommsen's hypotheses for the reconstruction of the *tabula* (p. 75) will have to be abandoned because of the compression of the distance between A and B and also between the left-hand margin of the bronze (viewed from the *lex rep.* face) and B (cf. my comments about a less drastic compression on pp. 78–9) or else D will have to be moved away from what appears to be a near join with E towards the centre of the bronze. The sheer plausibility of the texts which can be reconstructed in the lower half of the bronze, with lacunae as short as six letters (pp. 80, 172), makes such a dislocation unattractive. On the other hand, if we retain the position of D relative to E, the closing of the gap between A and B (even assuming that A is moved so that its left-hand edge, viewed from the *lex rep.* face, is almost at the margin of the bronze) is even tighter than Mattingly thought plausible, when he proposed his reduced line-length (45 letter-spaces rather than 35). This would render, for example, *lex rep.* 25 and 26, *lex agr.* 22 and 27, completely unintelligible, not to mention the problem of an introductory formula in *lex agr.* 16. In the light of this, it seems that Mommsen's hypotheses about the upper half of the bronze should not be abandoned. We seem, therefore, constrained to lose the intelligibility of the present arrangement of the lower half of the *tabula*, since D will have to be separated from E by an enormous lacuna. Yet there is one hypothesis, which, even if it is not an easy assumption, would obviate these difficulties – that is, that the *tabula* was not, as a whole, a parallelogram, but two rectangles probably of different breadths, one asymmetrically superimposed on the other (I refer to its overall form here, not to the shape of any component parts). The upper rectangular 'crossbar' would have made a right-angle with the lower rectangle about the level of *lex rep.* 45. This would allow fragment A to be placed to the left of the apex of E (viewed from the *lex rep.* face), as Mommsen and Mattingly wanted, without the necessity of drawing it in a peculiar shape to fit the geometry of the parallelogram of the *tabula*. Whether the exact joins postulated by them could all be maintained is open to question (see the commentary on *lex rep.* 45–7 and *lex agr.* 51–3, but their general location of the base of A would be plausible.

INDEX

References to the texts (e.g. ***lex rep.* 29**) are to the line-numbers of the two laws; those to both the introductory chapters and the commentaries are by page-number.

For EU product safety concerns, contact us at Calle de José Abascal, 56–1°,
28003 Madrid, Spain or eugpsr@cambridge.org.

www.ingramcontent.com/pod-product-compliance
Lightning Source LLC
LaVergne TN
LVHW090309210926
848480LV00001B/189